Historical Modernisms

Historicizing Modernism

Series Editors

Matthew Feldman, Professorial Fellow, Norwegian Study Centre, University of York; and Erik Tonning, Professor of British Literature and Culture, University of Bergen, Norway

Assistant Editor: David Tucker, Associate Lecturer, Goldsmiths College, University of London, UK

Editorial Board

Professor Chris Ackerley, Department of English, University of Otago, New Zealand; Professor Ron Bush, St. John's College, University of Oxford, UK; Dr Finn Fordham, Department of English, Royal Holloway, UK; Professor Steven Matthews, Department of English, University of Reading, UK; Dr Mark Nixon, Department of English, University of Reading, UK; Professor Shane Weller, Reader in Comparative Literature, University of Kent, UK; and Professor Janet Wilson, University of Northampton, UK.

Historicizing Modernism challenges traditional literary interpretations by taking an empirical approach to modernist writing: a direct response to new documentary sources made available over the last decade.

Informed by archival research, and working beyond the usual European/American avant-garde 1900–45 parameters, this series reassesses established readings of modernist writers by developing fresh views of intellectual contexts and working methods.

Series Titles

Arun Kolatkar and Literary Modernism in India, Laetitia Zecchini
British Literature and Classical Music, David Deutsch
Broadcasting in the Modernist Era, Matthew Feldman, Henry Mead and Erik Tonning
Charles Henri Ford, Alexander Howard
Chicago and the Making of American Modernism, Michelle E. Moore
Ezra Pound's Adams Cantos, David Ten Eyck
Ezra Pound's Eriugena, Mark Byron
Ezra Pound's Washington Cantos and the Struggle for Light, Alec Marsh
Great War Modernisms and The New Age Magazine, Paul Jackson

Historicizing Modernists, Edited by Matthew Feldman, Anna Svendsen and Erik Tonning
James Joyce and Absolute Music, Michelle Witen
James Joyce and Catholicism, Chrissie van Mierlo
John Kasper and Ezra Pound, Alec Marsh
Judith Wright and Emily Carr, Anne Collett and Dorothy Jones
Katherine Mansfield and Literary Modernism, Edited by Janet Wilson, Gerri Kimber and Susan Reid
Late Modernism and the English Intelligencer, Alex Latter
The Life and Work of Thomas MacGreevy, Susan Schreibman
Literary Impressionism, Rebecca Bowler
Modern Manuscripts, Dirk Van Hulle
Modernist Lives, Claire Battershill
The Politics of 1930s British Literature, Natasha Periyan
Reading Mina Loy's Autobiographies, Sandeep Parmar
Reframing Yeats, Charles Ivan Armstrong
Samuel Beckett and Arnold Geulincx, David Tucker
Samuel Beckett and the Bible, Iain Bailey
Samuel Beckett and Cinema, Anthony Paraskeva
Samuel Beckett and Experimental Psychology, Joshua Powell
Samuel Beckett's 'More Pricks than Kicks', John Pilling
Samuel Beckett's German Diaries 1936–1937, Mark Nixon
T. E. Hulme and the Ideological Politics of Early Modernism, Henry Mead
Virginia Woolf's Late Cultural Criticism, Alice Wood
Christian Modernism in an Age of Totalitarianism, Jonas Kurlberg
Samuel Beckett and Experimental Psychology, Joshua Powell
Samuel Beckett in Confinement, James Little
Katherine Mansfield: New Directions, Edited by Aimée Gasston, Gerri Kimber and Janet Wilson
Modernist Wastes, Caroline Knighton
The Many Drafts of D. H. Lawrence, Elliott Morsia
Samuel Beckett and the Second World War, William Davies

Upcoming Titles
Samuel Beckett and Science, Chris Ackerley

Historical Modernisms

Time, History and Modernist Aesthetics

Jean-Michel Rabaté and Angeliki Spiropoulou

BLOOMSBURY ACADEMIC
LONDON • NEW YORK • OXFORD • NEW DELHI • SYDNEY

BLOOMSBURY ACADEMIC
Bloomsbury Publishing Plc
50 Bedford Square, London, WC1B 3DP, UK
1385 Broadway, New York, NY 10018, USA
29 Earlsfort Terrace, Dublin 2, Ireland

BLOOMSBURY, BLOOMSBURY ACADEMIC and the Diana logo are trademarks of Bloomsbury Publishing Plc

First published in Great Britain 2022
This paperback edition published 2023

Copyright © Jean-Michel Rabaté and Angeliki Spiropoulou, 2022

Jean-Michel Rabaté and Angeliki Spiropoulou have asserted their rights under the Copyright, Designs and Patents Act, 1988, to be identified as Editors of this work.

Cover design: Eleanor Rose

All rights reserved. No part of this publication may be reproduced or transmitted in any form or by any means, electronic or mechanical, including photocopying, recording, or any information storage or retrieval system, without prior permission in writing from the publishers.

Bloomsbury Publishing Plc does not have any control over, or responsibility for, any third-party websites referred to or in this book. All internet addresses given in this book were correct at the time of going to press. The author and publisher regret any inconvenience caused if addresses have changed or sites have ceased to exist, but can accept no responsibility for any such changes.

A catalogue record for this book is available from the British Library.

A catalog record for this book is available from the Library of Congress.

ISBN: HB: 978-1-3502-0296-2
PB: 978-1-3502-0300-6
ePDF: 978-1-3502-0297-9
eBook: 978-1-3502-0298-6

Series: Historicizing Modernism

Typeset by Integra Software Services Pvt. Ltd.

To find out more about our authors and books visit www.bloomsbury.com and sign up for our newsletters.

In memory of Hayden White

Contents

List of illustrations	x
Notes on contributors	xiii
Preface	xviii
Foreword: Modernism, time and history *Terry Eagleton*	xix
Historical modernisms: Introduction *Jean-Michel Rabaté and Angeliki Spiropoulou*	1

Part I Historicizing modernism

1. 'The Last Witnesses': Autobiography and history in the 1930s *Laura Marcus* — 33
2. Spatial histories of magazines and modernisms *Andrew Thacker* — 55
3. Rethinking the modernist moment: Crisis, (im)potentiality and E. M. Forster's failed *Kairos* *Vassiliki Kolocotroni* — 73
4. 'Well now that's done: And I'm glad it's over': Modernism, history and the future *Max Saunders* — 91
5. Historical and rhetorical emplotments of modernism: An interview with Hayden White by Angeliki Spiropoulou — 111

Part II Stories and histories of the avant-gardes

6. Medium-New *Tyrus Miller* — 121
7. Time assemblage: History in the European avant-gardes *Sascha Bru* — 141
8. Clement Greenberg's modernism: Historicizable or ahistorical? *Rahma Khazam* — 159
9. Beer in Bohemian Paris: A symbol of the Third Republic *Alexandra Bickley Trott* — 175
10. From the marvellous to the managerial: Life at the Surrealist Research Bureau *Rachel Silveri* — 197
11. History and active thought: The Belgrade surrealist circle's transforming praxis *Sanja Bahun* — 215

Bibliography	234
Index	253

Illustrations

2.1 Cover of the Journal *Blast*, no.1, 1914. Image courtesy of The Modernist Journals Project. Brown and Tulsa Universities, www.modjourn.org. — 64

2.2 Cover of the Journal *Légitime Défense*, 1932 — 65

4.1 To-Day and To-Morrow: Classified Index from Ralph de Pomerai, *Aphrodite; or, The Future of Sexual Relationships* (London: Kegan Paul, Trench and Trubner, 1931), end-matter — 96

7.1 Pablo Picasso, *Guitar, Sheet Music, Glass* (1912). Cut-and-pasted wallpaper, newspaper (*Le Journal*, 18 November 1912), sheet music, coloured paper, paper and hand-painted faux bois paper, charcoal and gouache on paperboard, 47.9 × 36.5 cm. McNay Art Museum, San Antonio. Bequest of Marion Koogler McNay © McNay Art Museum/Art Resource, NY/Scala, Florence © 2021 Succession Picasso/SABAM Belgium — 146

7.2 Max Ernst, *Katharina Ondulata d.i. frau wirtin a.d. lahn* (1920). Gouache, pencil and ink on printed paper, 31.2 × 27 cm. Inscribed: 'Katharina ondulata d.i. frau wirtin a.d. lahn erscheint als der deutschen engelin u. perlmütter auf korksohlen im tierbild des krebses'. Scottish National Gallery of Modern Art, Edinburgh. Purchased with the support of the Heritage Lottery Fund and the Art Fund 1995. © Scala, Florence © 2021 SABAM Belgium — 149

7.3 Sophie Täuber & Hans Arp, *Untitled* (Duo-Collage, 1918). Paper, board and silver leaf on board, 82 × 62 cm. © bpk, Nationalgalerie, Staatliche Museen zu Berlin, Jörg P. Anders © 2021 SABAM Belgium — 153

9.1 Claude Monet, *Rue Montorgueil*, 1878, oil on canvas, Musée d'Orsay, Paris. Reproduction permission granted by Musée d'Orsay, Paris — 176

9.2 Édouard Manet, *Rue Mosnier*, 1878, oil on canvas, J. Paul Getty Museum, Los Angeles. Digital image courtesy of the Getty's Open Content Programme — 176

9.3	Édouard Manet, *Le Bon Bock*, 1873, oil on canvas, Philadelphia Museum of Art: The Mr. and Mrs. Carroll S. Tyson, Jr., Collection, 1963, 1963–116-9	185
9.4	Eugène Cottin, 'La Lutte à Entreprendre', *Le Bon Bock*, no. 1, 21 February 1885, p.3. Courtesy of BnF	186
9.5	Eugène Cottin, 'Les Effets de la Bière en Allemagne', *Le Bon Bock*, no. 10, 2 May 1885, p. 1. Courtesy of BnF	186
9.6	Eugène Cottin, 'Les Effets de la Bière Française', *Le Bon Bock*, no. 11, 9 May 1885, p.1. Courtesy of BnF	187
9.7	Eugène Cottin, 'Expertise sur les Bières d'Allemagne', *Le Bon Bock*, no. 13, 23 May 1885, p.1. Courtesy of BnF	189
9.8	Eugène Cottin, 'Un Rêve', *Le Bon Bock*, no. 5, 28 March 1885, p.3. Courtesy of BnF	189
9.9	Léonce Petit, 'G. Courbet', *Le Hanneton*, 13 June 1867, p.1. Léonce Justin Alexandre Petit (1839–1884), Public domain, via Wikimedia Commons	191
9.10	Eugène Cottin, 'Un Toast à l'armée française au Tonkin, *Le Bon Bock*, no. 7, 11 April 1885, p. 3. Courtesy of BnF	191
9.11	Eugène Cottin, 'Notre Armée dans l'est', *Le Bon Bock*, no. 16, 13 June 1885, p.1. Courtesy of BnF	192
10.1	Man Ray, *Surrealist Group 'Waking dream séance'*, 1924. Photograph of the Bureau de recherches surréalistes (Surrealist Research Bureau) in November 1924. Standing (left to right): Max Morise, Roger Vitrac, Jacques-André Boiffard, André Breton, Paul Éluard, Pierre Naville, Giorgio de Chirico, Philippe Soupault. Seated (left to right): Simone Breton, Robert Desnos, Jacques Baron. © Man Ray 2015 Trust/Artists Rights Society (ARS), NY/ADAGP, Paris [2020], image: Telimage, Paris	205
10.2	Man Ray, *Centrale surréaliste (Surrealist group)*, 1924. Photograph of the Bureau de recherches surréalistes (Surrealist Research Bureau) in November 1924. Standing (left to right): Jacques Baron, Raymond Queneau, André Breton, Jacques-André Boiffard, Giorgio de Chirico, Roger Vitrac, Paul Éluard, Philippe Soupault, Robert Desnos, Louis Aragon. Seated (left to right): Pierre Naville, Simone Breton, Max Morise, Louise (Mick) Soupault. © Man Ray 2015 Trust/Artists Rights Society (ARS), NY/ADAGP, Paris [2020], image: Telimage, Paris	205

10.3 Detail of advertisement for La Machine Comptable Ellis, *Mon Bureau* 164 (October 1927): page 603. Source gallica.bnf.fr/ Bibliothèque nationale de France 208
10.4 Advertisement for Société des Machines à Écrire MAP, *Mon Bureau* 139 (September 1925): page 664. Source gallica.bnf.fr/ Bibliothèque nationale de France 208
11.1 Vane Bor (Stevan Živadinović), *Milica S. Lazović as a Shadow, or Two Minutes Before Crime*, 1935, vintage photograph, 90 × 60 mm, Inv. No. M112. Courtesy of the Museum of Contemporary Art, Belgrade 221
11.2 Vane Bor (Stevan Živadinović), *One Minute Before Murder*, 1935, vintage photograph, 87 × 62 mm, Inv. No. M111. Courtesy of the Museum of Contemporary Art, Belgrade 221

Contributors

Sanja Bahun is Professor of Literature and Film and the Dean of Postgraduate Research and Education at the University of Essex. She is the author of *Modernism and Melancholia: Writing as Countermourning* (2014) and the co-editor of *The Avant-garde and the Margin: New Territories of Modernism* (2006), *Violence and Gender in the Globalized World: The Intimate and the Extimate* (2008, 2015), *From Word to Canvas: Appropriations of Myth in Women's Aesthetic Production* (2009), *Myth and Violence in the Contemporary Female Text: New Cassandras* (2011), *Language, Ideology, and the Human: New Interventions* (2012), *Myth, Literature, and the Unconscious* (2013), *Cinema, State Socialism and Society in the Soviet Union and Eastern Europe, 1917–1989: Re-Visions* (2014) and *Thinking Home: Interdisciplinary Dialogues* (2018).

Sascha Bru is Professor at the Faculty of Arts of the University of Leuven (KU Leuven), where he is also a director of the MDRN research lab. His work studies European modernism and avant-garde culture. His books include *Democracy, Law and the Modernist Avant-Gardes* (2009), *The European Avant-Gardes, 1905–1935* (2018) and, as co-editor, *The Oxford Critical and Cultural History of Modernist Magazines: Europe, 1880–1940* (2013), *The Aesthetics of Matter* (2013), *Futurism: A Microhistory* (2017) and *Realisms of the Avant-Garde* (2020). His current research projects include a book on children in the avant-gardes, and a study of issues of time and history in twentieth-century artistic experiments.

Terry Eagleton is Distinguished Professor of Literature at Lancaster University and the University of Notre Dame. A renowned public intellectual, he has authored a number of books, including *The Event of Literature* (2012), *Why Marx Was Right* (2011), *Reason, Faith, and Revolution: Reflections on the God Debate and On Evil* (2009), *How to Read a Poem* (2008), *Trouble with Strangers* (2008), *The Meaning of Life* (2007), *After Theory* (2003), *The English Novel: An Introduction* (2004), *Sweet Violence* (2003), *The Gatekeeper* (memoir, 2001), *Modernity, Modernism, Postmodernism: Essays* (2000), *The Illusions of Postmodernism* (1996), *Marxist Literary Theory: A Reader* (co-editor, 1996), *The Ideology of the Aesthetic* (1990), *Literary Theory* (1983), *Body as Language: Outline* of a 'New Left' Theology (1970), *Directions: Pointers for the Post-Conciliar Church* (editor, 1968) and *The New Left Church* (1966).

Rahma Khazam is a Paris-based researcher and art historian affiliated to Institut ACTE, Sorbonne Paris 1. She received her PhD from the Sorbonne in aesthetics and art theory. Her research, which spans the fields of modernism, American art from the 1940s to the 1970s, image theory and speculative realism, has been published in exhibition catalogues, edited volumes and academic journals. She received the 2017 AICA France Award for Art Criticism, and is the editor of *A Pragmatic Poetics* (2018). She is currently a researcher at ENSAD, Paris.

Vassiliki Kolocotroni is Senior Lecturer in English Literature at the University of Glasgow. She works on international modernism and the avant-garde, theory, classical reception, travel and film. She is the co-editor of *The Edinburgh Dictionary of Modernism*, *Modernism: An Anthology of Sources and Documents* and a European literature editor of *The Routledge Encyclopedia of Modernism*. She has also co-edited *In the Country of the Moon: British Women Travelers to Greece, 1718–1932* and *Women Writing Greece: Essays on Hellenism, Orientalism and Travel*. She is currently at work on a study of modernism and Hellenism.

Laura Marcus is Goldsmiths' Professor of English Literature at the University of Oxford, and a Fellow of the British Academy. Her research interests include life-writing, modernist literature and culture, and early cinema and film theory and aesthetics. Her monograph publications include *Auto/biographical Discourses: Theory, Criticism, Practice* (1994), *Virginia Woolf: Writers and Their Work* (1997/2004), *The Tenth Muse: Writing about Cinema in the Modernist Period* (2007, winner of the 2008 James Russell Lowell Prize of the MLA), *Dreams of Modernity: Psychoanalysis, Literature, Cinema* (2014) and *Autobiography: a very short introduction* (2018). Co-edited publications include *The Cambridge History of Twentieth-Century English Literature* (2004) and *Late Victorian into Modern: Oxford Twenty-First Approaches to Literature* (2016). She is currently completing an interdisciplinary study of the concept of rhythm in the late nineteenth and early twentieth centuries and starting a book on early twentieth-century life-writing.

Tyrus Miller is Dean of the School of Humanities and Professor of English and Art History at University of California, Irvine. He is the author and editor of several books on modernism and the avant-garde, including *Late Modernism: Politics, Fiction, and the Arts between the World Wars* (1999), *Singular Examples: Artistic*

Politics and the Neo-Avant-Garde (2009), *Modernism and the Frankfurt School* (2014) and the *Cambridge Companion to Wyndham Lewis* (2016). He has also edited and translated Georg Lukács's post–Second World War essays in Hungarian, *The Culture of People's Democracy: Hungarian Essays on Literature, Art, and Democratic Transition, 1945–1948* (2013).

Jean-Michel Rabaté is Professor of English and Comparative Literature at the University of Pennsylvania, co-editor of the *Journal of Modern Literature*, co-founder of Slought Foundation and a Fellow of the American Academy of Arts and Sciences. He is the author or editor of more than forty books on modernism, psychoanalysis, philosophy and literary theory. Recent titles include *Rust* (2018), *Kafka L.O.L.* (2018), *After Derrida* (2018), *Rire au Soleil* (2019), *New Beckett* (2019), *Understanding Derrida/Understanding Modernism* (2019), *Knots: Post-Lacanian Readings of Literature and Film* (2020), *Beckett and Sade* (2020) and *Rires Prodigues* (2021).

Max Saunders is Interdisciplinary Professor of Modern Literature and Culture at the University of Birmingham. He was Director of the Arts and Humanities Research Institute at King's College London. He studied at the universities of Cambridge and Harvard, and was a Fellow of Selwyn College, Cambridge. He is the author of *Self Impression: Life-Writing, Autobiografiction, and the Forms of Modern Literature* (2010); and *Imagined Futures: Writing, Science, and Modernity in the To-Day and To-Morrow Book Series, 1923–31* (2019). In 2013 he was awarded an Advanced Grant from the ERC for a five-year collaborative project on digital life writing called 'Ego-Media'.

Rachel Silveri is Assistant Professor in the School of Art and Art History at the University of Florida, where she specializes in modern art from Europe and North America. She is currently at work on her first book manuscript, *The Art of Living in the Historical Avant-Garde*. Her work has appeared in collections published by The Museum of Modern Art, including the exhibition catalogue *Francis Picabia: Our Heads Are Round So Our Thoughts Can Change Direction* (2016) and the Museum Research Consortium Dossier *Picasso's Sculpture* (2017). With Trevor Stark, she is the co-editor of *Selva: A Journal of the History of Art* n.2, special issue on 'Reactionary Art Histories' (2020). Recipient of grants from The Getty Foundation, the Alliance Programme, and The Pierre and Tana Matisse Foundation, among others, she received her PhD from Columbia University in 2017.

Angeliki Spiropoulou is Professor of Modern European Literature and Theory at the University of the Peloponnese and Research Fellow at the Institute of English Studies-School of Advanced Study, University of London. She is the author of *Virginia Woolf, Modernity and History: Constellations with Walter Benjamin* (2010), *Topoi of the Modern: European Literature and Modernity* (2021) and co-author of *History of European Literature: 18th–20th C* (2008). She is the editor or co-editor of 'Gender Resistance' (*ESSE* 2012), *Walter Benjamin: Images and Myths of Modernity* (2007), *Culture Agonistes: Debating Culture, Rereading Texts* (2002) and *Contemporary Greek Fiction: International Orientations and Crossings* (2002). She has contributed to collective volumes, dictionaries and encyclopaedias of modernism and is currently working on history writing by major European modernists. She is a board member of the European Society of Comparative Literature and is on the advisory board of the European Consortium of Humanities Institutes and Centres.

Andrew Thacker is Professor of Twentieth-Century Literature at Nottingham Trent University. He is the author or editor of several books on modernism, including the three volumes of *The Oxford Critical and Cultural History of Modernist Magazines* (2009–13), *Geographies of Modernism* (2005), *Moving through Modernity: Space and Geography in Modernism* (2003) and *Modernism, Space and the City* (2019). He was a founder member and the first Chair of the British Association for Modernist Studies, and is an editor of the journal *Literature & History* and co-director of the Modernist Magazines Project. He is currently working on two projects: a cultural history of the modern bookshop and a new series of volumes for Oxford University Press on global modernist magazines.

Alexandra Bickley Trott is Senior Lecturer in Fine Art Theory at Oxford Brookes University, where she leads the Art and Design programmes in the School of Arts. Her research often focuses on lesser-known figures and collectives in the nineteenth- and twentieth-century avant-garde and her PhD, awarded in 2015, presented the first critical monograph of the original Fumiste collective, the *Cercle des Hydropathes* (1878–80). She has previously published on the Ballets Suédois's interaction with the Parisian avant-garde (*Across the Great Divide: Modernism's Intermedialities, from Futurism to Fluxus*, (2015); and on the satirical caricatures of Hydropathe artist Georges Lorin (*The Power of Satire* (2015)). Recent work includes a study of Duncan Grant's *Kinetic Scroll* (1914) as part of a Tate 'In Focus' project; as well as a larger research project examining the interactions between the avant-garde and working-class artists ('The Working-Class Avant-Garde', *OLH* Special Collection (2020); and *Kahoon Projects* (2019)).

Hayden White (1918–2018†) was Bonsall Professor of Comparative Literature at Stanford University. He specialized in Modern European cultural history, philosophy of history, literary theory, social theory and literary history. White served as University of California Exchange Professor at the University of Venezia, the University of Bologna (Italy), and as a visiting professor of history at the University of Poznan (Poland). Among many other awards, he was an elected Fellow to the American Philosophical Society and the American Academy of Arts and Sciences. Among his many books, which have been translated in many languages, is the groundbreaking 1973 study *Metahistory: The Historical Imagination in Nineteenth-Century Europe* as well as the volumes *Figural Realism: Studies in the Mimesis Effect* (1999); and *The Content of the Form: Narrative Discourse and Historical Representation* (1986).

Preface

This book series is devoted to the analysis of late-nineteenth- to twentieth-century literary modernism within its historical contexts. *Historicizing Modernism* therefore stresses empirical accuracy and the value of primary sources (such as letters, diaries, notes, drafts, marginalia or other archival materials) in developing monographs and edited collections on modernist literature. This may take a number of forms, such as manuscript study and genetic criticism, documenting interrelated historical contexts and ideas, and exploring biographical information. To date, no book series has fully laid claim to this interdisciplinary, source-based territory for modern literature. While the series addresses itself to a range of key authors, it also highlights the importance of non-canonical writers with a view to establishing broader intellectual genealogies of modernism. Furthermore, while the series is weighted towards the English-speaking world, studies of non-Anglophone modernists whose writings are open to fresh historical exploration are also included.

A key aim of the series is to reach beyond the familiar rhetoric of intellectual and artistic 'autonomy' employed by many modernists and their critical commentators. Such rhetorical moves can and should themselves be historically situated and reintegrated into the complex continuum of individual literary practices. It is our intent that the series' emphasis upon the contested self-definitions of modernist writers, thinkers and critics may, in turn, prompt various reconsiderations of the boundaries delimiting the concept 'modernism' itself. Indeed, the concept of 'historicizing' is itself debated across its volumes, and the series by no means discourages more theoretically informed approaches. On the contrary, the editors hope that the historical specificity encouraged by *Historicizing Modernism* may inspire a range of fundamental critiques along the way.

Matthew Feldman
Erik Tonning

Foreword: Modernism, time and history
Terry Eagleton

There is no doubt that modernism signifies a crisis of language and representation, of how to depict a world which appears increasingly fragmented and opaque; but it is equally a crisis of history. This is so in a double sense: modernism is itself the product of a peculiarly fraught historical moment, breaking out most spectacularly in the years surrounding the First World War; but it also poses the problem of how to represent that history, not least when (as in T. S. Eliot's two-way-street idea of tradition, in which the present shapes the past as much as vice versa) one can no longer plausibly see time as either smoothly unfurling or moving steadily onwards and upwards. That whole ideology of history, which had served the Western middle classes superbly well in their heyday, now lies broken and rusting on the battlefields of Gallipoli and the Somme, along with a good deal more detritus which was once a set of noble ideals. A rather more wretched form of history, this time that of the colonized rather than colonialists, is the nightmare from which James Joyce's Stephen Dedalus is seeking to awaken – though one of the worst kinds of nightmare is the one in which you imagine you have woken up only to discover by some slight slippage of meaning or warping of perception that you have done no such thing, and are still fast asleep. Many a political revolution, including the one which came to an end in Ireland in the year of publication of *Ulysses*, is familiar with such false dawns.

What is now deeply in doubt is not progress itself, since even the most ardent postmodernist must allow that it is preferable to live after the invention of an aesthetics than before it, but Progress; and if this is called into question, it is because any general scheme of history at all, even a deteriorationist one of the kind promoted by Oswald Spengler, strikes the mind of post-Nietzschean Europe as less persuasive than a sense of history as an enigmatic, utterly incoherent text as resistant to sense as Dadaist sound poetry or surrealist theatre. Marx takes a rather different view: for him, modernity represents an enthralling narrative of emancipation and, simultaneously and inseparably, one prolonged nightmare. There is indeed a grand narrative, but it is ironically double-edged. This, however, was in the days when there was still something known as dialectical thought, which in the course of time was to yield to an ideology of difference.

Once one becomes in the habit of reading narratives which begin *in medias res*, curve back to some origin which turns out to be only one possible starting-point, then leap into the future only to land up back in the present, it is clear that what is at one level a crisis of literary form is also, more fundamentally, the loss of a traditional kind of storytelling under turbulent historical conditions. The genetic fallacy (the assumption that to investigate the causes of a phenomenon is to understand it for what it is) and the teleological fallacy (the faith that to know the ultimate goal of a process is the key to comprehending it) have both been thrown into question. This is not the case with classical realism. The finest specimen of that form in England is George Eliot's *Middlemarch*, which for all its disenchantment with the failure of social reform continues to believe in 'the growing good of the world', and implicitly portrays the history it recounts as being in a middle march from a lower to a higher state. Contrast this faith, then, with Joseph Conrad's portrayal of his protagonist Mr. Verloc being driven in a cab in *The Secret Agent*:

> The cab rattled, jingled, jolted; in fact, the last was quite extraordinary. By its disproportionate violence and magnitude it obliterated every sensation of onward movement; and the effect was of being shaken in a stationary apparatus like a mediaeval device for the punishment of crime, or some very new-fangled invention for the cure of a sluggish liver. (Ch. 8)

This impression of getting nowhere fast, of bouncing agitatedly up and down on the spot, is the ultimate riposte to the creed of progress, of which the conservative Conrad was deeply sceptical. The very idea of motion has now become something of a metaphysical mystery.

For the classical realist, there is a narrative inherent in reality itself, quite independent of how we might happen to construe it, and it is the task of fiction to excavate this story and reduplicate it in the shapely design of one's own work. Modernism, by contrast, comes in the wake of Friedrich Nietzsche's conviction that the world is no way in particular, and that only by foisting our own arbitrary fictions upon it can any coherent sense be hammered out of the stuff. There is no longer any such thing as what is the case – an epistemology that postmodernism continues to promote while at the same time maintaining that women really are oppressed and that (post)colonial exploitation is more than a convenient frame for making sense of things. Nor in Nietzsche's eyes is history itself more than a collection of gruesome accidents and random events, with its murky roots in blood, toil and perpetual violence. It is, of course, Hegel whom he has in his sights – a philosopher of history who was in fact far from the sanguine spirit he is so often mistaken for, believing as he did that episodes of peace and fulfilment were rare indeed in the annals of human history.

The term 'modern' derives, ironically enough, from classical antiquity – from the word *modernus*, which became current in the medieval period and which can be roughly translated as 'the time of the now'. The idea of the new is not new at all. *Modernus* means what is current or contemporary, but one should note that much of what is contemporary is not new. Air travel is contemporary, but it now has quite a history behind it. The phrase 'the time of the now' is paradoxical, since the 'now' is both in and out of time, to be discovered at the very heart of temporality but also its polar opposite. Nor is the new desirable in itself: crack cocaine is relatively new, and so is failing to notice the murder of a fellow passenger on a tube train because you are too busy fiddling with your smart phone. Famine and sexual slavery are also bang up to date. There is nothing inherently precious about innovation, as the victims of chemical weapons might testify if they are still alive to do so. All new things have one feature in common, namely their novelty, which then tends to reduce them all to the same level rather as the commodity form does for Marx. There are times when modernism in purely formalist spirit regards the past as its adversary simply because it is the past, not on account of any grave offence it may have perpetrated.

What is also typical of the new is its fugitive, transient quality. It is with Charles Baudelaire that the idea of the modern as ephemeral – as a kind of perpetual vanishing act – is born. To celebrate the transient is a way of subverting the classical. If novelty is no virtue in itself, why should permanence be? Warfare and poverty have been constant factors in human history, yet we do not think the better of them for that. So why not scribble your poems on people's shirt fronts, or build a self-implosion device into your piece of sculpture? Why not seek to annihilate the past altogether in the manner of the various revolutionary avant-gardes of the early twentieth century, burning Raphael and placing bombs in libraries so as to create for yourself that pure space, akin in its luminous vacancy to the space which existed before the Creation, which might then become the matrix for your own absolutely original work?

One problem with this audacious aesthetic is that there is in fact nothing which is absolutely original. If there were, we would not be in possession of the language in which to identify it, let alone give an account of it. We can only extrapolate from what we know already. This is one reason why aliens are so disappointingly non-alien. They may be only three foot high, speak in robotic voices, smell strongly of sulphur and display a morbid interest in the human genitalia when they stretch us out on their couches, but otherwise they look pretty much like Tom Cruise. Aliens are testimony to the paucity of the human imagination. The real aliens are those who are squatting in our laps at this very moment. There is nothing that is not fashioned out of pre-existing materials, and that is therefore (as Henrik Ibsen well knew) mortgaged to the past. That this is so is part of what Jacques Derrida means by textuality. The call to make it new, to be (in Arthur Rimbaud's phrase) 'absolutely modern', to create a historical tabula rasa, turns out to be a fantasy. It is the Oedipal dream of being self-creating, without parentage, sprung triumphantly from one's own loins. Works of art which are out to liquidate the past in the name of the ineffably new tend to overlook Sigmund Freud's warning that those who do not confront the past are doomed to repeat it. All you are likely to do is thrust past history into the political unconscious, where it will begin to fester. Not even the most outlandishly unfamiliar work of art can give the slip to T. S. Eliot's all-encompassing Tradition, which will always manage to incorporate it into its own unfathomable depths. It is as though the Tradition has seen innovation coming and reorganized itself in order to accommodate it.

Avant-gardism is an act of oblivion, since it involves consigning all previous cultural history to the ashcan of tradition. The past is immolated on the altar of the present. The present and future are defined by their rupture with the past – so that once that past is indeed buried in oblivion, avant-gardism becomes impossible to sustain. Another problem with this avant-garde aesthetic is that wiping the historical slate clean is far from simple. This is partly because history is what we are for the most part made of, but also because to seek to erase history is itself a historical act, and thus ends up simply piling more historical material on to whatever it is you were hoping to annul. We can only transform history with the few poor, contaminated instruments which we have inherited from it. No thinker was more ironically aware of this than Marx, who held that only on the basis of the fabulous accumulation of spiritual and material riches of the middle class (the most revolutionary agent in human history, he notes in *The Communist Manifesto*) might a genuine socialism be conceivable. Since that enthralling, emancipatory narrative is simultaneously a tale of misery and exploitation, the realm of future freedom is in part the fruit of non-freedom. Whether what might emerge at the end of this process is then worth the fearful price in human blood and sweat the human race has paid for it is a question on which Marxism has been curiously silent.

Modernism, one might claim in too glib a formulation, is fascinated by time but disenchanted with history. In fact, the former becomes often enough a surrogate for the latter. There are modernist artists who seek a victory over time by compressing it to an infinite singularity, a timeless instant which is the closest one can approach to the Absolute. As Stephen Dedalus announces, we must cling to the now, the here, through which all future plunges to the past. The modernist attraction to the void or vortex, 'vertical' irruptions into the forward flow of time, belongs with this vision. So too do attempts to spatialize temporality, as with Walter Benjamin's project of 'constellating' disparate historical moments into a single dialectical image. The linear gives way to the synchronic, motion to montage. One source of this project is the city, modernism being for the most part an urban, rather than rural, affair. It is the city, in which different sensations besiege you at every moment on all sides, which is one source of modernism's love affair with incongruous juxtapositions and unpredictable affinities – with what Benjamin calls inconceivable analogies and connections. Another source of this disaffection with the linear is modern physics, for which a Newtonian world of solid objects, fixed laws and stable temporality is giving way to an indeterminate, multidimensional sphere of flux and energy. Time for Einstein's special theory of relativity does not run on rails, which is no doubt one reason why some of the Dadaists regarded him as an honorary member of their group, along with Charlie Chaplin.

There is also, however, what one might call phenomenological time. If you want to defeat the time of clocks and calendars, you can try turning inward, perhaps under the influence of Henri Bergson or Martin Heidegger, to the lived, irregular, multilayered time of the human subject, the most magnificent literary example of which is Marcel Proust's *Remembrance of Things Past*. Yet the contrast between this existential richness and the dull, dreary, one-damn-thing-after-another evolution of history is a false antithesis. For history, too, is irregular and multilayered, an array of mini-narratives which are by no means always synchronizable. It is a view of the historical more congenial to the colonial margins than the metropolitan centre. Different currents of history move at different tempos, sharply diverge or randomly intersect, curve back on themselves or suddenly accelerate, as the structure of Conrad's *Nostromo* would suggest. If history is less linear than complexly stratified and interwoven, then you can shake its various bits and pieces free of their chronological frame and slice into it at any point. To a certain modernist eye, everything is perpetually present, it is to the eye of God. The possibility of a Surrealist history, one which brings the very old and the very new into shockingly unfamiliar juxtaposition, is now on the agenda.

Alternatively, you can adopt the Futurists' tactic of trying to outrun time, beat it at its game, live so fast and furiously that the present is no sooner here than it is eclipsed by what is still to arrive. Even the contemporary is obsolete. If you cannot transcend temporality, at least you can intensify it to the point where it begins to warp and bend. By caricaturing conventional notions of progress, pressing them to an extreme limit, they begin to come apart at the seams. This is because the middle classes require a firm framework of order within which their technological advances may take place; but if you speed those advances up in the manner of Futurism, you risk undermining the moral and political stability which is supposed to contain them, and history bucks wildly out of control. In classical Marxist parlance, one is speaking of a contradiction between base and superstructure. The capitalist economy is agitated, ungovernable, endlessly mutable and mercurial, while the bourgeois values which hold it in place are staid, stable and supposedly unchanging. What happens with certain currents of (post)modernism is that the turbulent energies of the base are, so to speak, lifted into the superstructure, so that art, culture and morality come to manifest all the flux, relativity and ungroundedness of market society itself. Modernism is one name for this momentous shake-up of the classical bourgeoisie, the kind of cultivated, reputable figures one finds in Proust or Thomas Mann, who by the time of postmodernism have more or less disappeared from the face of the planet; but the price one pays for this cultural revolution is a steep one. It means that the superstructure is no longer able to fulfil its classical function of *legitimating* the base– which is to say, of providing pious rationales for profane activities, justifying injustice and inequality by reference to eternal verities.

To be modern is to be post-mortal. Modern men and women die, of course, but they also acquire a kind of ersatz immortality by belonging to a history that will never end. The ideology of progress means that human powers are indefinitely expandable and know no natural closure. If you cannot vanquish death as an individual, then, you can certainly do so as a species. If history has no inherent end then it is a form of infinity, and thus among other things a substitute for a celestial paradise which to some in the nineteenth century is beginning to look increasingly implausible. Heaven, so to speak, is horizontalized. The future may be inconceivable, but at least it exists on the same plane as ourselves, even if it lies at an immeasurable distance from our own historical moment. There is, to be sure, a certain wilful self-delusion at issue here, since the fact that our age is pregnant with the infinite may lead us to regard it with a certain pride, even though we know that this all-consuming Now will soon be an insignificant Then. There is no reason, for example, why our most productive scientific hypotheses should not turn out to be just as defective as the scientific speculations of the past. There is thus a secretly tragic dimension to this triumphalistic version of the modern. Besides, the more of the past we pile up behind us, the more likely it is to weigh upon us as a tainted legacy or undischarged debt (one thinks of Ibsen once more), thereby obstructing the birth of a finer future. The problem with the past is that there is so much more of it than the present. And what is transmitted from generation to generation is barbarism as well as civilization.

Modernism divides, roughly speaking, into those artists for whom there is no salvation to be found in history, and those more buoyant, wide-eyed avant-gardists for whom the future is what redeems the present. Both groups predate one of the most fundamental of all historical developments: the point at which humanity gains the ability to exterminate itself, and in doing so confirms its universality as a species in the most frightful way imaginable. Nobody will be exempt from the effects of nuclear war or ecological catastrophe, however much the postmodernists may denounce the concept of universality as spuriously ideological. One needs, then, an alternative to the idea of Progress, and one modernist way of outflanking it is the eternal Now. This, to be sure, is no more than a convenient fiction, since there is no pure contemporaneity – no sheerly self-identical moment which could be lifted free of the perpetual conversion of the past into the present. If there were indeed such a moment, it would be insulated from both past and present and thus out of time, which is the etymological root of the word 'eternity'. Progress is infinite, but the moment is eternal. As Ludwig Wittgenstein suggests, eternal life can only be here and now, which is one reason why it cannot be represented. If, by virtue of an utterly impossible realism, we could truly see things as they are, peer into the very heart of them, then as William Blake maintains we would see in a cleansing of the doors of perception that their roots run down to eternity, and that our everyday vision is in this sense a necessary form of false consciousness. It is one of many legacies that the modernists inherit from the Romantics.

There is, however, another modernist strategy for defeating the sad waste of time stretching before and after, as *Four Quartets* puts it. This is to see history not as linear but as cyclical, which combines the linear with the eternal. It also involves a return to the pre-modern. Such a conjuncture of the atavistic and the avant-garde, the very old and the very new, is characteristic of modernism as a whole, which in order to find its paradigms of the future looks back over the barren waste of modernity to some pre-modern, prelapsarian paradise, all the way from the Fisher King to ancient China, the south sea island to the native rituals of Mexico, the so-called organic society of early-seventeenth-century England to the medieval world of Dante. Cyclical time is closed, as modern temporality is not, and innovation is of no particular value, History is locked into Nature and the cosmos, into the seasonal and liturgical round, which furnishes it with the stoutest of foundations. This is not true of the time of the modern, which lacks a grounding in reality and thus must improvise, become its own norm, make itself up as it goes along. In the pre-modern sphere of the cyclical, by contrast, time is meaningfully organized: there is a season for planting and for harvesting, fading and flourishing, fasting and abundance, feast days and secular occurrences. For modernity, time is the matrix of meaning but is not itself meaningful, which is why Philip Larkin's question 'What are days for?' is the very model of a pseudo-question. There can be no significant shape to a temporality which is infinite. The time of the modern, however progressive it may be, is potentially tragic, since actions, once performed, cannot be recuperated, whereas cyclical time is anti-tragic since everything will return again with a slight difference, and nothing in this eternal recurrence can be permanently lost. Like the idea of Progress, it is a fantasy of imperishability. If such a vision lies at the basis of Joyce's cosmic comedy, with its 'neverchanging-everchanging' view of reality, it also lies at the root of W. B. Yeats's desperate, last-ditch assurance that the ousted Anglo-Irish Ascendency to whom he has hitched his middle-class wagon will one day be restored, and all will run on that unfashionable gyre again.

It is customary to think of the past as finished and the present as open-ended, but this is not the view of one of the greatest of all modernist documents of historiography, Walter Benjamin's 'Theses on the Philosophy of History'. In Benjamin's view, the past itself is unfinished, and it is the present which has an opportunity of bringing it to fruition. What happens, happens; but the significance of such apparently dead-and-done-for events lies in the keeping of the present, so that it is up to us to determine whether, say, a man or woman of the Neolithic age belonged to a species which ended up destroying itself. Similarly, it is we who can invest the tradition of the oppressed with significance by ensuring that past defeats are transformed into political victories. Until then, past history will remain in a state of fluidity, and our judgement on it must remain suspended. Those throughout the centuries who lost their lives in various struggles for justice cannot literally be compensated; but their battles can be retrospectively imbued with a different meaning by our own actions in the here and now. So it is that for Benjamin, the tradition of the oppressed is constructed backwards, and will be intelligible as a coherent narrative only on

Judgement Day – a Day on which the secret affinities between this or that strike for justice over the course of human history will be revealed.

Modernism represents the most magnificent cultural flowering of the modern age. Nothing that has happened in its wake has remotely matched its depth and scope – one which involves nothing less than the fashioning of whole new forms of human subjectivity. Many of the supposedly distinctive motifs of postmodernism are merely reprises of its mighty predecessor. Yet the historical span of the modernist project, as opposed to its well-nigh global geographical reach, is notably brief: a few decades of the last century. Realism, by contrast, has a far lengthier pedigree. But this is because realism is inseparable from the emergence of a social class which took several centuries to establish itself, and in doing so transformed the face of the earth; whereas modernism marks a specific point of crisis in that class's late evolution. It is from being bound up so intimately with that highly particular historical moment that the movement derives much of its extraordinary force; and it is thus an arresting paradox that its relation to that history should so often take the form of negation, repression and imaginary transcendence.

Historical modernisms: Introduction
Jean-Michel Rabaté and Angeliki Spiropoulou

The pandemic generated by the spreading of Covid-19 (the date of the inception of the disease had to be grafted to its moniker) has led many public intellectuals to voice worries about an unprecedented disruption of social interactions and international politics. This would have ushered in a radically new situation. Indeed, there is a widespread belief that 'events' like the fall of the Berlin Wall, the attacks of 9/11 on the United States, the Arab Spring rebellions, the economic crises of 2008, etc., gave birth to configurations that were so novel that nothing would be the same after. As Walter Benjamin observes, this is an optical delusion stemming from the fact that each epoch believes itself to be at the vanguard of the modern: 'Each age unavoidably seems to itself a new age. The "modern" however, is as varied in its meaning as the different aspects of one and the same kaleidoscope.'[1] Our ambition in this collection is to explore the images of the kaleidoscope and show that their coloured pageantry makes sense when duly historicized. Whoever has kept a longer view of history, not necessarily of the *longue durée* type we associate with Fernand Braudel and the *Annales* school, but going back more than three generations, can call up vignettes dating from the Spanish flu that started in 1918, a global pandemic that affected more than 500 million people worldwide and killed about 50 million in three years, thus much more lethal than the preceding world war.[2] This 'epidemic' (a Greek word meaning literally 'about the people') was of importance for modernism, not least because one of the main modernist poets and critics, an activist tirelessly advocating 'the new' in the arts, was to succumb to it: Guillaume Apollinaire was one of the first victims of the global infection. One of the last was Freud's cherished daughter, Sophie, who died of complications from the Spanish flu in January 1920. Whereas the last bubonic plague took forty years to go round the globe, the influenza took two years to spread everywhere, whereas the Covid-19 virus took less than four months. Speed and spread have become the hallmarks of the modern, for better and for worse.

Even if we have not completely forgotten the influenza of 1918 to which Joyce (or a friend of his) is still alluding in 1929, when 'A Litter' quotes the song 'I opened the window and in flew Enza'),[3] most readers of Joyce are blithely unaware of his first literary project, a 1900 play entitled *A Brilliant Career*. In *A Brilliant Career*, the hero is a young doctor who has been elected as mayor in a town where cases of bubonic plague have been reported. The mayor first shows signs of callousness when he spurns his true love in order to marry well socially, but then he acts resolutely, albeit with the help of the rejected lover in disguise: together, they save the city from the pandemic. His victory is shown to be hollow when he realizes that he has lost his true love who proved most efficient in the struggle against the plague.[4] This plot was completed in 1900, at a time when Joyce was under the sway of Ibsen. He sent the play to the renowned critic William Archer whose answer, polite and understanding though it was, ended up being so devastating that Joyce destroyed the play soon afterwards.[5] If Joyce was probably right and his first play was a pale imitation of Ibsen's *An Enemy of the People*, nevertheless we can regret that the only play about a pandemic by a famous modernist (I bracket off Camus's *Plague*, a novel only) vanished to leave no trace.

Apart from the coincidence of identical preoccupations 120 years apart, we may want to consider that Joyce's ambition was clear: he meant to illustrate himself as a playwright because for him, in 1900, Ibsen embodied modernity, and modernity was in touch with life and the actual problems of the people. Ibsen had tackled issues of public health, the subjugation of women even in marriage and the need for democratic governments. Joyce had a point when he failed to see these themes treated by Shakespeare, and as late as 1916, when he was already writing *Ulysses*, he would still praise Ibsen above the Bard.[6] Unhappily, very few people read Ibsen today and his plays are rarely staged, whereas Shakespeare is still performed all over the world, and in all languages. Thus it was Joyce's unwavering reverence for Ibsen that made his one surviving play, *Exiles*, less of a bad play than a dated play.

One can try to defend *Exiles* against all odds, at least by arguing that a sound knowledge of the play's plot, characters and philosophy will provide one with keys opening up some of the locked doors of *Ulysses*, but this is a hard task because the play sounds so wooden and unmodern. If one agrees that *Ulysses* succeeds where *Exiles* fails, the failure of one may have been necessary for the success of the other – such a failure is what allowed Joyce to write the 'Circe' episode, a brilliant variation on *Peer Gynt, Faust* and *La Tentation de Saint Antoine* together. Of course, this is only a matter of perspective. Should one imagine *Exiles* as written in 1900, instead of *A Brilliant Career,* it would not appear as such a bad play but if one compares *Exiles* with beacons of theatrical modernity like Alfred Jarry's *Ubu Roi* (1896), Synge's *Playboy of the Western World* (1907), Maeterlinck's *Les Aveugles* (1890), Claudel's *Tête d'Or* (1889–94), Malevitch's *Victory over the Sun* (1913) or Yeats's *At the Hawk's Well* (1916), to offer only few markers, one will be sorely disappointed. Joyce, who had revolutionized the novel with *A Portrait of the Artist as a Young Man* and *Ulysses,* clearly lags behind as a playwright.

One way to save *Exiles* is to 'modernize' it by performing the kind of surgical intervention Harold Pinter had the courage to undertake. Samuel Beckett understood fully what Pinter was doing when in April 1969 he wrote to him: 'You're a brave man to take on *Exiles.* I understand your excitement. I often wondered how it could be done, that speech be overcome and the deep wounding played.'[7] Pinter had sent Samuel a typescript of *Silence* and was planning to direct *Exiles* at the Mermaid Theater in London; it opened on 12 November 1970. Beckett highlighted the difficulties of the play, its overabundance of speech given that very little is happening and the task of conveying suffering when the main characters appear either too masochistic or sadistic. Beckett and Pinter both considered the problem as a practical problem – Pinter solved it by reducing the text considerably, which had the effect of making it sound like a Beckett play.

Can one save the play differently, that is, by historicizing it? We know that Joyce finished writing his play during the war, and was conscious of the ongoing slaughter and the impending armed struggle for the independence of his native country. When in his notes he calls *Exiles* 'three cat and mouse acts',[8] he refers to the bill passed in 1913 that allowed the British police to free suffragettes and bring them back to jail immediately. Endless political discussions point to a new Ireland that should be free and independent. Thus Robert tells Richard in Act I: 'If Ireland is to become a new Ireland she must become European. And that is what you are here for. Some day we shall have to choose between England and Europe.'[9] One could imagine a creative rewrite of Joyce's play in the aftermath of Brexit, pointing to Ireland's role in a reduced Europe in which it is now the only English-speaking country.

These preliminary remarks aim at showing that if one should 'always historicize', especially when modernism is concerned, considerations of history are complex and more often than not complicate the issues. We have learned that history is not the linear progression from date to date, from king to queen via a few battles in between. It moves by jumps and starts and rarely follows a linear development. At the same time, the usual rejection of *Exiles* as a waste of effort is predicated on a correct reflex. Those who discard it follow their gut feelings that tell them that this was not Joyce at his best, or that one can be a genius in prose and an amateur playwright. In other words, even if they were to accept a historicization saving the play in the name of a more capacious comprehension of Joyce, they would still want to assert literary values and draw the line between superb prose and shoddy theatrical dialogue. The same discussion would also apply to Joyce as a poet: periodically, his poetry is exhumed to be 'saved' but it cannot compete with that of his peers like Pound, Eliot and Stevens. This leads to the next question: do we take modernism to mean simply a historical period, in which case anything that would have been produced between certain dates – say 1910 to 1954, to remain conservative – falls under the heading of modernism, or should it appear as a qualitative concept, and be regulated by criteria thanks to which we decide who is modernist and who is not? The point has not been settled. It has generated endless discussions about whether authors who remain at the cusp, like Edith Wharton and Willa Cather, or John Galsworthy and George Bernard Shaw, can be called modernist.

Is *Exiles* modernist because it is Joyce's only surviving play, and Joyce is an undisputed modernist? Is *Exiles* then modernist because it belongs to the workshop of *Ulysses*, one of the monuments of modernism? Or is *Exiles* modernist because it follows and furthers patterns launched by Ibsen, who himself can be considered an earlier modernist? Or is it *not* a modernist play because its scenic language has not been rethought, and resembles the language of the most classical theatre of the time unlike the way Jarry, Yeats, Synge, Pirandello and a few others like Beckett revolutionized it? Again: what do we mean by 'modernism'? It is simply the literary and artistic vanguard of any given period? This is the extended meaning that has been given to it by Susan Stanford Friedman in a number of provocative essays and books.

Friedman's maximalist thesis is that there is a 'planetary modernism' and that modernity is a recurrent feature moving across centuries and various cultures.[10] Thus there were pre-1500 modernities in the Tang dynasty China, and there have been Indian or Arab modernities. Such an ample vision is seductive and conjures up a modernism of *longue durée*, passing from continent to continent, from language to language, crisscrossing the most diverse cultures. It includes today's modernisms in Iran, Brazil, Nigeria, Turkey, the Arab countries and much more. Although we agree with the idea that modernism has been unduly limited to a group of European and American writers, all white and usually well educated, and that it gains by expanding its horizons, we believe that there is a confusion between 'modernity', which, as Baudelaire knew, combines the sense of the eternal and the transient, and 'modernism' as we used to know it, say as defined by a few masterpieces produced in 1922. It is exciting to imagine a transnational and transhistorical modernism. Even though we accept the idea that modernism cannot be limited to one country, we remain sceptical about the idea of a transhistorical modernism, as do all the contributors to this volume. We all argue that modernism needs to keep some kind of historical grounding. For instance, it seems counter-intuitive to call Claus Sluter (1340–1406), the author of masterpieces like the '*puits de Moïse*' in the Chartreuse de Champmol (1405), a 'modernist' sculptor because his work invents naturalist realism in portraits at the court of Burgundy and thus in Europe, also because he would exemplify an early transnationalist ethos, being both Dutch and Bourguignon. Let's agree to call him 'modern', a term linked with 'modernity' and not 'modernism'.

Another difficulty is to agree on criteria that allow one to decide what is most 'modern' in a given culture and at a given time. Should one measure this by the effect of scandal created by some works? Victor Hugo became famous with *The Battle of Hernani* in 1830, in which pitted battles opposed the Romantic school and the 'Classics'. The notorious trials of *Madame Bovary* in 1857 and the censorship of Baudelaire's *Les Fleurs du Mal* the same year opposed the whole group of progressive artists to Bourgeois morality. As Thomas Crow has shown, *l'Art pour l'Art* was subversive in mid-nineteenth-century Paris.[11] By the end of the nineteenth century, realism and naturalism were considered subversive; Zola would denounce the conditions of the workers, and Gerhart Hauptmann's play *Die Weber* (The Weavers) of 1892 was banned because it made heroes of the rebellious Silesian weavers in the 1848 revolt.

On the other hand, one cannot deny that sense of being 'modern' defines early Anglo-American modernism. It was in the minds of all of the writers and artists we call 'modernist'. Hence we have that famous letter sent by Ezra Pound to Harriet Monroe, when he reports his 'discovery' of T. S. Eliot, who, he claims, 'has actually trained himself and modernized himself on his own'. Pound, having just read 'The Love Song of Alfred E. Prufrock', was truly startled when he saw how much more advanced (and autonomous) his fellow American was. This story has often been narrated, and too often omits what was most distinctive in the posture of Pound and Eliot: they were both reclaiming a certain tradition, whether defined by troubadour poetics for the former or by French poets like Gérard de Nerval and Jules Laforgue for the latter, so as to keep thinking the past and writing the future at the same time.

Indeed, one might want to argue that what modernism brought to the fore is an awareness that its history has been underpinned by Freud's *Nachträglichkeit* much more than by any evolutionist teleology. There is first the fact that modernism has not been a movement as such, unlike surrealism or Dadaism, but a label applied retroactively by critics, poets and reviewers who were trying to make sense of the amazingly original works that were produced four years after the First World War or so. This 'retrospective arrangement', to quote Joyce again, or more precisely his character Tom Kernan, who keeps using the phrase, concerns events that often were of a traumatic nature and thus could not be described directly. An emblematic novel from the anus mirabilis of 1922 would be Virginia Woolf's *Jacob's Room*, a novel of silences, absences and gaps, all predicated on the death of the main protagonist, lost in the Great War. Similarly, masterpieces like *Ulysses* and *À la recherche du temps perdu* were impacted by the war, and the welcome delay allowed them to grow exponentially in size and ambition. But modernism did not happen all at once in 1922, and it was present before the war, in 1913 already, if not by the turn of the century.

What we call 'history' is most of the time imperceptible, marked by apparently minor changes, shifts in habitus, details that betray huge shifts like the apparently meaningless modifications of taste, as shown, for instance, by sartorial fashion. The 2009 film *Coco Chanel & Igor Stravinsky* begins perfectly by presenting as accurately as possible the first performance of Stravinsky's *Rite of Spring* at the Théâtre des Champs Elysées in 1913. This is done in order to prepare for a later torrid affair between the married composer and a single and single-minded Gabrielle Chanel. The most laudable effort in Jan Kouen's *Coco Chanel & Igor Stravinsky* is to provide an accurate reconstitution of the original performance of the *Rite of Spring* – to this day, it feels shocking, new and energetic.

The main thesis of the film is accurate: there is genius in music and there is genius in fashion. The launching of the most modern of perfumes, Chanel number 5, in 1921, with its iconic square bottle, now in all the museums of design, and its innovative use of synthetic components, may be as revealing as the scandal surrounding the *Rite of Spring* in 1913 and its being accepted as a modernist masterpiece in 1921. Fashion can be seen as a true marker of change. The fashion specialist Valerie Steele provides an accurate assessment when she describes a revolution in taste between the years 1907 and 1913. Interestingly, she insists that the First World War did not play a major role:

> Within only a few years, roughly between 1907 and 1913, a fashion world dominated by the corset, frou-frou skirts, and pastel shades turned into one where women increasingly wore brassieres and high-waisted 'Empire' frocks

or 'Oriental' fantasies in bright, 'barbaric' colors. They sometimes even wore trousers. This is not to say that World War I had not impact, but the cultural factors leading to change were already influencing fashion before 1914. The war itself primarily accelerated changes that were already happening.[12]

Books and essays have been written on modernist fashion and Paul Poiret who initiated a new look. Poiret asserted that he had been the first to wage war on the corset in his 'Art Deco' creations; however, from today's vantage point, his creations look rather dated. Mario Fortuny and Madeleine Vionnet both claimed to have abolished the corset by 1907, even before Poiret claimed that he was responsible for this iconic gesture of freedom defining modernity. Moreover, in 1903 already, the famous actress Gabrielle Réjane told an interviewer that she had no need for a corset. At the same time, Leon Bakst's designs for the *Ballets Russes* became fashionable in 1910, after the first Paris performance of *Schéhérazade*. Bakst gave rise to a mixture of exoticism and eroticism as he displayed naked male and female torsos.

In his novel that served as a basis for the film, Chris Greenhalgh had the wonderful idea of making Igor Stravinsky and Coco Chanel glimpse each other not after the war, when they became lovers for a brief time, but in 1913, at the première of the *Rite of Spring*. Indeed, as biographers agree, Chanel attended that eventful performance. Greenhalgh describes her costume in opposition to rich society women who came to the performance wearing lush Poiret dresses:

> They regard her, these women, with disapproval, without quite knowing why. It's not as if she's more decorative. Quite the opposite. If anything, the cut of her clothes is austere. The simplicity of her gown, its restrained elegance, makes them seem almost gaudy by comparison. And her silhouette is intimidatingly slim. It is this quality of understatement, this *nonchalance de luxe*, they find disrespectful. The impressions she gives is that she's not even trying. It seems so effortless, they feel undermined.
>
> To Coco, conscious of the disdainful glances she's attracting, these others seem ridiculous in their plumes and feathers, their taffeta gowns and heavy velvet dresses. If they want to look like chocolate boxes, that's their affair, she reasons. As for her, she prefers to look like a woman.[13]

Here is no projection or anachronism – if the 'little black dress' was created by Chanel in 1926 and launched by *Vogue* as a garment comparable to Ford's Model T., Chanel already opened her first boutique at the famous address of 21, rue Cambon, in 1910, where she specialized in hats. In 1913, when she opened a fashion boutique in Deauville, she had the original idea of combining high fashion and casual clothing, garments suitable for sports and leisure. Her creations in Deauville in the summer of 1913 were indeed made just after she had heard *The Rite of Spring*. These 1913 creations announced a simple style that clashed with the sumptuous extravagance of Fortuny and Poiret outfits. Chanel's simplicity was quite artful, but it would be wrong to interpret it as a consequence of the austerity created by the Great War – in fact, as with the arts, fashion anticipated these radical changes that Lisa Chaney evokes aptly in her description of the Deauville boutique:

> In Gabrielle's boutique, with its stripped awning proudly bearing the name 'Gabrielle Chanel', she offered clothes and hats based on simplified elements. There were open-collar blouses; simple sweaters; loose, belted jackets and long skirts for relaxed and outdoor living. Most famously, Gabrielle had taken familiar items of men's practical clothing and turned them to her advantage. The fisherman's shirts, turtlenecks and oversize sweaters, the polo sweater (…), all these she modified for women. The polo shirt, for example, became an open-necked, belted tunic with sleeves rolled up. Borrowing from those workaday wardrobes, she amazed and delighted her audience by demonstrating that the practical and the everyday could be the sources of high style, until then invariably rooted in luxury and the exotic.[14]

Greenhalgh's wonderfully audacious concept was to link this new simplicity with the primitivism unleashed by Stravinsky's fierce rhythms and stylized dance style. Should we try to define modernism by a few keywords? Insofar as it provides an umbrella term for a whole period, it would have to be opposed to Romanticism, Symbolism on the one hand, and post-modernism on the other. If we look for more formal markers, it is clear that the minimalism of Chanel's black dresses forces us to look at one major tendency of modern painting, namely abstraction. Do these terms offer sufficient criteria?

Unhappily, as soon as one historicizes, one finds more messy situations. This will be illustrated with two vignettes, drawing on the work of the two editors of *transition*, Eugène Jolas and Georges Duthuit, the first one appearing before the Second World War, and the second after. Here is why the study of little magazines is a productive and convenient way of historicizing modernism, as Andrew Thacker shows in his essay 'Spatial Histories of Magazines and Modernisms'. Drawing on his work on the transnational 'Modernist Magazines Project', Thacker emphasizes the problems of periodization and even of definition that emerge if a history of modernism is approached *via* avant-garde periodicals on a global level. In assessing the role of magazines for sketching a history of modernism, new critical tools, specific to the notable heterogeneity of the genre, are on call while this history itself is constantly revised alongside the questioning of traditional literary terms, such as 'work' or 'author'. A genealogy of modernism through magazines expands the movement's geopolitical calibre to include non-Western forms and colonial politics while a comparative perspective between and across continents reveals international collaborations, transnational connections and global peregrinations which remap modernism's history and prove periodicals to be more significant agents of the movement than the published book. Such an ever-expanding spatial history of modernism also questions the ideology of 'lateness' or 'lagging behind' North European and American modernity that informs much of the discourse around the history of modernism.[15]

Little magazines present to the reader the 'monuments' in instalments as well as some of the controversies they trigger before they are published. For instance, it is rewarding to read *Ulysses* and *Tarr* next to the other essays in *The Egoist*. The role of editors like Dora Marsden, Eugène Jolas and Georges Duthuit then comes to the fore. What we see confirmed here as a recurrent feature of modernism is the need to reinvent a certain past, whether a German Romantic tradition as with Jolas, or a Byzantine tradition as with Duthuit. Eugène Jolas can be given pride of place as a critic, agitator, editor and impresario of international modernism. He has not survived as a poet but his reviews, interviews and critical essays[16] point to a keen intelligence and sketch a consistent programme that presents modernism as threading a way between the arts, philosophy and literature. Jolas was a cosmopolitan '*passeur*' (to use the Bishop's term),[17] a translator in an intellectual sense, a mediator capable of establishing intercultural bridges between Joyce and Novalis, Gide and Benn, Martin Heidegger and André Breton, Ernst Jünger and African-American spirituals. We will argue in these pages that modernism is not limited to one language, and indeed that it should be understood as a cross-fertilization between several idioms. Their interaction requires new modes of narrative, linking a general meta-history with micro-narratives, as Hayden White, to whom this collection is dedicated, has tirelessly argued.

In the case of Jolas, it was his upbringing that accounted for his trilingualism. He was born in Union City, New Jersey, but his Franco-German parents returned to their native Lorraine. He spent his school years in what was Germany then before returning to New York at the age of fifteen. A journalist in Pittsburgh, he then presented cultural life in Paris for the *Chicago Tribune*. When he came back to France, he saw himself as a naive American reporter who met, interviewed and befriended a host of artist and writers in excellent vignettes that capture the gist of the Parisian spirit. Jolas could translate into simple vignettes his sudden immersion in the culture of the roaring twenties. If James Joyce figures there in good place ('My admiration for Joyce is such that I am sure that he is, of all contemporaries, the only one who will pass into posterity' (CW, 9)), his predilection for his Alsatian stomping grounds appears when discussing Strasbourg, a city felt to be at the '*carrefour du monde*' (CW, 11). Joyce reappears in July 1924 through the voice of Margaret Anderson, when her interview surveys the difficulties met by the Little Review after the censorship of several chapters of Ulysses. Tristan Tzara confesses that Dada is over, but he announces a return to classicism in the arts and literature. Jolas agrees with Breton's diagnosis in Les Pas Perdus: Dadaism and cubism can blend together; thus, surrealism will provide a workable solution. Jolas formulates a maxim that he tirelessly repeated throughout his career: 'All of the work of the moderns is decidedly vertical and tends toward a new metaphysics' (CW, 33).

Jolas's respect for Breton's radicalism did not sway him from an earlier affiliation with an Alsatian avant-garde embodied by Claire and Ivan Goll, who had launched their own 'sur-realism', for a while a rival for Breton's more visible movement. The Golls argued that Breton was too dogmatically Freudian. Jolas had held the belief that Goll's sur-realism would work better because it gathered a wider array of talents, like Joseph Delteil and Pierre Reverdy. Goll helped Jolas express his faith in the 'new mythos' by rooting the new 'international psyche' in a German-Romantic ground – which shows the need to link the local and the global when talking about high modernism.

Jolas's flirtation with surrealism was lasting, to the point that *transition* was considered a Surrealist magazine in English. However, when he launched it, his model was not the Surrealist reviews or the *Nouvelle Revue Française*, but *Commerce*, a high-end magazine whose internationalist angle derived from the polyglottism of Valery Larbaud, a writer-translator-initiator grounded in a cosmopolitan tradition. Jolas's work for *transition* was tireless, and his critical writings are broken down into sections like 'Revolution of the Word: *Transition* Manifestoes and History', 'The Language of the Night', 'From Romanticism to the Avant-Garde' and 'Crisis of Man and Language: Verticalist/Vertigralist Manifestoes'. Above all, Jolas became Joyce's publisher, friend and confidant, finding in his work the embodiment of his main tenets: literary language must be revolutionized, the loose syntax of dreams gives access to universal myths, the language of the night offers access to new truths. While *transition* gave Joyce a steady outlet to publish his fragments, it also featured authorized commentaries.

Jolas was establishing a forceful link between Modernism and Romanticism, which clashes with the systematic critique of Romanticism one finds with modernists like Eliot and Pound. In fact, Jolas's model of Romanticism was not the British or French type (neither Rousseau nor Wordsworth, anathemas both to Pound and to Eliot) for it derived from the earliest programme of German Romanticism; it expanded the theory what Philippe Lacoue-Labarthe and Jean-Luc Nancy have called *the Literary Absolute*.[18] Jolas aimed at completing the unfinished programme of German Romanticism in order to found a new 'mythos'. He tapped the Romanticism of Hölderlin, Schelling, Novalis and the Schlegels, and thus Jolas's endorsement of Jung's collective unconscious is not so surprising. He believed in universal archetypes bridging the gap between individual dreams and ancient religions.

However, Jolas realized after the war that German Romanticism had brought about the assertion of the exceptionalism of the German nation, and thus contributed to the emergence of the worst aspects of the Nazi ideology. He played a political role in Germany then, for he had been put in charge of a new German press agency, with the mission of de-Nazifying the language of journalism corrupted by the regime. During the post-war years, Jolas reframed his Romantic tenets. In 1941, he still held that *transition* had been 'pan-Romantic' and that Romanticism was not dead. After the Second World War, Jolas meditated on the links between Nazi ideology and the thought of Herder, Fichte and even Novalis. He saw the myth of the pure German *Volk* as a reaction against an Enlightenment that was felt to be too dry, rationalistic and 'French'. One observes a similar attitude facing Heidegger who is mentioned in a 1933 article on 'Primal Personality' for *transition* no 22. Jolas gives a solid account of the philosopher's critique of logic, the discovery of a Nothing apprehended via fear and anxiety, and then enlists Heidegger in the cohort of thinkers who were to launch a new metaphysic: 'Man is beginning to think about the structure of his being. Being as such is questioned. Metaphysics has become revolutionized' (CW, 272). Jolas became more critical after the war. He could also report with a smile that the German philosopher thought that the best French book was Saint Exupéry's *Le Petit Prince*: according to him, it contained a new philosophy of technology (CW, 486).

After the Second World War, *Transition* was revived by Georges Duthuit; it had folded in 1938. Beckett figures in both runs. In a letter to Duthuit from June 1949, we hear him reminiscing: 'Here in the loft I find an old copy of *transition* (1938), with a poem of mine, the wild youthful kind, which I had quite forgotten, and an article (also by me) on a young Irish poet (young then) who had just published a volume of poems in the same series as *Echo's Bones*.'[19] The poem was 'Ooftisch', typical of Beckett's *transition* style, and the Irish poet was Denis Devlin. Beyond nostalgia, Beckett raises the issue of repetition, a key question if we consider the radical pronouncements made in the 1930s by the Surrealists and the first transition group. Could one believe in an avant-garde after the war had made such a term sound somewhat militaristic? Could there be a 'Revolution of the Word' while a new division of Europe was ushered in by an incipient Cold War?

Duthuit, connected by marriage to Henri Matisse, was interested less in taking the flame from Jolas (Jolas was never excluded and had been invited to contribute, writing an excellent survey of the evolution of experimental poetry),[20] than in promoting a different programme. Duthuit did not believe in a universal and polyglottic language whose models would be the experimental writings of Joyce and Stein. The names that appear in the first issues of the newly capitalized *Transition* are Jean-Paul Sartre, Georges Bataille, René Char, Jean Wahl, Antonin Artaud, Max-Pol Fouchet, André Malraux, Maurice Nadeau and Jean Genet. Some of these authors were known to French readers before the war. Joyce himself remained quite present as the fourth issue announced a *James Joyce Yearbook* edited by Jolas with the *transition* press. The second *Transition* belongs to a post-war mentality when discussions were polarized by Existentialism, Marxism and left-wing Catholicism with philosophers like Gabriel Marcel. New names emerged like René Char and André du Bouchet next to established writers like André Gide, Saint-John Perse and Antonin Artaud.

Duthuit had specialized as an art critic with an expertise in Byzantine art. His main theme was how Western art after Cézanne returns to earlier forms such as Byzantine art. Matisse's work gives the same sense of space as Byzantine mosaics; Masson's new paintings and drawings open up a Zen space. What Duthuit praises in those efforts is an ability to bridge the gap between pragmatics and metaphysics. For the Byzantines and the Japanese, art was not meant to be exhibited in a museum but served to elicit contemplation. 'For what Byzantium produces is not works of art to be exhibited or appreciated, but practical tools overflowing with spiritual life.'[21]

In Venice, Duthuit saw the resurgence of the true Byzantine spirit, kept alive in the dark vault and nave of Saint Mark, a monument bridging the gap between religion and paganism. Such a syncretism would have been missed by Nietzsche, according to Duthuit: 'Nietzsche strangely undervalued this religion, yet it seems to have accomplished as nearly as possible, through its etiquette and pomp, what he himself on the threshold of madness dreamed of achieving: the absorption of all anguish in joy and the alliance of the sun-god and the god of the cross.'[22] Likewise, modern painters should relinquish their individuality and fuse with a collective delirium reached mythically or mystically. A central insight

Duthuit shared with the painters Tal Coat and André Masson was that there was a 'crisis of the imaginary', which had been created by the fusion of cubism and surrealism. Artists and writers should begin questioning a 'reality' whose lack of substance had been denounced by Breton. Reality did not exist by itself and took shape under the impact of desire. The issue was to combine desire and a progressive political programme.

Duthuit had met Clement Greenberg when he was living in New York during the war. He and Greenberg agreed on the connection between late surrealism and early American abstract expressionism – one living link had been André Masson when he had worked in Connecticut; Greenberg, who hated surrealism, makes an exception for Masson. He notes that Masson got rid of 'the monstrous, the epically brutal, and the blasphemous'.[23] Now, 'Self-control, elimination, and simplification would seem to be the solution for Masson'.[24] The single risk is that it might lead to 'impoverishment, not simplification'.[25] Masson has been harnessed in Greenberg's historical teleology. Masson's evolution that led to simplification can thus enlist him in the programme of modernism as defined in 1960 in the groundbreaking definitions of 'Modernist Painting', an essay that begins with a parallel between painting and philosophy:

> Modernism includes more than art and literature. By now it covers almost the whole of what is truly alive in our culture. It happens, however, to be very much of a historical novelty. Western civilization is not the first civilization to turn around and question its own foundations, but it is the one that has gone furthest in doing so. I identify Modernism with the intensification, almost the exacerbation, of this self-critical tendency that began with the philosopher Kant. Because he was the first to criticize the means itself of criticism, I conceive of Kant as the first real Modernist.[26]

It is in this context that Rahma Khazam's essay 'Clement Greenberg's Modernism: Historicizable or Ahistorical?' introduces an important shift in the current view, as it problematizes the alleged ahistoricism constitutive of artistic modernism so often associated with Greenberg's forceful theorization. If Khazam argues for the failure of Greenberg's attempt to purify modernism from history by defining it in terms of formal autonomy, she also historicizes Greenberg's dualist model of historical/ahistorical. As she explains, such a dualism can take its full meaning only when it is located in a comparative context in which it moves along older and later theories. This is how it manages to bring into play the category of the contemporary whose perspective presents modernism not as a break but rather as an encompassing of an ethos of separation, division and, ultimately, sequentiality. The lesson of this analysis is that a re-reading of modernism in its context of both its production and its reception, such as proposed by *Historical Modernisms*, will involve a historicizing of the critical framework in which it was received. Such a historicization entails a greater scepticism towards the easy *topos* of evolution.

In the same manner, Beckett, as we saw, refused a historical narrative that would present modernism as an inevitable evolution in the art of painting; for him, there is no teleology moving from representation to abstraction because there is no progress in the arts and literature, a position shared by Walter Benjamin and also Tristan Tzara when he rejected Breton's historical optimism. Adorno was notoriously hesitant on this issue, moving from a teleological analysis of music in which Schönberg was progressive and Stravinsky regressive, to the later theses of *Aesthetic Theory* in which he comes very close to the position of his old friend and mentor Benjamin. How can progress and evolution accommodate repetition? In *The Rules of Art*, Bourdieu quotes a remark by Marcel Duchamp, who was sceptical about the second school of abstract art in New York or Paris, about the return of the same in art. Duchamp understood the evolution as a consequence of the culture industry in quest of the new at any cost; the capitalistic 'market for symbolic goods' always wants to have the illusion of the new. Duchamp, who knew Beckett through his chess-playing, was opposed to the spirit of the 1950s that requested 'purity' of the medium in art, which led him to reject pure abstraction as promoted by Greenberg. Bourdieu writes, quoting Marcel Duchamp:

> The characteristic of the century that is ending is to be like a double-barrelled gun: Kandinsky and Kupka invented abstraction. Then abstraction died. One wouldn't talk about it any more. It came back thirty-five years later with the American abstract expressionists. You could say that Cubism reappeared in an impoverished form with the postwar Paris school. Dada has similarly reappeared. Second shot, second wind. It is a phenomenon particular to this century.[27]

There would be no difference between the rapid waves of fashion and the swift sequence of -isms. Rejecting such a temporal awareness, Beckett opts for an ethical position that appears even more radical than Duchamp's famed humour. Beckett thus wishes to find a new lever with an ethical refusal of the heroic struggle with the object or reality. For Beckett, who cannot be excluded from the modernist camp, an ethics of impoverishment should take precedence over an aesthetics of abstraction as a new and 'modernist' sublime.

So far, our examples have shown the impossibility of reducing modernism to a concept like abstraction or anti-Romanticism. It seems difficult to reduce modernism to formal issues like the reinvention of language or the belief in the autonomy of art. Or if we walk down this slippery slope, we will soon be stuck in a corner, and will then allow for the production of an 'other' of modernism, an anti-modernism defined by a list of the opposite characteristics. The programme of this collection would consist in examining modernism historically, but without trying to 'overcome' or 'surpass' it with a new term. This logic has been analysed and attacked with great gusto by Andrew McNamara in *Surpassing Modernity*.[28]

McNamara focuses on current discussions in the art world and notices ironically that all the new movements attempt to sell themselves by inventing a new term that will then surpass – surpass what? not the precedent labels, only modernism. He lists the postmodern, the anti-aesthetic, the post-postmodern, contemporary, contemporaneity, hypermodern, non-modern, digi-modernism, auto-modernism, relational aesthetics, altermodern, metamodernisme, remodernism, militant modernism, liquid modernity, multiple modernities, *nachmoderne*, the off-modern, polymodern.[29] He even provides a series of criteria that are tabulated to show that each time modernism is taken as a straw man that the 'new' movement will supplant or overcome.

Modernism	Contemporary (or 'Contemporaneity')
Purity and rationalization	Paradox and ambiguity
Demarcation/binaries	Hybridity
Simplification/top down hierarchies	Complexity
Eurocentrism, primitivism.	Non-Western, transcultural
Elitist	Democratic
Universal	Cultural relativism
Aesthetic	Anti-aesthetic
Synthesis, resolution.	Contradiction, antinomy[30]

Noting wryly that none of these labels has been able to live very long, with the relative exception of the 'post-modern', although the term has now lost most of its purchase, McNamara insists that this game of one-upmanship should stop. Moreover, in his examples that come from recent controversies in the visual arts, he observes a recurrent paradox: many third world artists or emergent artists keep denouncing the evil nature of the old modernism while resorting to the same criteria, like praising the autonomy of art against corrupted regimes that want to enlist artists in false praise for local regimes.

In another interesting move, McNamara focuses on Walter Benjamin who was notoriously ambivalent about the new, as suggested earlier. Following the intuitions of the Hungarian-Australian philosopher György Márkus, McNamara highlights a creative vacillation in Benjamin.[31] On the one hand, Benjamin attacks all the theories of progress, but on the other hand he seems to trust technology, at least for media like photography and film, with the power to dispel Romantic and lyrical illusions associated with the 'aura'. As McNamara summarizes the issue, this would come from the fact that Benjamin has well perceived the 'deep ambiguities of cultural modernity' which derives from the 'confluence of the most archaic and the most modern, of the unconscious and the conscious', thus combining regressive aspects with utopian or transcending gestures.[32]

Benjamin was aware of the difficulties involved in any definition of time; of delineating its philosophical, cosmological, technical or historical nature or indeed its very existence, also questioned by Aristotle in his *Physics* where he asks: does time 'belong to the class of things that exist or to that of things that do not exist? Then secondly, what is its nature?'[33] Aristotle's treatment of these questions is more open-ended than it has generally been recognized, but the formal division he made of time into different 'nows', albeit not necessarily successive, has been interpreted as a foundational moment in spatializing and homogenizing time in Western culture culminating in the establishment of a uniform and global time measure in the nineteenth century.[34]

However, modernity's ideological conflation of chronological sequence with causality and historical progress has been most forcefully contested by Benjamin, alongside a long line of modernists critical of modern times, who pinpointed the political implications of a teleological notion of history that legitimates modernity as the most advanced epoch in relation to the past. Such a notion, he warns, must be rejected because it rests on the succession of 'homogeneous, empty time', creating a phantasmagoria of modernity as by definition progressive.[35] The famous commentary in his IX Thesis on a philosophy of history on Paul Klee's 1920 picture 'Angelus Novus' he held in his possession as depicting the 'Angel of History' offers a dialectical image of a historical consciousness that looks to rescue the past and the passing present from the catastrophic storm of what is generally called Progress.[36] Moreover, Benjamin's idea that there is a past new to every present, or that any past which is not recognized by the present threatens to disappear, resonates with Ezra Pound's extreme presentism when he writes in 1938: 'We do NOT know the past in chronological sequence. It may be convenient to lay it out anesthetized on the table with dates pasted on here and there, but what we know we know by ripples and spirals eddying out from us and from our time.'[37]

Sharing more than a common rejection of linear temporality with modernist artists, Benjamin's seminal contribution to a philosophy of history through his imaginative topography of Parisian modernity modelled on Baudelaire's work does not only continue to inspire critical readings of modernist history, as is evinced by the references to his thought in nearly all essays of the present volume, but also, and importantly, it reads like a constructivist modernist work in its use of montage of citations, constellations of dialectical images and micrological approach. 'To write history thus means to cite history', he writes, aspiring to render a heightened 'graphicness' to the Marxist understanding of history, by carrying over

> the principle of montage into history. That is, to assemble large-scale constructions out of the smallest and most precisely cut components. Indeed, to discover in the analysis of the small individual moment the crystal of the total event. And, therefore, to break with vulgar historical naturalism. To grasp the construction of history as such. In the structure of commentary. -Refuse of History-[38]

However ambivalent he was of the modern cult of novelty as 'the return of the eversame', Benjamin nevertheless sought to define the truly new and progressive as is revealed by art. We read:

> In every true work of art there is a place where, for one who removes there, it blows cool like the wind of a coming dawn. From this it follows that art, which has often been considered refractory to every relation with progress, can provide its true definition. Progress has its seat not in the continuity of elapsing time but in its interferences – where the truly new makes itself felt for the first time, with the sobriety of dawn.[39]

Inversely, however, it is modernism's pursuit of novelty, its inwardness, formal reflexivity and abstraction that has provoked its dominant perception as being a-historical. In contrast with the factually rich and concretely figurative realist genre, which is concomitant with the prevailing nineteenth-century positivist spirit of historicism, modernism and the avant-garde broke away from mimetic standards typically associated with historical referentiality. This criticism, expressed most influentially by Georg Lukács, spurred a long-standing debate on the political progressiveness of modernism. The 'negation of history' appears to be part of the human ontology of modernist literature and, as he explains, it manifests itself in two forms:

> First, the hero is strictly confined within the limits of his own experience. There is not for him [...] any pre-existent reality beyond his own self, acting upon him or being acted upon by him. Secondly, the hero himself is without personal history. He is 'thrown-into-the-world': meaninglessly, unfathomably. He does not develop through contact with the world; he neither forms nor is formed by it.[40]

On a closer reading, Lukács implicitly admits modernism's attachment to its historical actuality when he proposes that this new abstract, disintegrated and solitary subjectivity, haunting modernist works, may be 'an attempt to escape from the dreariness of life under capitalism'. However, he insists that modernism separated 'time from the outer world of objective reality'.[41] Lukács's expressed supposition of the pre-existence of an objective and representable reality that modernist art fails to reflect rests on the division between fact and fiction, between history and literature and is the product of the disciplinization of history as a science in the nineteenth century, defined in opposition to the putatively purely fictitious nature of literature. The universal law of historiography became the revelation of the particulars, the reconstruction of 'objective' facts and the historical context of the past 'as it really was' [*wie es eigentlich gewesen ist*] in the Rankean historicist vocabulary. Nevertheless, historically speaking, the terms of this antithesis were not always the same. In Aristotle's famous distinction between poet and historian, found in his *Poetics*, literature's privileged access to universals, ensuing from its dealing with probability, is valued more than the singularities of what has been. Compare the following passage:

> The distinction between historian and poet is not in the one writing prose and the other verse – you might put the work of Herodotus into verse, and it would still be a species of history; it consists really in this, that the one describes the thing that has been, and the other a kind of thing that might be. Hence poetry is something more philosophic and of graver import than history, since its statements are of the nature rather of universals, whereas those of history are singulars. By a universal statement I mean one as to what such or such a kind of man will probably or necessarily say or do – which is the aim of poetry, though it affixes proper names to the characters.[42]

Interestingly, for Aristotle, the difference between the two types of discourse is not one of form and, significantly, neither is it one of truth value. Facts are not considered more truthful than poetic construction; on the contrary, poetry is argued to have more cognitive and epistemological weight (it is 'more philosophic'). Artistic *mimesis* is thus problematized since its object does not axiomatically coincide with empirical, historical facts as realist aesthetics would suggest. Following from this and contrary to what is commonly thought, neither can modernism be considered as generically anti-mimetic.

However, the formal distinctiveness between history and literature set by scientific historicism has also been questioned in twentieth-century thinking, for example, in Paul Ricoeur's study *Time and Narrative* (1983) whose 'touchstone' is the 'classical problem of the relation of narrative, be it historical or fictional, to reality', posing the thorny question of the referentiality of historical narrative to events that 'really' happened in the past.⁴³ Importantly, Ricoeur also draws attention to the common linguistic basis of both history and literature when he writes that:

> The relation between fiction and history is assuredly more complex than we will ever be able to put into words. And, of course, we have to combat the prejudice that the historian's language can be made entirely transparent, to the point of allowing the things themselves to speak; as if it sufficed to eliminate the ornaments of prose to be done with the figures of poetry.⁴⁴

The problematization of the objective status of historical fact and a stress on the linguistic basis of historical narrative lie at the heart of Hayden White's radical critique of modern historiographical assumptions, emphasizing the common ground between literature and history. His critique of the truthfulness or objectivity of realism's factuality is based on his laying bare the mechanism by which a fact really becomes 'historical' along a series of disciplinary conventions. He writes:

> The factuality of the events themselves would have to be treated as having been based on evidence of a kind not to be admitted in historical (or, more precisely, historiological) discourse. [...] On this account, a historical fact would differ from other kinds of fact by virtue of the rules prevailing in historical discourses for determining when a given event could be described as the kind of event properly characterized as 'historical'.⁴⁵

White's underlining of our always already linguistically mediated access to the historical past and the constructed nature of historical narration of 'facts' along literary modes and figures of speech evokes Roland Barthes's earlier pinpointing of the paradox that 'the fact never has any but a linguistic existence', and 'yet everything happens as if this linguistic existence were merely the pure and simple "copy" of another existence, situated in an extra-structural field, the "real" '.⁴⁶

Indeed, any contemporary investigation of narrative and history, of history as narrative, is directly indebted to White's quintessentially modernist theory of history. His foregrounding of the linguistic foundation of historiography and its narrative conventions have had a major effect on both recent historical thinking and literary criticism which took a historical turn at the end of the twentieth century in reverse analogy to the earlier linguistic turn of historical science that White also steered. More particularly, White's work brings into relief the process and strategies of encoding historical experience in narrative plots, thus also pushing the boundaries of historiography itself. This volume is dedicated to his memory as a minor tribute not only for his path-breaking contribution to contemporary historical thought but also because the book would have hosted an essay by him had its completion not been prevented by his unfortunate death in 2018. The essay he had promised to contribute was provisionally entitled 'History *as* Exception', and was intended, provocatively as ever, to explore the reasons why post-structuralist thinkers as a rule did not attempt to deconstruct historiography, apart from attacking it as 'grand narrative', after Jean-François Lyotard, or as a mere ideology of progression. He was interested in discussing how 'history' was used as a counterpoint to 'constructionist pseudo-foundationalism' and felt that it needed to be further radicalized. His interview – sadly, probably the last one to be published while he was still alive – is included in the volume *in lieu* of that undelivered chapter. However, albeit standing as substitute to his undelivered chapter, this interview is highly pertinent to the theme of the volume as it summarizes some important ways in which White conceives the complex and productive relation of modern and contemporary literature with history writing.

Not just the literariness of historiography but, mutually, the power of literature as historical world-making, as an act of *poesis* that has the power to create the past in any present, is also pinpointed by Wilhelm Dilthey in his 1887 essay, 'The Imagination of the Poet: Elements of a Poetics'.[47] Dilthey's claim that 'our philosophical conception of history was developed from literary history' is prescient of White's groundbreaking work. Similarly, in his book *The Names of History*, Jacques Rancière identifies a 'poetics of knowledge', a literary epistemology as well as methodology at the heart of particular historical schools. However, what he calls 'regimes of art', inversely, bring out art's and art criticism's own historicity since such regimes define the specific ways in which a given historical epoch conceives of the nature and logic of artistic representation or the 'poetic systems'; in other words, they evoke the modalities of the relationship between 'thought, language and world', which determine the understanding of art in the modern world.[48]

In view of the acknowledged porosity between art and history, *Historical Modernisms* contests modernism's alleged ahistoricism and joins in recent and growing research which, spurred by New Historicist critical trends appearing in the late twentieth century, is devoted to exploring the complex relation of modernism and the avant-garde with history, historiography and conceptualizations of time.[49] The volume aims to shed new light on aspects of the historical-mindedness of modernism and the artistic avant-gardes cutting across Anglophone and European traditions, also paying heed to the imperialist overtones of dominant definitions of time and the modern. Drawing on empirical cases of both literary and artistic modernism, it poses fundamental theoretical questions on the subject and symptoms of history, revealing the multifaceted relationship of modernist and avant-garde movements with historical thinking and history making.

More specifically, the essays in the volume reassess modernism's complex modes of historicity across different genres of art and publications, from autobiography, the visual arts and literature to little magazines and editions, and address the radical contribution of literary and artistic avant-gardes on new tropes of temporality and historiography. At the same time, they offer selective close-ups on some of their own histories transnationally, from the Anglophone and French paradigms to the less explored traditions of Central Europe and the Balkans, connecting the historical trajectories of modernist and avant-garde movements with both micropolitics and geopolitics. By investigating how modernist and avant-garde artworks (re)define and practice time, historical conjuncture and historiography itself, the book attempts to complicate and revise modernism's own history, its production and reception in response to the new material and conceptual conditions of modernity.

The intensely fluid and antinomical nature of modernity is pinpointed by Woolf in her 1927 essay, tellingly entitled 'Poetry, Fiction and the Future', where she wonders about the direction of contemporary writing and links it with the historical circumstances of the modern epoch which she perceives as a break from the past. The modern age, she contends, is 'an age clearly when we are not fast anchored where we are; things are moving round us; we are moving ourselves'. 'The modern mind', she goes on,

> is full of monstrous, hybrid, unmanageable emotions. That the earth is 3,000,000,000 years; that human life lasts but a second; that the capacity of the human mind is nevertheless boundless; that life is infinitely beautiful yet repulsive; that one's fellow creatures are adorable but disgusting; that science and religion have between them destroyed belief; that all bonds of union have broken.[50]

Although few modernists chose to allude directly to the dense historic facts of the period, most adumbrated their effects by undertaking a critical historiography of the present in its everyday, microhistorical, anthropological dimension, associated with the *Annales* School of historiography, through the simultaneous mapping out of the struggles of modern subjectivity and social life. The historical subjects of modernism became ultimately dissolved in the large spaces of urban modernity and of the unconscious, newly discovered by the modern science of psychoanalysis that pioneered the reconstructing of individual psychic histories. Modernists' quest for alternative models of historical movement ranged from the nostalgic flight to an idealized past, common origins and universal time patterns to the futurity of catastrophe or utopian dreams of a new, liberated world, often sprinkled with allusions to primordial, mythical and ritual material.

In his 'Foreword' to the collection, Terry Eagleton succinctly reviews the vicissitudes of the relationship of modernism with history in the context of modern times. He emphasizes the double-edgedness of this relationship which is conceived as 'crisis', alternating between disenchantment and emancipation, redemption and doom, the secular and the mythical, progress and decline, and embedded in the paradox of the recurrent 'new' caught in a movement of transience forming discontinuous or cyclical patterns. Eagleton stresses that, against progressive linearity associated with realism, modernism privileges the synchronic, the simultaneous, the multidimensional, while it marks a discordance between collective and individual life, and exhibits an acute sense of a secularized present apparently adopting an attitude of 'negation, repression and imaginary transcendence' toward history, proclaiming to turn inwards instead.[51]

A rejection of linear development was one of the reasons why autobiography, similarly with the historical novel, was generally unpopular with modernists, as Laura Marcus notes in her contribution, entitled '"The last witnesses"': Autobiography and History in the 1930s'. Marcus goes on to assert the genre's link with both history and modernism not only by arguing that autobiography as a form of history writing was displaced in other literary genres, such as the *Bildungsroman*, the *Künstlerroman*, journals, diaries and autobiographical fiction, but also by discussing the attempt at the genre taken by major modernist writers. In their different ways and despite their categorical inwardness, modernist autobiographical works present intricate connections with the turbulent historical era of their production in tandem with an exilic sense of modern subjectivity. Thus they produce new configurations of the narrative and conceptual entwinement between the inner self and the outer world, the dual temporalities of suspension and flow, the psychological and the historical approach which is endemic to the genre. Refracting the historical atmosphere of the 1930s, these works problematize the assumption of causal sequence informing traditional autobiographical narrative by introducing discontinuity and loss into the supposed continuum of history and of bios, while they also reflect on the state of autobiographical 'witnessing' and remembrance, as both foundational motives and tropes of historical writing.

The problem of joining internal consciousness with outside world endemic to the autobiographical genre is paramount in modernist and avant-garde experiments with temporality against progressive clock-time. These are routinely connected with new philosophies of time, such as those condensed in Henri Bergson's concepts of *durée réelle* and *élan vital*,[52] as well as the trend of presentism and the consciousness of the 'now' which punctuates historical, temporal flow in modernism which etymologically derives from the Latin 'modus'. The evocation of the notion of the 'moment' could thus be seen as a symptom of the anachronistic movement of art whose 'moments' become the vantage point of the intelligible. However, in the essay, entitled 'Rethinking the Modernist Moment: Potentiality, Crisis and *Kairos*', Vassiliki Kolocotroni presents this time determinator not merely as interruption of linear chronological sequence or a synecdoche of the present but rather as a critical and potentially transformative temporal mode analogous to other time markers, as, for example, the 'event', reactivated by Alain Badiou, and '*kairos*', drawing on Erwin Panofsky. These 'moments' are then read as charged points of subjective crisis pregnant with opportunity at the same time as they entail the possibility of failure, thus acquiring a historical momentum.

Beyond the purely temporal axis emphasizing significant moments as history making or unmaking, the history of modernism and the avant-gardes may be said to coincide with a history of the new as 'Medium-new', as is suggested by the title of Tyrus Miller's contribution to the volume. Setting the discussion of the poetic medium in the context of the separation of space and time, image and language, painting and literature that runs through artistic discourse in modernity in an affirmative or negative mode, modernist experimental emphasis on medium, its re-invention and assemblage is viewed as an outcome of history than a mere formalist concern. Being more than just technique, it 'mediates' an artist's creative intention and the tradition between the artist and his audience, that is, historically inherited conventions of aesthetic communication. In modernism, and especially its avant-garde branches, the delegitimation of tradition is actually inseparable from the demand for new medium-categories as the object of art, thus marking the modernist sense of crisis as medium reflexivity. T. S. Eliot's 'historical sense' aptly expresses this paradoxical interdependence of tradition and the new, transposing the historical past to the realm of the aesthetic, when he claims that the poet writes not only 'with his own generation in his bones, but with a feeling that the whole of literature of Europe from Homer and within it the whole of the literature of his own country has a simultaneous existence and composes a simultaneous order'.[53] What is stressed in defence of the historicity of modernism is how the medium of modernist poetry, even when it seemingly withdraws from history, is nevertheless a transfiguration of the historically determined language of tradition or the everyday.

Furthermore, modern literature's contested connection with the real in view of its claim for artistic autonomy is related to its break of causality; it undoes the intelligible link between successive moments, thus rendering the category of the plausible inoperative. However, as Jacques Rancière has argued in tacit response to modernism's claim to historical autonomy, art's plots have always been autonomous since they have always had a time and space proper to them.[54] The question is if the rupture of causality renders modernism ahistorical. The dialectical character of modernist novel, for example, lies rather in its dealing with the antithesis between 'the shower of atoms' falling on an ordinary human mind on an ordinary day, as Virginia Woolf has described 'life', with some arranged plot.[55] Nevertheless, modernism's historicity or lack thereof is determined by the paradox of antagonistic trends, especially in activist avant-garde, of seeking to dissolve the literary and artistic practice into life, thus merging with history on the one hand, and on the other seeking autonomy from the sphere of history through purity of form as was suggested by Clement Greenberg, as noted earlier.

Apart from addressing questions of time and history in modernism, the volume attempts to enrich its recorded history as well as foreground its unique historiographical force. Challenging the conception that history is necessarily about the past even if the latter is a construct of the present, Max Saunders's contribution, entitled '"Well now that's done: and I'm glad it's over": Modernism, History, and the Future', pays heed to the publishing landscape of the interwar period, and, importantly, to what is often neglected: modernism's concern with the future. Contributing to cultural history as well as to the examination of the historical awareness of the modernist period, Saunders focuses on the 'futurological experiment' of the multi-volume series 'To-Day and To-Morrow' launched by C. K. Ogden and published by Kegan Paul throughout the 1920s. Each volume presented the current state of a topic, and then predicted its future practicing the oxymoron of 'future history'. Saunders also considers a parallel series by Ogden on the 'History of Civilization' and argues for the significance of the series for modernist imaginings of the future, including the future of historiography itself, read in the context of innovative contemporary theories that predicted its dissolving into economics and psychology. These forward-looking, popular series mark the epoch's emphasis on history and the future seeking new paradigms to serve both.

Precisely because 'history is not a single genre but can be written in many genres,'[56] it can be read in different forms of modernist art. The historiographical imagination of the avant-garde, turning away from conventional temporal boundaries and pointing to new historiographical directions, is taken up in the essay, 'Time Assemblage: History in the European avant-gardes'. In this chapter Sascha Bru provides an overview of the variety of modes of figuring (past) time in the visual field of the artistic avant-gardes, looking closely on selected works of emblematic modernist artists. Bru examines how the regime of historicity assigned to the avant-garde, against the temporalities of classic historicism and beyond futurism (Renato Poggioli) and presentism (François Hartog), appears to be the 'future anterior' that describes both the anticipatory quality of the avant-garde and the intrusion of the past in the present as a history of tomorrow. More than this, he argues, by exploiting the essentially anachronic function of all art, the avant-garde movements encompassed interchronicity and polytemporality (according to Bruno Latour), acceding ontological primacy to no particular temporal category in the end.[57] Similarly to the claim made by Saunders, Bru views avant-garde historiographical experiments as both running parallel and contributing to the development of new theories of history in the twentieth century and beyond. This attests to art's potentiality as not purely material of historical study but as an 'organon' of history.[58]

The volume is also dedicated in historicizing avant-garde movements and works by placing them in their proper historical context. As Walter Benjamin urges in his 1931 essay 'Literary History and the Study of Literature', in any literary (or art) history we need to include the history of a work's entire life and effects, its reception by its contemporaries, its translations, its fame, alongside that of its composition.[59] Alexandra Bickley Trott's chapter, entitled 'Beer in Bohemian Paris: A Symbol of the Third Republic', reflects on the histories of modern art movements, pushing them earlier into the nineteenth century, according to a current critical trend in modernist studies.[60] The chapter reveals the iconographic importance of beer for the bohemian Hydropathes and the Bon Bock club of *fin de siècle* Paris, as expressive of a hidden socio-political agenda. The Hydropathes are linked with the development of *laïcité*, and the emergent secularism in liberal republican France, while the Bon Bock group's apparent obsession with beer is connected to a nationalist history in the wake of the Franco-Prussian war. The discussion draws on original research into the bohemianism of *fin de siècle* Paris and historicizes its cultural production by viewing less studied groups as these in the light of the period's political tensions.

Surrealism is also pinned in its historical everydayness in Rachel Silveri's archival study presented in the essay 'From the Marvellous to the Managerial: Life at the Surrealist Research Bureau', which reassesses the movement's mode of production at its early stages. The practices of the Surrealist Research Bureau are historicized in relation to a broader set of social discourses, including the rationalization of the office space, the rise of bureaucracy and the prevalence of management practices in interwar France. Silveri argues that despite the Surrealist demand for revolutionary action and liberated desire, the artists themselves were mired in a network of power relationships typical of enterprise structures. The essay, thus, revises and enriches the history of one of the most prominent avant-garde movements, revealing its genetic oppositions.

Also focused on obscure aspects of surrealism producing new and expanded histories of modernism and the avant-garde through archival research of geographically or historically peripheral versions of the movement is Sanja Bahun's essay, 'History and Active Thought: The Belgrade Surrealist Circle's Transforming Praxis'. This chapter delves into the lesser known Belgrade Surrealist Circle placing it in the historical context of monarchical Yugoslavia, drawing on literary, philosophical and visual material. Such historicizing attempts indeed render a fuller view of the political affiliations, implications and charge of the movements examined. Following surrealism's political tendentiousness internationally, but also due to its location at the liminal intersection of two demising empires (Austro-Hungarian and Ottoman), and between the demands of an imported notion of nation-state and the indigenous styles of political action, The Belgrade Surrealist Circle produced politically engaged theories. They focused on the aesthetic modes and strategies of representation suitable for continual rebellion and self-critique against Western individualism and passivity leading to reification, thus proposing an historical intervention, a revolutionary approach to matter, history and art-making, through the category of the irrational stemming from the unconscious.

An insistence on art as a 'praxis', transforming material as well as subjective history for the future, is a constant feature of modernist and avant-garde poetics that may in turn account for its continuing actuality. However, this does not necessarily accord with Paul de Man's notion, expressed in his essay, 'Literary History and Literary Modernity',[61] that modernity is part of the historical process found in every epoch and every act of literature, which in fact ontologizes the concept of modernity and thus dehistoricizes it. Rather, historicizing modernism is meant to pay heed to the historically specific mode of thinking and/in art-making ushered by that historical moment associated with 'modernism' in all its capaciousness and its political, affective and aesthetic effects.

All the essays in the volume testify to the resilience of modernism, a term that has been much used and abused and that still fulfils a function even without a coherent definition. Our collection will have reached its aim if it can persuade that one point must be maintained: modernism is historical, but this history is not stable or written in stone, it is still in the making, which entails that we have to keep historicizing it.

Notes

1. Walter Benjamin, *The Arcades Project*, trans. Howard Eiland and Kevin McLaughlin (Cambridge, MA: Harvard University Press, 1999), 545.
2. See Laura Spinney, *Pale Rider: The Spanish Flu of 1918 and How It Changed the World* (New York: Public Affairs), 2017.
3. 'A Litter to James Joyce', in *Our Exagmination Round His Factification for Incamination of Work in Progress*, ed. Samuel Beckett and others (London: Faber, 1972), 193.
4. This play is summarized by Stanislaus Joyce in *My Brother's Keeper: James Joyce's Early Years* (Cambridge: Da Capo Press, 2003), 115. As Stanislaus mentions, there had been a few cases of bubonic plague in Glasgow in 1900. It was stopped relatively fast. It spread from China in 1882, and then reached India, Madagascar, Egypt, Paraguay, Portugal, South Africa, Scotland, Russia, Australia, until it ended in Cuba and Puerto Rico in 1912.
5. See Richard Ellmann, *James Joyce*, rev. ed. (Oxford: Oxford University Press, 1982), 78–80.
6. Ibid., 398.
7. Letter of 21 April 1969, in Samuel Beckett, *Letters Vol. IV: 1966–1989* (Cambridge: Cambridge University Press, 2016), 158.
8. James Joyce, *Exiles*, in *Poems and Exiles*, edited with an Introduction by C.C. Mays (London: Penguin, 1992), 351.
9. Ibid., 158.
10. Susan Stanford Friedman, *Planetary Modernisms: Provocations on Modernity across Time* (New York: Columbia University Press, 2018).
11. See Thomas Crow, *Modern Art in the Common Culture* (New Haven: Yale University Press, 1998).
12. Valerie Steele, *Paris Fashion: A Cultural History*, rev. edition (New York: Bloomsbury, 2017), 193.
13. Chris Greenhalgh, *Coco Chanel & Igor Stravinsky* (New York: Riverhead books, 2002), 16–17.
14. Lisa Chaney, *Coco Chanel: An Intimate Life* (New York: Viking), 92.
15. See, for example, Dipesh Chakrabarty's dismantling the master narrative of European history, according to which ' "Europe" remains the sovereign, theoretical

subject of all history, including the ones we call Indian, Chinese, Kenyan, and so on'. In 'Postcoloniality and the Artifice of History: Who Speaks of Indian Pasts? *Representations*, no. 37 (Winter, 1992): 1.
16 Collected in Eugène Jolas, *Critical Writings, 1924–1951*, edited and with an introduction by Klaus H. Kiefer and Rainer Rumold (Evanston: Northwestern University Press, 2009). Hence abbreviated as CW followed by page number.
17 See Tom Bishop, *Le Passeur d'Océan: carnets d'un ami américain* (Paris: Payot, 1989).
18 Philippe Lacoue-Labarthe and Jean-Luc Nancy, *The Literary Absolute: The Theory of Literature in German Romanticism*, trans. Philip Barnard and Cheryl Lester (Albany: State University of New York Press, 1988).
19 Samuel Beckett, *Letters Vol. II: 1941–1956* (Cambridge: Cambridge University Press, 2012), 161.
20 Eugène Jolas, 'From Jabberwocky to "Lettrism"', *Transition Forty-Eight*, no 1, ed. Georges Duthuit (January 1948) : 104–20.
21 Georges Duthuit, 'Matisse and Byzantine Space', *Transition Forty-Nine*, no. 5 (1949): 20.
22 Ibid., 29.
23 Clement Greenberg, 'Review of Exhibitions of Joan Miró and André Masson' (1947), in *Collected Essays and Criticism, 1939–1944, Vol. 1*, ed. John O'Brian (Chicago: The University of Chicago Press, 1986), 208.
24 Ibid., 209.
25 Ibid.
26 Clement Greenberg, *The Collected Essays and Criticism, Vol. 4, Modernism with a Vengeance, 1957–1969* (*Chicago*: Chicago University Press, 1993), 85.
27 Pierre Bourdieu, *The Rules of Art: Genesis and Structure of the Literary Field*, trans. Susan Emanuel (Stanford: Stanford University Press, 1995), 160.
28 Andrew McNamara, *Surpassing Modernity: Ambivalence in Art, Politics and Society* (New York: Bloomsbury, 2019).
29 Ibid., 2.
30 Ibid., 9.
31 Benjamin's structural oscillation has also been noted by other scholars, such as John McCole, in *Walter Benjamin and the Antinomies of Tradition* (Ithaca, NY: Cornell University Press, 1993).
32 Ibid., 35.
33 Aristotle, *Physics, Vol. 1: Books 1–4*, trans. P. H. Wicksteed and F. M. Cornford, (Cambridge, MA: Harvard University Press, Loeb Classical Library, 1989), Book 4 §10 217b29–218a3.
34 Since the invention of pendulum clock in the seventeenth century and the establishment of World Standard Time in 1884, time has become connected with modern imperialism and globalization. See, for example, Stephen Kern, *The Culture of Time and Space, 1880–1918* (Cambridge, MA: Harvard University Press, 1983),

1 and 314. On the modern history of measuring time in relation to literature, see Randall Stevenson, *Reading the Times: Temporality and History in Twentieth-Century Fiction* (Edinburgh: Edinburgh University Press, 2018).

35 Walter Benjamin, 'On the Concept of History' (1940), in *Selected Writing, Vol. 4: 1938*, ed. Howard Eiland and Michael W. Jennings (Cambridge, MA: Harvard University Press, 2006), 394–5.

36 Ibid., 392.

37 Ezra Pound, *Guide to Kulchur* (New York: New Directions, 1970), 60.

38 Benjamin, *The Arcades Project*, Convolute NII,3 and N2,6. And further in Nl1,2., he claimed: 'To write history means giving dates their physiognomy'. On time, progress and historical method, see also N9a,7.

39 Ibid., N9a,7.

40 George Lukács, 'The Ideology of Modernism', in *The Meaning of Contemporary Realism*, trans. John & Necke Mander (London: Merlin Press, 1963), 20–1.

41 Ibid., 29, 39.

42 Aristotle, *Poetics*, trans. Ingram Baywater, in *The Complete Works of Aristotle; The Revised Oxford Translation Vol. 2*, ed. Jonathan Barnes (New Jersey: Princeton University Press, 1984), 9.1451b 1–10.

43 Paul Ricoeur, *Time and Narrative Vol. 1*, trans. Kathleen Mclaughlin and David Pellauer (Chicago: University of Chicago Press, 1984), 100.

44 Ibid., 154.

45 Hayden White, 'The Historical Event', *Differences; A Journal of Feminist Cultural Studies* 19, no 2 (2008): 13.

46 Roland Barthes, 'The Discourse of History' (1963), in *The Rustle of Language*, trans. Richard Howard (New York: Hill & Wang, 1986), 138.

47 Wilhelm Dilthey, *Selected Writings Vol. 5: Poetry and Experience*, ed. R. Makkreel and F. Rodi (Princeton, NJ: Princeton University Press, 1985), 36.

48 See Jacques Rancière, *The Names of History: On the Poetics of Knowledge*, trans. Hassan Melehy (Minneapolis: University of Minnesota Press, 1994); *and Mute Speech: Literature, Critical Theory, and Politics*, trans. James Swenson (New York: Columbia University Press, 2011).

49 Such questions were also addressed and tested during the two-day conference, entitled 'Historical Modernisms' which took place at the Senate House, University of London, on 13 December 2016 and was organized by the Institute of English Studies at the School of Advanced Study in the framework of the Institute's 'Comparative Modernisms' Seminar convened by Angeliki Spiropoulou.

50 'Poetry, Fiction and the Future', in *The Essays of Virginia Woolf Vol. 4*, ed. Andrew McNeille (London: The Hogarth Press, 1984), 429. This essay was first published in *New York Herald Tribune* in 1927 and later reprinted under the title 'The Narrow Bridge of Art' in the posthumous collections of Woolf's essays, *Granite and Rainbow* and the *Collected Essays*, both edited by Leonard Woolf.

51 In his book *The Culture of Time and Space 1880–1918,* Stephen Kern argues that 'a series of sweeping changes in technology and culture created distinctive new modes of thinking about and experiencing time and space', in the *fin de siècle* when the sense of the present was 'distinctively new, thickened temporally with retentions and protentions of past and future and, most important, expanded spatially to create the vast, shared experience of simultaneity', also related to the introduction of World Standard Time in 1884 and a combination of technological innovations – the telephone, wireless telegraph, X-ray, cinema, and the bicycle, automobile and airplane – and cultural ones, in particular the 'affirmation of private time' with its radical interiority of experience (1, 314).

52 See Henri Bergson's 1907 book, *Creative Evolution,* trans. Arthur Mitchell (Henry Holt and Company, 1911). Earlier in his 1889 doctoral thesis, *Time and Free Will: An Essay on the Immediate Data of Consciousness* (London: Routledge, 2003), Bergson made a distinction between *durée réelle* (duration) and the mechanical, spatialized measuring of time. See also Mary Ann Gillies, *Bergson and British Modernism* (Montréal Que: McGill-Queen's University Press, 1996).

53 T. S. Eliot, 'Tradition and the Individual Talent', in *Selected Essays 1917–1932* (London: Faber & Faber, 1980), 14.

54 Rancière, *Mute Speech,* 28.

55 See Woolf, 'Modern Fiction', in *The Essays of Virginia Woolf Vol. 4,* 160.

56 See Sanjay Subrahmanyam, 'On World Historians in the Sixteenth Century', *Representations* 91, no. 1 (Summer 2005): 26–8.

57 See Renato Poggioli, *The Theory of the Avant-Garde,* trans. by Gerald Fitzgerald (Cambridge, MA: The Belknap Press of the Harvard University Press, 1968); François Hartog, *Régimes d'historicité. Présentisme et expériences du temps* (Paris: Seuil, 2003); and Bruno Latour, *Nous n'avons jamais été modernes: Essai d'anthropologie symétrique* (Paris: La Découverte, 1991).

58 Walter Benjamin, 'Literary History and the Study of Literature' (1931), in *Selected Writings Vol. 2: 1927–1934,* ed. Marcus Bullock, Howard Eiland and Garry Smith (Massachusetts: Harvard University Press, 1999), 464.

59 Ibid.

60 See, for example, *Late Victorian into Modern,* ed. Laura Marcus, Michèle Mendelssohn, and Kirsten E. Shepherd-Barr (Oxford: Oxford University Press, 2016), which addresses the continuities between Victorian and modern against their mutual exclusion in standard accounts of literary history.

61 Paul de Man, 'Literary History and Literary Modernity', in *Blindness and Insight: Essays in the Rhetoric of Contemporary Criticism* (London: Routledge, 1989).

Part I

Historicizing modernism

1

'The Last Witnesses': Autobiography and history in the 1930s

Laura Marcus

Explorations and definitions of modernist historiography, which rest so substantially on critiques of the linear (or teleological) and historicist (or relativist) models associated strongly with nineteenth-century historians (and criticized by Nietzsche in the nineteenth century and by many others after him), have not been brought to bear to any great extent on accounts of autobiography in the modernist period, though autobiography as a genre could certainly be understood as a mode of history-writing or, at least, as occupying the border territory between history and literature.

Autobiography is by definition concerned with the relationship between the past and the present. The tendency of the genre to construct a linear and continuous life-narrative (though there are of course many exceptions to this) was one reason for modernist writers to stand apart from the form. Few of the most prominent modernist writers produced self-declared autobiographies, and this, accompanied by a focus on modernist 'impersonality', meant that for many decades modernism was perceived as a movement and a period either hostile or indifferent to autobiographical representation. (There is a parallel in the perceived opposition of modernists to history and the historical novel, though, as Seamus O'Malley has shown with particular reference to Conrad, Ford Madox Ford and Rebecca West, this is also a misconception.[1]) It now seems clear that autobiography lay at the heart of much modernist literary production, though most often in displaced forms: the *Bildungsroman* and *Künstlerroman*, autobiographical fiction and the fragmentary forms of journal and diary.

The writers I discuss in this chapter, which include Virginia Woolf, Stefan Zweig and, in its second part, Bryher (Winifred Ellerman) and Walter Benjamin, did, however, produce explicitly autobiographical texts, even if they distanced this work, as did Benjamin, from autobiography *per se*. Born into the nineteenth century or at the turn of the century, they subsequently experienced the rapidly changing conditions of early-twentieth-century modernity. The historical and political contexts of the late 1930s, with the increasing threat and then declaration of war, produced a sense, implicit or explicit, of the profound uncertainties of the present and of the shape of the future. The autobiographical writings of Benjamin and Zweig raise particular questions about historical fragmentations, brought about by the condition of exile, but there is a more general theme of sharp discontinuity that runs throughout this period.[2]

Benjamin is central here, in that his engagements with the philosophy of history are some of the most radical in the twentieth century, and are predicated on concepts of rupture, a deep antithesis towards conventional models of 'progress', an understanding of, in Christian Emden's phrase, 'the dynamic of historical time strata in the simultaneity of the non-simultaneous' (a conception shared by Karl Mannheim in his 'Historismus' essay[3]) and a method which involved constellations of juxtaposed images.[4] 'Articulating the past historically,' Benjamin famously wrote in 'On the Concept of History', 'does not mean recognizing it "the way it was". It means appropriating a memory as it flashes up in a moment of danger.'[5] 'Now-time' (*Jetztzeit*) is not mere 'presentism' but 'a past ... blasted out the continuum of history'.[6] Zweig also stresses the decisive moments (*Sternstunden*) of history – his autobiography, *The World of Yesterday*, represents the end of the pre–First World War era (and the empire) and the collapse of European culture in the face of fascism[7] – but at the same time he was deeply concerned with the time-dimensions of history and life-writing in a more philosophical sense. Hence the lecture which he wrote at the close of the 1930s in which he talked of history as a literary artist (*Dichterin*).[8] The historical sketches he wrote under the category of *Sternstunden* revolve around charged moments (of varying duration) within the individual and/or the collective life and the relationship between inner experience and outer event.

Writing in 1928 of Thomas De Quincey, whose *Confessions of an English Opium-Eater* appeared in 1821, Virginia Woolf argued that both autobiography 'as the eighteenth century knew it' and biography[9] had been transformed by a more penetrating focus on the interior life of the individual. Yet, she asserts:

> external events also have their importance. To tell the whole story of a life the autobiographer must devise some means by which the two levels of existence can be recorded – the rapid passage of events and actions; the slow opening up of single and solemn moments of concentrated emotion. It is the fascination of De Quincey's pages that the two levels are beautifully, if unequally, combined. For

page after page we are in company with a cultivated gentleman who describes with charm and eloquence what he has seen and known – the stage coaches, the Irish rebellion, the appearance and conversation of George the Third. Then suddenly the smooth narrative parts asunder, arch opens beyond arch, the vision of something for ever flying, for ever escaping, is revealed, and time stands still.[10]

The connection between the outer and the inner is thus linked, in Woolf's account, as in Zweig's, to two different temporalities: the flow of time (the historical continuum) and its suspension or hollowing out from within.

A dominant image in the autobiographies of the period is that of the altered speed of the twentieth century. Stefan Zweig was representative of many when he wrote of the middle-European world into which he was born and educated as

an ordered world with definite classes and calm transitions, a world without haste. The rhythm of the new speed had not yet carried over from the machines, the automobile, the telephone, the radio, and the aeroplane, to mankind; time and age had another measure.[11]

Describing the cultural passions of his generation, he writes of the 'solid masters of our father's time' that 'they no longer interested us. Instinctively we felt that their cool, well-tempered rhythm was alien to our restless blood and no longer in keeping with the accelerated tempo of our time'.[12] But from the perspectives of the late 1930s (and 1940, when Zweig was writing his autobiography), it was not just that the old world had been superseded but that the world that had replaced it was already undergoing extinction.

While autobiographical narrative must of necessity be predicated on a degree of continuity between past and present selves, there is also a sense, in the texts of this particular period, of a marked difference between, in Virginia Woolf's words, the 'two people: I now, I then'.[13] While for Goethe, the imperative was that 'the individual know himself *and his century*, himself as the same in the midst of all the circumstances',[14] the modernist autobiographer is much more likely to represent a self in flux or mutation over time.[15] The autobiographical form may, however, serve to hold these disparate selves together within a single frame and to create a relatively stable 'platform of time', in Woolf's phrase, from the circumstances of the present on which to stand and observe the flow of time.

Opening the first lines of her memoir, posthumously published as 'Sketch of the Past', with a date – 'Two days ago – Sunday 16 April 1939 to be precise – Nessa said that if I did not start writing my memoirs I should soon be too old' – Woolf pointed both to the immediate time of the work's composition and to a different point of origin: 'I begin: the first memory.' The vivid recall of her impressions of the past led her to write that they 'can still be more real than the present moment',[16] seeming to possess 'an existence independent of our minds', and to imagine a future device which would make it possible to 'tap' into time past:

> Instead of remembering here a scene and there a sound, I shall fit a plug into the wall; and listen into the past. I shall turn up August 1890. I feel that strong emotion must leave its trace; and it is only a question of discovering how we can get ourselves again attached to it, so that we shall be able to live our lives through from the start.[17]

The writing of the memoir continued into 1940 with the gap of a year between '19 June 1939' and '8 June 1940'. 'The present' was now that of wartime, though Woolf mentions this circumstance very briefly in the intermittent passages with which she begins different sections of the text.

> *The present.* 19 June 1940. As we sat down to lunch two days ago, Monday 17th, John [Lehmann] came in, looked white about the gills, his pale eyes paler than usual, and said the French have stopped fighting. Today the dictators dictate their terms to France. Meanwhile, on this very hot morning, with a blue bottle buzzing and a toothless organ grinding and the men calling strawberries in the Square, I sit in my room at 37 M[ecklenburgh] S[quare] and turn to my father.[18]

Woolf's account of the emotional demands made by her Victorian father, the philosopher and writer Leslie Stephen, and, indeed, of his 'tyranny' after her mother's death suggests that the link suggested in the paragraph between fathers and dictators is neither accidental nor unmotivated; it was a line of thinking Woolf had already explored in detail in *Three Guineas* (1938). 'Two different ages,' she writes of her father in *A Sketch of the Past*, 'confronted each other in the drawing room of Hyde Park Gate [her childhood home]. The Victorian age and the Edwardian age ... We looked at him with eyes that were looking into the future.'[19] She writes of her adolescent years that 'it was the tyrant father – the exacting, the violent, the histrionic, the demonstrative, the self-centred, the alternately loved and hated father – who dominated me then.'[20] 'It was only the other day,' Woolf writes, 'when I read Freud for the first time, that I discovered that this violently disturbing conflict of love and hate is a common feeling; and is called ambivalence'.[21]

Virginia and Leonard Woolf had met Freud in London in January 1939, some four months before his death. Her reading of Freud at the end of the 1930s took her to his 'Massenpsychologie und Ichanalyse' ('Group Psychology and the Analysis of the Ego') (1921) and to his late works on civilization and its vicissitudes. There is a connection here to the very different work of Arthur Koestler and Stefan Zweig. Their encounters with the exiled Freud in his final months form a culminating point to their memoirs of Europe in the first decades of the twentieth century, marking an end point to a culture whose demise was brought about by the forces of destruction which it was his life's work to analyse. 'We must agree with Freud,' Zweig wrote at the opening of *The World of Yesterday*, 'to whom our culture and civilization were merely a thin layer liable at any moment to be pierced by the destructive forces of the "underworld".'[22] At the autobiography's close, Zweig writes of his final discussions with the dying Freud in London: 'In those hours I frequently spoke with Freud about the horror of Hitler's world and the war. The outburst of bestiality deeply shocked him as a humanitarian, but as a thinker he was in no way astonished.'[23] Yet Freud, with whom he had been in contact since 1908, also represents, for Zweig as for others, turn-of-the-century Vienna in its intellectual flowering; a culture which is understood to be much more than a thin veneer over a fundamental barbarism.

For those whose lives were made particularly turbulent by the historical forces of the early twentieth century, assumptions of continuity had frequently become meaningless. Psychological, and psychoanalytic, models of the self's multiplicity were combined, and at times subordinated to, a sense of the radical dispersal of identity imposed by external events. 'My today and each of my yesterdays,' Zweig wrote,

> my rises and falls, are so diverse that I sometimes feel as if I had lived not one, but several existences, each one different from the others ... My feeling is that the world in which I grew up, and the world of today, and the world between the two, are entirely separate worlds ... All the bridges between our today and our yesteryears have been burned.[24]

The turn to the past in autobiographical writing of this time thus took a variety of forms, but there was a shared sense that what was being recaptured in recall and writing was either long-lost or on the brink of disappearance. Zweig, contemplating in 1939 the work that would become *The World of Yesterday* (largely composed in exile in New York and Brazil in 1940/1), wrote to his friend Felix Braun, a younger writer who had, like Zweig, fled to Britain:

> Wouldn't it perhaps be the right thing to do, some time when you have some leisure, to provide a portrait of Vienna and our youth, and even if they live only as memories, still to allow them to rise again intensively and thus creatively? I myself want to write such a book some time, not as an autobiography but a

farewell to that Austrian-Jewish-bourgeois culture culminating in Mahler, Hoffmannsthal, Schnitzler and Freud. For this Vienna and this Austria will never exist again and never come again. We are the last witnesses.[25]

While Zweig, in working on the book, referred to it as an autobiography and as the 'story of his life', he also insisted that it was predominantly the story of an epoch. The text, though it is unusually frank about the sexual experiences of his generation (a focus undoubtedly inspired by Zweig's close relationship with Freud, to whom he had written that, under his influence, autobiography had become 'more clear sighted and audacious'[26]), is not intimate or introspective. Zweig, in the first chapters of the text in particular, instead charts his encounters, in the different cities of Europe, with some of the most significant cultural figures of the early twentieth century – Rudolf Steiner in Berlin, Emile Verhaeren in Brussels, Rilke and Romain Rolland in Paris, Yeats and Symons in London. The Preface to *The World of Yesterday* opens with a disclaimer about the act of autobiography (a familiar rhetorical gesture throughout the entire tradition of autobiographical writing):

> I have never attached so much importance to my own person that I would have been tempted to tell others the story of my life. Much had to occur, infinitely more events, catastrophes, and trials than are usually allotted to a single generation had to come to pass ... Nothing is further from my thought than to take so pivotal a place unless it be in the role of a narrator at an illustrated lecture. Time gives the pictures; I merely speak the words which accompany them. Actually, it is not so much the course of my own destiny that I relate, but that of an entire generation, the generation of our time, which was loaded with a burden of fate as was hardly any other in the course of history.[27]

In Zweig's conception of history as a literary artist (*Dichterin*),[28] he compared historical truth to an artichoke, where peeling off the leaves never reveals the ultimate core. Beginning to write his autobiography in Bath, without access to his personal archive of notes and correspondence, reinforced the invented, *gedichtet*, quality of the text. As one of his earliest biographers, Donald Prater, wrote, in both his autobiography and in his historical works Zweig saw himself as 'the instrument of history herself as an artist'.[29]

Arthur Koestler, in his autobiography *Arrow in the Blue*, outlined the two modes which he saw as the autobiographer's primary choices – 'the Chronicler's urge', which 'expresses the need for the sharing of experience related to external events' and 'the *Ecce Homo* motive' which 'expresses the same need with regard to internal events'.[30] He had attempted in writing his own autobiography, he stated at the close of *The Invisible Writing*, to combine 'the historian's and the psychologist's approach'.[31] There was, however, for many writers a marked tension between the model of autobiography as an inward turn and the perception that the role of the writer, even when narrating his or her own experiences, was to record the times – even to 'bear witness'. 'My desire', the Russian poet Osip Mandelstam wrote, in an autobiographical piece composed in the late 1920s, 'The Noise of Time', 'is not to speak about myself but to track down the age, the noise and the germination of time. My memory is inimical to all that is personal ... and it labours not to reproduce but to distance the past'.[32]

Mandelstam's work of distancing contrasts with Zweig's acts of memory, which have been criticized for their apolitical nostalgia and their failure to engage with anti-Semitism in the Vienna of the early twentieth century which he seeks to recapture.[33] The trajectory described in *The World of Yesterday* is one in which Zweig and his compatriots move from a position as a 'citizen of the world' to, in exile, becoming a citizen of nowhere: 'I have no compunction about admitting that since the day when I had to depend upon identity papers or passports that were indeed alien, I ceased to feel as if I quite belonged to myself. A part of the natural identity with my original and essential ego was destroyed for ever.'[34] As George Prochnik suggests, Zweig was haunted by 'the great fear of the exile ... the notion that uprooting translates into terminal disconnection'.[35] The autobiography charts this disconnection, though it could be said that its very composition was an attempt not only to create some form of continuity between past and present lives but, more problematically, to smooth over the embarrassing fact of his Austrian-German patriotism at the beginning of the First World War.[36]

In the Preface to *The World of Yesterday*, one of whose working titles was 'My Three Lives', Zweig writes that 'it often happens that when I carelessly speak of "my life," I am forced to ask, "which life?" – the one before the World War, the one between the first and second, or the life of today ... My feeling is that the world in which I grew up, and the world of today, and the world between the two, are entirely separate worlds'. For many, it was the outbreak of war in 1914 that marked an absolute break with the past: Koestler wrote that 'though born in 1905', he had been a 'a true child of the nineteenth century – the century of crude philosophies and arrogant over-simplifications which lingered on into the twentieth, until the First World War brought it to a close with a bang'.[37] Benjamin, in his essay 'The Storyteller', wrote of the First World War as producing an end to transmittable experience, and effecting absolute and 'overnight' changes in 'our image not only of the external world but also of the moral world':

For never has experience been more thoroughly belied than strategic experience was belied by tactical warfare, economic experience by inflation, bodily experience by mechanical warfare, moral experience by those in power. A generation that had gone to school on horse-drawn streetcars now stood under the open sky in a landscape where nothing remained unchanged but the clouds and, beneath those clouds, in a force field of destructive torrents and explosions, the tiny, fragile human body.[38]

For others, the temporal divide between the centuries – the year 1900 – acted as a particularly charged historical marker, and one which often became an integral part of autobiographical narratives, as in *The Education of Henry Adams*, the autobiography, written in the third person, of the US historian and politician Henry Adams. Between the two is 1910, 'on or around' which, Woolf wrote, 'human character changed.' Gottfried Benn, writing in 1955, the year before his death, also cited 1910 as the year in which 'the scaffolds began to crack,'[39] while Henri Lefebvre, in 1974, wrote that 'around 1910 a certain space was shattered. It was the space of common sense, of knowledge (savoir), of political power ... This was truly a crucial moment.'[40] For Thomas Harrison, the year 1910 saw some of the most important developments in European cultural formations and artistic expression, but was also marked by its nihilism and its uncertainties in relation to past, present and future: 'Nothing in 1910 is definitively over and nothing definitively begun .... The prewar years were a workshop of *futurisme* and *passéisme* alike ... Ten years into the century both a death and a birth seem to have taken too long in coming.'[41]

Bryher and Benjamin

The English writer Bryher (the name by which Annie Winifred Ellerman, born in 1894, was known) did not publish her full autobiography (of the years from birth up until the outbreak of the Second World War), *Heart to Artemis*, until 1963. From the opening paragraphs of *The Heart to Artemis* onwards, Bryher made clear her intention to position her life and experience in their literary, historical and geographical contexts:

> When I was born in September, 1894, Dorothy Richardson's Miriam was a secretary. Mallarmé had just retired and was no longer teaching English to French schoolboys. The death duties that were to obliterate most of our feudal estates had been introduced in that year's budget while the *Fram* was drifting through the polar ice and would-be explorers dreamed about Bokhara, a

fabulous city that was then more difficult to access than Tibet. I opened my eyes upon the end of not only the nineteenth century but of a second Puritan age. An epoch passed away while I was learning to speak and walk. Its influence remains as the start of memory and as a measuring rod for progress that even Edwardian survivors lack.[42]

Sections that would be incorporated into this text had been printed some decades earlier. In the July 1937 issue of *Life and Letters To-Day*[43] Bryher published an autobiographical essay titled 'Paris, 1900'. This short memoir focused on a family visit in early childhood to the 1900 Paris Exposition, the experience of which had been described by Henry Adams as creating an absolute rupture between the centuries, as he found himself, overwhelmed by the power of the 'dynamo' which was the Exhibition's source of power, 'lying in the Gallery of Machines at the Great Exposition of 1900 with his historical neck broken by the sudden irruption of forces totally new'.[44] These 'forces' (material, dynamic, electrical) radically undermine the historian's arrangement of sequences, and his former faith in the relations of cause and effect, as well as the 'stories or histories' which supported them.[45] We might, for all the radical differences between Adams' and Benjamin's circumstances and thought, find some connection between the fracturing of historical causality and sequence which Adams describes, and Benjamin's critique of historicism as contenting itself with 'establishing a causal nexus among various moments in history'. The historian who understands this fallacy 'ceases to tell the sequence of events like the beads of a rosary'.[46]

Bryher's 'Paris, 1900' was published during the months of the 1937 Exposition, the last of its kind in Paris, in which Nazi Germany and the Soviet Union competed for symbolic power through the monumental architecture of their pavilions, which flanked the Eiffel Tower. It opens with these lines: 'All my life I have suffered from "geographical emotions". Cities are so much easier to understand than people.'[47] Bryher represents the sea-voyage to Dieppe, and the boat-train to Paris, from a perspective which is at once a child's eye view and makes claims to capture the spirit of the age or the signs of the times: 'Everything was heavy; where possible it was solid. A historian without other chronicle to guide him might reconstruct the age from the pictures of its luggage.'[48] The daughter of the industrialist and shipping magnate Sir John Ellerman, Bryher was from an early age travelling the world; the journey to Paris was the first of many voyages abroad. She records in the memoir that in 1900 there were strong hostilities between the French and the English (Britain was in disgrace at the time over the Boer War, and on a subsequent visit to France two years later

Bryher saw Kruger making a speech from a balcony) and that her childhood self was both nationalistic and pugilistic:

> To read of fascism now is to see the picture of that Paris street. I fulfilled all nationalistic obligations, in complete confidence that I was right, merely because I had been born in England. Brutality is a part of primitive nature and it is a need of childhood, atom in so vast a world, to assert its ego … Only, civilisations should be built, not by children, but by men.[49]

From this observation, Bryher moves directly to an account of the Exposition. She recalls 'the entrance and the symbol of the Exhibition'; 'an immense arch in plaster', which she calls 'the magnified twin of a hair-ornament of the period, a two-pronged comb over which convolvulus of many decorations ramped in flowery dots. Everything at that time had to curl; there should exist a name to describe the horror of 1900 over a blank space'.[50] This entrance was 'La Porte Monumentale', designed by the architect René Binet, an enormous, ornately decorated arch, crowned by a statue (created by Moreau-Vauthier) called 'La Parisienne' which was clothed in modern Parisian fashion and illuminated at night by thousands of light bulbs. Both the statue and the electrical illuminations were intended and received as celebrations of modernity; 'La Porte Monumentale' was a flamboyant example of the Art Nouveau style of the 1890s and 1900s, the aesthetic which dominated the Exhibition as a whole. Bryher links the period style not to the new century but to the previous one, represented as a dying epoch. She writes of the galleries they visited:

> Everything was carved; was either giant or dwarf. Mermaids wriggled from mother-of-pearl water lilies that opened into a vase, the legs of a table bent like bamboos in the wind. The glass cases were crowded; they were a snail's shell of surfaces, coral, garnet, enamel, or amber …. And perhaps because all sincerity of emotion was repressed, the age, as it felt itself dying, redoubled outward forms and put the emphasis of life upon ownership of thousands of small possessions. It was at the Paris exhibition that modern art was born. The unconscious mind of thousands must have begun to imagine blank spaces and straight lines, while the eyes stared at cabinets full of miniatures, toy clocks, jewelled thimble cases, and Fragonard paintings reproduced in beads upon tiny bags.[51]

Her five-year-old self was, Bryher writes, far more interested in the pavilion containing 'Krupp's exhibit of long and shining guns', at which her parents expressed horror, than in a gallery of toys ('[The soldiers'] red trousers displeased me, everybody knew that the new English khaki blended much better with the landscape').[52] The memoir is striking in the vividness of its description of her early memories of Paris and of the tension between her delight in France, including her first taste of *galettes*, and her nationalistic impulses. While her childhood patriotism and pugilism were linked, she indicates, to her keen desire to be a boy (a theme that runs throughout her writing and her life),[53] she ends the memoir with these words: 'Though my later way was to be in a different direction and in another country, it was in France that I first learned to be a European.'[54]

A version of 'Paris, 1900' was translated into French in 1937 by Adrienne Monnier and Sylvia Beach, who owned the Paris bookshop *Shakespeare and Company*.[55] Beach and Monnier had been close friends of Bryher's since the 1920s: 'there was only one street in Paris for me, the rue de l'Odéon' – Bryher later wrote in *Heart to Artemis*.[56] In 1940 Monnier published a short piece in the final issue of *La Gazette des Amis des Livres* (May 1940), 'Our Friend Bryher', in which she wrote of Bryher's commitment to France and French literature and culture. She also referred to her French translation of 'Paris, 1900', 'the account of the journey [Bryher] made to Paris as a child, during the 1900 Exposition', which the *Nouvelle Revue Française* had published in its December 1937 issue, adding that 'I had a small book made of them [Bryher's memories], the appearance of which has been delayed by events and which is coming out now'.[57] This last issue of the *Gazette*, published in the month in which the German army entered France, also contained an article by Walter Benjamin on Georges Salles's *Regard*.

In a letter dated 19 December 1937, Walter Benjamin, who came to know Monnier and Beach well in the Paris of the 1930s and was helped by them, and by Bryher[58] during the Nazi Occupation, wrote to Bryher, with whom he had previously been in contact, saying how much he admired 'Paris, 1900' and that he looked forward to reading the whole of it:

> I have at last had the pleasure of reading something by you. *Paris 1900* certainly attracted me because it is by you. It won me over by its own merits.
>
> It is a completely pure-spirited text. It has something which is rare in childhood reminiscences, the *loyauté* which downplays nothing and thereby expresses the grace of childhood by displaying its often dark background. In this dark background your little heroine sometimes recalls children in the paintings of Reynolds and Gainsborough. In others she has the still, martial decisiveness which one could read in the face of Alice in Wonderland in my childhood edition. Just as you march out from the station into the midst of the contemptible (*verächtlichen*) French.
>
> I have often reflected on the importance of giving free rein to the aggressivity (in fantasy) of children. You surely know Struwwelpeter – one of the most read

children's books in Germany. It takes full account of this aggressivity of children. That is why they love it so much. the real horrors confronting them lie elsewhere. As you describe in relation to the white-faced clown, 'un danger au-delà de l'imagination.'

One of the passages which most deeply affected me was that of the crêpes. And how true that the highest degree of reality which something can have for a child is that it 'emerges' directly out of one of their books!

You have found the redeeming word for the entrance arch of the world fair which has often worried me. You have recognised in it the *comb* which crowns the allure of Paris!

I should like one day to be able to read this text in full. Perhaps it could lead to a small exchange. As I began to realise in 1932, at first more unconsciously than not, that I was facing exile, I practised a kind of immunisation which would preserve me from nostalgia for the city in which I had spent my childhood.[59] At that time I wrote, under the title 'Berlin Childhood around 1900', a series of short sketches. Most of them are still in print and I would be glad to send you some.[60]

The letter was written shortly after the closure of the 1937 Exposition, which had provided an opportunity for Bryher, Beach and Monnier to publicize *Life and Letters To-Day* in a display of French literature, on the basis that *Shakespeare and Company* was its Paris distributor. Benjamin, who had in 1936 corresponded with Bryher about the possible translation and publication of his long essay 'The Work of Art in the Age of Mechanical Reproducibility' in *Life and Letters To-Day*, refers to the details of her memoir which connect closely to his own preoccupations and writings: children's play and fantasies, modes of recollection and reminiscence, city portraits, urban spectacle, the telling detail which encapsulates an epoch (here the 'comb' of 'La Parisienne' at the 1900 Exposition), the ornamentality and 'stylizing style', in Benjamin's phrase,[61] of *Art Nouveau/ Jugendstil*. In the work now known as *The Arcades Project*, his radically non-linear, image-based exploration of the Paris of the nineteenth century, Benjamin wrote of the World Exhibitions as 'places of pilgrimage to the commodity fetish'[62] which 'construct a universe of spécialités'[63] and of 'the world dominated by its phantasmagorias – this, to make use of Baudelaire's term, is "modernity"'.[64] In a brief fragment on the 1900 Exhibition, in the file ('Konvolut') on 'Fashion', Benjamin referred to 'a Palais du Costume, in which wax dolls arranged before a painted backdrop displayed the costumes of various peoples and the fashions of various ages',[65] a slightly flat observation which takes its colouration from the quotations and observations surrounding it, as in the assertion that 'Fashions are a collective medicament for the ravages of oblivion'.[66]

Benjamin closes his letter to Bryher with the mention of his own autobiographical 'sketches'. He had composed his *Berlin Chronicle* in 1932 in Ibiza; a substantial part of the text was subsequently included in his *Berlin Childhood around 1900*, which he wrote between 1932 and 1938. He did not himself define the texts as autobiographies, writing in *A Berlin Chronicle*, that:

> Reminiscences, even extensive ones, do not always amount to an autobiography. And these quite certainly do not, even for the Berlin years that I am exclusively concerned with here. For autobiography has to do with time, with sequence and what makes up the continuous flow of life. Here, I am talking of a space, of moments and discontinuities.[67]

In this passage, in which Benjamin self-reflexively defines the task he is undertaking, he argues that the city evoked in his reminiscences is not on the side of 'life' – the 'bios' of autobiography – but bears witness to death, and in particular the 'brief, shadowy existence' of the people he knew in his Berlin childhood:

> They steal along its walls like beggars, appear wraithlike at windows, to vanish again, sniff at thresholds like a *genius loci*, and even if they fill whole neighbourhoods with their names, it is as a dead man's name fills his gravestone.[68]

Benjamin intertwines childhood memories, which have 'a quality that makes them at once as evanescent and as alluringly tormenting as half-forgotten dreams' with 'images' that belong to the second half of the nineteenth century and which 'constantly detach themselves from things and determine our perception of them'. The autobiographical writings thus bear a close relationship to *The Arcades Project*, which brought together the cultural constellations of nineteenth-century Paris, in which the Paris arcades were to be explored as paradigms of a 'past become space'.[69] They are also profoundly shaped by the increasingly exigent political situation in the 1930s. In an afterword to the posthumously published *A Berlin Childhood*, Theodor Adorno wrote that

> the historical archetypes that [Benjamin] wished to develop [in the *Passagen-Werk*] out of their pragmatico-social and philosophical origin were, in the Berlin book, to flash up abruptly out of the immediacy of memory – with the force of pain felt for the irretrievable which, once it is lost, coagulates into an allegory of one's own demise.[70]

Marcel Proust was a crucial influence on Benjamin's writings about his Berlin childhood. In discussing Proust in *A Berlin Chronicle*, Benjamin refers to the endless unfolding of images and 'the fan of memory',[71] but we might also find deep resonances between Benjamin's models of illumination and Proust's description of the merging of present and past in the coming together of an experience and a memory, producing 'for a moment briefly as a flash of lightning – what normally it never apprehends: a fragment of time in a pure state'.[72] These are, Proust writes, 'Fragments of existence withdrawn from Time'.[73] But, as Peter Szondi suggests, Benjamin's 'lost time', unlike that of Proust, 'is not the past but the future'.[74]

Eschewing linear sequence as it does, *A Berlin Chronicle* is a complex text to navigate, and this difficulty indicates how much we habitually rely not only on narrative sequence but also on the model of a life in relation to formation or a journey. In *A Berlin Chronicle* Benjamin refers to a long-standing idea 'of setting out the sphere of life – *bios* – graphically on a map'[75] on which, using a system of signs, he would mark out the houses, assembly halls, hotel rooms, cafes, etc., of his childhood and youth. Later in the text, he refers to the slight role played in memory by people and recalls an afternoon in Paris 'to which I owe insights into my life that came in a flash, with the force of an illumination. It was on this very afternoon that my biographical relationships to people, my friendships and comradeships, my passions and love affairs, were revealed to me in their most vivid and hidden intertwinings'.[76] What was made clear to him was the kind of hold 'cities keep over imagination'[77] – a phrase which resonates with Bryher's 'geographical emotions' – so that 'the veil it has covertly woven out of our lives shows images of people less often than those of the sites of our encounters with others or ourselves'.[78]

It is this veil that was broken through in the moment of illumination, offering him a representation of the patterns of human relationships in his life which seemed to transcribe itself. Sitting in the Café des Deux Magots, 'I was struck by the idea of drawing a diagram of my life, and knew at the same moment exactly how it was to be done'. The sheet of paper was subsequently lost, and he was never able to 'restore it as it rose before me then, resembling a series of family trees': 'reconstructing its outline in thought',[79] he would instead 'speak of a labyrinth'. In the conditions of the modern city, it is suggested, the patterns of relationships in lives are subordinated to, or subsumed by, the dominance of space and its modes of social organization. But the labyrinth is also a particularly charged image for Benjamin which, in the 'Tiergarten' section of *A Berlin Childhood*, takes the idea of a labyrinthine 'straying in the city' back to 'the labyrinths scrawled on the blotting paper of my [childhood] notebooks' and, behind or before that, to the language of nature.[80]

Benjamin's explicit engagement with Freud's work is limited, but there are nonetheless important connections between his writings and Freud's concepts of mental topography and, later, the language of the unconscious, as well as, centrally, the 'dream-work' (with its displacements and condensations of images) and memory-work. 'Remembrance', Benjamin writes in *A Berlin Chronicle*, 'must not proceed by way of narrative, much less by way of reports, but must, in the strictest and epic and rhapsodic manner, assay its spade in ever-new places, and in the old ones delve to ever-deeper layers.'[81] This passage, also produced in 1932 as a separate fragment, titled 'Excavation and Memory' uses an archaeological motif – bringing it into relationship with Freud's models of memory and the unconscious. Benjamin refers to the ways in which one might seek to approach the buried past: memory, he writes, is only a medium, like the earth in which an ancient city lies buried, and it must be turned over and over in order to yield up its 'long-sought secrets': 'That is to say, they yield those images, that severed from all earlier associations, reside as treasures in the sober rooms of our later insights – like torsos in a collector's gallery.'[82]

While *A Berlin Childhood* includes a substantial part of the material in *A Berlin Chronicle*, it presents it in a series of images and longer and shorter titled sections or fragments: 'Loggias', 'Imperial Panorama', 'The Telephone', 'Butterfly Hunt', 'Cabinets', etc. At the opening of the final version (completed in 1938), Benjamin refers to the beginnings of the project: 'In 1932, when I was abroad, it began to be clear to me that I would soon have to bid a long, perhaps lasting farewell to the city of my birth.'[83] Calling to mind 'images of childhood' was to be a way, as he wrote to Bryher, of inoculating himself against homesickness: the intention was not to 'limit its effect through insight into the irretrievability – not the contingent biographical but the necessary social irretrievability – of the past'. 'Biographical features', as well as the 'physiognomies' of family and comrades, which 'stand out more readily in the continuity of experience than in its depths, altogether recede in the present undertaking'.[84] In other words, this is not to be a restoration of a personal, 'biographical' past but 'an effort to get hold of the *images* in which the experience of the big city is precipitated in a child of the middle class'. What is crucial is not the 'continuity of experience' – the continuity of personhood – but the radical break between present and past, brought about both by the extraordinarily rapid changes wrought upon a modernized Berlin and by his own exile from that city. 'Like a mollusk in its shell,' he writes, 'I had my abode in the nineteenth century, which now lies hollow before me like an empty shell. I hold it to my ear.'[85] In a chapter on 'Shells' in *The Poetics of Space*, Gaston Bachelard writes that 'an empty shell, like an empty nest, invites daydreams of refuge'.[86] Benjamin, by contrast, seems not to be dreaming of reinhabiting the shell but of using it as a listening device (comparable to Woolf's imaginings of the radio-like apparatus by means of which she would be able to 'listen in to the past') in which might be captured the sounds of the past, and, indeed, 'the noise of time'.

The childhood imagination, as Benjamin depicts it, entails a merging with the object world – the key terms are 'mimicry' (or 'mimesis'), which is related both to becoming similar (to dwelling places, furniture, clothes)[87] and to the recognition of similarities between things, and distortion (*Enstellung*) (which Benjamin often framed as a mishearing of words and names which led to its own form of magical invocation). Benjamin referred to 'the world distorted in the state of resemblance' in his 1929 essay on Proust: 'He lay on his bed racked with homesickness, homesick for the *world distorted in the state of resemblance* ... To this world belongs ... the image.'[88]

While one interpretation of Benjamin's project is that it is historiographical rather than biographical, the 'images' he conjures up are by no means generalized or impersonal. The 'empty shell' held to the ear yields less the sounds of the public city than those of domestic space. He described the text as 'the most precise portrait I shall ever be able to give of myself' and as 'a kind of self-portrait'.[89] In writing of Berlin's 'loggias' – internal balconies – Benjamin refers to 'the images and allegories which preside over my thinking' and to the rhythms of the city – of the railways and of carpet-beating – which 'rocked me to sleep. It was the mold in which my dreams took shape'. Describing the highly decorated Tiergarten villas of his childhood, Benjamin writes: 'Among the caryatids and atlantes, the putti and pomonas, which in those days looked on me, I stood closest to those dust-shrouded specimens of the race of threshold dwellers – those who guard the entrance to life, or to a house. For they are versed in waiting.'[90] There is a strongly implied connection between the condition of exile and the appeal, even the security, of liminal spaces – courtyards, thresholds, passageways. The loggias, he writes, have stayed with him 'on account of their uninhabitability for one who himself no longer has a proper abode'.[91]

The condition of exile, both from place and from the past (whether the latter is mourned or seen as a world well lost), runs throughout many of the autobiographies of the early twentieth century. Closely connected to this theme is the perception of a fracturing of history. There are here two forms of time-consciousness and historicity. One relates to events which are so extreme that they fracture history's flow and create an absolute divide between then and now; the other to a philosophy of history focussed on the different rhythms, speed and intensity of historical processes. This bears closely on a resistance to what are viewed as the false certainties of narrative sequence and causality, bringing modernist autobiography and twentieth-century historiography into a closer relationship than has yet been explored.

Notes

1. Seamus O'Malley, *Making History New. Modernism and Historical Narrative* (New York: OUP, 2014). See also Michael Sayeau, *Against the Event. The Everyday and the Evolution of Modernist Narrative* (Oxford: OUP, 2013), and Laura Marcus, 'Experiments in Form: Modernism and Autobiography in Woolf, Eliot, Mansfield, Lawrence, Joyce, and Richardson', in *A History of English Autobiography*, ed. Adam Smyth (New York: Cambridge University Press, 2016), 298–312.
2. For an in-depth comparative discussion of Woolf's and Benjamin's representations of the past and practices of historiography, see Angeliki Spiropoulou, *Virginia Woolf, Modernity and History: Constellations with Walter Benjamin* (London and New York: Palgrave Macmillan, 2010). See also Sanja Bahun, 'The Burden of the Past, The Dialectics of the Present: Notes on Virginia Woolf's and Walter Benjamin's Philosophies of History', *Modernist Cultures* 3, no. 2 (2008): 100–15.
3. Karl Mannheim, 'Historismus', *Archiv für Sozialwissenschaft und Sozialpolitik* 52, no. 1 (1924): 1–60. Translated in Karl Mannheim, *Essays in the Sociology of Knowledge*, ed. Paul Kecskemeti (London: Routledge, 1952), 84–133.
4. Christian J. Emden, *Walter Benjamins Archäologie der Moderne: Kulturwissenschaft um 1930* (Munich: Wilhelm Fink Verlag, 2006), 85–6.
5. Walter Benjamin, *Selected Writings Vol. 4 1938–1940*, ed. Howard Eiland and Michael Jennings (Cambridge, MA: The Belknap University of the Harvard Press, 2003), 391.
6. Ibid., 395.
7. See David Turner, 'History as Popular Story: On the Rhetoric of Stefan Zweig's 'Sternstunden der Menschheit', *The Modern Language Review* 84, no. 2 (April 1989): 393–405.
8. This lecture was intended for delivery in Stockholm at a PEN conference, cancelled because of the outbreak of war. Zweig, 'Die Geschichte als Dichterin', Reed Library – Stefan Zweig Collection, SZ-AP2/W-H234.1. In: stefanzweig.digital, Ed. Literaturarchiv Salzburg, Last Update 17.12.2019, URL: stefanzweig.digital/o:szd.werke#SZDMSK.211.
9. Woolf was greatly involved with the 'new biography' of Lytton Strachey, André Maurois, Harold Nicolson and others, which was defined against the terms of Victorian biography and had as its central tenets the levelling of the relationship

between biographer and subject, the use of fictional techniques and a focus on a 'key' to personality. See her essays 'The New Biography' and 'The Art of Biography'.
10 Virginia Woolf, 'De Quincey's Autobiography', in *The Essays of Virginia Woolf Vol. 5, 1929 to 1932*, ed. Stuart N. Clarke (London: Hogarth Press, 2009), 457–8.
11 Stefan Zweig, *The World of Yesterday* (London: Cassell, 1987), 30.
12 Ibid., 45.
13 Virginia Woolf, 'Sketch of the Past', in *Moments of Being*, ed. Jeanne Schulkind (London: Pimlico, 2002), 87.
14 'inwiefern es unter allen Umständen dasselbe geblieben'. Johann Wolfgang von Goethe, *Dichtung und Wahrheit. Aus meinem Leben* (Munich: Carl Hanser, 1960), Preface, 6. My italics.
15 Paul Ricoeur, in *Time and Narrative, Vol. 3*, 244–9, points to the limits of narrative identity and the need to 'link up with the "non-narrative" components in the formation of an acting subject' (249).
16 Woolf, 'Sketch', 80.
17 Ibid., 81.
18 Ibid., 116.
19 Ibid., 149.
20 Ibid., 123.
21 Ibid., 116. The term 'ambivalence' had been introduced into psychology in 1910 by the Swiss psychiatrist Eugen Bleuler.
22 Zweig, *World of Yesterday*, 15.
23 Ibid., 318.
24 Ibid., 6.
25 Letter of 20 June 1939, cited in Ulrich Wienzierl, 'Autobiografie als Epochendarstellung', in *Stefan-Zweig-Handbuch*, ed. Arturo Larcati, Klemens Renoldner and Martina Wörgötter (Berlin: De Gruyter, 2018), 340.
26 Cited in Freud, Sigmund, Stefan Zweig. *Correspondance* (Paris: Rivages, 1995).
27 Zweig, *World of Yesterday*, 5.
28 This concept was explored in the lecture he wrote immediately after working on his autobiography, as mentioned in note 8.
29 D. A. Prater, *European of Yesterday. A Biography of Stefan Zweig* (Oxford: Clarendon Press, 1972), 307.
30 Arthur Koestler, *Arrow in the Blue* (London: Readers Union, William Collins and Hamish Hamilton, 1954), 17.
31 Arthur Koestler, *The Invisible Journey. Autobiography 1931–53* (London: Collins with Hamish Hamilton, 1954), 430.
32 Osip Mandelstam, *The Noise of Time and Other Prose Pieces*, trans. Clarence Brown (London: Quartet, 1988), 109–10.

33 For critiques of Zweig's nostalgic picture of imperial Vienna, see for example Hannah Arendt, 'Stefan Zweig: Jews in the World of Yesterday', in *The Jewish Writings*, ed. H. Arendt (New York: Schocken, 2007), 317–28; also Robert S. Wistrich, 'Stefan Zweig and the 'World of Yesterday', in *Stefan Zweig Reconsidered. New Perspectives on His Literary and Biographical Writings*, ed. Mark H. Gelber (Tübingen: Max Niemeyer Verlag, 2007), 59–77. On the background to Arendt's critique, see Michael Steinberg, 'Hannah Arendt and the Cultural Style of the German Jews', *Social Research* 74, no. 3 (Fall 2007): 879–902.

34 Zweig, *World of Yesterday*, 310.

35 George Prochnik, *The Impossible Exile. Stefan Zweig at the End of the World* (London: Granta, 2014), 11.

36 On this, see Nikolaus Unger, 'Remembering Identity in *Die Welt von Gestern*: Stefan Zweig, Austrian German Identity Construction and the First World War', *Focus on German Studies*, 12 (2005), 95–116. As Unger notes, even later in the war he rejected Zionism as an alternative version of the nationalism which had been discredited in its German/Austrian form.

37 Koestler, *Arrow*, 38.

38 Walter Benjamin, 'The Storyteller', in *Selected Writings Vol. 3, 1935–1938*, ed. Howard Eiland and Michael Jennings (Cambridge, MA: The Belknap Press of the Harvard University Press, 2002), 143–4.

39 Thomas Harrison takes Benn's remark as his epigraph in his *1910: The Emancipation of Dissonance* (Berkeley: University of California Press, 1996). Jane Goldman opens her account of modernism in 1910 in her book *Modernism, 1910–1945: Image to Apocalypse* (Basingstoke: Palgrave Macmillan, 2004).

40 Focusing on the flowering of cultural life in 1913 in his book *1913: The Cradle of Modernism* (Malden, MA: Blackwell, 2007), Jean-Michel Rabaté chooses that year as his reference point. This is also Harrison's emphasis, though he stresses the strongly pessimistic current in intellectual life of 'the seven years to either side of' 1910.

41 Harrison, *1910*, 8.

42 Bryher, *The Heart to Artemis: A Writer's Memoir* (London: Collins, 1963), 7.

43 Bryher had purchased the journal in 1935; it was edited by Robert Herring, who also wrote film criticism for her earlier journal *Close Up*, and Dorothy Petrie Townshend.

44 Henry Adams, *The Education of Henry Adams. An Autobiography* (Cambridge, MA: The Riverside Press, 1918), 382.

45 Ibid.

46 Walter Benjamin, 'On the Concept of History', in *Selected Writings Vol. 4*, 397.

47 Bryher, 'Paris, 1900', *Life and Letters To-day* 16, no. 8 (Summer 1937), 33.

48 Ibid.

49 Ibid., 34.
50 Ibid.
51 Ibid., 36.
52 Ibid., 35.
53 See my 'European Witness: Analysands Abroad in the 1920s and 1930s', in Laura Marcus, *Dreams of Modernity* (Oxford: OUP, 2014), chapter 8, 151–77.
54 Ibid., 42.
55 The French version, presumably based on a revised text by Bryher, is more focussed on her Paris experiences, with less material on her English childhood. The references to contemporary politics are also somewhat different.
56 Bryher, *Heart to Artemis*, 211.
57 Reprinted in Adrienne Monnier, *Les Gazettes d'Monnier 1925–1945* (Paris: René Julliard, 1953), 245.
58 Bryher, *Heart to Artemis*, 278.
59 In his foreword to the 1938 version, not published until 1950, Benjamin gives a fuller account of this immunization strategy. He had earlier published some extracts in his own name or pseudonymously.
60 Walter Benjamin, *Gesammelte Briefe*, ed. Christoph Gödde (Frankfurt am Main: Suhrkamp, 1999), Vol. 5, 628–9.
61 Walter Benjamin, *The Arcades Project*, trans. Howard Eiland and Kevin McLaughlin (Cambridge, MA: Harvard University Press, 1999), 556.
62 Ibid., 7.
63 Ibid., 17–18.
64 Ibid., 26.
65 Ibid., 73.
66 Ibid., 80.
67 Walter Benjamin, 'A Berlin Chronicle', in *Selected Writings Vol. 2*, ed. Michael W. Jennings, Howard Eiland, and Gary Smith (Cambridge, MA: Harvard University Press, 1999), 612.
68 Ibid., 612–13.
69 See Sigrid Weigel, *Body- and Image-Space. Re-reading Walter Benjamin* (London: Routledge, 1996), 112.
70 Theodor W. Adorno, 'Nachwort', in Walter Benjamin, *Berliner Kindheit um neunzehnhundert* (Frankfurt: Suhrkamp, 1987), 111.
71 Benjamin, *Berlin Chronicle*, 597.
72 Marcel Proust, *In Search of Lost Time*, trans. Andreas Mayor and Terence Kilmartin, revised by D. J. Enright (London: Chatto and Windus, 1992), book VI, 224. See also Walter Benjamin, 'On the Image of Proust', in *Selected Writings Vol. 2*, ed. Michael W. Jennings, Howard Eiland, and Gary Smith (Cambridge, MA: The Belknap University of the Harvard Press, 1999).

73 Ibid., 227.
74 Peter Szondi, 'Nachwort', in Walter Benjamin, *Städtebilde* (Frankfurt: Suhrkamp, 1963), 82.
75 Benjamin, 'Berlin Chronicle', 596.
76 Ibid., 614.
77 Ibid.
78 Ibid.
79 Ibid.
80 See Weigel, *Body- and Image-Space*, 138.
81 Benjamin, *Berlin Chronicle*, 611. Despite the image of the spade, Gerhard Richter suggests that Benjamin's argument is that memory is not an instrument 'but rather a scene, space or site, a spectacle or stage (*Schauplatz*).' See *Walter Benjamin and the Corpus of Autobiography* (Detroit: Wayne State University Press, 2000), 42–3.
82 Ibid.
83 Walter Benjamin, *Selected Writings Vol. 3, 1935–1938*, ed. by Howard Eiland and Michael Jennings (Cambridge, MA: The Belknap University of the Harvard Press, 2002), 344.
84 Ibid., 345.
85 Ibid., 392.
86 Gaston Bachelard, *The Poetics of Space*, trans. Maria Jolas (Boston: Beacon Press, 1994), 107.
87 Benjamin, 'Berlin Childhood', 391.
88 Benjamin, 'On the Image of Proust', 240.
89 Walter Benjamin, *The Correspondence of Walter Benjamin, 1910–1940*, ed. Gershom Scholem and Theodor Adorno, trans. Manfred Jacobson and Evelyn Jacobson (Chicago: University of Chicago Press, 1994), 424, 427.
90 Benjamin, 'Berlin Childhood', 354.
91 Ibid., 346.

2

Spatial histories of magazines and modernisms
Andrew Thacker

Introduction

What happens to our histories of modernism when the route commences not with individual authors, artists or texts, but by taking the plethora of magazines, whether 'little', 'big' or something in-between, as our point of origin? If we agree with Scholes and Wulfman's assertion that 'modernism began in the magazines',[1] then how is our historical understanding of modernism altered by engaging more closely with a different kind of material? Modernism as canonized in the Western academy since the 1930s with the development of New Criticism, the critical criteria of T. S. Eliot or the claims of Ezra Pound for the 'men of 1914' has for several decades now been the focus of critique from various sources: in particular, we might note the questioning around 'gender and modernism' in the 1980s and 1990s, the emergence of the New Modernist Studies at the end of the last century and, mostly recently, the work being done on queer modernism.[2] The selection of what constitutes the object of study has thus been criticized, revised and reorientated in multiple ways and, as Mao and Walkowitz note in their overview of the 'new modernist studies', the keyword of this process has been that of 'expansion': we now know, study and teach a much different canon of modernism, with diverse senses of its history.[3] However, the *material form* of much of the literature studied has remained, to an extent, the same: novels, short stories, poems, plays – mostly to be analysed in individual books, anthologies and textbooks, or course readers. How many undergraduate courses in modernism, we might wonder, survey the history of the subject predominantly via its magazines? Since 1995, with the founding of the digitization work of the Modernist Journals Project (MJP), teachers and critics have had access to the material culture of Anglo-American modernism as it emerged in a wide range of magazines; other digitization projects such as the Blue Mountain Project or Monoskop have widened the focus to include the European avant-garde, while other work on middlebrow culture and pulp magazines has similarly expanded our access to other forms of modern periodicals.[4] The study of magazine culture is thus more established now as part of the materialist and historicist turn within modernist studies (and within English as a discipline more widely), but have we really started to imagine what the history of modernisms would look like if we approached it primarily via magazines rather than by means of its books?

The Modernist Magazines Project that I have been co-directing since 2006 has aimed to trace the contribution that the little magazine, and many of its variants, has made to the construction of modernism, a project that has so far produced three volumes of essays on the modernist magazine in Britain and Ireland, in North America and in Europe. The second stage of the project, which aims to produce another set of volumes exploring the modernist magazine in the rest of the world, has recently begun.[5] Building upon this work this chapter explores some of the significant challenges for historicizing modernism when we take seriously the idea that magazines should be considered as our primary texts. These challenges revolve around the issues of method, periodization and spatial history. The chapter starts by exploring these three issues in turn, before turning to consider some examples from the future project on Global Modernist Magazines that poses a fresh set of questions for how we historicize modernism.

Method

If we are to really understand the role of magazines in the history of modernism it has become increasingly clear that we require radical new methods for the literary analysis of a textual object, the magazine, which differs greatly from a poem, a novel or a play. Many of the basic interpretive strategies of literary history and criticism are problematic when faced with the run of a magazine: 'what constitutes the work?' or 'who is the author?' are not easy questions to answer in relation to periodicals. It is difficult to imagine a modernist magazine as a 'well-wrought urn', to evoke Cleanth Brooks's famous New Critical image for the individual work of art. Is an individual issue the essential unit, the 'work', or is the entire run of the magazine the single 'work'?[6] And how should we balance 'the multivocal authorship' of a periodical with the 'more or less coherent vision of its editors'?[7] Such theoretical questions around form have been explored and debated within Victorian Periodicals research for a number of years,[8] but it seems that the issues facing attempts to historicize magazines within modernism are somewhat different. The categories of modernism and the avant-garde themselves create complex problems for the analysis of twentieth-century periodicals as textual objects; this is not the case for Victorian periodicals, where work upon theorizing serials is able to explore their variety without having to engage constantly with definitions of the 'Victorian' as a category of analysis. As Laurel Brake asserts, in nineteenth-century periodical studies, 'the focus of research is seldom on their *Victorian* identity'.[9] This is in contrast to scholars in modernism, who spend an awful lot of time debating the nature of the modernism they locate in magazines, as well as the parameters of what constitutes a *modernist*, rather than merely *modern*, magazine.[10] Here, of course, scholars of Victorian periodicals are aided by the fact that 'Victorian' offers a ready-made category for literary history, in contrast to the more historically nebulous concept of 'modernism'. The notion of the modernist magazine is – as is modernism itself – perhaps too heterogeneous to be readily reduced to the familiar generic categories of the nineteenth-century serial (the review, the weekly, the quarterly, the newspaper).

So we need new methods of analysis. I've suggested a couple of these in the introductions to the already published volumes, referring to the idea of *periodical codes* and the *periodical field*.[11] Do we also need to think about employing some version of Franco Moretti's 'distant reading' methodology for magazines? Probably.[12] However, the irregular nature of many modernist magazines hampers their ability to be analysed by means of a 'distant reading' approach, as has been carried out upon the large corpora of Victorian periodicals by critics such as Dallas Liddle and Jim Mussell.[13] For example, though the Vorticist magazine *Blast* (1914–15) was advertised as a quarterly – a well-established genre of the nineteenth-century serial – it only ever produced two issues, a year apart, rather than separated by three months. Similarly, Robert Graves's *The Owl* purported to be another quarterly, but managed only two issues in 1919, with a final issue in 1923. Alfred Kreymborg's important magazine of poetry, *Others*, ran for four years from 1915, but was only a monthly for the first year; thereafter, as Jay Bochner notes, it appeared 'quite irregularly, in spurts of three to four months at a time'.[14] Thus the generically unstable label of the 'miscellany', or the temporally disjunctive term 'irregular', is a familiar descriptor of many modernist magazines. In order, then, to apply some form of Moretti's 'distant reading' to individual modern periodicals we need a more substantial and stable corpus than is often available in a number of modernist magazines: many lack the quality of being what Mussell terms 'repetitive serial forms'.[15] Which perhaps suggests that 'close reading' still has a significant role to play when facing textual objects defined as 'irregular' or 'occasional'.[16]

Certain critics working in modern periodical studies have argued for shifting attention from the 'much studied modernist little magazine' to a wider 'print media ecology' in the early twentieth century, exploring pulp or glossy magazines, newspapers or newsletters.[17] Collier, for example, argues that 'there is a more urgent need for mapping the much larger, nonmodernist locales of the vast landscape of twentieth century print culture than for filling in the blank spots on the already well-sketched map of modernism'.[18] Such arguments are stimulating and productive in opening up periodical studies and print culture, helping to understanding the little magazine within the wider field of contemporary periodicals. This was certainly the aim in the first two volumes of the *Oxford Critical and Cultural Histories*, which included essays on many magazines that cannot be easily defined as modernist 'little' magazines, such as the *London Mercury*, *New Yorker* or *The Smart Set*. However, I would argue that there still remains very much that is *not* studied in the *modernist* little magazine: even if we just took the corpus of the MJP, with its digitized versions of some twenty-five magazines, there still exist thousands of pages to be analysed further; unknown authors and artists to ponder; editorials, adverts and images to digest.[19] In many ways this is not really a 'well-sketched map of modernism' at all. For instance, if we do persevere with some form of close reading of periodicals, then many little magazines of modernism are only scantily treated, if at all, in comparison to the work carried out texts that are normally encountered within books. Consider, for example, how much 'close reading' has been conducted on the 500 lines or so of Eliot's *The Waste Land*, whether in a Faber edition or a Norton Anthology, in comparison to the 5,000 pages or so (85 issues of *c.* 68 pages) of *The Little Review* from 1914 to 1922 that have been digitized by the MJP.[20] And even if we reach for a 'distant reading' methodology to help with the labour of analysing this vast corpus, what are we to do about the seven years of *The Little Review* that are not currently digitized and online due to copyright restrictions, and thus not readily accessible to the probing tools of digital humanities?[21] A focus only upon those magazines available in digital form up to 1923, due to US copyright laws, inevitably skews our historical conception of what happened to modernism in the many periodicals published after this date. For example, the two magazines in which Eliot first published *The Waste Land* in 1922 prior to book publication – *The Criterion* in Britain and *The Dial* in the United States – are currently not digitized, and hence a reading of the poem in the context of the rest of the contents of these magazines is much harder to access. Analysis of the contents of these two major magazines, *The Criterion* as edited by Eliot from 1922 to 1939, and *The Dial* in the version revived by Scofield Thayer and James Sibley Watson (1920–9), and edited by Marianne Moore from 1925 onwards, is, arguably, only starting to be sketched out by scholarship.[22] Some of the famous Anglophone transnational magazines edited in Paris in the 1920s and 1930s are also not digitized, such as Ford Madox Ford's *transatlantic review* (1924) or Eugène Jolas's *transition* (1927–38). A more deeply historicized modernism thus needs to take account of the great unread pages of existing magazines and of the many magazines not readily available for 'distant reading' in the digital archive.

Periodization

The burgeoning field of modern periodical studies has significantly revised both the literary history and the geographical understanding of modernism. This work has shown that the periodization of modernism and its magazines needs to be greatly expanded beyond that of traditional accounts that suggest that modernism (as often conceived in the Anglophone world) starts in the 1910s and concludes in the late 1930s. All of the volumes in the first Modernist Magazines series pushed the starting point back into the nineteenth century, in order to trace a fuller genealogy of the 'little magazine'. In Britain the most often cited precursor 'little magazine' of modernism was that of *The Yellow Book* (1894–7), but our research indicated the importance of other magazines such as the 'Arts and Crafts' periodical *The Century Guild Hobby Horse* (1884–94), the English symbolist publication *The Dial* (1889–97) or the magazine of the Pre-Raphaelite movement, *The Germ* (1850). Such magazines pioneered the independent ethos and anti-commercial qualities that form the core of definitions of the modernist 'little magazine'.[23] In North America the 1890s saw the flourishing of large numbers of 'ephemeral bibelots', as F. W. Faxon labelled them in a bibliography of some 200 such publications in 1903.[24] Short-lived magazines with low circulations and bizarre names (*The Freak, The Lark, The Fly Leaf, The Ghorki*) constitute what Kirsten MacLeod has described as a 'fin-de-siècle modernism'.[25] Turning to Europe we find the 1880s as the point of origin for the ideas and attitudes of the modernist magazine shown in France with the appearance of symbolist magazines such as *La Plume* (1889–1905) or *La Revue Blanche* (1889–1903), as well as other 'petites revues' such as *Le Scapin* (1885–6), and *Le Chat Noir* (1881–95). The first work of historiography on the 'little magazine' also appeared in France, with Remy de Gourmont's *Les Petites Revues*

(1900).²⁶ Operating with an earlier genealogy for Spain brought into view the Catalan magazines of 'modernisme' and 'noucentrisme', as well as the influence of Nicaraguan poet Ruben Dario's 'modernismo', and the work of the Generation of '98'.²⁷ Including such material demonstrates a theorization of modernity and the modern that predated many Anglophone versions, thus producing another challenge to our historical understanding of modernism.²⁸

Extending the genealogy of the modernist magazine back into the late nineteenth century therefore enables us to understand the emergence of the 'petites revues' formula as a response to changes in mainstream publishing, the development of new (and cheaper) forms of print technology and the emergence of an aesthetic ideology of cultural production which emphasized formal experimentation and a rejection of mainstream norms: all features that were crucial to the explosion of the little magazine in the twentieth century.²⁹

Of equal significance for the historicizing of modernism has been the extension of the chronology of the modernist magazines beyond the 1930s.³⁰ This enabled us to explore, for example, in a magazine such as *The Kenyon Review* (1939–70) the emergence of New Criticism as it codified a certain version of 'high modernism' associated with Ezra Pound and T. S. Eliot. We could also, therefore, consider how formations such as the Beats, the New York Poets and the Black Mountain group attempted to revive the revolutionary spirit of early-twentieth-century modernist experimentation in a different place and time, in magazines such as *Origin* (1951–2007) or *Yugen* (1959–62).³¹ There is also a persuasive argument to be made that the modernist little magazine is very much alive today – in the shape of online poetry publications such as *Jacket*, *Shearsman*, *m58*, along with myriad others.³² This temporal expansion of modernism in magazines later into the twentieth century is, as discussed below, important when venturing beyond an Anglo-European framework. Studying the history of modernism through the lens of its magazines thus suggests that periodization must, in particular, be flexible and attentive to specific national histories of modernism and their evaluations of what it means to be modern.

New spatial histories

A new spatial history of modernism begins to emerge strongly when we expand the geography of the modernist magazine beyond Europe and Anglo-America. From the earliest stages of bibliographic research, however, I was aware that there were forms of modernist magazine published beyond the chosen geography of these three volumes. Even in the foundational study of Frederick Hoffman et al., *The Little Magazine* (1946), there are entries for *Angry Penguins* (Melbourne, Australia, 1946), *Australian New Writing* (Sydney, 1943) and *Voorslag* (Durban, South Africa, 1926).[33] The flourishing study of modern periodicals over the last two decades is thus part of an expansion in modernist studies itself, particularly in the considerable new work on transnationalism and globalization.[34] Such innovations have made more visible the fact that the continents of South America, Africa and Asia all have publications we can understand as modernist little magazines, and analysing these in more detail will be the principal aim of the next volumes on Global Modernist Magazines. As Eric Bulson argues persuasively in *Little Magazine, World Form*, the little magazine was something like a 'world form' that was crucial in transporting modernism as a movement around the world, but which was also involved in complex negotiations with existing forms of national print culture.[35]

The transnational dimension of the modernist magazine, for instance, emerged strongly in the first series of volumes, with stories of networks of international contributors as well as the peregrinations of particular magazines across continents, such as the 'American' magazine *Broom* (1921–4) in Rome, Berlin and New York (in which the editors utilized the strength of the dollar in post–First World War Europe by moving the magazine to places where publication costs were cheaper). The avant-garde's complex interactions between and across continents can also be traced, for example, in the history of Dada as it zig-zagged between various cities in magazines such as *Cabaret Voltaire* (Zurich, 1916), *The Blind Man* (New York, 1917), *Dada* (Paris, 1920–1), *Der Dada* (Berlin, 1919–20) and back to *New York Dada* (New York, 1921). The affiliations between *291* (1915–16) magazine, begun in New York by Alfred Stieglitz, and Francis Picabia's *391* (1917), with three issues published in New York, followed by four issues in Barcelona, and a final issue published in Zurich in 1919, demonstrate the complex transnational geography of the avant-garde at this point: tellingly, Tristan Tzara described *391* as a '*revue en voyage*'.[36]

The issue of magazines '*en voyage*' created certain problems for the structure of the original Modernist Magazines Project, and also for its next stage. For, in locating magazines by their places of publication, we sometimes miss the other geographical affiliations they have, and their travelling tendencies. This was always an issue the original series editors were aware of: there was, for instance, an early discussion about where to place the English-language film journal *Close-Up*: published in Switzerland, it was also very engaged with the German film industry in Berlin, but institutionally linked to the London Film

Society. On the advice of Laura Marcus (who contributed the chapter on the magazine) it was placed in the first volume on Britain and Ireland. But the closer you look, the more you realize that *Close-Up* is not alone. *Dyn*, for example, was a surrealist magazine published in Mexico City between 1942 and 1944 but which seems mainly to address debates in London, Paris and New York.[37] In the North American volume I wrote upon the poetry magazine *Palms* – edited by a US national, Ida Purnell, and published in Guadalajara 1923–30, but hard to describe as a Mexican magazine because of its Anglophone contents, minimal reference to its location, along with an address to networks and audience in the United States and, to a certain extent, Europe.[38]

Such magazines might thus be considered to possess multiple spatialities. Though they were physically located in one or more places of publication, to a weaker or stronger degree, they also spoke to or for a readership that was sometimes located in a quite different place. Though closely tied to avant-garde circles in London, for example, *Close-Up* frequently engaged with German expressionist cinema witnessed by the editors in Berlin. Magazines thus contributed significantly to the historical spread of modernism across Europe and beyond, demonstrating how modernist ideas travelled around the globe, interacting with national cultural traditions to produce new forms of modernist expression. In exploring the transnational travels of modernist little magazines we are, therefore, studying what Andreas Huyssens, drawing upon the work of Arjun Appadurai, describes as 'modernisms at large', that is, 'the cross-national cultural forms that emerge from the negotiation of the modern with the indigenous, the colonial and the postcolonial in the "non-Western" world'.[39]

A particularly interesting example of Huyssens' 'modernism at large' is that of the single-issue magazine *Légitime Défense*. This was part of a group of magazines edited by students from French colonial territories who came together while studying in Paris, and which clearly demonstrates how some magazines display the concept of multiple spatialities. Strongly linked with the late colonial theorists of negritude, Aimé Césaire and Leopold Senghor, this group of magazines included *Revue du monde noir* (Paris, 1931–32), *Légitime Défense* (Paris, 1932), *L'Etudiant Noir* (Paris, 1934–5) and *Tropiques* (Martinique, 1941–5). These *'revue en voyage'* oscillate between the geographies of Europe and the Caribbean, powerfully addressing various aesthetic and political discourses within Paris and Martinique simultaneously, in a kind of Bakhtinian double-voiced discourse, while also reaching out to address emerging anti-colonial voices in African literature and black writers and artists in the United States.[40]

Légitime Défense was produced by a collective of eight middle-class Martinique students in Paris (Etienne Léro, René Ménil, Jule-Marcel Monnerot, Michel Pilotin, Maurice-Sabas Quitman, Auguste Thésée and Pierre Yoyotte) and emerged out of the collapse of *Revue du monde noir* after six issues. Léro, Ménil and Monnerot had all contributed to the earlier magazine and wanted to position *Légitime Défense* as a more radical critique of political conditions in the Caribbean. *Légitime Défense* thus contained a heady mixture of Marxist critique, anti-colonial discourse and an engagement with one of the most dominant avant-garde movements in Paris in the early 1930s, surrealism. It also reached out to Black American writers and other transnational modernist formations by publishing a section of Claude McKay's novel *Banjo* and a polemic by Etienne Léro on the *Scottsboro* case in Alabama.[41] As Lori Cole notes, in drawing upon both Marx and André Breton (the title of the magazine was adapted from a 1926 essay by Breton) the magazine 'appropriated Communist and Surrealist rhetoric for the purposes of initiating a Caribbean literary and political consciousness'.[42] In particular the *Légitime Défense* collective embraced the way in which both the surrealists and the French Communist party denounced the 1931 Colonial Exposition held in Paris.[43] What the magazine provides, then, is a complex example of the 'negotiation' between a European modernism and a colonial modernity forged in the Francophone Caribbean, with its own particular history and politics.[44] Until its absorption into France as a *département* in 1946, Martinique was one of France's *vieilles colonies*, which had bestowed a limited and subaltern form of French citizenship upon its inhabitants without the enabling structures of local democratic government.[45] The students from the country that studied in Paris brought together their complex geopolitical identities in the pages of the magazine and attempted, in Cole's words, to 'insert themselves within a discourse from which they were previously excluded by their status as other, a gesture that inaugurates black consciousness into both Western and Caribbean discourse'.[46] This strategy was particularly evident, as Cole demonstrates, in the magazine's adoption of a key discursive feature of much avant-gardist discourse, that of the manifesto form.[47] By negotiating both with the manifesto tradition of Marxism and that of surrealism, the group articulated a unique voice of dissent for their own anti-colonial voices, as witnessed in this early proclamation in the magazine: 'We are speaking to those who are not already branded as killed established fucked-up academic successful decorated decayed provided for decorative prudish opportunists.'[48]

If Marxism and surrealism form the immediate intellectual influences behind *Légitime Défense* a more intriguing concept of 'negotiation' between European and Caribbean modernisms can be explored if we place the front cover of *Légitime Défense* (Figure 2.2) alongside a paradigmatic instance of the Anglo-American little magazine tradition, Wyndham Lewis's *Blast* (Figure 2.1), in its first issue of 1914.

What is interesting here is the obvious resemblance of format, or what I would call the shared periodical codes of these two modernist magazines:[49] there are striking similarities between the use of colour (black print on a puce/pink

Figure 2.1 Cover of the Journal *Blast,* no.1, 1914. Image courtesy of The Modernist Journals Project. Brown and Tulsa Universities, www.modjourn.org.

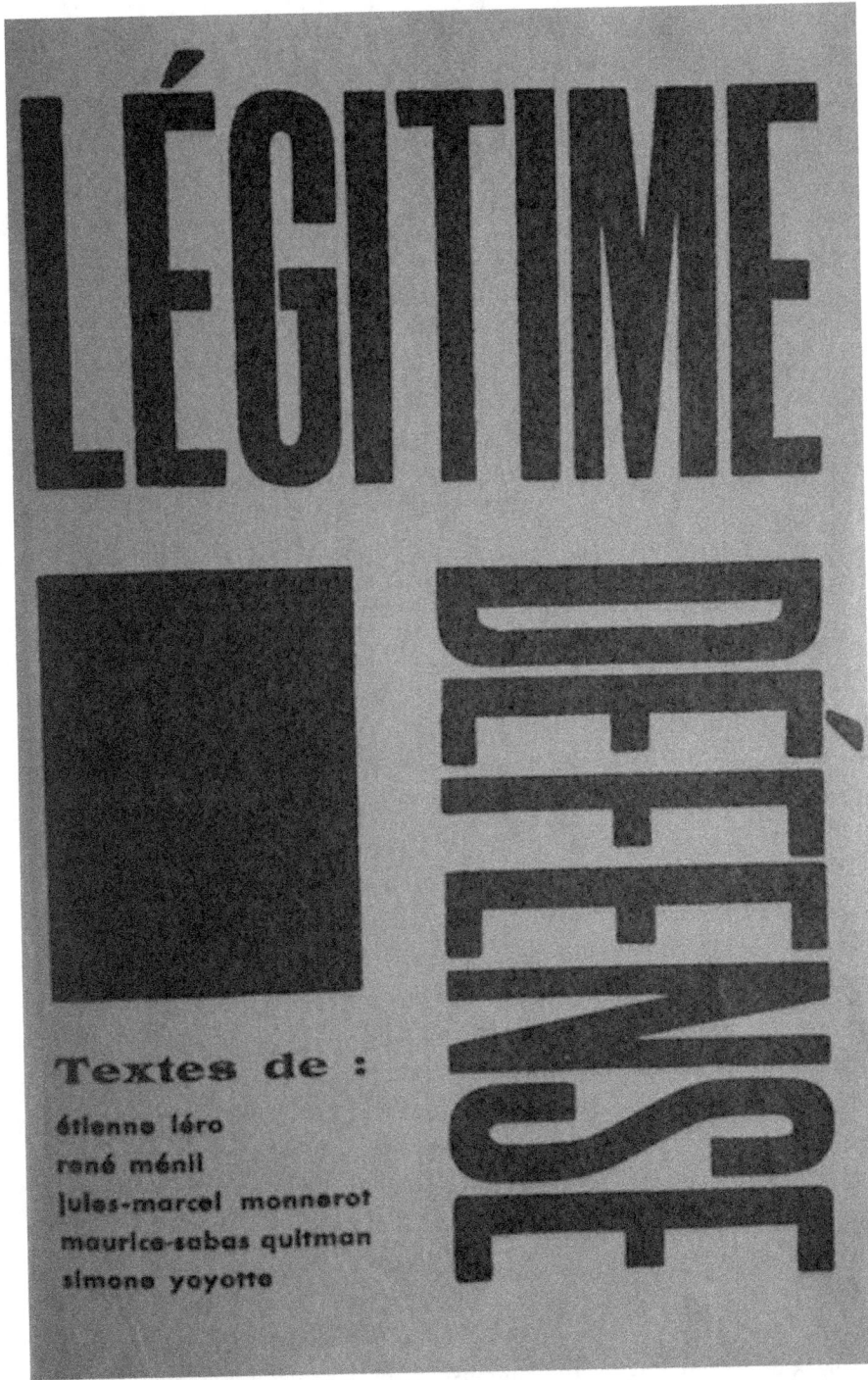

Figure 2.2 Cover of the Journal *Légitime Défense*, 1932.

background) and a sans-serif typeface, laid out in an affront to the horizontality of normal typography. There is no obvious evidence to indicate that the *Légitime Défense* group were consciously copying the stylings of *Blast*: rather, the point is that the two magazines seem to illustrate Huyssens' notion of 'the cross-national cultural forms' that we can detect once we widen the spatial history of modernism to study the 'negotiations' between Western and non-Western instances of magazine publication. *Blast* and *Légitime Défense* not only share a sustained use of the manifesto format within their pages but also exhibit a similarity in tone: the famed 'blasts' of Lewis's magazine against English Victorian culture or Italian Futurism are echoed in the opening manifesto statement in *Légitime Défense*, which attacks the Black bourgeoisie in the Caribbean as 'one of the most depressing things on earth' and then continues,

> we declare (and we shall not retract this declaration) that, faced with all the administrative, governmental, parliamentary, industrial, commercial corpses and so on, we intend – as traitors to this class – to take the path of treason so far as possible. We spit on everything they love and venerate, on everything that gives them sustenance and joy.[50]

Clearly the attack in *Légitime Défense* has a more political cast than is found in *Blast*, which was aimed primarily at what Lewis perceived as the backward aesthetic and cultural formations that prevailed in Britain, and which Vorticism might readily replace. The critique in *Légitime Défense* is more self-directed (Edwards memorably terms it a 'kind of class suicide'), aimed at a Martinique bourgeoisie (from which the editors all came) that celebrated French culture above all as a model for Caribbean writing.[51] However, both magazines share a certain attitude, that of the voice of the confrontational modernist magazine aiming to *épater les bourgeois*, willing to 'spit on everything they love and venerate' in a manifesto. It is this shared tone that is marked by the striking similarity of the covers of the two magazines.

Légitime Défense is not then 'influenced' by *Blast*, consciously or unconsciously, but can be seen as exemplifying certain of the features of the 'cross-national cultural form' (Huyssens) of the modernist magazine that previous histories of modernism have tended to view as an exclusively 'Western' form. In particular *Légitime Défense* finds its voice by a negotiation between the multiple spatialities encountered in its pages: living in Paris as colonial outsiders these young students review both their native Caribbean home and its Black bourgeoisie, while drawing inspiration for this reassessment from the Western intellectual formations of Marxism and surrealism; simultaneously they look to Black America for inspiration, a strategy which opens onto another geography, that of Africa. Etienne Léro's account of the 'poverty' of Caribbean poetry thus ends by bringing these diverse spatial locations together when he writes, 'Let's hope the wind rising from black America will quickly cleanse our Caribbean of the aborted fruits of a decrepit culture'.[52] He then looks to two 'black revolutionary poets, Langston Hughes and Claude McKay' to bring to the Caribbean their 'African love of life, the African joy of love, the African dream of death'. The outcome, imagines Léro, will be that 'the black proletariat – sucked dry in the Caribbean by a parasitic hybrid caste in the pocket of degenerate whites – will manage, by breaking this double yoke, to establish that one has a right both to eat and have a life of the mind, from that day forth alone will a Caribbean poetry exist'.[53]

Légitime Défense is, then, a fascinating example of what Bulson describes as the 'strange amalgam of print media' that characterizes modernist little magazines emerging out of conditions of colonial modernity.[54] Placing it alongside a magazine such as *Blast*, which has a paradigmatic position in the history of the avant-garde in the Anglophone world, continues a conversation about the transnational and international formations of modernism that is ongoing in our discipline. It would be far too easy to view a magazine such as *Légitime Défense* as simply a 'belated' version of the modernism of *Blast*, drawing upon similar periodical codes in its use of the manifesto or experimental typographic formatting. Rather the best way to understand *Légitime Défense* is as a magazine viewed through the lens of its multiple spatialities and its particular historical moment, where its coding and content are produced by the dynamic interaction of its diverse geopolitical and aesthetic affiliations.

Modernism thus starts to look different when we view it primarily through the history of its magazines; it begins to look even more different – diverse, strange, provocative– when we juxtapose magazines from one familiar iteration of modernism (the Western avant-garde), with that of periodical forms from elsewhere: *Blast* next to *Légitime Défense*; the Tokyo avant-garde production, *Mavo* (1924) alongside Bauhaus magazines; the *Transition* from Uganda (founded in 1961 by Rajat Neogy and then edited by Wole Soyinka in 1973) alongside Eugène Jolas' Paris-based *transition*.[55] And in the case of *transition/Transition* it is worth pondering further the differing historical nuances embodied in the title of the respective magazines: from a slogan in Paris searching for the next iteration of the avant-garde (such as the promotion in its pages of Joyce's 'Work in Progress') to a (post)colonial notion of a shift to national independence (Uganda gained formal independence from Britain a year after the first issue of *Transition*). For this reason the next volumes of the Modernist magazine project will aim to consider carefully the material print culture of specific nations when tracing the diffusion of the little magazine across the globe, along with the complex travels and multiple spatialities of these '*revues en voyage*'. In this way we hope to productively trouble the story we tell ourselves about how modernism emerged in the magazines, and the historical understanding we have of modernism itself.

Notes

1. See Robert Scholes and Clifford Wulfman, *Modernism in the Magazines: An Introduction* (New Haven: Yale University Press, 2010), 73.
2. For an indication of this work see, inter alia, Bonnie Kime Scott, ed., *The Gender of Modernism: A Critical Anthology* (Bloomington: Indiana University Press, 1990) and Sandra M. Gilbert and Susan Gubar, *No Man's Land: The Place of the Woman Writer in the Twentieth Century*, 3 vols (New Haven: Yale University Press, 1988, 1989, 1994); Douglas Mao and Rebecca L. Walkowitz, 'The New Modernist Studies', *PMLA* 123, no. 3 (2008): 737–48. There have been three Queer Modernisms conference held in Britain since 2017 (see https://queermodernismconference.wordpress.com) and see also Benjamin Kahane, 'Queer Modernism', in *A Handbook of Modernism Studies*, ed. Jean-Michel Rabaté (Oxford: Wiley, 2013), 347–61.
3. Mao and Walkowitz, 'New Modernist Studies', 737.
4. For the MJP, see http://modjourn.org//; Blue Mountain Project http://bluemountain.princeton.edu/bluemtn/cgi-bin/bluemtn; Monoskop magazines https://monoskoorg/Avant-garde_and_modernist_magazines; Pulp magazines https://www.pulpmags.org; Middlebrow network https://www.middlebrow-network.com.
5. The first series consisted of *The Oxford Critical and Cultural History of Modernist Magazines Vol. I: Britain and Ireland 1880–1955* (Oxford: Oxford University Press, 2009); *Vol. II: North America, 1894–1960* (2012), eds. Peter Brooker and Andrew Thacker; *Vol. III, Europe 1880–1940* (2013), eds. Peter Brooker, Sascha Bru, Andrew Thacker, and Christian Weiko. All subsequent references to these volumes will be by short title and volume number. The second series of volumes will be called *The Oxford Critical and Cultural History of Global Modernist Magazines,* and the series editors are Eric Bulson and Andrew Thacker. The first volume, on magazines in South America and the Caribbean, will be edited by Andrew Thacker and María del Pilar Blanco.
6. See Matthew Philpotts, 'Defining the Thick Journal: Periodical Codes and Common Habitus', paper from the MLA 2013 Special Session, 'What Is a Journal? Towards a Theory of Periodical Studies,' available at http://blogs.tandf.co.uk/jvc/files/2012/12/mla2013_philpotts.pdf.

7   Jeff Drouin, 'Close and Distant Reading Modernism', *Journal of Modern Periodical Studies* 5, no. 1 (2014): 115. For a discussion of periodical editors using Bourdieu's notion of habitus, see Matthew Philpotts, 'The Role of the Periodical Editor', *Modern Language Review* 107, no. 1 (Jan. 2012): 39–64.
8   See, for example, the special issue of *Victorian Periodicals Review*, Fall 2015, on 'The Return to Theory', itself a reprise of an issue of the same journal from 1989.
9   Laurel Brake, 'The Case of W. T. Stead', in *Transatlantic Print Culture, 1880–1940: Emerging Media, Emerging Modernisms*, ed. Ann Ardis and Patrick Collier (Basingstoke: Palgrave Macmillan, 2008), 152.
10 For a provocative argument that the category of 'modernism' is something of a hindrance to the development of a theory of 'modern periodical studies', see Patrick Collier, 'What Is Modern Periodical Studies?', *Journal of Modern Periodical Studies* 6, no. 2 (2015): 92–111.
11 See Andrew Thacker, 'General Introduction: Magazines, Magazines, Magazines!', *Oxford Critical and Cultural History of Modernist Magazines Vol. II*, 1–30.
12 For one such attempt, see the special issue on 'Visualizing Periodical Networks', *Journal of Modern Periodical Studies* 5, no. 1 (2014).
13 See, for example, Dallas Liddle, 'Genre: "Distant Reading" and the Goals of Periodicals Research', *Victorian Periodicals Review* 48, no. 3 (Fall 2015): 383–402.
14 Jay Bochner, 'Others', in *American Literary Magazines: The Twentieth Century*, ed. Edward E. Chielens (Westport, CN: Greenwood Press, 1992), 232.
15 James Mussell, 'Repetition: Or, "In Our Last"', *Victorian Periodicals Review* 48, no. 3 (Fall 2015): 345; Franco Moretti, *Distant Reading* (London: Verso, 2013).
16 See Drouin, 'Close and Distant Reading Modernism', for an argument in favour of combining distant and close reading methodologies. Collier suggests an approach that draws upon the notion of 'surface reading' initially proposed by Stephen Best and Sharon Marcus and related to periodicals by Margaret Cohen; see Collier, 'What Is Modern Periodical Studies?' 107–8.
17 See Ardis and Collier, 'Introduction' to *Transatlantic Print Culture*, 5; 8. See also Faye Hammill, Paul Hjartarson, and Hannah McGregor, 'Introduction' and Patrick Collier, 'What Is Modern Periodical Studies?' in the special issue, 'Magazines and/ as Media: Periodical Studies and the Question of Disciplinarity', *Journal of Modern Periodical Studies* 6, no. 2 (Nov. 2015): iii–xiii and 92–111.
18 Collier, 'What Is Modern Periodical Studies?' 99.
19 See Thacker, 'General Introduction', 20–1.
20 For the MJP digital editions of *The Little Review*, see http://www.modjourn.org/render.php?view=mjp_object&id=LittleReviewCollection.
21 Roxanne Shirazi argues that one way past the impasse of copyright is for digital humanities to access the underlying data rather than the page images of copyrighted periodicals. See Roxanne Shirazi, 'A Digital Wasteland: Modernist Periodical Studies, Digital Remediation, and Copyright' in *Creating Sustainable*

Community: The Proceedings of the ACRL 2015 Conference, March 25–28, Portland, Oregon, edited by Dawn M. Mueller (Chicago: Association of College and Research Libraries, 2015), 192–9. http://www.ala.org/acrl/sites/ala.org.acrl/files/content/conferences/confsandpreconfs/2015/ACRL2015_A.pdf.

22 For work on these two magazines, see Jason Harding, *The Criterion: Cultural Politics and Periodical Networks in Interwar Britain* (Oxford: Oxford University Press, 2002); and Victoria Bazin, *Modernism Edited: Marianne Moore and the Dial Magazine* (Edinburgh: Edinburgh University Press, 2019).

23 See, for example, the definition given by Frederick Hoffman, Charles Allen, and Carolyn F. Ulrich, *The Little Magazine: A History and a Bibliography* (Princeton, NJ: Princeton University Press, 1947), 2, and a more recent one by Suzanne Churchill and Adam McKible, 'Little Magazines and Modernism: An Introduction', *American Periodicals: A Journal of History, Criticism and Bibliography* 15, no.1 (2005): 3.

24 See Frederick Winthrop Faxon, *Ephemeral Bibelots: A Bibliography of the Modern Chap Books and Their Imitators* (Boston: Boston Book Company, 1903).

25 Kirsten MacLeod, 'The Fine Art of Cheap Print: Turn of the Century American Little Magazines', in *Transatlantic Print Culture,* 184. MacLeod's recent book demonstrates a larger corpus of material in the category of American 'ephemeral bibelots' and also poses some excellent questions about how we should understand these magazines within the wider history of modernism; see MacLeod, *American Magazines of the Fin de Siècle: Art, Protest, and Cultural Transformation* (Toronto: University of Toronto Press, 2018).

26 Remy De Gourmont, *Les Petites Revues, essai de bibliographie* (Paris: Librairie du Mercure de France, 1900).

27 See Lori Cole, 'Madrid: Questioning the Avant-Garde' and Geoffrey West, '"Noucentrisme" and the Avant-Garde in Barcelona', in *Modernist Mazagines Vol. III*, 369–91 and 392–412.

28 For a succinct discussion of this issue, see Gerard Aching, 'The Temporalities of Modernity in Spanish American *Modernismo*: Darío's Bourgeois King' in *The Oxford Handbook of Global Modernism*, ed. Mark Wollaeger and Matt Eatough (Oxford: Oxford University Press, 2012).

29 For a discussion of these features, see the 'General Introduction' to both *Modernist Magazines Vol. I: Britain and Ireland* and *Vol. II: North America.*

30 For Europe the complications attendant upon the effect of the Second World War, such as the redrawing of national borders, meant that we decided to stop at 1940.

31 For a discussion of these magazines, see chapters 40–44 of *Modernist Magazines Vol. II: North America.*

32 For *Jacket* see http://jacket2.org; for *Shearsman* see https://www.shearsman.com/shearsman-magazine; for *m58* see https://www.m58.co.uk.

33 Hoffman, *The Little Magazine*, 351, 364, 388.

34 See, inter alia, Jessica Berman, *Modernist Commitments: Ethics, Politics, and Transnational Modernism* (New York: Columbia University Press, 2011); Susan Stanford Friedman, *Planetary Modernisms: Provocations on Modernity across Time* (New York: Columbia University Press, 2015); and *The Oxford Handbook of Global Modernisms*, ed. Mark Wollaeger with Matt Eatough (New York: Oxford University Press, 2012).

35 See Eric Bulson, *Little Magazine, World Form* (New York: Columbia University Press, 2017).

36 Tristan Tzara in *Dada* 4–5, quoted in Debbie Lewer 'The Avant-Garde in Swiss Exile 1914–20', in *Modernist Magazines Vol. III*, 1047.

37 See Annette Leddy and Donna Conwell, eds, *Farewell to Surrealism: The Dyn Circle in Mexico* (Los Angeles, CA: Getty Research Institute, 2012).

38 See Andrew Thacker, 'Poetry in Perspective: The Melange of the 1920s', in *Modernist Magazines Vol. II*, 320–46.

39 Andreas Huyssens, 'Geographies of Modernism in a Globalizing World', in *Geographies of Modernism*, ed. Peter Brooker and Andrew Thacker (London: Routledge, 2005), 9. See also Arjun Appadurai, *Modernity at Large: Cultural Dimensions of Globalization* (Minneapolis, MN: University of Minnesota Press, 1996).

40 For a discussion of these magazines, see Brent Hayes Edwards, *The Practice of Diaspora: Literature, Translation, and the Rise of Black Internationalism* (Cambridge, MA: Harvard University Press, 2003).

41 Etienne Léro, 'Civilisation', *Légitime Défense*, no. 1 (1932): 9. On the significance of McKay for black intellectuals in Paris, see Edwards, *Practice of Diaspora*, 187–240.

42 Lori Cole, '*Légitime Défense*: From Communism and Surrealism to Caribbean Self-Definition', *Journal of Surrealism and the Americas* 4, no. 1 (2010): 15. The question of whether, or if at all, *Légitime Défense* predates the theory of negritude is the subject of much critical debate; for an overview of this issue, see Edwards, *Practice of Diaspora*, 194.

43 Cole, '*Légitime Défense*', 21–2.

44 There is considerable discussion upon the nature of the 'modernity' found in the various territories of the Caribbean, many of which have diverse, rather than shared, histories of colonial and political rule. To refer to the 'colonial modernity' of the Caribbean is to signal a complex set of questions surrounding how these various islands engaged with the impact of colonization and the forms of social and economic modernity attendant upon these, including centrally the fact of slavery and the development of the plantation, and the types of modernism that emerged out of these multiple interactions. As Mary Lou Emery notes, in an essay that reads Caribbean literature as a kind of 'contramodernism', we can 'read Caribbean modernism as constitutive of a previously defined modernism and also

counter to it: simultaneously interconnected with alternative modernisms', such as 'Latin American surrealism ... the Harlem Renaissance, and the Francophone cultural and political movement of Négritude'. See Mary Lou Emery, 'Caribbean Modernism: Plantation to Planetary', in *Oxford Handbook of Global Modernisms*, 51.

45 For more context, see Gary Wilder, *The French Imperial Nation-State: Negritude and Colonial Humanism between the Two World Wars* (Chicago: Chicago University Press, 2005).

46 Cole, 'Légitime Défense', 26.

47 See ibid., 17–19.

48 *Légitime Défense*, 2; I am using the translation given in *Refusal of the Shadow: Surrealism and the Caribbean*, eds. Krzysztof Fijałkowski and Michael Richardson (London: Verso, 1996), 42.

49 For the concept of periodical codes, see 'General Introduction', *Modernist Magazines, Vol. 1*, 6–8.

50 'Declaration', *Légitime Défense*, 2 (translation from *Refusal of the Shadow*, 43).

51 Edwards, *Practice of Diaspora*, 191.

52 Etienne Léro, 'Misère d'une Poésie', *Légitime Défense*, 12 (translation from *Refusal of the Shadow*, 58).

53 Ibid., 58. Edwards is critical of *Légitime Défense* for its use of terms such as 'black proletariat', arguing that the magazine could neither grasp conceptually what this term entailed nor help organize it; Edwards, *Practice of Diaspora*, 198.

54 Eric Bulson, 'Little Magazine, World Form', in *The Oxford Handbook of Global Modernisms*, 268.

55 For a brief discussion of *Mavo*, see Bulson, *Little Magazine, World Form*, 62–4; for *Transition*, see Peter Benson, *Black Orpheus, Transition, and Modern Cultural Awakening in Africa* (Berkeley, CA: University of California Press, 1986).

3

Rethinking the modernist moment: Crisis, (im)potentiality and E. M. Forster's failed *Kairos*

Vassiliki Kolocotroni

Bookended by two world wars, and as many twists in imperialist fortunes, inspired by a number of revolutionary movements and fuelling many militancies to more or less successful emancipatory ends and ongoing practices of dissent, modernism can be said (*pace* Eliot's Prufrock) to have had 'the strength to force the moment to its crisis'. A close relative of the Paterian prescription of passionate intensity for 'the given time'[1] (itself an early figuration of Alain Badiou's diagnosis of the modernist century's 'passion for the real'),[2] and similarly concerned with relegating the possibility of climax to aesthetic sublimation, the moment in modernism is the generic bearer of crisis, in both its quantitative and qualitative aspects – in the temporal sense with its qualities of suddenness,[3] evanescence, fleetingness, spontaneity, presentness and their attendant affective, epistemological and ethical associations: shock, wonder, quickening of the senses, estrangement, defamiliarization, *jouissance*, sense of liberation, connectedness/disconnectedness, transience. In formal terms, modernist writing often relies on the moment for its signature effects: Helen Carr and Richard Parker,[4] for instance, have read the Poundian doctrine of the 'Image' ('that which presents an intellectual and emotional complex in an instant of time'),[5] as well as Zukofsky's early Objectivist writing as enacting the Paterian aesthetic moment, and one could argue that even the caesurae that introduce *The Waste Land*'s abject metamorphoses ('Twit twit twit/*Jug jug jug jug jug jug/* So rudely forc'd/Tereu') rely as much on the sudden appearance of the aesthetic moment as on an apocalyptic synchronicity. In the case of T. E. Hulme's imagistic flourishes, in poems such as 'The Sunset' (1909), the 'intellectual and emotional complex' flashing (the reader) 'in an instant of time', may also be viewed as an effect of crisis, both of lyrical and cultural convention, and potentially more violently perhaps, of masculinity too:

> A coryphée, covetous of applause,
> Loth to leave the stage,
> With final diablerie, poises high her toe,
> Displays scarlet lingerie of carmin'd clouds,
> Amid the hostile murmurs of the stalls.[6]

Along the same trajectory one encounters other modernist staple devices, such as Woolf's 'moments of being' and Joyce's epiphanies, recorded experiences of '"luminous" correspondence between an internal predisposition and a powerfully felt external perception', as Ashton Nichols puts it,[7] which critics have classified variously within spiritual or vitalist or psychoanalytical or other scientific frameworks,[8] and whose provenance has also been traced to Victorian motifs, such as Robert Browning's 'good minute' or 'infinite moment'.[9] In turn, the visual and spatial signature of these sudden and transformative recognitions connects them to devices integral to other modernist techniques such as collage, Eisensteinian montage and surrealist *trouvailles* ('lucky finds'), the latter appearing under the auspices of another variant of the critical moment, 'objective chance' [*le hasard objectif*].[10] This panoply of related formal events may be associated in a sweeping gesture with modernism's critical construction of a personal history within, or as Alan Wilde put it, '*vis-à-vis* large, imposing structures' and its 'intense need to shape a disordered world – not, in the first instance, either to reform or escape it but, instead, to establish, if only negatively, a relationship with it.'[11]

The paradoxical effect of this kind of concatenation, however, that is of the classification of these cognate effects under a common rubric, is the normalization of crisis and its moment into what can appear at times as a phenomenological impressionism, a phantasmagoria of perceptions and responses in a somewhat forced, seemingly necessary disunity or random order. The quotidianizing of the crisis moment, a guiding principle in many accounts of the modernist everyday, posits a problem, both methodological and strategic. It is perhaps with good reason that Leon Trotsky balked when André Breton outlined his theory of 'objective chance' at their meeting in Mexico in 1938:

> At other times he took up this or that concept which he considered worthy of putting before me, submitting it to a sharp critique. He thus said one day: 'Comrade Breton, your interest in phenomena of objective chance does not appear clear to me. Yes, I know well that Engels referred to this notion, but I ask

myself if, in your case, it isn't something else. I am not sure you aren't interested in keeping open (his hands described a little space in the air) a little window on the beyond.'[12]

For someone like Trotsky, concerned with the 'revolutionary expansion of the concept of the everyday' and 'the concrete analysis of the concrete situation'[13] anything vaguely smacking of 'the beyond' would be anathema.[14] Marxist post-revolutionary thought concerned itself exhaustively with matters of the everyday, of course, through relating them to radical concepts of reality, the present, class consciousness, alienation and the philosophy of praxis more broadly, all paths that lead us firmly away from crisis and towards critique. In a temporal and formal sense, these concerns may also lead us away from the modernist moment as symptom of crisis, and the motif of the sudden, fleeting awareness of it.

What still remains, however, is the need to think about those irruptions of critical content in the continuum of represented experience as they are re-collected in modernist tranquillity. I would like to suggest two ways in which one might rethink modernist crisis, without making of it a generalized, normal condition, with the moment as its symptom or saving grace, working its magic on the individual. Both involve retrospection, a sense of (at least possible) *collec*tivity and *connec*tivity and a sense of urgency. The first by way of a concept that has gained much currency recently, mainly through the work of Alain Badiou, namely the event. The event in a Badiouan sense creates subjects, and fidelity to the event 'binds the subject to a truth'. As Badiou puts it:

> Every process of truth begins with an event. An event is unpredictable and incalculable – it is a supplement of the situation. Every truth, and therefore every subject, depends upon an eventual emergence. A truth and a subject of truth do not derive from what there is, but from what happens, in the strong sense of the term 'happens'.[15]

An event in that sense will puncture time and inaugurate a new subject, who in turn will commit to that eventual transformation. In other words, it is the aspect of active, subject-forming intervention and innovation, that strong sense of 'happens' rather than 'appears', that distinguishes the concept of 'event' from the 'moment'. Though there is no reason why a moment can't be isolated as partly inaugurating an event, the event is only thinkable (and formative of subjects and truth processes) with the immediate hindsight afforded by the new experience of time after the event – put crudely, it is about action, not perception, about the new militancy and praxis arising from it rather than about the moment of its coming to pass. Eventality thus outlasts the moment and sets in motion a transformative *durée* which confirms the subject through its fidelity to the originary act. Woolf's *Mrs Dalloway*, for instance, may be considered in this light as recording evental subject formations and deformations, as seen in the retrospections of Septimus, Clarissa or Miss Killman, though the truth processes inaugurated in their lives may ultimately lead to an impossible existence in the now. That's one example – Yeats's 1916, Eliot's conversion may be read eventally through their writing too.

I want to move swiftly and speculatively to another cognate concept, however, which I would propose as equally relevant for an attempt to finesse our understanding of modernism's moment and as alternative to its association with epiphanic and evanescent shock effects. The concept which offers us these alternative inflections is that of '*kairos*',[16] with its multiple associations with crisis, exception, emergency, urgency, temporal disjunction, inaugural potentiality, freedom and pleasure. In the Foreword to a collection of essays on *Rhetoric and Kairos*, Carolyn R. Miller cites Erwin Panofsky's description of the iconic representation of *Kairos* in classical art:

> 'Kairos'; that is, the brief, decisive moment which marks a turning-point in the life of human beings or in the development of the universe. This concept was illustrated by the figure vulgarly known as Opportunity [...], a man (originally nude) in fleeting movement, usually young [...] equipped with wings both at the shoulder and at the heels. His attributes were a pair of scales, originally balanced on the edge of a shaving knife, and, in a somewhat later period, one or two wheels. Moreover his head often showed the proverbial forelock by which bald-headed Opportunity can be seized.[17]

Originally denoting the strategically aimed mortal blow (as in the *Iliad*), later adopted by rhetoricians to define the appropriate, exact delivery of the clincher line in an argument or oration, and by early Christian writers as 'the time of the now' as urgent, messianic time, *kairos* is antithetical to the psychoanalytical logic of trauma, that is to the repressed or latent aspect of experience, or indeed to the very logic of forgetting itself. It is instead the assumption of a heightened reality in the present that signals the dissolution of temporal boundaries: even in its eccentric, chemically induced configuration as the union with the cosmos afforded by the psychedelic experience as preached by Ken Kesey and the Merry Pranksters of the 1960s, *kairos* takes on the form of a release from the limits of time and space – as Tom Wolfe recalled:

> Gradually the Prankster attitude began to involve the main things religious mystics have always felt, things common to Hindus, Buddhists, Christians,

and for that matter Theosophists and even flying-saucer cultists. Namely the *experiencing* of an Other World, a higher level of reality. And a perception of the cosmic unity of this higher level. And a feeling of timelessness, the feeling that what we know as time is only the result of a naïve faith in causality – the notion that A in the past *caused* B in the present, which will *cause* C in the future, when actually A, B, and C are all part of a pattern that can be truly understood only by opening the doors of perception and experiencing it ... in this moment ... this supreme moment ... this *Kairos*.[18]

Though partaking of qualities of liminality (especially if configured in a spatial as well as temporal sense, that is, when referring to the exact place in which a strike is made, which presupposes an inexact – *ákairos* – spot),[19] *kairos* is of the order of the strong potentiality, of now-time as seized time, or as Giorgio Agamben puts it, 'the only real time, the only time we have':[20]

> What do we have when we have *kairos*? The most beautiful definition of *kairos* I know of occurs in the *Corpus Hippocraticum* which characterizes it in relation to *chronos*. It reads: *chronos esti en ho kairos kai kairos esti en ho ou pollos chronos*, *chronos* is that in which there is *kairos*, and *kairos* is that in which there is little *chronos*.[21]

In other words, for Agamben, '[w]hereas our representation of chronological time, as the time *in which* we are, separates us from ourselves and transforms us into impotent spectators of ourselves [...], messianic time, as operational time in which we take hold of and achieve our representations of time, is the time *that* we ourselves are.'[22] Here, Agamben glosses *kairos* via the concept of the messianic event in the writing of Saint Paul:

> Paul's technical term for the messianic event is *ho nyn kairos*, 'the time of the now'; this is why Paul is an apostle and not a prophet. [...] [T]he messianic event is not the end of time, but the *time of the end* ... What interests the apostle is not the last day, it is not the instant in which time ends, but the time that contracts itself and begins to end ..., or if you prefer, the time that remains between time and its end.[23]

Agamben embraces the eschatological associations of the term, though he reads them through a Benjaminian lens which accords our consciousness of the time that remains a '*weak* messianic power'.[24] Agamben relates this reflection to Paul's statement in the second letter to Corinthians: 'power fulfils itself in weakness.'[25] The implications of this line of thinking for a critique of power are of broader interest for Agamben, especially in his reading of Aristotle's discussion of 'impotentiality',[26] and Heidegger's interpretation of it in his 1931 lecture course on Aristotle's *Metaphysics*.[27] In a stronger, materialist reading, closer to Badiou's eventalism, however, Antonio Negri has read *kairos* as the precipitation, or as he puts it, '*decision of a new being*':[28]

> If consciousness perceives *kairòs* ambiguously, as 'being on the brink', as 'being on a razor's edge', i.e. as the instant in which the 'archer looses the arrow', then *kairòs* becomes the restlessness of temporality – the name we wanted for that experience. But if it is so, we will then be able to ask ourselves if *kairòs* is not equally real insistence in that point of time defined by the point of that arrow; that is to say, being's act of leaning out over the void of the time *to-come*, i.e the adventure beyond the edge of time. In third place, we will be able to ask ourselves if *kairòs* is not – *simpliciter* – power to experience temporality.[29]

Concerned (like Badiou) with the transformation of 'the ontology of temporality into a production of truth', and more specifically with praxis, Negri posits a 'decisive function' for *kairos* as 'an event of generation', 'the arrow that has been released'.[30] The extension of *kairos* into the *to-come* opens up utopian potentialities, but also acts of creation in the now, imagination as a 'linguistic gesture, hence a common gesture', as Negri puts it; 'the gesture which throws a web over the *to-come* so as to know it, construct it, organize it with power'.[31] In what follows, I consider briefly how the concept of *kairos*, in both its strong and weak expressions, might add a resonance to modernist formulations of the supreme instant.

One could read much modernist poetry kairologically, along the lines of this restless temporality: Eliot's later reflections, for instance, where *kairos* is subsumed, pacified in *chronos*, as in these lines from 'East Coker': 'Not the intense moment/Isolated, with no before and after,/But a lifetime burning in every moment'; Yeats's questions (as in the last lines of 'Leda and the Swan') could be read as kairotic moments as formulated this time by Heidegger, that is as moments 'that impos[e] [their] own time by apprehending us through a genuine asking of questions',[32] moments, as Heidegger puts it, 'when we are pushed out into the open'.[33] Or, to return to modernism, the caesura of Pound's 'In a Station of the Metro' may be read as the kairotic moment of a seized potentiality of transformation, not merely an interruption in perception. For Gregory Mason, this moment would be a variant of the kairoticism (and one might add, eventalism) of the haiku, the effect of which he approaches in Paterian terms:

> Each haiku poem could be said to build upon its own particular *kairos*, its 'haiku moment.' This 'haiku moment' denotes a kind of *kairos* when a seemingly

commonplace event becomes the inspiration for a poem. The event presents an intersection of the transient with the enduring, and the concrete image embodying it resonates with associations and connotations. The haiku form is radically kairotic, urging a sensitivity to experience that enhances the quality of each passing moment.[34]

For Theodor Adorno, it is the 'snatched instant', or the captivating detail that in its intensity kairotically confirms the totality of the artwork – as he puts it in *Aesthetic Theory*:

> That in many of its elements the artwork becomes more intense, thickens, and explodes, gives the impression of being an end in itself; the great unities of composition and construction seem to exist only for the purpose of such intensity. Accordingly, contrary to current aesthetic views, the whole in truth exists only for the sake of its parts – that is, its καιρός, the instant – and not the reverse.[35]

Equally resonant, but more complex in their associations with potentiality and praxis, as well as a 'weak messianic power', are the kairoticisms of those modernist events which arise from a moment whose truth was *not* fully lived, yet whose momentousness has cast a shadow of protracted potentiality over life, a kind of radical waiting, as identified by Adorno in his reading of Beckett:

> [H]is consciousness was correct that the need for progress is inextricable from its impossibility. The gesture of walking in place at the end of *Godot*, which is the fundamental motif of the whole of his work, reacts precisely to this situation. Without exception his response is violent. His work is the extrapolation of a negative καιρός.[36]

There are many such moments in Woolf's writing (who can also be kairotic in a positive sense, as in *Orlando* or *To the Lighthouse*), but also and perhaps most strikingly in E. M. Forster's many staged encounters between the 'tame and the savage', between classes and 'races'. In his various 'panics', rare 'happy endings', where two men 'fall in love and remain in it for the ever and ever that fiction allows',[37] but mainly in the recurrent 'No's, "not yet … not there" of his characters' prospects,[38] Forster seems to be constructing a form of queer *kairos*, which encompasses the desire to 'only connect the prose and the passion', as in the famous, ambiguous final maxim of *Howards End*,[39] its power and its impossibility. As Frank Kermode has shown in his classic exploration of fictions of 'the End', narrative endings are the very stuff of *kairotic* temporality: 'The fictive end purges the interval of simple chronicity. It achieves a "temporal integration" – it converts a blank into a *kairos*, charges it with meaning.'[40] For Kermode, '[t]his is the time of the novelist, a transformation of mere successiveness which has been likened, by writers as different as Forster and Musil, to the experience of love, the erotic consciousness which makes divinely satisfactory sense out of the commonplace person.'[41] Kermode's discussion of the formal kairoticism of narrative time per se may provide a broad and still useful entry point, but in the final part of this essay, I would like to explore further the specificity and, *pace* Kermode, the 'divinely' *unsatisfactory* sense of Forsterian *kairos*.

In terms of our discussion so far, Forster's queer *kairos* is both evental and negative in the sense that while it may be experienced as 'the time of the instant, the moment of rupture and opening of temporality', a 'restless temporality', as Negri glosses it in his reading of *kairos* (except for *Maurice*'s wilful, all-that-heaven-will-allow ending), usually inaugurates a *betrayal* rather than a *fidelity* to the event. The 'plain, simple man, with no pretensions to literary style' who narrates 'The Story of a Panic', fails to understand the salutary 'laughter of the escaping [English] boy', or the sudden death of the Italian 'fisher-lad', after their kairotic, Pan-presided encounter in the Ravello wood;[42] in 'The Road from Colonus', the ageing, babbling Mr. Lucas betrays the experience of the 'supreme event' awaiting him 'in that place and with those people' in Greece, which for a 'tremendous moment' he was certain 'would transfigure the face of the world',[43] as does the 'authoress' Miss Raby, in 'The Eternal Moment', whose inability genuinely to 'connect the prose and the passion' in her romanticized rendition of the place of her 'missed moment' with the Italian porter has only the effect of turning the idyllic small town into a hot spot for the wrong kind of tourist.[44]

It is in the suppressed, openly homoerotic stories, however, that Forster writes out the full ramifications of a queer *kairos*, most notably in 'The Life to Come' (1922), which casts a moment of Christian conversion in the light of queer love. In its failed (and in that sense strong) messianism and the fatal inversions on which it relies, its insistence on the 'no more' as a 'not yet', Forster's linguistic gesture here seems suspended over the precipice of time conceived as crisis and *kairos*. The story is based on a typically Forsterian encounter between the young English missionary, Paul Pinmay, stationed in an unspecified foreign country, and the young native chief Vithobai-*cum*-Barnabas, as he is named after his conversion to Christianity. The choice of names for both missionary and convert is significant, and points to a set of foundational but troubled couplings: in the New Testament, Barnabas, meaning 'the son of consolation', is the mediator of the converted Saul to the suspicious disciples at Jerusalem (*Acts* 9.27), the one who brings Saul-*cum*-Paul back from Tarsus to join the church at Antioch and goes out with him on the first missionary journey (*Acts* 11.25f), and between whom and Paul there is a decisive later rupture (*Acts* 15.26-40).[45] For Badiou, who 'ha[s] never really connected Paul with religion', Paul is 'a poet-thinker of the event', a 'militant figure'.[46] Though his approach could not be further from Forster's adaption of the figure of Paul, as we will see, Badiou's gloss on the critical moment of the future apostle's life resonates with our discussion and the kairotic terms of Forster's story: 'Is the term "conversion" appropriate to what happened on the road to Damascus? It was a thunderbolt, a caesura, and not a dialectical reversal.'[47] The opening of 'The Life to Come' introduces Paul and Vithobai, unnamed, in a post-caesura scene, in a spatial and temporal setting of potentiality, immediately reverting through another caesura of shameful recognition to regret and resignation:

> Love had been born somewhere in the forest, of what quality only the future could decide. Trivial or immortal, it had been born to two human bodies as a midnight cry. Impossible to tell whence the cry had come, so dark was the forest. Or into what worlds it would echo, so vast was the forest. Love had been born for good or evil, for a long life or a short. [...] A remote, a romantic spot ... lovely ... lovable. And then he caught sight of a book on the floor, and he dropped beside it with a dramatic moan as if it was a corpse and he the murderer. For the book in question was his Holy Bible. [...] 'Oh, what have I done?' [...] 'Only one end to this, he thought.'[48]

Written in reverse order in four sections, 'Night', 'Evening', 'Day', 'Morning', the story is the violent extrapolation (to paraphrase Adorno) of a fatal betrayal of a kairotic event. Having converted through and for love, rejected but faithful (in a double, queer sense, that is, faithful in Christ, but also faithful to his first night with Paul, as well as to his language), Vithobai/Barnabas pleads with Paul to fulfil his promise of a love and life to come:

> Tepid, impersonal, as if he still discussed public affairs, the young man said: 'Let us both be entirely reasonable, sir. God continues to order me to love you. It is my life, whatever else I seem to do. My body and the breath in it are still yours, though you wither them up with this waiting. Come into the last forest, before it is cut down, and I will be kind, and all may end well. But it is now five years since you first said Not yet.'
> 'It is, and now I say Never.'
> 'This time you say Never?'
> 'I do.'[49]

In a kairotic context, the clergyman's 'I do' is a lying word, a denial proffered as an affirmation; conversely, when urged to confess to his love as a sin, the convert's 'No' is a truth and a conviction:

Do you repent of your words?

No.

Then you must be punished. As the head of the community you are bound to set an example. You are fined one hundred pounds for backsliding.

'No.' Then as if to himself he said: 'First the grapes of my body are pressed. Then I am silenced. Now I am punished. Night, evening and a day. What remains?'[50]

What remains is a betrayal of 'the time when it was still time' (as Beckett might have put it),[51] and a waiting for Vithobai/Barnabas, whose conversion translates his desire into a messianic idiom and the invocation of 'the life to come', which ironically he elicits from the clergyman in the final scene. The story closes with the end of the two lovers (as now old, consumptive Vithobai/Barnabas stabs an urgently repenting Paul – false or weak apostle that he has proved to be) at the moment of his own death:

> The jerk the knife gave brought his own fate hurrying upon him. He had scarcely the strength to push the body onto the asphalt or to spread the skein of blue flowers. [...] He dragged himself up, he looked over the parapet. Below him were a horse and cart, beyond, the valley which he had once ruled, the site of the hut, the ruins of his old stockade, the schools, the hospital, the cemetery, the stacks of timber, the polluted stream, all that he had been used to regard as signs of his disgrace. But they signified nothing this morning, they were flying like mist, and beneath them, solid and eternal, stretched the kingdom of the dead. He rejoiced as in boyhood, he was expected there now. Mounting on the corpse, he climbed higher, raised his arms over his head, sunlit, naked, victorious, leaving all disease and humiliation behind him, and he swooped like a falcon from the parapet in pursuit of the terrified shade.[52]

Here, Forster engages obliquely with Plato's *Phaedrus*, another foundational tale of homoerotic love: 'Phaedrus. My tale, Socrates, is one of your sort, for love was the theme which occupied us – love after a fashion.'[53] The famous dialogue, set in a pleasant wooded spot in the hot midday and ending with a very Forsterian prayer to god Pan, features Socrates's defence of philosophy as the true art of speaking, his appreciation of the knowledge of *kairos*, or the 'times and seasons' for speaking truth and justice, and of course the elaborate figure of the soul as 'a pair of winged horses and a charioteer'; of the many variants of this figure in Socrates's telling, there are those that pertain to the lover:

> Now the lover who is taken to be the attendant of Zeus is better able to bear the winged god, and can endure a heavier burden; but the attendants and companions of Ares, when under the influence of love, if they fancy that they

have been at all wronged, are ready to kill and put an end to themselves and their beloved.

Forster had already turned to Plato as an authority on the 'malady' of homosexual love: in *Maurice* (written in 1913–14), he presents the *Phaedrus* as a corrective gloss on the Bible, though in terms which neither Clive himself nor the characters of the later story can actually live out:

> The boy [Clive] had always been a scholar, awake to the printed word, and the horrors the Bible had evoked for him were to be laid by Plato. Never could he forget his emotion at first reading the *Phaedrus*. He saw there his malady described exquisitely, calmly, as a passion which we can direct, like any other, towards good or bad. Here was no invitation to license. He could not believe his good fortune at first – thought there must be some misunderstanding and that he and Plato were thinking of different things. Then he saw that the temperate pagan really did comprehend him, and, slipping past the Bible rather than opposing it, was offering a new guide to life. 'To make the most of what I have.' Not to crush it down, not vainly to wish that it was something else, but to cultivate it in such ways as will not vex either God or Man.[54]

As he put it in 'What I Believe' (1938), his 'law-givers [were] Erasmus and Montaigne, not Moses and St Paul',[55] and in 'The Life to Come', Forster places the latter pair, or at least one of their namesakes, in the terrible situation of an impossible 'what if'. Like Nietzsche's Socrates, failing to heed fully Dionysus's command to 'make music!' and fearing that 'like some barbarian king, he did not understand the noble image of some god',[56] Forster's Paul is a cautionary example, a missed opportunity to affirm life in the now. His end bears out the catastrophic consequences of 'crushing [love] down', while through a queering of the Biblical promise, it is Vithobai/Barnabas who assumes the mantle of the messiah: 'But he survived for a moment longer, and it was the most exquisite he had ever known. For love was conquered at last and he was again a king, he had sent a messenger before him to announce his arrival in the life to come, as a great chief should.'[57] The reversal of the circumstances of redemption is deeply ambivalent: the references to 'a king' and 'a great chief' are both paratactic and paradoxical, suggesting a slippage from the symbolic language of Christianity to that which it failed to dominate or extinguish. The reborn Vithobai ('sunlit, naked, victorious') is a radicalized, rebel angel: '"I served you for ten years," he thought, "and your yoke was hard, but mine will be harder and you shall serve me now for ever and ever."'[58] In Christopher Lane's reading, though 'gratuitous and bathetic' to almost farcical effect, Vithobai's act 'seems consistent with Forster's anxiety and the problem of managing colonial and sexual fantasy.'[59] For

Lane, the story's final image 'not only forges a comparison between sexual desire and colonial insubordination, but also assumes, as its corollary, an analogy between the unconscious and a state of savagery'.[60] In fact, Lane quotes Forster's 'confession' to Siegfried Sassoon (in a letter dated 21 July 1923) that he 'wish[ed] the story could have [had] another ending'.[61] The brief sketch in the letter of an abandoned final chapter, in which 'Pinmay enters Eternity as a slave while Vithobai reigns with his peers', is read by Lane as 'Forster's insistence that sexual inequality persists in Heaven'. For Lane,

> In his determination to retain Pinmay's and Vithobai's intimacy – a determination that went hopelessly awry in the narrative's execution – Forster could not conceive of homosexual desire without accompanying elements of violence, slavery and distress. Thus we might argue that Forster's expectation of redemption precipitates an astonishing burden on his texts, forcing them to buckle under the strain of reconciling impossibly conflicted sexual and racial desires.[62]

Yet, as I would argue, it is in the very impossibility of resolving the conflict while retaining the intimacy that the kairotic power of Forster's writing lies.[63] Read through this lens, the master–slave dialectic and its double reversal in Forster's tale (as Vithobai's conversion through the promise of love, a 'not yet', turns into a waiting for what will never be, and forces a reversion to the moment of union, the original 'Night' when all was still possible) intercepts the message of redemption and interprets or converts it into that temporal modality 'through which being opens itself, attracted by the void at the limit of time', as Negri puts it.[64] The final image of Vithobai's demonic flight invokes the trajectory of a rebel angel, or in different terms, to bring Benjamin back into the frame, of the angel of history – I am cross-reading Forster with Agamben here:

> There must be a critical demolition of the ideas of process, development, and progress whereby historicism seeks to reinsert the pseudo-meanings of the Christian 'history of salvation' into a history which it has itself reduced to a pure chronology. Against the empty, continuous, quantified, infinite time of vulgar historicism must be set the full, broken, indivisible and perfect time of concrete human experience; instead of the chronological time of pseudo-history, the cairological time of authentic history; in place of the total social process of a dialectic lost in time, the interruption and immediacy of dialectic at a standstill.[65]

The fact that the story was thought 'wholly unpublishable' by Forster at the time of its composition adds a further nuance to this discussion of critical temporality: 'Have this moment burnt my indecent writings or as many as the fire will take

[…] I am not ashamed of them,' he wrote in his diary on 8 April 1922, '[i]t is just that they were a wrong channel for my pen.'[66] Luckily, he changed his mind and salvaged that writing, even as he remained ambivalent about its prospects and literary suitability. There is a poignancy, or a kairotic urgency, about the perceived danger of that creative moment, a recognized 'action on the edge of being', in Negri's phrase.[67] For us now, in our time still, as for Forster, the story in its queer kairoticism, its unresolved conflict, and weak, though rebellious, messianism poses an open question about the 'not yet, not there' of such 'indecent' moments.

Notes

1 See Walter Pater, 'Conclusion', in *Studies in the History of the Renaissance*, ed. Matthew Beaumont (Oxford: Oxford University Press, 2010). For discussions of the resonance of the Paterian moment in modernism, see Perry Meisel, *The Absent Father: Virginia Woolf and Walter Pater* (New Haven, CT: Yale University Press, 1980) and *The Myth of the Modern: A Study in British Literature and Criticism after 1850* (New Haven, CT: Yale University Press, 1989).
2 Alain Badiou, *The Century*, trans. Alberto Toscano (Cambridge: Polity Press, 2007), 21, *passim*.
3 See Karl Heinz Bohrer, *Suddenness: On the Moment of Aesthetic Appearance*, trans. Ruth Crowley (New York: Columbia University Press, 1994).
4 See Helen Carr, *The Verse Revolutionaries: Ezra Pound, H.D. and the Imagists* (London: Jonathan Cape, 2009) and Richard Parker, 'Walter Pater – Imagism–Objectivist Verse', *Victorian Network* 3, no. 1 (Special Bulletin [2011]): 22–40.
5 Ezra Pound, 'A Few Don'ts by an Imagiste', *Poetry* 1, no. 6 (March 1913): 200–6, 200.
6 T. E. Hulme, *Selected Writings*, ed. Patrick McGuinness (New York: Routledge, 2003), 9.
7 Ashton Nichols, 'Browning's Modernism: The Infinite Moment as Epiphany', *Browning Institute Studies* 11 (1983): 81–99, 96.
8 For a detailed account, see Sharon Kim, *Literary Epiphany in the Novel, 1850–1950: Constellations of the Soul* (New York: Palgrave Macmillan, 2012).
9 See Nichols, 'Browning's Modernism'.
10 On the finer points of 'objective chance' and Breton's attempts to convince Trotsky of its revolutionary relevance, see E. San Juan Jr., 'Aimé Césaire's Insurrectionary Poetics', in *Surrealism, Politics and Culture*, ed. Raymond Spiteri and Donald LaCoss (Aldershot: Ashgate, 2003), 226–45.
11 Alan Wilde, 'Modernism and the Aesthetics of Crisis', *Contemporary Literature* 20, no. 1 (Winter 1979): 13–50, 47.

12 Quoted in André Breton, *What Is Surrealism? Selected Writings*, ed. Franklin Rosemont (New York: Pathfinder, 1978), 239.
13 See John Roberts, *Philosophizing the Everyday: Revolutionary Praxis and the Fate of Cultural Theory* (London and Ann Arbor: Pluto Press, 2006), 27, 28.
14 As it happens, Breton later claimed to have landed his point after clarifying that those 'phenomena' of objective chance were only seemingly magical and disturbing 'in the present state of knowledge' (Breton, *What Is Surrealism?* 239).
15 Alain Badiou, 'A Poetic Dialectic', in *Handbook of Inaesthetics*, trans. Alberto Toscano (Stanford: Stanford University Press, 2005), 55.
16 The term/name (Gr. καιρός/Καιρός respectively) variously appears in English renditions as 'kairós', 'kairos' (that is, with or without an accent or italics) or 'cairos'. Unless quoting another author's spelling, I will be using the non-accented, non-capitalized, italicized version.
17 Carolyn R. Miller, 'Foreword', in *Rhetoric and Kairos: Essays in History, Theory, and Praxis*, ed. Philip Sipiora and James S. Baumlin (Albany: State University of New York Press, 2002), xii.
18 Tom Wolfe, *The Electric Kool-Aid Acid Test* (London: Black Swan, 1989), 129–30. See also pp. 117–18, 131. I am grateful to Adam Piette for bringing this use of *kairos* to my attention. The term also appears in the related, contemporary context of therapy culture; see, for instance, Pauline B. Bart, 'The Myth of Value-Free Psychotherapy', in *The Sociology of the Future: Theory, Cases, and Annotated Bibliography*, ed. Wendell Bell and James A. Mau (New York: Russell Sage Foundation, 1971), 113–59, 130: 'A striking example of therapy both as recreation and as social movement can be found in the [1967] booklet describing Kairos, the mental health spa in San Diego, where self-actualizing encounter therapy takes place. Not only can individuals join the Kairos Club, but they can give gift certificates of from $25 to $100 "for that person whom you know is open and really right for such an experience"'.
19 See Phillip Sipiora, 'Introduction: The Ancient Concept of *Kairos*', in *Rhetoric and Kairos: Essays in History, Theory, and Praxis*, ed. Philip Sipiora and James S. Baumlin (New York: State University of New York Press, 2002), 2.
20 Giorgio Agamben, *The Time That Remains: A Commentary on the Letter to the Romans*, trans. Patricia Dailey (Stanford, CA: Stanford University Press, 2005), 68.
21 Agamben, *The Time That Remains*, 68–9.
22 Ibid., 68–9.
23 Ibid., 61, 62.
24 'The past carries with it a secret index by which it is referred to redemption. [...] [L]ike every generation that preceded us, we have been endowed with a *weak messianic power*, a power on which the past has a claim' (Walter Benjamin, 'On

the Concept of History', in *Selected Writings: Vol. 4, 1938–1940*, ed. Howard Eiland and Michael W. Jennings; trans. Harry Zohn (Cambridge, MA.: Harvard University Press, 2006), 390.
25   See Paul 2 Corinthians 12:9-10, quoted in Agamben, *The Time That Remains*, 140.
26   Giorgio Agamben, 'On Potentiality', in *Potentialities: Collected Essays in Philosophy*, ed. and trans. Daniel Heller-Roazen (Stanford, CA: Stanford University Press, 1999), 182.
27   Agamben, 'The Passion of Facticity', in *Potentialities*, 201. See also Heidegger's related concept of *Augenblick*, or 'glance of the eye', also sourced from Aristotle, which connotes for Heidegger a decisive instant, a moment of vision and transformation. For a discussion, see Suvi Alt, 'Darkness in a Blink of an Eye', *Angelaki* 21, no. 2 (June 2016): 17–31 and William McNeill, *The Glance of the Eye: Heidegger, Aristotle, and the Ends of Theory* (Albany: State University of New York Press, 1999).
28   Antonio Negri, '*Kairòs, Alma Venus, Multitudo*', in *Time for Revolution*, trans. Matteo Mandarini (London: Continuum, 2003), 154. Emphasis added. For a discussion of Negri's deployment of the concept in Biblical and revolutionary contexts, see Roland Boer, 'The Immeasurably Creative Politics of Job: Antonio Negri and the Bible', *SubStance* 41, no. 3 (2012): 93–108 and 'Revolution in the Event: The Problem of Kairós', *Theory, Culture & Society* 30, no. 2 (2013): 116–34.
29   Negri, '*Kairòs, Alma Venus, Multitudo*', 152.
30   Ibid., 152, 154.
31   Ibid., 156.
32   Melissa Shew, 'The *Kairos* of Philosophy', *Journal of Speculative Philosophy* 27, no. 1 (2013): 55.
33   Martin Heidegger, 'The Fundamental Question of Metaphysics', quoted by Shew, 'The *Kairos* of Philosophy', 64.
34   Gregory Mason, 'In Praise of *Kairos* in the Arts: Critical Time, East and West', in *Rhetoric and Kairos: Essays in History, Theory, and Praxis*, 207. The effect of associative enhancement is noted too by Sergei Eisenstein, whose 1929 essay 'The Cinematographic Principle and the Ideogram' considers the haiku (alongside other examples of Japanese poetic and pictorial art) as analogous to cinematic form. See *Film Form: Essays in Film Theory*, ed. and trans. Jay Leyda (New York and London: Harcourt Brace Jovanovich, 1949), 32.
35   T. W. Adorno, *Aesthetic Theory*, ed. and trans. Robert Hullot-Kentor (London and New York: Continuum, 2002), 187.
36   Ibid., 30.
37   Forster, 'terminal note' to *Maurice* (London: Penguin Classics, 2005), 220.
38   See, for instance, the final words of *A Passage to India*: ' "No, not yet," and the sky said "No, not there" ' (London: Penguin Classics, 2005), 306.
39   E. M. Forster, *Howards End* (London: Edward Arnold, 1910), 183–4.

40 Frank Kermode, *The Sense of an Ending: Studies in the Theory of Fiction* (Oxford and New York: Oxford University Press, 2000), 192.
41 Ibid., 46.
42 'The Story of a Panic', in *Selected Stories*, ed. Davis Leavitt and Mark Mitchell (New York and London: Penguin Books, 2001), 1, 23.
43 'The Road from Colonus,' *Selected Stories*, 86.
44 'The Eternal Moment,' *Selected Stories*, 161–92.
45 I owe this gloss to my erudite colleague Donald Mackenzie. For a detailed reading of the blend of 'sex and exegesis' in the story, see Gregory W. Bredbeck, 'Missionary Positions: Reading the Bible in E. M. Forster's "The Life to Come"', in *Reclaiming the Sacred: The Bible in Gay and Lesbian Culture*, Second edn., ed. Raymond-Jean Frontain (New York: Harington Park Press, 2003), 137–60, 138.
46 Alain Badiou, *Saint Paul: The Foundation of Universalism*, trans. Ray Brassier (Stanford CA: Stanford University Press, 2003), 1–2.
47 Ibid., 17.
48 E. M. Forster, 'The Life to Come', in *The Life to Come and Other Stories*, ed. Oliver Stallybrass (London: Edward Arnold, 1972), 65–82, 65–6.
49 Ibid., 75.
50 Ibid., 76.
51 Samuel Beckett, 'Gloaming', quoted by James Knowlson in *Damned to Fame: The Life of Samuel Beckett* (London: Bloomsbury, 1997), 432.
52 Forster, 'The Life to Come', 81–2.
53 Plato, *Phaedrus*, trans. Benjamin Jowett. http://classics.mit.edu/Plato/phaedrus.html.
54 Forster, *Maurice*, 59–60.
55 E. M. Forster, *Two Cheers for Democracy* (London: Edward Arnold, 1972), 65.
56 Friedrich Nietzsche, 'The Birth of Tragedy Out of the Spirit of Music', in *The Birth of Tragedy and Other Writings*, ed. Raymond Geuss and Ronald Spiers; trans. Ronald Spiers (Cambridge: Cambridge University Press, 1999), 71.
57 Forster, 'The Life to Come', 81.
58 Ibid., 81.
59 Christopher Lane, *The Ruling Passion: British Colonial Allegory and the Paradox of Homosexual Desire* (Durham, NC: Duke University Press, 1995), 169.
60 Ibid., 169.
61 Ibid., 170.
62 Ibid.
63 In this sense, I am in broad agreement with Bredbeck, who reads the story's ending as 'ironically suggest[ing] that which it will not say. [...] Forster's truth is different: that some things remain – and *should* remain – uncapturable' ('Missionary Positions,' 156).

64 Negri, 'Kairòs, Alma Venus, Multitudo', 152.
65 Giorgio Agamben, 'Project for a Review', in *Infancy and History: The Destruction of Experience*, trans. Liz Heron (London and New York: Verso, 1993), 148.
66 Quoted by Oliver Stallybrass in the Introduction to *The Life to Come and Other Stories*, xii.
67 Negri, '*Kairòs*', *Alma Venus, Multitudo*, 159.

4

'Well now that's done: And I'm glad it's over': Modernism, history and the future

Max Saunders

When does Tiresias see the encounter between the typist and her lover, the 'young man carbuncular', in *The Waste Land*? His present tense may suggest he is reporting it as it happens. But then he tells us he has 'foresuffered all/Enacted on this same divan or bed'. He foresaw it in the past, that is; as a seer would be expected to do. So is he witnessing the scene he foresuffered now happening in the present in front of his (blind) eyes; saying, 'I foretold you so'? If so, that would be the opposite sequence to the one he gives us, saying he 'Perceived the scene, and foretold the rest'. That way round may get at the depressing predictability of modern degradation (we all know where this is heading …). But it also tells us that modernism's relation to history, to time, to the future, has been radically disconcerted. The event is in the past, the present and the future. A figure from the classical past speaks to us – from when? – about an event in the reader's era, which he has predicted, or is predicting …

Modernism is generally cast as backward looking: classicising; allusive; declinist. Yes, it talks of innovation – of 'the new (the really new) work of art' (Eliot); of the need to 'Make it New!' (Pound).[1] But the It to be made new, the context for the really new work, is the past; the tradition; history. While a writer like H. G. Wells was portraying Edwardian drapers and Suffragettes, and imagining time machines and alien invasions, Eliot, Joyce and Pound were reanimating Tiresias, Ulysses, Propertius and Dante.

Modernism's relation to the past seems familiar. Its relation to the future is less often told, even though modernists themselves foretold it. This chapter will argue that what Eliot called 'the immense panorama of futility and anarchy which is contemporary history', while it may express nostalgia about past history, primarily expresses anxiety about the future.[2] It will show how, in order to understand modernism's relation to history, both terms need to be triangulated with the future; and it will recover some key texts from the modernist period in which thinking about history and about the future co-exist. Joyce's 'mythical method', like Eliot's own, may have offered a reassuring sense of how post-war disorder might be reordered. What is disturbing about such moments of new world disorder, though, as we are reminded now, is what they presage. We call events historic not because they are over, settled and written down, but because they disturb such order.

Eliot's phrase 'contemporary history' might give us pause. Wait a minute: isn't all history *past* history? What does it mean to speak of 'contemporary history'? It could indicate the recent events which have led up to the present moment. One might think that 'recent history' would be a more colloquial way of expressing that. The term 'contemporary history' had some currency, since the early nineteenth century, as simply a description of the most recent period under investigation.[3] That may have been what Eliot meant. Yet the phrase is also susceptible of a different reading: one which expresses a specifically modernist attitude to temporality.

Ford Madox Ford, for example, recalling his effort to reconstruct himself as a writer after his experiences on the Western Front, said: 'I wanted the Novelist in fact to appear in his really proud position as historian of his own time. Proust being dead I could see no one who was doing that.'[4] Again, being the historian of your own time could mean writing the history of your own lifetime; looking back, but only as far as the span of your life, to your childhood (Ford was sixty when wrote these words). That is the sense he appears to invoke when, at the same time that he was composing the preceding volume of reminiscences, *Return to Yesterday* (1931), he drafted *A History of Our Own Times*; a work which sketched out world history from the time of his youth to the present.[5]

But the phrase 'historian of his own time', as with 'contemporary history', will bear a more radical reading: as pushing the time frame right into the present, and writing the history, not of the past at all, but a paradoxical history of *now*.[6] That sense comes to the fore when Eliot wrote 'Little Gidding' during the Second World War:

A people without history
Is not redeemed from time, for history is a pattern
Of timeless moments. So, while the light fails
On a winter's afternoon, in a secluded chapel
History is now and England.[7]

But the pattern, as Eliot had written in 'East Coker' in 1940, 'is new in every moment/And every moment is a new and shocking/Valuation of all we have been'.[8] The modernist sense of history, according to this view, is of a dynamic process. History does not remain fixed, because the meaning of events in the past is changed by events in the future. This was an understanding of a situation which both thrilled and terrified Thomas De Quincey, in a superb passage of the *Confessions of an English Opium Eater* which Eliot appears to have been recalling. De Quincey elaborates a metaphor for experience as an exploration of the unknown:

> In fact, every intricate and untried path in life, where it was from the first a matter of arbitrary choice to enter upon it or avoid it, is effectually a path through a vast Hercynian forest, unexplored and unmapped, where each several turn in your advance leaves you open to new anticipations of what is next to be expected, and consequently open to altered valuations of all that has been already traversed.[9]

The extraordinary temporal gyration in that sentence enacts the vertiginous sense of a life's pattern, as each 'turn' produces first 'anticipations' of future choices and then 'altered valuations' of your past course. As he teases out the implications, he develops the classic statement of the indeterminacy of autobiographical meaning:

> Even the character of your own absolute experience, past and gone, which (if anything in this world) you might surely answer for as sealed and settled for ever – even this you must submit to hold in suspense, as a thing conditional and contingent upon what is yet to come – liable to have its provisional character affirmed or reversed, according to the new combinations into which it may enter with elements only yet perhaps in the earliest stages of development.

What is true for individual experience is true for collective experience. What is true of auto/biography is true of history.

Where Romantic writers like De Quincey or Wordsworth work construct a labyrinthine syntax threading between different moments of time to bring out their shifting interrelationships, modernists tend to operate through fragmentation and collage. That is one way of making moments 'timeless' – by breaking them out of their temporal location and sequence, and throwing them into a melee of moments from other times. A sexual encounter of the jazz age signifies differently when seen by Tiresias, and the typist juxtaposed with Cleopatra or Philomel.

Timelessness is itself an equivocal quality, or lack of quality. Is a timeless moment for all time, or of no time? What possibilities of meaning are available to a moment once broken out of its historical context? Eliot saw the 'mythical method' in *Ulysses* (and doubtless *The Waste Land* too) as 'manipulating a continuous parallel between contemporaneity and antiquity'. It makes patterns across time, rather than sequences through time. It is opposed to narrative – the primary mode of historical understanding: 'Instead of narrative method,' says Eliot, 'we may now use the mythical method.' The results are transhistorical. Neither the Trojan wars, nor Dublin in 1904, but a pattern of wandering and return; neither the classical past of Greece, Rome and Egypt, nor post-war Europe, but patterns of death and rebirth, waste and fertility.

The mythical method has become the most familiar version of modernism's engagement with history, by disintegrating it. The prestige of Eliot and Joyce, and of other modernists using it – Ezra Pound, H. D., David Jones, Yeats – together with the influence of Eliot's criticism through the mid-twentieth century, has effectively displaced alternative modernist reconceptualizations of history. These reconceptualizations take three forms, which are the subject of the rest of this chapter. Unlike Eliot's 'mythical method', they remain based in narrative, though they all transform that narrative in different ways.

The first is what Ford, describing his decade-long collaboration with Joseph Conrad, referred to as the 'time shift'.[10] This is an elaboration of the flashback or prolepsis, used not for the racking up of tension or the filling in of the back-story (as in the classic example, analysed by Erich Auerbach, in *Mimesis*, of 'Odysseus' Scar'), but to produce a sense of fracture in both the time-sequence and the narrative. Conrad uses it in *The Secret Agent*, the botched explosion of the bomb at Greenwich not being represented directly in the text, but causing the narrative to flash forward in time to its aftermath, then back to its causes.[11]

The questions of what trauma does to narrative, and what narrative does to trauma, were at the heart of the most substantial of the Conrad–Ford collaborations, *Romance*: a novel based on the story of the last Englishman tried for piracy, in which the protagonist John Kemp goes on a Bovaryesque quest for adventure, is drawn into the world of Cuban pirates, escapes death there and then faces it again before the law. Like Madame Bovary, the novel wants to make the reader feel the glamour of romance as something real, but also to ironize the way retrospect casts a romantic glow over the past, and even its traumatic episodes. Ford wrote a poem for the book's epigraph, which includes the lines:

> If we could have remembrance now
> And see, as in the days to come
> We shall, what's venturous in these hours.[12]

Thomas Moser describes this wish as symptomatic of Ford's 'characteristic longing to leap out of the present so that he can look back at it'.¹³ To achieve 'remembrance now' is to become the historian of your own time; to experience the contemporary as if it were already history. (The elegiac connotations of the term 'remembrance' also suggest that what's at stake here is wanting to be remembered as if respectfully after one's own death.) There are two points to make about this move. First, as the parallels with Eliot, Joyce and Conrad suggest, the quest for forms which move beyond the narrative present is 'characteristic' not just of Ford but of modernism more generally; and we shall see more evidence of it in other writers. Second, the desire to look back may sound like a form of escapist nostalgia. But it is enabled by something much more surprising: a leap into the future.

Modernism's mythical method, its allusiveness, like its classicizing, characterize it as preoccupied with the past; with tradition; with history (Pound's *Cantos* are what he called – defining epic – 'a poem including history').¹⁴ But again, this emphasis has obscured its engagements with the future. So much so that the main collection of writings in the modernist period about the future has remained largely unknown for nearly a century.

This is the extraordinary book series called 'To-Day and To-Morrow', published by Kegan Paul in the United Kingdom from 1923 to 1931, and issued in the United States by E. P. Dutton. There were 110 volumes: small, pamphlet-length books on a wide range of topics, as can be seen from the Classified Index (Figure 4.1) that began to be included after about sixty had appeared, and seemed to require organizing into categories:

This is our second type of modernist reconceptualization of history. The series was edited by the polymath and maverick intellectual C. K. Ogden, and included many of the leading thinkers, scientists and writers of the period, combining established talents like Bertrand Russell and James Jeans with brilliant young writers yet to make their names, such as J. B. S. Haldane, Robert Graves, Vera Brittain, J. D. Bernal and Hugh MacDiarmid.

Why such a project is interesting with respect to history is its lack of concern with the past. Unlike a comparable series, *Essays of To-day and Yesterday*, published by Harrap from 1926, and including conservative and reactionary writers like Hilaire Belloc, A. C. Benson and G. K. Chesterton, To-Day and To-Morrow largely ignores 'yesterday'. The inverse of Walter Benjamin's 'Angel of History', whose 'face is turned toward the past', and who is propelled by the storm of progress into 'the future to which his back is turned', Odgen's contributors resolutely face the future and turn their back on the past.¹⁵ They

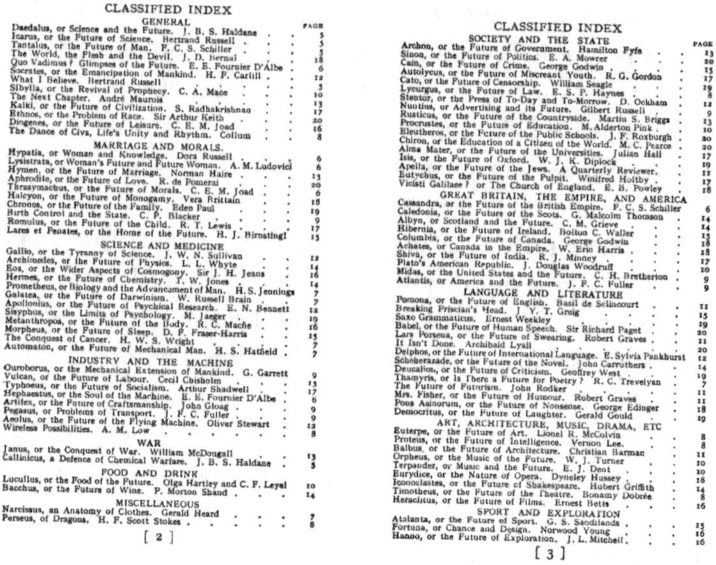

CLASSIFIED INDEX

GENERAL

PAGE

Daedalus, or Science and the Future. J. B. S. Haldane . . 5
Icarus, or the Future of Science. Bertrand Russell . . . 5
Tantalus, or the Future of Man. F. C. S. Schiller . . . 5
The World, the Flesh and the Devil. J. D. Bernal . . . 18
Quo Vadimus? Glimpses of the Future. E. E. Fournier D'Albe . . 6
Socrates, or the Emancipation of Mankind. H. F. Carlill . . 12
What I Believe. Bertrand Russell 5
Sibylla, or the Revival of Prophecy. C. A. Mace . . . 10
The Next Chapter. André Maurois 13
Kalki, or the Future of Civilization. S. Radhakrishnan . . 17
Ethnos, or the Problem of Race. Sir Arthur Keith . . . 20
Diogenes, or the Future of Leisure. C. E. M. Joad . . . 16
The Dance of Civa, Life's Unity and Rhythm. Collum . . 8

MARRIAGE AND MORALS.

Hypatia, or Woman and Knowledge. Dora Russell . . . 6
Lysistrata, or Woman's Future and Future Woman. A. M. Ludovici 6
Hymen, or the Future of Marriage. Norman Haire . . . 13
Aphrodite, or the Future of Love. R. de Pomerai . . . 20
Thrasymachus, or the Future of Morals. C. E. M. Joad . . 6
Halcyon, or the Future of Monogamy. Vera Brittain . . . 18
Chronos, or the Future of the Family. Eden Paul . . . 19
Birth Control and the State. C. P. Blacker 9
Romulus, or the Future of the Child. R. T. Lewis . . . 17
Lares et Penates, or the Home of the Future. H. J. Birnstingl 15

SCIENCE AND MEDICINE

Gallio, or the Tyranny of Science. J. W. N. Sullivan . . 12
Archimedes, or the Future of Physics. L. L. Whyte . . . 14
Eos, or the Wider Aspects of Cosmogony. Sir J. H. Jeans . 16
Hermes, or the Future of Chemistry. T. W. Jones . . . 14
Prometheus, or Biology and the Advancement of Man. H. S. Jennings 7
Galatea, or the Future of Darwinism. W. Russell Brain . . 7
Apollonius, or the Future of Psychical Research. E. N. Bennett 12
Sisyphus, or the Limits of Psychology. M. Jaeger . . . 19
Metanthropos, or the Future of the Body. R. C. Macfie . . 16
Morpheus, or the Future of Sleep. D. F. Fraser-Harris . . 15
The Conquest of Cancer. H. W. S. Wright 7
Automaton, or the Future of Mechanical Man. H. S. Hatfield . 7

INDUSTRY AND THE MACHINE

Ouroborus, or the Mechanical Extension of Mankind. G. Garrett 9
Vulcan, or the Future of Labour. Cecil Chisholm . . . 13
Typhoeus, or the Future of Socialism. Arthur Shadwell . . 17
Hephaestus, or the Soul of the Machine. E. E. Fournier D'Albe . 6
Artifex, or the Future of Craftsmanship. John Gloag . . . 9
Pegasus, or Problems of Transport. J. F. C. Fuller . . . 9
Aeolus, or the Future of the Flying Machine. Oliver Stewart . 12
Wireless Possibilities. A. M. Low 8

WAR

Janus, or the Conquest of War. William McDougall . . . 13
Callinicus, a Defence of Chemical Warfare. J. B. S. Haldane . 5

FOOD AND DRINK

Lucullus, or the Food of the Future. Olga Hartley and C. F. Leyel 10
Bacchus, or the Future of Wine. P. Morton Shand . . . 14

MISCELLANEOUS

Narcissus, an Anatomy of Clothes. Gerald Heard . . . 7
Perseus, of Dragons. H. F. Scott Stokes 8

[2]

CLASSIFIED INDEX

SOCIETY AND THE STATE

PAGE

Archon, or the Future of Government. Hamilton Fyfe . . 13
Sinon, or the Future of Politics. E. A. Mowrer . . . 20
Cain, or the Future of Crime. George Godwin . . . 15
Autolycus, or the Future of Miscreant Youth. R. G. Gordon . 17
Cato, or the Future of Censorship. William Seagle . . . 19
Lycurgus, or the Future of Law. E. S. P. Haynes . . . 8
Stentor, or the Press of To-Day and To-Morrow. D. Ockham . 12
Nuntius, or Advertising and its Future. Gilbert Russell . . 9
Rusticus, or the Future of the Countryside. Martin S. Briggs . 13
Procrustes, or the Future of Education. M. Alderton Pink . . 10
Eleutheros, or the Future of the Public Schools. J. F. Roxburgh . 20
Chiron, or the Education of a Citizen of the World. M. C. Pearce . 20
Alma Mater, or the Future of the Universities. Julian Hall . 17
Isis, or the Future of Oxford. W. J. K. Diplock . . . 19
Apella, or the Future of the Jews. A Quarterly Reviewer. . 11
Eutychus, or the Future of the Pulpit. Winifred Holtby . . 17
Vicisti Galilaee? or The Church of England. E. B. Powley . 18

GREAT BRITAIN, THE EMPIRE, AND AMERICA

Cassandra, or the Future of the British Empire. F. C. S. Schiller 6
Caledonia, or the Future of the Scots. G. Malcolm Thomson . 14
Albyn, or Scotland and the Future. C. M. Grieve . . . 14
Hibernia, or the Future of Ireland. Bolton C. Waller . . 15
Columbia, or the Future of Canada. George Godwin . . . 18
Achates, or Canada in the Empire. W. Eric Harris . . . 18
Shiva, or the Future of India. R. J. Minney 17
Plato's American Republic. J. Douglas Woodruff . . . 10
Midas, or the United States and the Future. C. H. Bretherton . 9
Atlantis, or America and the Future. J. F. C. Fuller . . 9

LANGUAGE AND LITERATURE

Pomona, or the Future of English. Basil de Sélincourt . . 11
Breaking Priscian's Head. J. Y. T. Greig 15
Saxo Grammaticus. Ernest Weekley 19
Babel, or the Future of Human Speech. Sir Richard Paget . . 20
Lars Porsena, or the Future of Swearing. Robert Graves . . 11
It Isn't Done. Archibald Lyall 20
Delphos, or the Future of International Language. E. Sylvia Pankhurst 12
Scheherazade, or the Future of the Novel. John Carruthers . . 14
Deucalion, or the Future of Criticism. Geoffrey West . . . 19
Thamyris, or Is There a Future for Poetry? R. C. Trevelyan . 7
The Future of Futurism. John Rodker 11
Mrs. Fisher, or the Future of Humour. Robert Graves . . 11
Pons Asinorum, or the Future of Nonsense. George Edinger . 18
Democritus, or the Future of Laughter. Gerald Gould . . 19

ART, ARCHITECTURE, MUSIC, DRAMA, ETC

Euterpe, or the Future of Art. Lionel R. McColvin . . . 8
Proteus, or the Future of Intelligence. Vernon Lee. . . . 8
Balbus, or the Future of Architecture. Christian Barman . . 11
Orpheus, or the Music of the Future. W. J. Turner . . . 10
Terpander, or Music and the Future. E. J. Dent . . . 10
Eurydice, or the Nature of Opera. Dyneley Hussey . . . 18
Iconoclastes, or the Future of Shakespeare. Hubert Griffith . 14
Timotheus, or the Future of the Theatre. Bonamy Dobrée . . 8
Heraclitus, or the Future of Films. Ernest Betts . . . 16

SPORT AND EXPLORATION

Atalanta, or the Future of Sport. G. S. Sandilands . . . 15
Fortuna, or Chance and Design. Norwood Young . . . 16
Hanno, or the Future of Exploration. J. L. Mitchell . . . 16

[3]

Figure 4.1 To-Day and To-Morrow: Classified Index from Ralph de Pomerai, *Aphrodite; or, The Future of Sexual Relationships* (London: Kegan Paul, Trench and Trubner, 1931), end-matter.

were predominantly progressive, atheist or at least agnostic, and utopian, committed to an Enlightenment belief that science, reason, communication and education would enable humanity to leave behind the storms of the past – a history of war, religious intolerance, ignorance and cruelty. To that extent, the conception of the series bears out Anthony Giddens' characterization of modernity as 'a society—more technically, a complex of institutions—which, unlike any preceding culture, lives in the future, rather than the past'.[16]

Yet To-Day and To-Morrow *does* engage with history in two illuminating ways. First, a number of its key contributors who would become leading public intellectuals were committed to a Marxist view of history, which claimed to have established a scientific basis for historical processes (in the material and economic bases of society, and its class relations). Since the collapse of the Soviet Union and the triumph of rampant neoliberalism, that view is discredited everywhere but – paradoxically – in economics. But at its core is the belief that if history can be conducted as science, then its results should be as predictable as those in the physical or biological sciences. Philosophers like Karl Popper and scientists like Stephen Jay Gould have contested this position, arguing that even in the history of science, too much depends on unforeseeable chance and inspiration to be susceptible of rigorous prediction.[17] But right at the turn of the century, H. G. Wells had given a compelling example of how the recasting of futurology from prophecy to scientific prediction could nevertheless provide useful hypotheses, approximations which could in turn direct future thinking. He argued that just as biologists and palaeontologists had been able to construct a sophisticated theory of evolution from a very patchy fossil record, so too thinkers about the future could construct patterns from the recent discoveries and emerging trends around them, and extrapolate hypotheses from them.[18] He doesn't claim that it would ever be possible to specify the future in all its detail. But it should be possible to glimpse what he would call in his 1933 projection *The Shape of Things to Come*. The method, that is, is the same whether you're engaged in history or futurology. It just points in opposite directions. Thus for example in his breathtakingly visionary *The World, the Flesh and the Devil* (1929), the X-ray crystallographer J. D. Bernal imagines humans bionically enhancing their bodies to increase their strength and sensory range, and to extend their longevity. But in elaborating the effects of such technological developments, he anticipates social tensions between those who have augmented themselves through bio-engineering, and those who have chosen not to, or cannot afford to do so. It is thus a vision of a future form the class struggle might take, using the familiar Marxist analysis, but simply applying it to a state of affairs that doesn't exist yet, but might in a possible future society. The working title for Bernal's book had been 'Possibilities'.[19] These scientific futurologists were not laying claim to a vatic vision of the truth of the future. They were conducting thought experiments, exploring possible futures to see which directions should be encouraged, and which might prove harmful. One of the classic defences of the value of history is that we understand the present better if we know where we have come from. Part of To-Day and To-Morrow's justification is that we understand ourselves better if we know where we might be heading.

The other way in which the series engages with history is by writing it. That is, several of the best volumes experiment with a technique J. B. S. Haldane uses in the first volume, *Daedalus; or, Science and the Future*: a complex time-shift in which the writer jumps forward to the distant future in order to look back at a period between then and now; a period still in the future for us, but described historically from the further future. In my study of To-Day and To-Morrow, *Imagined Futures*, I call this technique 'future history'.[20] It's like Ford's 'remembrance now'; but instead of letting *present* experience feel like future memories of that experience, 'future history' imagines our *future* already feeling as if it were our past. In the middle of *Daedalus* Haldane switches into 'some extracts from an essay on the influence of biology on history during the 20th century which will (it is hoped) be read by a rather stupid undergraduate member of this university to his supervisor during his first term 150 years hence'.[21] The book originated in a paper read to Ogden's 'Heretics' debating society, so the denigration of the typical undergraduate is a knowing Cambridge in-joke. But it also has more interesting effects. First, it is a realist device. Casting speculation into the register of history makes it sounds like the hypothetical scenario has already happened. Futurology is presented as fact. This can make radical transformation feel less threatening. Vera Brittain's *Halcyon* invents excerpts from a book by a feminist Oxford professor (itself a future history idea in 1929) called the *History of English Moral Institutions in the Nineteenth, Twentieth, and Twenty-first Centuries*. It charts the progressive achievements of women's freedom through a sequence of legislation which had not happened yet at the time of writing; such as the 'Sexual Instruction (Schools and Welfare Centres) Act of 1948' (38), the 1949 'Married Women's Independence Act' (38) and the 'Matrimonial Causes Act of 1959' (40), which broadened the possible grounds for divorce, and made consensual divorce legal. These seem obviously necessary to us now that equivalents have become law (or nearly have, in the case of 'no fault' divorces in the UK). They still seemed controversial to many when proposed in the 1920s. But presenting them as part of the Whig interpretation of future history makes them seem unobjectionable; part of the deal of civilized modernity; not mere possibility, but actuality.

Daedalus uses the future history device for comparable effects. The book's most audacious prediction – what Haldane calls 'ectogenesis': the rearing of human embryos in artificial wombs outside the mother's body – is presented as so widespread and familiar to the stupid undergraduate that he is rather bored by the idea. Yet the aim of presenting the really new as if it were already entirely familiar can have a double edge. Yes, it might accustom people to ideas they would otherwise chafe at. But equally, the vision of a world in which people accept the outlandish as if it were the most normal thing can produce a powerfully satiric effect. That's how Haldane's friend Aldous Huxley works it in his novel about ectogenesis, *Brave New World* (1932), in which not just the human 'Hatcheries', but the paraphernalia of the 'feelies', 'hypnopaedia', Malthus Belts – any of which may have been suggested by To-Day and To-Morrow[22] – are all taken for granted by everyone in the World State, and are shocking only to John Savage, the representative of the twentieth century.

Future history, that is, can conduce paradoxically to satire as well as realism. But that satire can itself be triple-edged. It can satirize the historian, as *Daedalus* pokes fun at the undergraduate's essay. Or it can ironize the content of the history. There are elements of this in *Daedalus* too, when, for example, overenthusiastic genetic modification has created algae which have turned the seas purple. (The undergraduate doesn't notice, but classically trained Haldane would have, that this ironically realizes the Homeric epithet for the sea as 'wine dark.') Haldane doesn't satirize ectogenesis though; he is seriously committed to the idea that science will transform human existence in liberating ways. One of the writers who does use future history so as to satirize the historical actors as well as speculative science is André Maurois. His witty volume, *The Next Chapter: The War against the Moon* (1927), shows the press barons having a video-conference (itself a shrewd bit of futurology in the very early days of television). They decide that in order to maintain world peace, a fictitious common enemy must be manufactured. So they work up popular opinion against the moon and persuade governments to attack it with a Wellsean death ray. Unpredictably, the Moon starts firing back (54–8). Maurois' science fiction is tongue-in-cheek, but his critique of media power is serious, and his predictions about human developments are stunningly accurate: a world war of 1947 (close, if too late and too short); and the resulting development of knowledge of 'energy within the atom' between then and 1951 (only two years out about the start of the atomic age).

The third possible target of satire in future history, in addition to the historian or the historical events, is the idea of history itself. *The Next Chapter* is presented as a 'Fragment of a Universal History' published in 1992 (little did Maurois foreknow that Francis Fukuyama would have announced the end of history three years before then).[23] Its focus on historiography was more evident in the title by which it was first advertised in other volumes: *Clio, or the Future of History*; though perhaps Maurois, or Ogden, felt that, when it was finished, its futuristic fantasy had predominated. The main point here, though, is that the games these writers were playing with the idea of history show how history itself had come into question.

In part that was an effect of the First World War. Even as it was declared, Henry James felt that the received account of contemporary history was no longer adequate:

> The plunge of civilization into this abyss of blood and darkness by the wanton feat of those two infamous autocrats is a thing that so gives away the whole long

age during which we have supposed the world to be, with whatever abatement, gradually bettering, that to have to take it all now for what the treacherous years were all the while really making for and *meaning* is too tragic for any words.[24]

How much more tragic after four and a half years of slaughter? At the beginning of the third volume of Ford's *Parade's End*, *A Man Could Stand Up* – (1926), the pacifist suffragette Valentine Wannop is teaching in a girl's school when the Armistice is announced. The other teachers are worried that in this euphoria they will lose control of their pupils:

> If, at this parting of the ways, at this crack across the table of History, the School – the World, the future mothers of Europe – got out of hand, would they ever come back? The Authorities – Authority all over the world – was afraid of that; more afraid of that than of any other thing.[25]

History is now and England. In the moment of the Armistice they feel that it can be described as a celebration of victory and relief, but also as revolution. That feeling of the redescribability of history is produced by the sense of a 'crack across the table of History'; a sense of a radical fissure between past and future; between the old and the new, old and young. History is the story of these transformations – in the world of work, the relations between the sexes and so on. But it is also cracked. The devastations of war, its trauma, its disturbances to the social and psychological order mean that it no longer seems possible to capture the past in narrative; or at least in a single narrative.

That a similar turn was occurring in biography after the war is well known, with Lytton Strachey's *Eminent Victorians* (1919) as prime exhibit. But Strachey's notorious 'debunking' of the individual biographies of Florence Nightingale or General Gordon is not just *ad hominem* (or *ad feminam*). His figures are eminent not only for their personal qualities, but as representatives of their respective institutions: the medical profession and the military for these two; the church and the educational system with Cardinal Manning and Thomas Arnold. In ironizing them, Strachey is simultaneously ironizing Victorian historiography. What Virginia Woolf said about biography also applies to history:

> There are some stories which have to be retold by each generation, not that we have anything new to add to them, but because of some queer quality in them which makes them not only Shelley's story but our own. Eminent and durable they stand on the skyline, a mark past which we sail, which moves as we move and yet remains the same.[26]

This was written at the time she was formulating her views on what she called 'The New Biography'. And in *Orlando*, published the following year, she would, precisely, retell much of English history from the Renaissance to the present, mocking biography and the biographer in the process.[27]

What is at stake here is a new sense, in the era of modernism, of the relativity of history; its multiplicity, provisionality, disputability. This is our third and final modernist reconceptualization of history. It is manifest not only in the modernists discussed already, but in the historiographical developments of the same period. Doubtless modernist self-consciousness about narrative experiment affected the way some readers read history, seeing it less as sheer presentation of facts, and more as narratives producing effects. The subject is an enormous one, beyond the scope of this chapter. But it will be indicated here via discussion of three examples, very disparate in kind, but again connected by the prodigious C. K. Ogden.

From 1920 Ogden edited the journal *Psyche*, devoted to psychology in the broadest sense (including anthropology, medicine, symbolization, communication, etc.). In 1926 he launched an associated series of small pocketbooks called Psyche Miniatures. This also ran to 110 volumes. Some recycled work from the journal. About half were on the same subjects as the journal; the latter half consisted mostly of works written in or translated into BASIC English, Ogden's simplified version of the language, reduced to 850 words, as an international auxiliary language. The seventh of the Pysche Miniatures was *On History: a Study of Present Tendencies* (1927); the first book by A. L. Rowse, who would go on to become one of the best known British popular historians of the twentieth century.[28] It was characteristic of Ogden's knack as a talent-spotter. This series is no better known now than To-Day and To-Morrow, but it too deserves to be rediscovered. The first volume was I. A. Richards's *Science and Poetry* (1926). Later contributors included Rudolf Carnap, Bronislaw Malinowski, Joseph Needham, J. B. Watson, John Wisdom, Otto Neurath, J. B. S. Haldane and Ogden himself. Just as To-Day and To-Morrow was followed by major modernists such as Joyce, Eliot, Waugh, Lewis, Huxley and Leonard Woolf, so the Psyche Miniatures, like all Ogden's editorial ventures, made their mark on the intelligentsia.[29] For example, my copy of *On History* bears Lytton Strachey's bookplate.

Rowse bemoans the prevalence of specialisation in history writing. 'The lay mind', he says, 'finds most modern work strangely inconclusive.' (19–20)

> And that not all is well is to some extent shown by the amount of argument and discussion that goes on, not only as to the writing of history, but also as to the reading and interpretation of history. (19)

Specialization has produced 'a widening gap between the researcher and the interpreter' (20). He disagrees with Chesterton's position, which he characterizes as drawing the moral 'of the futility of attempting to get at the truth of the matter by reading the historians, ultimately arriving at a kind of scepticism with regard to history' (22). But that he voices this view shows his awareness of its currency. Rowse's own prescription is the one to which he would devote his life's work: to seek to combine specialist expertise with popular presentation. He quotes G. M. Trevelyan on the need for 'the synthesis of the scientific and the literary views of history' (27). The 'scientific' view of history here appears to denote scrupulous evidencing from the archives; the adducing of *Quellen* ('sources') seen as the bedrock of the German academic industry devoted to the Leopold von Rankean mission of establishing '*wie es eigentlich gewesen ist*' (how it truly was). Harold Nicolson (the husband of Virginia Woolf's lover, Vita Sackville-West) made a comparable distinction in his book of the same year, *The Development of English Biography*, between, on the one hand, a 'pure' biography in pursuit of 'historical truth' and 'complete and accurate portraiture'; and on the other, an 'impure' or applied biography, adulterated by hagiography, didacticism and excessive subjectivity.[30]

Rowse's *On History*, however, makes a case for a different form of scientific history.[31] He argues that the historiography of the previous century was outmoded. Its view of an essentially static society, explicable in terms of the machinations of a privileged elite (36–7), had been challenged by the impact of Darwinian theory on the social sciences, leading to a view of society as in a constant state of evolution as a result of struggle (35–6); and challenged in parallel (50) by Marx's account of the decisive influence of the material basis of society and its relations of production, and the class struggle (46–7; 93). Rowse is careful to present himself as not doctrinaire in his Marxism. He sees it not as the be-all and end-all, but as a 'framework' which 'does not seek to include, though it underlies, other studies', and which he is thus able slyly to characterize as 'libertarian' (68). Nevertheless, 'the historical province is first and foremost that of men in the mass' (65).

The crucial point is that what Rowse thinks history needs to re-energize itself is a theory. At a time of such excitement over the theories of genetics, Relativity, psychoanalysis, behaviourism and the atom, he argues that history too seems in need of one – especially in England, where 'there has been a notorious dislike of the abstract discussion of theories or of the ideas which are often implied in historical work' (92). And that is what his book offers. At least, the chapter headings for the third and longest chapter read 'A Theory of History'; the title itself offers, more tentatively, a 'Sketch of a Theory of History'. The theory will allow the 'return to synoptic writing' which he feels is needed; and the 'greater breadth of conception' (31) that makes the synthesis between 'the analytic and the generalizing methods' possible (30). These 'generalizing principles will involve a different conception of historical processes' (32), he says. They will provide the 'integrating force' of the future (32, 56), building on the insights from anthropology, psychology and 'social studies' (40; 95). Historical materialism is not unprecedented; but what is needed is 'to systematize the results of such speculations' (32). What is also apparent is that what Rowse is writing is not so much an analysis of present history, but a manifesto for what he wants it to be in future. In fact, it could just as well have appeared in the To-Day and To-Morrow series.[32]

The writing is oddly convoluted, to the point that the advocacy of Marxism can easily be missed. Perhaps that was the point. Rowse had been made a Fellow of All Souls College, Oxford, in 1925, and it's as if he didn't want to risk his colleagues there being able to realize what a socialist Trojan Horse they had elected. It would be nice to believe that he saw himself as gently preparing his fellow academics for the methodological onslaught; though his dismissal of 'the reactionary stupidity of the professional intelligentsia' (90) makes it implausible that the offensive would operate through charm.

On History is far from parochial. Rowse quotes Marx and Trotsky, cites German philosophers and French historians. Indeed, his theory challenges 'the all-sufficiency of the nation as a historical unit' (93), seeking to replace it with an internationalism based on class. But he appears bizarrely out of touch with what was happening in his own discipline, at least outside of Oxford.[33] He seems unaware that the historical development he was advocating for the future had in fact already begun to manifest itself; and in Britain, and, again, thanks to C. K. Ogden, in yet another series he edited, launched three years earlier in 1924.

This was entitled the History of Civilization, and in its conception was arguably the most audacious of his book series. Like Ogden's other major textbook series, the International Library of Psychology, Philosophy and Scientific Method, the History of Civilization involved an internationalist mission to translate leading European scholarship. The core of the series consisted of translations of the French collection *L'Evolution de l'Humanité*, to which newly commissioned works written in English were added. The book history of the series remains to be written, and could fill a book, not fit a chapter conclusion. But the series list included in a 1929 volume gives an idea of its scope and organization.

The volume that was probably published first, and was included as the first in the listings, *Social Organization* by W. H. R. Rivers (1924), included a brief prospectus as end-matter with this short description:

> This series, which will eventually comprise upwards of 200 volumes, is designed to form a complete Library of Social Evolution. The field has been carefully mapped out, both as regards subjects and periods; and, though the first instalments will be published as they are ready, the necessary degree of chronological sequence will be secured by the fact that the volumes of 'L'Evolution de l'Humanité' will be used as a nucleus and translated as they appear.[34]

This was followed by a list of only eighty-four volumes, suggesting that the careful mapping out was sketchier than claimed.

The projections flickered as the series developed. The undated prospectus at the end of Eugène Pittard's 1926 volume, *Race and History*, expands the description to over two pages, claiming that:

> The series marks one of the most ambitious adventures in the annals of book publishing. Its aim is to present in accessible form the results of modern research and modern scholarship through the whole range of the Social Sciences – to summarize in one comprehensive synthesis the most recent findings and theories of historians, anthropologists, archaeologists, sociologists, and all conscientious students of civilization.[35]

It appends a 'plan, comprising of upwards of eighty titles, though not definitive'. Not definitive at all, as it turns out, since the following list includes ninety-one. The jacket of *Prophets and the Rise of Judaism* (1937) is comically unable to put a number on the eventual run, saying only that the series will provide 'A Complete History of Mankind from Prehistoric Times to the Present Day in Numerous Volumes [...]'; but that 'More than fifty' had already appeared by then. A 1939 catalogue bound in as end-matter to what looks like the first impression of Jacques de Morgan's *Prehistoric Man* (1924) lists 'just under one hundred' projected titles, saying that more than sixty were then available.[36] The 1944 catalogue bound into G. Renard's *Life and Work in Prehistoric Time* (1929), when combined with the list given on the verso of the half-title amounts to just sixty titles, indicating that the war years had shut the series down. The British Library catalogue doesn't record any further volumes published after 1939, and only records sixty-six under the series title.

The jacket of *Prophets and the Rise of Judaism* (1937) also includes two telling quotations about the series from the reviews. The *Manchester Guardian* called it 'an heroic attempt to bring some light into the vast mass of ill-organized knowledge which we owe to modern research'. For *Nature* it was 'the most important contribution so far undertaken towards the task of organization and systematization of the social studies'.[37]

That idea that 'modern research' in history was too specialized and disconnected to be intelligible and accessible was Rowse's diagnosis too. The fact that Ogden and/or Kegan Paul included these quotations as promotional material indicates that that was the view of the series they wanted to present. History is seen not as about producing yet more knowledge of the past – because the table of History is cracked. Historical sources alone have come to seem problematic. The thing is to organize and systematize that knowledge; or, as we would now say, to theorize it. The organizing principle of the French series was both evolutionary and humanist; that of the British counterpart, to recast history as social science. *Social Organization*, that is, was the volume that sounded the note of the series, because its title was also the project's rationale.

Both the History of Civilization and the Evolution of Humanity must have seemed doomed titles during and after the Second World War; so it's unsurprising that the series ground to a halt in 1939. It is also possible that the ambitious scale was self-defeating. Besides the money and shelf-space required for even fifty or a hundred volumes, let alone two hundred, the aim to bring order and system to piecemeal research may have seemed defeated by the quest for completeness of period, region and topic.

Ogden carried on building two of his series: the International Library and the Psyche Miniatures. His driving interests until his death in 1957 were psychology and BASIC English. But he took on a very different historical project in 1938, which seems the place to conclude this survey, since it brings together most of the themes discussed here. It was a collaboration with E. H. Carter ('Formerly H. M. Inspector of Schools and Training Colleges'), and miniature in scale compared to the book series: a single volume, providing a *General History: in Outline and Story*. World History, that is, from the pre-Historic to the contemporary; all in fewer than 300 pages. It was written in BASIC and aimed at a young as well as international audience. Again, the terms in which they introduce it echo the idea we have seen in Rowse and in the reviews of the History of Civilization:

> The purpose of this book is to give a bird's eye view of history from the earliest times to the present day. It is hoped that it may be of value in two ways: first, by offering a framework with the help of which details of history outside the range of the book itself may be seen with a certain order and relation; second, by putting in a clear light the connection between the histories of different countries, so that the story of any one of them is seen as but one thread in the complex design which is the story of them all.[38]

Just as Ogden edited the vast International Library, then published his own *ABC of Psychology* (1929) as a sketch-map of the terrain it covered, so here he and Carter are providing a form of 'ABC' of History – the History of Civilization which that series had mapped out.³⁹ Here, too, the task is seen as one of organization and systematization: providing a sense of 'order and relation' that enables us to make sense of the details of history. This organizing motive operates at two levels. The 'framework' gives a context to the details of a single national history. The opening section on the Stone Ages doesn't mention Stonehenge, for example. But its 'General History' of the Ice Age, the discovery of copper, then tin, then their combination as bronze, enabling the development of better tools to work stone, gives us a narrative ordering which allows us to place particular stone edifices into relation with it. That narrative is already international, moving between Australia, Europe, Egypt and America. The point is that its range gives the details – which are necessarily of one place and time – their significance. At the second level, the relation is worked the other way. The weaving together of the different national narratives shows that their ultimate meaning lies in being part of an international order.

Ogden's and Carter's title was a nod to H. G. Wells's 1920 bestseller, the *Outline of History*. And though they describe their history as extending up to 'the present day', in fact the last chapter asks, 'What of the Future?', as Wells had too, concluding his *Outline* with a consideration of 'The Next Stage in History'. That was what contemporary history meant above all for modernism between the wars, as for science, as for politics, as for the arts: not only the culmination of the past, but the beginning of the future.

Notes

1 T. S. Eliot, 'Tradition and the Individual Talent', in *Selected Essays*, third enlarged edition (London: Faber and Faber Limited, 1951), 13–22; Ezra Pound first used the phrase 'Make It New' in his translation entitled Ta Hio: *The Great Learning, Newly Rendered into the American Language* (Seattle: University of Washington Bookstore, 1928). As Michael North explains, it was in fact 'a dense palimpsest of historical ideas about the new': 'The Making of "Make It New": Ezra Pound's slogan was itself the product of historical recycling', Guernica (15 August 2013): https://www.guernicamag.com/the-making-of-making-it-new/, accessed 24 July 2019.
2 T. S. Eliot, '*Ulysses*, Order, and Myth' (1923), in *Selected Prose of T. S. Eliot*, ed. Frank Kermode (London: Faber, 1975), 177.
3 See, for example, the *Edinburgh Review* 12 (1808): 480. 'There is this general distinction between contemporary history and all other history,—that the

former is a witness, the latter a judge.' The Institute of Contemporary History was established in the early 1930s in the Netherlands. See Michael D. Kandiah, 'Contemporary History', https://www.history.ac.uk/makinghistory/resources/articles/contemporary_history.html.

4   Ford Madox Ford, *It Was the Nightingale* (London: Heinemann, 1934), 180.
5   Ford Madox Ford's *A History of Our Own Times* was published posthumously, ed. Sondra Stang and Solon Beinfeld (Bloomington: Indiana University Press, 1988; Manchester: Carcanet Press, 1989).
6   See David Garland, 'What Is a "history of the present"? On Foucault's Genealogies and Their Critical Preconditions', *Punishment & Society* 16, no. 4 (2014): 365–84. DOI:10.1177/1462474514541711.
7   T. S. Eliot, 'Little Gidding', V, from *Four Quartets* in *The Poems of T. S. Eliot, Vol. 1*, ed. Christopher Ricks and Jim McCue (London: Faber, 2015), 208.
8   T. S. Eliot, 'East Coker', II; ibid., 187.
9   Thomas De Quincey, *Confessions of an English Opium Eater* (Harmondsworth: Penguin, 1986), 181–2.
10 Ford, *It Was the Nightingale*, 143.
11 See R. W. Stallman, 'Time and *The Secret Agent*', in *Texas Studies in Literature and Language* 1, no. 1 (Spring 1959): 101–22; Michael Mageean, '*The Secret Agent*'s (T)extimacies: A Traumatic Reading beyond Rhetoric', in *Seeing Double: Revisioning Edwardian and Modern Literature*, ed. Carola M. Kaplan and Anne B. Simpson (London: Macmillan, 1996), 235–58; and Adam Parkes, *A Sense of Shock: The Impact of Impressionism on Modern British and Irish Writing* (New York: Oxford University Press, 2011), 241.
12 Ford Madox Ford and Joseph Conrad, *Romance* (London: Smith, Elder & Co., 1903), [v]; see Max Saunders, *Ford Madox Ford: A Dual Life*, 2 vols (Oxford: Oxford University Press, 1996), *Vol. 1*, 69–70.
13 Thomas C. Moser, *The Life in the Fiction of Ford Madox Ford* (Princeton: Princeton University Press, 1980), 49.
14 Ezra Pound, *The ABC of Reading* (London: Faber, 1951), 46.
15 Walter Benjamin, 'Theses on the Philosophy of History', in *Illuminations*, ed. Hannah Arendt, trans. Harry Zohn (New York: Schocken Books, 1969), 249.
16 Anthony Giddens, *Conversations with Anthony Giddens: Making Sense of Modernity* (Stanford, Calif.: Stanford University Press, 1998), 94.
17 Karl Popper, *The Poverty of Historicism* (London: Routledge, 2002), xi–xii. Stephen Jay Gould, 'Unpredictable Patterns', in *Predictions*, ed. Sian Griffiths (Oxford: Oxford University Press, 1999), 145–6. For further discussion, see Max Saunders, *Imagined Futures, Writing, Science, and Modernity in the To-Day and To-Morrow Book Series, 1923–31* (Oxford: Oxford University Press, 2019), Introductions.
18 H. G. Wells, *The Discovery of the Future* (London: T. Fisher Unwin, 1902).

19 Bernal's volume was advertised as *Possibilities* in the end-matter of Vera Brittain's *Halcyon* (1929), 4.
20 See Saunders, *Imagined Futures,* Chapter 2.
21 J.B.S. Haldane, *Daedalus; or, Science and the Future* (London: Kegan Paul, Trench and Trübner, 1923), 56–7. Place of publication and publisher should be taken to be the same for all subsequent references to Ogden's series unless stated otherwise.
22 Bonamy Dobrée's *Timotheus; the Future of the Theatre* (1925) imagine emotions being controlled by psychotropic gases; *Daedalus* discusses potential future applications of hypnosis; several volumes discuss contraception, particularly C. P. Blacker's *Birth Control and the State* (1926).
23 Francis Fukuyama, 'The End of History?' *The National Interest* no. 16 (1989): 3–18.
24 Henry James to Howard Sturgis, 4–5 August 1914: *Letters of Henry James*, ed. Percy Lubbock, 2 volumes (New York: Charles Scriber's Sons, 1920), *Vol. 2*, 384.
25 Ford Madox Ford, *A Man Could Stand Up*, ed. Sara Haslam (Manchester: Carcanet, 2011), 17–18.
26 Virginia Woolf, 'Not One of Us', A review of *Shelley; His Life and Work*, by Walter Edwin Peck, October 1927, in *The Death of the Moth, and Other Essays* (London: The Hogarth Press, 1942), 78.
27 For an extended discussion of these texts and issues, see Max Saunders, *Self Impression: Life-Writing, Autobiografiction, and the Forms of Modern Literature* (Oxford: Oxford University Press, 2010).
28 A. L. Rowse, *On History: A Study of Present Tendencies*, (London: Kegan Paul, Trench, Trübner & Co., 1927). Henceforth page references to Rowse's book will be noted inside brackets in the text.
29 See *Imagined Futures*, Ch. 6, on modern writers engaging with To-Day and To-Morrow.
30 Harold Nicolson, *The Development of English Biography* (London: The Hogarth Press, 1927), 9–11. 'But in general literary biography will, I suppose, wander off into the imaginative, leaving the strident streets of science for the open fields of fiction', he opined (155–6) – rather self-congratulatorily, since that is exactly what he did in his autobiografictional sketches published the same year as *Some People*. See Saunders, *Self Impression*, Chapter 11.
31 *On History* was published in the United States as *Science and History: A New View of History* (New York: W. W. Norton, 1928) in the American version of the Psyche Miniatures series, called the New Science Series.
32 There was some cross-over between the two series, volumes being the same length for both. See *Imagined Futures*, 386.
33 Rowse quotes the Master of Balliol A. D. Lindsay's *Karl Marx's Capital* on the economic antecedents of Puritanism, (*On History*), 71.
34 W. H. R. Rivers, *Social Organization*, ed. W. J. Perry (London: Kegan Paul, Trench and Trübner, 1924), end-matter.

35 Eugène Pittard, *Race and History*, (London: Kegan Paul, Trench and Trübner, 1926), 3.
36 This was common practice with Kegan Paul – see *Imagined Futures*, Appendix A.
37 Fuller texts of these reviews are reprinted in the end matter to some of the volumes, such as Jacques de Morgan's *Prehistoric Man* (1924) or Eugene Pittard's *Race and History* (1926).
38 *General History: In Outline and Story* by E H Carter and C K Ogden (London: Thomas Nelson, 1938), ix. The book was reprinted at least four times, in 1943, 1944, 1946 and 1950.
39 Ogden, *ABC of Psychology* (London: Kegan Paul, 1929).

5

Historical and rhetorical emplotments of modernism: An interview with Hayden White by Angeliki Spiropoulou

Few historians delved into the porosity between literature and history, or indeed the arbitrariness of their distinction, as systematically and convincingly as the American history and cultural theorist Hayden White. In his path-breaking study, *Metahistory: The Historical Imagination in Nineteenth-Century Europe* (1973),[1] White questioned the objectivist claims of historical science by stressing the linguistic and narrative foundation of historiography. White's radical recognition of the narrative nature of history and, inversely, of the epistemic quality of literature is encapsulated in his statement that 'history is no less a form of fiction than the novel is a form of historical representation'.[2] The influence of his work, marking the so-called linguistic turn in historian science, has been formative for twentieth-century historical theory and contemporary literary criticism. It is significant that after serving as a Professor in the History of Consciousness programme at the University of California-Santa Cruz, when he formally retired in 1994, he became Bonsall Professor of Comparative Literature at Stanford University.

One of White's most fundamental arguments is that historical events are made into familiar stories using 'all of the techniques that we would normally expect to find in the emplotment of a novel or a play'.[3] In seeking to lay bare a 'poetics of history', he presented a typology of nineteenth-century historical writing arranged according to patterns of literary 'emplotment' it tacitly employs and he then matched the emerging narrative tropes to particular modes of consciousness. Significantly, for White, traditional historiography actually competes with the long realist novel in the way it 'emplots' facts and events to render a 'truthful' sense of historical reality. Even more radically, White stressed the paradox of how historiography in effect defines what is considered a historical 'fact', even though facts are axiomatically taken as history's raw material in standard historical thinking and writing.

Suspicious of the facticity and putative objectivity of realist verisimilitude and by focusing on form as content, White sides with a modernist poetics of subjectivism and technical self-reflection, also refuting the realist/historicist division between fact and fiction. Relevantly for this volume, drawing on his study of major modernist authors and thinkers, White not only challenged modernism's putative ahistoricism but also, and significantly, he modelled the demand for a new historiographical imagination on the features and effects of modernist art. In his 1996 essay, 'The Modernist Event',[4] for example, White notes that the plotless, characterless narratives associated with modernism put into serious doubt the standard forms and premises of traditional narrative and call for a reconfiguring of historiography itself. But further than this, in what he calls a 'modernist event', such as the Holocaust, White recognizes a constitutional resistance to representation presented by the events of modernized life and discusses modernism's pioneering 'anti-narrative non-stories' as responses to this resistance, marked by the collapse of the distinction between form and semantic content and by the 'de-realization' of the event.

As explained in more detail in the Introduction to the present volume, which is dedicated to the memory of this pioneering thinker, the 2015 interview that follows is offered in lieu of the chapter White had generously promised to contribute, just some months before his sudden death in 2018, on the subject of deconstruction and history. However, the interview lucidly highlights some of White's original thinking on the relation of history and literature, the nature of the fact and the historical past, rhetorical tropes of narration and modernist and contemporary art's contribution to new historiographies. Apart from his brilliance, erudition and originality, his replies also reveal his immense kindness and intellectual generosity.

A.S.

Interview

Angeliki Spiropoulou: Your work evokes Walter Benjamin's notion that every present invents its own past or Benedetto Croce's idea that all history is contemporary history. What would the role of the subject and the context be in historical narratives?

Hayden White: I would have to know which 'subject' you are talking about: the subject of history (i.e., the actors and agencies of historical changes) or history's subjects (i.e., the specific kinds of people who are deemed worthy of appearing in a history because they are the kind of people who 'make' history). Or by the subject of history, do you mean the historian or whomever it is that assumes the authority to speak for history? As you know, I distinguish between the past of history, which places history within a larger time-portion of 'the past', and history's past (which subordinates the past to the historians who produce it). In the former, history is treated as a part of the past in general, while in the latter, the past is treated as historical only insofar as it yields to history's criteria of significance.

A.S.: You have insightfully pointed out that historical discourse is not defined by a specific method of approaching the past and neither is its subject matter (e.g., past events, facts, experiences) exclusive to it. On the contrary, historical study, in common with literary writing/theory, principally involves a narrative reconstruction or interpretation of its subject matter. In view of this thesis, what would the role of the artwork in historical studies be and, additionally, what is special in the relationship between history and literature?

H.W.: If we are looking for similarities between history and literature, we have to do so by examining the linguistic protocols by which some part of the past is constructed as 'history' or as 'historical.' One way to do this is to treat historiography and literature as kinds of artistic writing, which is to say that both differ from 'ordinary speech/language' by virtue of the use of certain devices, tropes, thematizations, and so on that are either not found in ordinary (communicative) speech or are only implicitly present in them (as in, for example, the use of metaphor or metonymy). Both kinds of literary writing, a history such as that of Herodotus and a novel such as DeLillo's *Underworld*, are products of the (Kantian) imagination or, following Jacques Lacan and Cornelius Castoriadis, dwell in 'the imaginary'. The older historiography, which sought to purge itself of both 'literary' and 'philosophical' language and thought, presupposed a condition of literalness or, in oral discourse, 'propriety', as a basis for a discourse purged of both rhetoricity and poiesis.

But as Ernesto Laclau argued in the last book before his death, *The Rhetorical Foundations of Society*, there is no degree-zero of rhetoricity. Speech and language are inherently rhetorical in the sense of being unable to avoid figures of speech and thought, use of tropes, and such devices as ablation and irony. Historians wish to speak literally, which is to say, properly – but the proper is a moral category, not an epistemic one, and what is meant by the literal meaning of a word or sign is nothing more than what a given group of speakers of a given language have decided by use and convention is the literal meaning. One thing that 'literature' always does, in contrast to non-artistic speech, is systematically experiment with the distinction between literal and figurative (or proper and improper) speech in order to render the language used to present a given reality more precisely, more concretely', or more 'dramatically'. This is why, when I am asked for an example of a modern literary treatment of historical reality, I cite one or another novel such as Toni Morrison's *Beloved*, De Lillo's *Underworld* or Roth's *American Pastoral*: following Barthes, I call these examples of 'novelesque history'. I might also have cited *Between the Acts* by Virginia Woolf – as interpreted by Angeliki Spiropoulou.

A.S.: In your discussion of modernism, you write that there are certain events, distinctive to modernity, which cannot be represented in the realist mode privileged by traditional historiography. They need to be represented in some new mode, proposed by plotless, multivocal modernist writing which is reflexive of the narrativization process. However, wouldn't this imply that you take historical experience, the historical referent, to be prior to the means of its representation since it appears to generate the demand for new forms? And if this is so, how is it related to your argument that 'the content is the form'?

H.W.: This is a good question, but like many such questions it ignores the distinction between events of the past and historical events. Events in the past (already written about in many cases) are what is 'given' in the sense of preceding the historian's interest in them. But not all events of the past are historical events; they must be 'worked up' as possible objects of a specifically 'historical' or 'novelistic' treatment before they can serve as 'referents.' The demand for new forms or modes or even genres of presentation arises with the appearance of events unclassifiable immediately by traditional modes of classification. In modernity, a case in point would be the kinds of microscopic events that are in principle not observable but must be inferred as having happened by virtue of the traces of their occurrence in, for example, bubble chambers for measuring the path of an electron or the beginning of the universe itself. The demand for new forms of presentation arises when someone or some group 'experiences' an event that, for that group, is unthinkable or unutterable. To grasp the 'meaning' of an event as 'historical' is to apprehend it as a pattern, a form of being in the world. Within what we think we already know as 'historical reality,' what Marx called the modes and means of production produce events unthought of in anyone's philosophy, such as destruction of the ozone layer around the earth. Indeed, the whole idea of ecohistory would have been unthinkable before modern technology.

A.S.: In many of your writings, you connect the experience and the structure of trauma with both modernist art and modernity as a historical period, evoking the Holocaust as an exemplar. It is particularly interesting that, inversely, you seem to be suggesting that a modernist mode of representing traumatic events, peculiar to modernity, resists the symbolic closure and mastery of anxiety or 'narrative fetishization' sought by realist narration. Perhaps you could elaborate on these connections around what you call 'the modernist event'. Could you also explain why you think the experience of trauma may not appropriately describe the experience of the nineteenth century, for example, and whether trauma can be considered a paradigmatic *topos* and trope of postmodern or contemporary, alongside modernist, writing?

H.W.: Well, of course, 'trauma' is a concept produced by psychoanalysis and can be applied to any event experienced by a group as disabling and omnipresent long after the event that caused it has passed, and demanding attention in whatever situation the traumatized person finds itself. The utility and relevance of the concept of trauma in the twentieth century has to do not only with the novelty of modernist techno-events, their scope, their reach, their shock value, but also with the speed of news of their occurrence by way of the electronic media. The transmission of news by vivid (colored) images, the number of images of any given event, and the violation of the privacy of those affected by events of an extreme nature, all of this has the effect of rendering extreme events palpable in a way that transmission by writing or print does not.

A postmodernist artistic movement such as Surrealism seems 'super-' or 'hyper-' real only in contrast to what we might call – from our perspective today – the 'coziness' of nineteenth-century events like 'the revolutions' of that century. Napoleon's campaign in Russia, the Paris Commune, and the Boer War appear in retrospect to be containable in well-wrought stories. But who can tell the story of Hiroshima or the Holocaust in a way that does justice to the 'quality' of the suffering endured by thousands of people on a single day of their 'surprising' occurrence.

A.S.: Interestingly, history is both an ostentatious concern and a method within contemporary literature, thus contrasting with modernism, whose emphasis on form resulted in a more controversial referential relationship to history than that evident in the classical historical novel. You have convincingly vindicated a historical concern for modernism. However, would you identify any qualitative differences between modernist and postmodernist art in treating history and history writing?

H.W.: Postmodernism is used in the Anglophone world as a term of derision, except for a few intellectuals such as Richard Rorty and on occasion me. Fredric Jameson is of course the writer who has studied postmodernism as the cultural equivalent of 'the cultural logic of late capitalism.' In his view, postmodernism manifests the total triumph of capitalism understood as the commodification of culture and the social relations of production. Postmodernism as thus understood is what comes after modernism, itself a mode of epochal self-consciousness produced by the conflict between the realities of agrarian and industrialized societies. This is quite different from Lyotard's conception of postmodernism as a repudiation of all 'grand narratives' and especially that of the 'hidden hand' and 'progress'. As a historian of culture, I see modernism (in the arts, fashion, architecture, literature, the social and human sciences, and the like) as a response (and not only a reaction) to the modernization of societies, which is to say, a response to capitalism, commodification, consumerism, value as exchange-value, etc. I do not see modernism as nostalgic for 'a world we have lost' but as a Nietzsche-like acceptance of the nihilism implicit in capitalism, its institutions and practices, and a commitment to go forth within this nihilism to the revivification of what remains valuable in spite of the commodification of culture.

According to this view, postmodernism is produced by the carrying out of this nihilistic impulse. It presupposes the ruination of traditional cultural institutions and asks what can be done with the 'waste' now produced. I agree with the late Arthur Danto that Marcel Duchamp was the herald of a genuinely postmodernist artistic practice: the art of the ready-made, the *objet-trouvé*, the copy and especially the mechanically re-produced copy, the simulacra which ironizes 'art' itself. Whereas the modernists were frightened by the loss of 'substance' effected by modernist science, postmodernists take this loss for granted, confront a world of pseudo-substantialized objects, a wasteland of things drained of all inherent value (which is what I mean by 'de-substantialization'). Marx tried to return thought to value (and substantiality) by the hypostatization of 'labor'. Modernist technology, now digitalized, substitutes the robot for the worker and pre-packaged work for 'service'. Postmodernism faces a world in which labor itself has been desubstantialized.

We can see the effects of this postmodernist *forma mentis* in the modern novel, in architecture (Frank Gehry), in theatre, music and in such human sciences as sociology, anthropology and political economy. As for history and history-writing, postmodernism manifests itself in various 'eccentric' or non-normative activities such as 'queer history', post-colonial and subaltern studies, and eco-, big data- and deep-historiography. But such movements gain little traction among professional historians insofar as both the content and the form of canonical historiography are constituted precisely to resist such deviancies. A postmodern historiography must begin not by treating its referent (the past, 'the seventeenth century', feudalism, the Renaissance, and so on) as given *a priori* but as constructions, the social functions of which, at the time of their invention as historiological objects, was to provide genealogical confirmation of 'the present' as 'the way things ought to be'.

A.S.: Your formalist perspective on historical thinking and your (post-) structuralist theoretical sympathies are uniquely combined with humanism. How does ethics come into your work? And where do you stand in relation to recent controversies about the nature of humanity itself?

H.W.: Humanism. The older I become, the more I think about this term. I am more inclined towards what Donna Haraway and others call 'inter-species' relations, between, say, humans and animals such as dogs, horses, and chickens. All forms of humanism end up being a kind of species-narcissism justifying the commodification of the whole of nature and its consumption.

A.S.: There are resonances of the Vichan philosophy of universal history in your 'poetics of history', the typology of rhetorical tropes corresponding to stages of historical consciousness and periods. However, how do you conceptualize the movement of history?

H.W.: 'History' cannot be conceptualized in the sense of finding or discovering the 'substance' of human evolution on the planet earth. Of course, one can stipulate what one means by 'History' but this runs counter to the empiricist ideology that serves as orthodoxy for modern professional historians. Stipulation of meaning for basic terms in a historiography is what engenders 'grand narratives' of the kind that postmodernists, according to Jean-François Lyotard, must eschew. 'The movement of history' is a metaphorical expression requiring the naming of the substance of this thing called 'history' that is supposed to be capable of 'movement'. Once you hypostatize 'history' you can present it as capable of all kinds of movements, including actions or intention-motivated movement. You can then proceed to chart a 'pathway' for this movement, posit an end, aim, or purpose of its 'journey', and so on. Benjamin speaks of history coming to a 'standstill', does he not? Of course, we don't have to be literalists in all this. We can stay within the metaphorical, which Spengler did in *The Decline of the West*. Rather than a conception of history as movement, we might speak of 'figures of history' (the title of a recent book by Jacques Rancière) and schemata of movement. Then you have allegory. Allegories of history – is that not what postmodernist novelists are all about? Try reading Toni Morrison's novel, *Beloved*, this way.

Notes

ACKNOWLEDGEMENT. This interview first appeared in the special issue on 'Contemporary Literature and History', edited by Christine Harrison and Angeliki Spiropoulou for the journal *Synthesis*, no 8 (Fall 2015): 118–24.

1. Hayden White, *Metahistory: The Historical Imagination in Nineteenth-Century Europe*. (Baltimore: Johns Hopkins University Press, 1973).
2. Hayden White, 'The Fictions of Factual Representation', in *Tropics of Discourse: Essays in Cultural Criticism* (Baltimore: Johns Hopkins University Press, 1978), 122.
3. Hayden White, 'The Historical Text as Literary Artifact' (1974), in ibid., 84.
4. Hayden White, 'The Modernist Event', in *Figural Realism: Studies in the Mimesis Effect* (Baltimore: Johns Hopkins University Press, 1999), 66–86.

Part II

Stories and histories of the avant-gardes

6

Medium-New

Tyrus Miller

I

Modernist theorizing about media might justifiably be seen as taking its point of departure from Gotthold Ephraim Lessing's 1766 treatise *Laocoön: An Essay on the Limits of Painting and Poetry*, a meditation on the capacities and limitations of these sister arts in response to the classical injunction *ut pictura poesis*, rearticulated in the Renaissance and elaborated in a range of artistic debates of the seventeenth and eighteenth centuries.[1] Lessing's fundamental contribution to aesthetics, his distinction of time- and space-based artforms and his prescriptive strictures against blending them, was an implicit (and often enough, explicit) touchstone of modernist media aesthetics. This is true whether Lessing's analytic was taken up affirmatively, as in Wyndham Lewis's militant advocacy of static, spatial art (*contra* time-art and its flux) in *Time and Western Man*,[2] in Clement Greenberg's evocation of an updated *Laocoön* to address the conditions of mid-twentieth-century modernism[3] and in Michael Fried's conjuring of minimalism's bad 'theatricality' to defend late modernist painting against a trend towards, in his view, literalist 'objecthood';[4] or negatively, in the transgressive blending of space and time in the mobilized aesthetics of Moholy-Nagy,[5] in the media-crossing experimentalism of Cage,[6] in the 'other criteria' applied by Leo Steinberg to the paintings of Pollock, Rothko, Dubuffet, Noland, Johns and Rauschenberg ('other', namely, than those criteria represented by the Lessing-esque pseudo-couple of Harold Rosenberg's 'action painting' theory and Clement Greenberg's assertion of painting's essential tendency towards flatness and 'all-over-ness');[7] and in Rosalind Krauss's correction of Lessing in her insistence on the time-dimension, the 'passages', of modern sculpture.[8] W. J. T. Mitchell sums up the stakes of a number of critical arguments for modernist abstract painting from Clement Greenberg to Rosalind Krauss, by noting how the terms of Lessing's antinomy of painting and literature were reiterated in a transmuted form. Painterly abstraction, Mitchell suggests, is the very means of enforcing a prescriptive separation of the one from the other:

> The project of abstract painting (as understood by some of its principal advocates) is only secondarily an overcoming of representation or illusion; the primary aim is the erection of a wall between the arts of vision and those of language. Sometimes this project expresses itself more generally as an attack on the 'confusion of the arts', the blurring of the boundaries between painting and other media.[9]

Basing his argument on the spatial (side-by-side) and temporal (one-after-another) essences of the media of pictures and speech, and on the corresponding objects of depiction (bodies) and narration (action), Lessing offered a critique, in the proto-Kantian sense of establishing the limits of validity, of artistic theories that in his view were tending to transgress the proper domain of the sister arts and leading to defects in composition and artistic rendering. Notably, Lessing employs the term 'medium' (*Mittel*) to designate not the raw material support of the artform, but rather the material characteristics of the work as a *means* (a more vernacular sense of *Mittel*) to accomplishing an intended artistic goal:

> Once more, then; I do not deny to speech in general the power of portraying a bodily whole by its parts ... but I do deny it to speech as the medium of poetry, because such verbal delineations of bodies fail of the illusion on which poetry particularly depends, and this illusion, I contend, must fail them for the reason that the *coexistence* of the physical object comes into collision with the *consecutiveness* of speech, and the former being resolved into the latter, the dismemberment of the whole into its parts is certainly made easier, but the final reunion of those parts into a whole is made uncommonly difficult and not seldom impossible.[10]

This usage similarly inflects an important monument in the history of modernist theories of the poetic medium, Ezra Pound's edition of Ernest Fenellosa's *The Chinese Written Character as a Medium for Poetry*, composed by Fenellosa around 1903 and published by Pound in 1919. The 'medium' is the Chinese written character, not 'poetry'; but poetry is the intentional framework that mobilizes and motivates aspects of the 'ideogram' as specifically poetic. Notably, Fenellosa makes explicit reference to Lessing's argument and categories, including a comparison of the Laocoön statue with lines from Robert Browning. The specific virtue of the ideogram as a medium of poetry, for Fenellosa, is that it overcomes the split between pictoriality and action in which Lessing grounded his aesthetics, and which Fenellosa/Pound now present as a linguistically contingent feature of Western alphabetic scripts and grammars.[11] Language has putatively become, in the crucible of the Chinese ideogram, a dramatic or even cinematographic enactment in which depiction and description are fused:

> One superiority of verbal poetry as an art rests in its getting back to the fundamental reality of *time*. Chinese poetry has the unique advantage of combining both elements. It speaks at once with the vividness of painting, and with the mobility of sounds. It is, in some sense, more objective than either, more dramatic. In reading Chinese we do not seem to be juggling mental counters, but to be watching *things* work out their fate.[12]

Fenellosa, having brought into unity Lessing's parallel antitheses of poetry and painting, speech and image, provides Pound with future theoretical justification for subsequently exploring a variety of poetic innovations in *The Cantos*, including the juxtaposition of heterogeneous materials without transitions, the relativizing of alphabetic orthography with Chinese characters and other graphic symbols, and the typographical treatment of the page as a hybrid of linguistic and pictorial meaning.

What we might view as a certain circularity in Lessing's reasoning – the constraints of poetry being defined by the nature of speech, but only speech's nature as delimited by the constraints of poetry – nevertheless highlights a salient ambiguity in the very definition of a medium. Medium signifies neither the pure materiality of artistic creation and communication nor a naturally given essence of the material; rather, a medium depends on an intentional structure of the act of artistic creation and on the sedimentation of precedent intentions in the historical traditions to which the current production of the work makes reference. 'Media', in this sense, can be viewed not as unchanging essences, but rather as relative constants or stabilities in the artistic appropriation of materials, and to this extent, media may exhibit a certain transhistorical validity despite the flux of historical variations and novelties in their use. Medium is an *outcome*, not an origin. It derives from iterative processes of artistic *Vermittlung*, mediation between the current act of creation and the tradition and between the artist and his audience. As Rosalind Krauss has recently underscored in her contemporary *plaidoyer* for medium-specificity, and in this regard with complete fidelity to Lessing: 'the medium [is] a form of remembering, since the various artistic supports, each represented by its individual muse, serve as the scaffolding for a "who you are" in the collective memory of the practitioners of that particular genre—painting, sculpture, photography, film'.[13] Raymond Williams, in his discussion of the concept of medium in *Marxism and Literature*, goes still further, reminding us of the work processes lying behind the artist's engagement with material and their embeddedness in the broad social relations of production and division of labour. He argues that the notion of medium, as used to characterize artistic labour in contrast to other forms of labour in capitalist society, bears the traits of what Lukács called reification; 'medium', in short, becomes, in aesthetic discourses, an ideologically charged cypher that conceals and deflects from more direct consideration the underlying social processes and practices of artistic production.[14] Despite this ideological distortion, however, Williams finds in the notion of medium an important diagnostic value, specifically for the social relations that undergird the development of artistic modernism:

> [S]ince the late nineteenth century, crises of technique—which can be isolated as problems of the 'medium' or of the 'form'—have been directly linked with a sense of crisis in the relationship of art to society which had previously been agreed or even taken for granted. A new technique has often been seen, realistically, as a new relationship, or as depending on a new relationship. Thus what had been isolated as a medium, in many ways rightly as a way of emphasizing the material production which any art must be, came to be seen, inevitably, as social practice; or, in the crisis of modern cultural production, as a crisis of social practice. This is the crucial common factor, in otherwise diverse tendencies, which links the radical aesthetics of modernism and the revolutionary theory and practice of Marxism.[15]

In light of the socio-historical dimensions that are encoded into and potentially legible in the notion of medium, the apparent circularity of Lessing's definition may, then, be less a logical flaw than a prescient formulation of the hermeneutic 'fusion of horizons' necessary to instance 'the medium' in individual works of art, to body forth the medium's 'effective history' in works, mediating the creative relations between present production and inherited tradition.[16]

Notably, T. S. Eliot, who exhibits in his criticism great sensitivity to the specific technical characteristics of the poetic uses of language, also carefully grounded his observations on the specific medium characteristics of poetry not in a material theory of the medium but in a hermeneutical argument about tradition. This is most evident in his renowned essay 'Tradition and the Individual Talent' (1919), which establishes the relationship between a self-sufficient, singular realization in the medium of poetry and an artistic process that extinguishes the contingencies of the self in order to submit to the selective necessity of tradition. What becomes evident from Eliot's own poetic practice in works such as 'The Waste Land', 'Gerontion' and 'The Hollow Men', however, is that the ideal poetic relation to tradition defined in 'Tradition and the Individual Talent' can only function as a *diagnostic* of the negative condition of modernity, as an index of what at present could be achieved only with the greatest ascetic efforts, through the most desperate contortions of crisis-consciousness, or perhaps ultimately not at all. 'Tradition and the Individual Talent' itself leaves this parlous state of affairs largely tacit (though perhaps legible between its elusive lines). Of Eliot's early essays, then, it is thus not 'Tradition and the Individual Talent' that offers the most salient analysis of medium in modernist writing, since it largely evades the question of what happen to media when the intentional structures embedded in tradition begin to erode, but rather his 1917 'Reflections on *Vers Libre*'. In this earlier essay, in contrast, Eliot diagnoses the emergence of technical formalism – a poetry whose heightened artifice derives from the isolation and intensive development of latent aspects of the material medium – as a symptom of a disturbance in tradition itself. Eliot notes that 'the decay of intricate formal patterns has nothing to do with the advent of *vers libre*. It had set in long before. Only in a closely-knit and homogeneous society, where many men are at work on the same problem ... will the development of such forms ever be carried to perfection.'[17] In the contemporary context of a heterogeneous, loosely structured modern society, immersion in technical problems of verse – Eliot's example is Swinburne's metrical complexities, but he could well be referring to Pound's early poetry – represents a problematic gambit. Given the general 'withdrawal of consensual language', as Christopher Butler has formulated modernity's progressive delegitimation of inherited artistic conventions,[18] any such elaborate techniques, even if inspired by the Troubadours or the Elizabethans, can only be speculative bids for a future recognition that is far from guaranteed. Swinburne, for Eliot, is exemplary for the failure of his metrical gambit: 'If anything promising for English poetry is hidden in the metres of Swinburne, it probably lies far beyond the point to which Swinburne has developed them.'[19]

In his essay 'How to Read', from the late 1920s, Pound famously formulated a typology of poetry that distinguished three distinct kinds of poetry, each based on alternative constitutions of the medium of language in poetry, according to how language is 'charged or energized in various manners'.[20] These include:

> MELOPŒIA, wherein the words are charged, over and above their plain meaning, with some musical property, which directs the bearing or trend of that meaning.
>
> PHANOPŒIA, which is a casting of images upon the visual imagination.
>
> LOGOPŒIA, 'the dance of the intellect among words', that is to say, it employs words not only for their direct meaning, but it takes count in a special way

of habits of usage, of the context we *expect* to find with the world, its usual concomitants, of its known acceptances, and of ironical play. It holds the aesthetic content which is peculiarly the domain of verbal manifestation, and cannot possibly be contained in plastic or in music. It is the latest come, and perhaps the most tricky and undependable mode.[21]

While Pound treats each type of poetry as legitimate in the light of tradition, he clearly conceives of logopœia as both the most contemporary ('the latest come') and the most consummately autonomous manifestation of language as a medium of poetry ('peculiarly the domain of verbal manifestation'). It is, for Pound, the mode in which language comes into its own as a *modern* poetic medium, emancipated from its heteronomous bonds to other media. Moreover, of the three kinds of poetry, as Pound formulates them, only logopœia contains an explicit index of contemporaneity in its relation to the social context of language usage, performance and pragmatics. Regardless of the ultimate validity of Pound's categories, they illustrate a key nuance in his understanding of medium as it pertains to poetry: far from simply focusing on language as a material support, much less on some isolated aspect of its sound or representational character, language as poetic medium, at its most distinct, is a particular relation to a social, cultural and, implicitly, historical context that is taken up into the artwork and that facilitates its capacity to communicate aesthetically.

II

The notion of the artistic medium, in sum, cannot be reduced either to the material support of the work of art or to a back-formation of the artist's techniques for mobilizing and intensifying properties that may be projected into or derived out of the artistic material. The commonly accepted artistic media took on their consistency and quasi-essential stability only against a background of long-evolving traditions of practice, chains of artistic exemplars, and conventions of composition and interpretation. However, one of the most salient conditions of modernist art and literature is the *disruption* of tradition, the *delegitimation* of inherited representational conventions, a process that the modernist avant-gardes, moreover, intentionally sought to intensify and accelerate into wholesale destruction. Whether this negative horizon of delegitimation was viewed by the modernist artist with anguish or with a sense of exhilaration, the artistic imperative it pronounced was to invent new forms, new idioms and paradoxically singular 'genres' of art. But this imperative to invent extended beyond the specific forms and styles to the domain of art itself, where the distribution and hierarchy of media was a defining feature. If traditional forms, idioms and genres were mutually implicated in stable artistic media and vice versa, then the general dialectic of modernism could not have left media unaffected. Accordingly, modernism expresses a paradoxical demand – given the mutually constitutive nature of media, conventions and traditions – to purify or reinvent old media, and, ultimately, to invent new media, freed from the burden of conventions and ungrounded in any precedent tradition, as if the media and the work they supported were to be co-equal objects of composition.

Modernism, and especially its activist wing in the avant-garde, proliferated nominalistic, performative attempts to call into being new medium-categories bearing new labels, exemplified, initially, by only one or a small number of works, or by a theoretical projection of future works, or by incomplete sketches, studies and notes towards their eventual realization.[22] We can multiply at will key such instances as Mallarmé's 'Book', the 'manifesto' developed by much of the historic avant-garde, the Cubists' 'collage', Marinetti's 'parole in libertà', Malevich's 'non-objectivity', Khlebnikov's and Kruchenykh's '*zaum*', Apollinaire's 'calligram', Pound's 'ideogram', Stein's 'geography', Lewis' 'vortex', Duchamp's 'readymade', Kandinsky's '*Geistige*', Klee's 'picture poems', Van Doesburg's '*Stijl*', Breton's '*poème-objet*', El Lissitzky's '*Proun*', Micić's '*Zenit*', Eisenstein's 'intellectual montage', the Productivists' 'factography', Hausmann's 'optophonetics', Schwitters' '*Merz*', the Surrealists' 'psychic automatism', the Bataille circle's *l'informe*, Moholy-Nagy's and Man Ray's 'photogram', and the Expressionists' '*neuer Mensch*'[23] (even before adding in a further iteration of neo-avant-garde bids for medium status such as 'concrete poetry', 'chance', 'graphic score', 'indeterminacy', 'instruction poem', 'shape', 'mesostic', 'mirror displacement', 'site/non-site', 'action', 'situation' and '*dérive*').

As Stanley Cavell has noted, 'One might say that the task is no longer to produce another instance of an art but a new medium within it … It follows that in such a predicament, media are not given *a priori*. The failure to establish a medium is a new depth, an absoluteness, of artistic failure.'[24] Cavell, who speaks of media as 'automatisms', in the sense of providing artists embedded, tacit ways of 'doing things' with words, images, sounds, etc., contrasts the traditional and modernist artist through their divergent relation to the medium as an ensemble of automatisms:

> In a tradition, the great figure knows best how to activate its automatisms, and how best to entice the muse to do most of the work. In a modernist situation, there is no such help … The automatisms of a tradition are given to the

traditional artist, prior to any instance he adds to it; the master explores and extends them. The modernist artist has to explore the fact of automatism itself, as if investigating what it is at any time that has provided a given work of art with the power of its art as such.[25]

As Rosalind Krauss notes (though referring to the re-invention of medium in the 'post-medium condition' of contemporary art):

> The invention of a medium will strike us as strange – since mediums develop over many centuries during which an entire guild uses their rules as a means of communication. An 'invented' medium would seem to be merely idiomatic.[26]

But it is, however, precisely upon the transmutation of this (potentially incommunicable) idiomaticity into communicable aesthetic validity that modernism stakes its artistic claim. As Cavell suggests, modernism turns 'tradition' into a reiterated series of foundational moments, a 'tradition of the new' (in Harold Rosenberg's words). Which might be restated, with a note of Benjaminian pathos: modernism generates the history of its media as a continuum of catastrophes: 'This is the meaning of the new fact of series, or the fact that a new medium establishes and is established by a series. Each instance of the medium is an absolute realization of it; each totally eclipses the other.'[27]

Modernism thus speculates on turning the authority of tradition over into a bid for posterior understanding and acceptance, with current incomprehension and even outrage as the necessary interest paid on that credit. This contract rests, that is, on the fallible potential for the artist to establish, through the reflexive action of the singular artwork itself, a code to accompany the work, to render its newly instituted language translatable into communicable experience and meaning. 'A medium', Krauss writes, 'is the articulation of such a code.'[28] But so too, we should add, may a supplementary theoretical statement or an externally furnished critical discourse serve this function, which, as Mitchell reminds us, often regularly accompanies the tacit statements of modernist media and addresses their typical lack of discursive explicitness. The sort of self-reflexively generated and work-immanent code from which Krauss conjures her prescriptive evaluations of artists and works is not, in historical perspective, the only way in which new, singular media have stated their case and bid for recognition. But by various means, one way or the other, the modernist work projects its own posterity forward from a foundational moment validating the artwork's forms and its medium in a singular act of present-tense co-creation.

III

We can see this media-renewing impulse at work already in Stéphane Mallarmé, in the last two decades of the nineteenth century, in his response to what he diagnosed as 'the crisis in poetry'. In a key passage, he writes:

> The pure work implies the disappearance of the poet as speaker, yielding his initiative to words, which are mobilized by the shock of their difference; they light up with reciprocal reflections like a virtual stream of fireworks over jewels, restoring perceptible breath to the former lyric impulse, or the enthusiastic personal directing of the sentence.[29]

Though apparently anticipating Eliot's 'continual extinction of personality', Mallarmé's evocation of 'the disappearance of the poet as speaker' more directly and more radically expresses an ideal of the purified medium, its liberation of a defining difference from 'speech', understood as language in its everyday, pragmatic acceptations, which constitutes in Paul Valéry's words, 'an extremely odd mixture of incoherent stimuli'.[30] Notably, unlike Eliot and Pound, Mallarmé makes no mention of 'tradition' or any other index of historicity or background climate of usage; indeed, the metaphors of jewels and fireworks suggest extremes of geological time and absolute presentness that preclude any middle-term duration in which history or tradition would be possible. Analogously, in his posthumously published notes towards *Le Livre*, Mallarmé also evokes the differential and distributed dimension of silence in speech, itself imagined as a sparkling crystalline form organized and composed through the constellations of white space on the page:

> poem,   held in space which isolates the stanzas and
> conceals itself and takes place
> amid the white of the paper; significative silence that it is
>   beautiful
> no less ~~difficult~~ to compose, than the
>   ~~meritorious~~
>   ~~glorious~~
> verses.[31]

It would, however, be misleading to consider Mallarmé's purification of the medium of writing as simply oblivious to background of history and tradition; far more, it represents an intentional and methodical withdrawal, in which everyday language remains as a negative horizon or even a resource to be transfigured by poetry. The white sheet of the virginal page is, prior to any writing deposited on it, the negation of the dark background, the night, of ordinary speech:

> To write – The inkstand, crystal as a conscience, within its depths its drop of shadow relative to having something be: then take away the lamp. You notice, one does not write luminously on a dark field; the alphabet of the stars alone, is thus indicated, sketched out or interrupted; man pursues black on white.[32]

The new literature as Mallarmé imagines it thus makes aesthetic use of the medium of typography derived from, but also defined by, an internal swerve from the newspaper, which despite the vulgar 'pressed' quality of its letters, also points the way to a new disposition of letters and spaces on visually arresting large format pages. In 'The Book: A Spiritual Instrument', in which 'instrument' may also be read as 'means' or 'medium', Mallarmé writes:

> The newspaper with its full sheet on display makes improper use of printing – that is, it makes good packing paper. Of course, the obvious and vulgar advantage of it, as everybody knows, lies in its mass production and circulation. But that advantage is secondary to a miracle, in the highest sense of the word: words led back to their origin, which is the twenty-six letters of the alphabet, so gifted with infinity that they will finally consecrate Language. Everything is caught up in their endless variations and then rises out of them in the form of the Principle. Thus typography becomes a rite. The book, which is a total expansion of the letter, must find its mobility in the letter; and in its spaciousness must establish some nameless system of relationships which will embrace and strengthen fiction.[33]

Mallarmé came closest to exemplifying this transformed medium practice in the constellative typography and 'significative' white space in his poem 'Un coup de dés jamais n'abolira le hasard', published in journal form in 1897 and in book form, posthumously, in 1914.

Taking up the lineage that Mallarmé helped establish in his essay 'Epstein, Belgion, and Meaning', published in *The Criterion* in 1930, Pound suggested that writing must evolve in the direction of a graphic diagrammatics, which would help establish art at the high level of non-linear, multidimensional thought already achieved by the sciences. Facilitated by Mallarmé's and Apollinaire's innovations in establishing a graphic-verbal medium, the French cousin to Pound's own Chinese-inspired ideograms, the poet can be 'as capable, or almost as capable as thinking thoughts that join like spokes in a wheel-hub and that fuse in hypergeometric amalgams'.[34] In his 1926 book of 'thought-images', the German critic Walter Benjamin expressed an analogous vision of the contemporary transfiguration of writing first adumbrated by the hermetic meditations of Mallarmé:

> Mallarmé, who in the crystalline structure of his manifestly traditionalist writing saw the true image of what was to come, was in the *Coup de dés* the first to incorporate the graphic tensions of the advertisement in the printed page. The typographic experiments later undertaken by the Dadaists stemmed, it is true, not from constructive principles but from the precise nervous reactions of these literati, and were therefore far less enduring than Mallarmé's ... Script – having found, in the book, a refuge in which it can lead an autonomous existence – is pitilessly dragged out into the street by advertisements and subjected to the brutal hetronomies of economic chaos ... If centuries ago it began gradually to lie down, passing from the upright inscription to the manuscript resting on sloping desks before finally taking itself to bed in the printed book, it now begins just as slowly to rise again from the ground. The newspaper is read more in the vertical than in the horizontal plane, while film and advertisement force the printed word entirely into the dictatorial perpendicular. And before a contemporary finds his way clear to opening a book, his eyes have been exposed to such a blizzard of changing, colorful, conflicting letters that the chances of his penetrating the archaic stillness of the book are slight ... [Q]uantity is approaching the moment of a qualitative leap when writing, advancing ever more deeply into the graphic regions of its new eccentric figurativeness, will suddenly take possession of an adequate material content. In this picture-writing, poets, who will now as in earliest times be first and foremost experts in writing, will be able to participate only by mastering the fields in which ... it is being constructed: statistical and technical diagrams.[35]

Both Benjamin and Pound, then, nearly contemporaneously predicted transformations of script as a poetic medium that develop from Mallarmé's typographic speculations to the explosion of literate thought beyond the linear, alphabetic and spatial boundaries of the book.[36]

Such speculations, at once, exploded the inherited conception of poetic language into new domains of immersive tactility related to modern technology and urban life and assimilated a vast new range of sonorous, luminous, graphic, chromatic, typographical, configurational and mobile stimuli to the expanded poetic medium/means of language. They exemplify a generalized modernist hypertrophy of 'language', which Geoffrey Galt Harpham has aptly called 'the critical fetish of modernity'. 'The modernist moment,' Harpham writes, 'is achieved when immediacy ... is renounced as an illusion [and] the limits of language are seen as the limits of the world, and linguistic mediation itself becomes the object of observation.'[37] He goes on to note that

> [D]uring this time and even beyond, artistic and cultural media were conceived as languages, with pigment, stone, tones, or human motion being credited with a 'syntax', a 'grammar', a 'rhetoric', even a 'phonology' ... The most programmatically modernist art did not affiliate itself with particular national traditions of expression, but cultivated an abstract 'language of art' that could address a broadly European, even a universal audience.[38]

Whatever its validity, the artistic productiveness of the modernist obsession with language-as-medium – language alone, but also language writ large – cannot be doubted. Mallarmé's path-breaking speculations on typography and the expanded book helped inspire further typographical, artistic and musical experiments throughout the twentieth century, from Apollinaire, Picasso and Pound to Cage, Boulez[39] and Broodthaers.

IV

In conclusion, I want to consider briefly one further modulation of the modernist impulse to invent new media, often 'nominalistically' – that is, as exemplified by a singular example, and provided a label that represents a bid for future validity. One of the ways that this occurred was the *assemblage* of individual works – in such modes as the avant-garde periodical, the performance venue, the collection and the exhibition – and their composition as, themselves, quasi-works of art. Often, this was accompanied by unconventional usage and labelling of the mode of presentation, implying, as well, that in editing or otherwise presenting a variety of modernist works, a 'metamedia' was also being invented and projected into the world. We might point, for instance, to key exhibitions as Kasimir Malevich's 0,10 exhibition, 'the Last Futurist Exhibition', the Cabaret Voltaire soirées, or to periodicals such as Theo Van Doesburg's *De Stijl* and Lajos Kássak's *MA* as instances in which the ensemble of works collected together and composed might themselves be seen as self-reflexive, aesthetically innovative instances of avant-garde form.

An illuminating example – because we can weigh an editor's own statement of his artistic and even political intentions – is Kurt Pinthus's celebrated collection of expressionist poetry *Menschheitsdämmerung* (Twilight/Dawn of Mankind). Pinthus's book assembles works by twenty-three of the younger generation of expressionist poets, collocating the poems into four 'chapters': 'Collapse and Cry',[40] 'The Heart's Awakening', 'Call and Outrage' and 'Love of Man'. It brings together such renowned poets as Gottfried Benn, Jakob Hoddis, Georg Heym,

Ivan Goll, Franz Werfel, August Stramm, Georg Trakl and Else Lasker-Schüler, as well as a number of now lesser-known figures such as Wilhelm Klemm, Rudolf Leonhard, Paul Zech, Walter Hasenclever and Karl Otten. Each section included poems from the twenty-three writers, arranged in an order determined by Pinthus's intuitive sense of interconnections between the works, rather than by external criteria such as alphabetical order, chronology, direct affiliations between the writers or independent presentation of a given poet's work.

Pinthus begins his preface by distinguishing *Menschheitsdämmerung* from an 'anthology'; the editor of this book, he claims, is an 'enemy of anthologies'.[41] 'Anthology' implies, he explains, a gathering of texts by poets who happen to live in the same time, and who are represented by alphabetical or chronological presentation of a few poems each. They may be connected by a common theme, or be presented as models of good poetry in the tradition of the forefathers. Instead, Pinthus insists for his own book on the term '*Sammlung*', which would typically be translated 'collection' or 'compilation'. However, he underscores that he means the term not only in this more obvious sense, but also in the sense of 'concentration' and 'composure' and further extending to the active, politically connotative sense of '*Versammlung*', 'assembly', a gathering of people together in action, a 'calling to order'. 'This book is not only called "a compiliation" (*eine Sammlung*)', he writes. 'It *is* assembly! (*Sammlung*): assembly of concussions and passions, assembly of desire, joy, and torment of an epoch—our epoch. It is the collected (*gesammelte*) projection of human movement out of and into time.'[42]

Pinthus goes on to contrast the organizational principle of his assemblage from the handling of cultural material by the twentieth-century humanities (*Geisteswissenschaften*). These latter, he suggests, took as their model the natural sciences and subordinated their materials to a conceptual, successive, and causal order. 'One saw things causally, vertically.'[43] His book, Pinthus argues, is assembled – called to order – in a different manner:

> One listens into the poetry of our time ..., one listen across and through, looking all around, ... not vertical, not successively, rather horizontal; one does not divide that which follows one from the other, rather one listens together, in an instant, simultaneously. One listens to the chiming together of poetic voices: one listens symphonically. The music of our time is intoned, the throbbing unison of heart and brain.[44]

If the book is symphonically organized – assembled, that is, through a network of immanent properties flowing out of the artworks into the new medium of the

Sammlung, rather than by the ordinary external principles by which anthologies are selected and arranged – what then is the underlying principle of composition?

> Their commonality is the intensity and radicalism of feeling, sensibility, expression, form; and this intensity, this radicalism, compels the poets in turn to struggle against the humanity of an epoch coming to its end and to longing preparation and demand for a new, better humanity.[45]

Pinthus suggests that it is the intensity of poetic subjectivity, of affective response to the historical condition of the age, that brings the poems together and represents, in the course of their meta-artistic composition and orchestration, the true object of their poetic striving: *Menschheit*, 'humanity' itself, in its twilight and new dawning. Subjectivity is, in this expressionist poetics, the expressive medium in which 'humanity' ebbs and emerges in historical time; the *Sammlung* of lyric poetry in a book is, in turn, the medium in which the temporalizing movements of this subjectivity can be made present and communicable to readers.

In moving from individual lyric expression in the medium of poetic language to the orchestrated collective subjectivity of a poetic generation in the medium of the 'compilation/assembly' to the universal voice of a historical horizon in the medium of a declining and dawning humanity, Pinthus reveals a logic of escalation in which the validity of unconventional artistic choices at one medium-level – the individual poems – is staked on the degree to which they can be assumed by the meta-artistic labour of the editor and eventually the meta-historical movements of toiling, suffering mankind as a whole. Indeed, if we take an admittedly extreme example, even for this collection of artistic extremities – August Stramm's often one-word-per-line ejaculations of pure feeling – it is hard to see how the work could be aesthetically justified on purely work-immanent grounds, without its being taken up by a meta-mediumistic and/or theoretical context that would legitimate its non-conventional poetic model and offer relevant interpretative framing for making sense of it as an instance of poetic art:

> Lips, lips
> Thirsty, curly, warm lips!
> Blooms! Blooms!
> Kisses! Wine!
> Red
> Gold
> Rapturous
> Wine!

You and I!
I and you!
You!⁴⁶

Pinthus's example, in conclusion, is also notable for its obvious overstraining of the aesthetic gambit of modernism, which is nevertheless far from exceptional in the history of modernist manifestoes and theories, and in its works of art and literature. Already upon the republication of *Menschheitsdämmerung* in 1922, after its blockbuster success of selling more than 20,000 copies, Pinthus's new foreword, entitled 'Reverberation' (*Nachklang*), sounded a note of profound disappointment and failure. Discussing his decision to republish the book unchanged from its original edition, Pinthus admits that '[t]he poetry of this generation died early'; 'faster than any other generation, this one entered literary history, became historical; their poetry became paradigm, schema for those who followed'.⁴⁷ Ultimately, however, the failure of the individual poetry – its petrification into a mere historical artefact – and the deadening of the book's living 'assembly' into a static, monumental tableau, indexes failure at the highest medium-level, 'mankind', which refused to be artistically composed and transfigured. 'The glow of this generation,' Pinthus laments, 'ignited itself in opposition to the past, to the decaying, and for a few moments was able to throw its illumination into the future, but it could not enflame humanity to the great deed or to great feeling.'

Notes

1. Gotthold Ephraim Lessing, *Laocoön: An Essay on the Limits of Painting and Poetry* (1766), in *Classic and Romantic German Aesthetics*, ed. J. M. Bernstein (Cambridge: Cambridge University Press, 2003), 25–129.
2. Wyndham Lewis, *Time and Western Man*, ed. Paul Edwards (Santa Rosa: Black Sparrow Press, 1993).
3. Clement Greenberg, 'Towards a New Laocoon', in *The Collected Essays and Criticism Vol. 1*, ed. John O'Brian (Chicago: University of Chicago Press, 1986), 23–41.
4. Michael Fried, 'Art and Objecthood', in *Art and Objecthood: Essays and Reviews* (Chicago: University of Chicago Press, 1998), 148–72.
5. László Moholy-Nagy, *The New Vision and Abstract of an Artist* (New York: Wittenborn, Schultz, 1947).
6. John Cage, *Silence* (Middletown, Connecticut: Wesleyan University Press, 1961).

7 Leo Steinberg, *Other Criteria: Confrontations with Twentieth-Century Art* (Oxford: Oxford University Press, 1972).
8 Rosalind Krauss, *Passages in Modern Sculpture* (Cambridge, MA: The MIT Press, 1981).
9 W. J. T. Mitchell, '*Ut Pictura Theoria*: Abstract Painting and Language', in *Picture Theory* (Chicago: University of Chicago Press, 1994), 216.
10 Lessing, *Laocoön*, 90.
11 For the connection of Lessing and Fenellosa, see Haun Saussy, *Great Walls of Discourse and Other Adventures in Cultural China* (Cambridge, MA: Harvard University Press, 2001), 40.
12 Ernest Fenellosa and Ezra Pound, *The Chinese Written Character as a Medium for Poetry: A Critical Edition*, eds. Haun Saussy, Jonathan Stalling, and Lucas Klein (New York: Fordham University Press, 2008), 45.
13 Rosalind E. Krauss, *Under Blue Cup* (Cambridge, MA: The MIT Press, 2011), 2. She is referring directly to Jean-Luc Nancy's essay 'Why Are There Several Arts and Not Just One?' in *The Muses*, trans. Peggy Kamuf (Stanford: Stanford University Press, 1994).
14 Compare, on this point, the Soviet Productivist theorist Boris Arvatov's framing of 'medium' as an alienation and mystification of bourgeois art's relations of production: '[N]ow artistic production was governed not by *socio-technical* tasks, but by *socio-ideological* tasks, the artist-productionist turned from an organizer of object into an organizer of ideas, turning the object into a "bare" medium, i.e. he introduced goals into his material process of production that were completely alien to this process' – Boris Arvatov, *Art and Production*, trans. Shushan Avagyan (London: Pluto Press, 2017), 26–7.
15 Raymond Williams, *Marxism and Literature* (Oxford: Oxford University Press, 1977), 163–4.
16 I refer to the hermeneutic framework set out by Hans-Georg Gadamer in *Truth and Method*, 2nd edn. (1st English edn, 1975, trans. W. Glen-Doepel, ed. by John Cumming and Garret Barden), revised translation by J. Weinsheimer and D. G. Marshall (New York: Crossroad, 1989).
17 T. S. Eliot, 'Reflections on *Vers Libre*', in *Selected Prose of T.S. Eliot*, ed. Frank Kermode (New York: Farrar, Straus and Giroux, 1975), 36.
18 Christopher Butler, *Early Modernism: Literature, Music and Painting in Europe 1900–1916* (Oxford: Clarendon Press, 1994), 4–14.
19 T. S. Eliot, 'Reflections on *Vers Libre*', 33.
20 Ezra Pound, 'How to Read', in *Literary Essays of Ezra Pound*, ed. T.S. Eliot (London: Faber and Faber, 1954), 25.
21 Ibid., 25.
22 I owe my discussion of label and example to Nelson Goodman's discussion of exemplification in *Languages of Art* (Indianapolis: Bobbs-Merrill, 1968). For

further application of this concept of exemplification to artistic works of the neo-avant-garde, see my *Singular Examples: Artistic Politics and the Neo-Avant-Garde* (Evanston, Illinois: Northwestern University Press, 2009).

23 For discussion of the notion of 'the new man' in the avant-garde, see Gottfried Küenzlen, *Der Neue Mensch* (Munich: Wilhelm Fink Verlag, 1994). For the even broader suggestion that in modernity there is an evolving reciprocity of the definition of 'man' and 'medium' in the human sciences, arts, and communication, such that modern 'man' could be defined as the 'medium of media', see Stefan Rieger, *Die Individualität der Medien: Eine Geschichte der Wissenschaften vom Menschen* (Frankfurt a/M: Suhrkamp Verlag, 2000). See also my essay of post-surrealist constructions of the 'new man' in the 1930s, 'Mimesis of the New Man: the 1930s from Ideology to Anthropolitics', *Encounters with the 30s* (Madrid: Reina Sofia, Museo Nacional Centro de Arte, 2012).

24 Stanley Cavell, *The World Viewed: Reflections on the Ontology of Film*, enlarged edition (Cambridge, MA: Harvard University Press, 1979), 103.

25 Ibid., 107.

26 Krauss, *Under Blue Cup*, 3.

27 Cavell, *The World Viewed*, 115. A more starkly catastrophic view, emphasizing the tendency of the serial 'new' to exhaust itself entropically, was expressed by Octavio Paz in *Children of the Mire: Modern Poetry from Romanticism to the Avant-Garde*, new and enlarged edition (Cambridge, MA: Harvard University Press, 1991). The notion of the new as a 'continuum of catastrophe' was most thoroughly explored by Walter Benjamin in his *Arcades Project* and his writings 'On the Philosophy of History', in which the angel of history views the entire past as an ever-escalating pile of rubble. Benjamin's figure is a sobering counter-image to the seriality of the new that Cavell celebrates as the achievement of modernity in art.

28 Krauss, *Under Blue Cup*, 3. Though he draws drastically different aesthetic conclusions than Krauss, Craig Dworkin offers an analogous view of media when he writes: 'Media … consist of analyses of networked objects in specific social settings. As much acts of interpretation as material things, as much processes as objects, media are not merely storage mechanisms somehow independent of the acts of reading or recognizing the signs they record' – Dworkin, *No Medium* (Cambridge, MA: The MIT Press, 2013), 22.

29 Stéphane Mallarmé, *Selected Poetry and Prose*, ed. Mary Ann Caws (New York: New Directions, 1982), 75.

30 Paul Valéry, 'Pure Poetry: Notes for a Lecture', in *The Art of Poetry*, trans. Denise Folliot (Princeton: Princeton University Press, 1958), 191.

31 Stéphane Mallarmé, *The Book*, trans. Sylvia Gorelick (Cambridge, MA: Exact Change, 2018), 5.

32 Mallarmé, 'Action Restricted', in *Selected Poetry and Prose*, 77.

33 Mallarmé, 'The Book: A Spiritual Instrument', in ibid., 82.
34 Ezra Pound, 'Epstein, Belgion and Meaning', *The Criterion* 9, no. 36 (April 1930): 475.
35 Walter Benjamin, *One-Way Street*, trans. Edmund Jephcott, in *Selected Writings Vol. 1, 1913–1926*, eds. Marcus Bullock and Michael W. Jennings (Cambridge, MA: The Belknap Press of the Harvard University Press, 1996), 456–7.
36 Notably, this was also the guiding thesis of Marshall McLuhan's media theory: that the homogeneous, visual space of thought constructed by literacy was, under the pressure of new technological and electronic media, as well with the impetus of as new scientific and technical paradigms, giving rise to a multidimensional, dynamically fluctuating space of experience and thought. It is out of the scope of this essay, but it is worth noting the central role of modernist literature and criticism – most importantly the writings of Wyndham Lewis, Ezra Pound, T. S. Eliot, James Joyce and I. A. Richards – in McLuhan's intellectual formation and as a touchstone throughout his career. For further on this connection, see Marshall McLuhan, *The Interior Landscape: The Literary Criticism of Marshall McLuhan, 1943/1962*, ed. Eugene McNamara (New York: McGraw-Hill, 1969); *Counterblast: 1954 Edition* (Berkeley: Ginko Press, 2011); *Understanding Media: The Extensions of Man* (Cambridge, MA: The MIT Press, 1994); Marshall and Eric McLuhan, *Laws of Media: The New Science* (Toronto: University of Toronto Press, 1988); and Glenn Willmott, *McLuhan, or Modernism in Reverse* (Toronto: University of Toronto Press, 1996). One could note an analogous modernist provenance of situationist thought, which has been highly influential in contemporary media theory. Lettrist and Situationist analyses of culture and their techniques of cultural intervention took inspiration from a heterogeneous range of avant-garde and neo-avant-garde practices from Mallarmé, Lautréamont and surrealism to the post-war COBRA group and continental *informelle* painting.
37 Geoffrey Galt Harpham, *Language Alone: The Critical Fetish of Modernity* (New York: Routledge, 2002), 4.
38 Ibid., 5–6.
39 Boulez's composition *Pli Selon Pli* (completed 1962), incorporating five Mallarmé poems, was, for example, a vehicle for Boulez to explore a problem of interartistic media relations. It represents, he writes, 'a number of solutions to the problems posed by the alliance of poetry and music, and these solutions range from a simple heading to total amalgamation. They give each piece a meaning and indicate the significance of its position in the complete cycle' – Boulez, 'Pli Selon Pli', in *Orientations: Collected Writings*, ed. Jean-Jacques Nattiez, trans. Martin Cooper (Cambridge, MA: Harvard University Press, 1986), 174. For a more extended treatment of the same issue, see also 'Sound, Word, Synthesis' (1958), in Ibid., 177–98.
40 Kurt Pinthus, *Menschheitsdämmerung: Ein Document des Expressionismus* (Hamburg: Rowohlt, 1955).

41 'Zuvor' (1919), in Pinthus, *Menschheitsdämmerung*, 22.
42 Ibid.
43 Ibid.
44 Ibid.
45 Ibid., *23*.
46 August Stramm, 'Blüte' (Blooms), in Pinthus, 142.
47 'Nachklang' (1922) in Pinthus, 34.

Time assemblage: History in the European avant-gardes

Sascha Bru

Given the rhetorical verve with which they claimed to break with the past, their pronounced desire to be of, or to transform, the present, and their strong futural thrust, the so-called classic or historical avant-gardes – Expressionism, Cubism, Futurism, Dadaism, Constructivism, Surrealism and many other isms – are generally considered to have been anti-passéist. Critics indeed most often side either with Renato Poggioli's claim that what ultimately tied all classic avant-gardes together was a generic futurism, an orientation towards the future,[1] or with the view put forth, among others, by François Hartog, that the dominant 'regime of historicity' of the avant-gardes was presentism, that is, their hermeneutical horizon of expectation was primarily geared towards the present.[2] Hardly anyone associates the classic avant-gardes with the past. To interpret the avant-gardes' alleged disregard of the past as emblematic of a joint a- or anti-historical stance, or to pit the avant-gardes, in a sort of Manichean conflict, on the side of a purely Kantian, historically disinterested, aesthetic that takes on the Hegelian, historical front of Realism, is jumping to conclusions too quickly, though. For it is, of course, not because we downplay the role of the past, and favour the present or the future, that we would be against history as such. Rather, this suggests that we operate with a different understanding of history, one that perhaps also recalibrates the relations between the past, the present and the future. What the avant-gardes' other understanding of history, and its 'medium', time, might have amounted to forms the topic of this essay.

I am profoundly grateful to Tyrus Miller, whose input has been vital to this essay. A first draft of this essay was read as a keynote at the conference *Realism(s) of the Avant-Garde*, organized by the European Network for Avant-Garde and Modernism Studies (EAM) at the University of Münster in September 2018. I am also much indebted to the organizer, Moritz Baßler, for inviting me to present it there.

Allegories of patience

One of the most undervalued aspects of the classic avant-gardes is their patience, for were we to take the words of many avant-gardists literally, then we can only conclude that they mainly awaited their own death, if not the end of times. In an oft-quoted patch from Filippo Tommaso Marinetti's 'Fondazione e Manifesto del Futurismo' (1909), for instance, we read that by the time the harbingers of Futurism will have turned forty, a younger generation will come to throw them out in the dustbin like 'manoscritti inutili', useless manuscripts.[3] Traditionally framed as a sign of Marinetti's insistence on youthfulness and generational conflict, this passage can also be interpreted as already prefiguring the end, that is, the moment upon which Futurism will have become a thing of the past, thereafter surviving only as a stack of archival manuscripts and artefacts in some new era. Right before Futurism is to meet its end here, the Futurists will encounter a phase of ferocious violence, Marinetti insisted. For as the manifesto goes on to state, he and his cohorts will not just be thrown in the dustbin. Younger artists, perhaps no longer Futurists, let alone humans – the manifesto says they will have 'hooked, predatory claws, sniffling like dogs'[4] – will come to the elders' houses and virulently slaughter them. Hence, to imagine the end of the present, or at least to appreciate the epoch of Futurism, Marinetti prefigured, we first have to envisage ourselves being killed and obliterated. Only at or from this projected point, only by imagining a future anterior that coincides with the end of life or human temporality, the meaningful nature of Futurism can become manifest.

The idea that the apocalyptic end to the epoch of the present was the condition of addressing oneself to the future constantly resurfaces in the classic avant-gardes. Quite a few Expressionists, for instance, saw the present as a mere intermediary phase pregnant with possibility, a phase that could only gain meaning in a cataclysmic temporality. In his famous 'Rede für die Zunkunft' (1919), for example, Kurt Pinthus described the present as 'a furtively receding nothing',[5] and even the ever-mild Kandinsky argued in *Über das Geistige in der Kunst* (1912) that an art which 'has no power for the future, which is only the child of the age, cannot become a mother of the future, is a barren art'.[6] The present to many avant-gardists was, in short, a nullity, a phase that awaited a calamitous overthrow. Only then would their art attain its proper functionality and value. In the meantime one of their principal tasks was to wait, to exert patience.

A most radical version of this view can be encountered in Russian Futurism. In 1913, in the Luna Park theatre in St Petersburg, the Union of Youth staged their

Pobeda nad Solntsem (Victory over the Sun). The story of this famous Futurist opera is well known – although we continue to argue over its exact tenor. A young aviator punctures the sun. The aviator, often read as a symbol of the new, the acme of the present, destroys the sun, emblem of the old forces that keep the universe from changing. By placing the destruction of the sun at the centre of the opera, Mikhail Matyushin, Aleksei Kruchenykh, Kasimir Malevich and Velimir Khlebnikov implied that to appreciate Russian Futurism as meaningful requires that we imagine the end of the present to coincide not just with our own death, but with a point beyond entropy, after the thermodynamic expiration of the universe as such. The future begins with extinction, in total darkness. The sun no longer exists. And only at this point does the new art become meaningful. All radical art begins after visibility, beyond legibility as currently coded. Indeed, it is an early version of the *Black Suprematist Square* (1915) icon that actually punctures the sun in this opera. Malevich in his later writings would go on to invite us to imagine the art of the future as being experienced on a desolated and arid land: '[Art] reaches a "desert" in which nothing can be perceived', adding, except 'feeling', a pure feeling of the materiality of art.[7]

Such reflections, when we take them at face value, tone down the naïve utopian zeal and buoyancy we usually associate with the Futurists, and the blind meliorism we attach to certain Expressionists. Instead, they accentuate the patience of the avant-gardes, an aspect we do not usually associate with them. When taken literally, many avant-gardists apparently awaited the end of times. Read allegorically, however, their projections of what on occasion resembles a post-human epoch, a world and time beyond human legibility from which their work becomes meaningful, can also be interpreted as prefiguring a different way of experiencing time and history, a temporality and historicity beyond any given understanding of history. It is worth seeing this allegorical reading through.

Historicism and realism

The intuition that the classic avant-gardes operated with a new or different notion of history is almost as old as the avant-gardes themselves. There is indeed a well-established tradition of research that in part finds its roots in the so-called Realism or Expressionism Debate as it was waged in the German-language exile journal *Das Wort* in the late 1930s,[8] but also in the work of Walter Benjamin and Frankfurt School representatives to, more recently, Jacques Derrida, Michel Foucault, Jean-François Lyotard, Gilles Deleuze, Michel Serres, Bruno Latour, Georges

Didi-Huberman, Jacques Rancière, W. T. J. Mitchell and Andreas Huyssen – all of whom have seized upon the work of the historical avant-gardes and their cognates to think differently about history. Lately, several scholars have also attempted to rethink the meaning of the term 'avant-garde' in our own seemingly post-avant-garde times. Whether we turn to Hal Foster, to Krzysztof Ziarek's conception of the avant-garde 'event-work',[9] Andrew Benjamin's reading of the 'avant-garde experience' as an 'anoriginal difference',[10] David Cunningham's understanding of the avant-garde as a concept of historical temporalization,[11] the work of Peter Osborne[12] and Susan Buck-Morss[13] – all these critics have revisited the (classic, neo- and more recent) avant-gardes' reflection on their own internal history within the last two centuries or so, in order to determine whether today, too, we could not think about the (or an) avant-garde differently, and from our contemporary point of view redraw or temporalize its history differently, or not at all.

However, all this critical energy has not led to a consensus on what the view or views of history in the avant-gardes amounted to, except perhaps in the negative. For at the risk of oversimplifying matters, all these scholars can be said to share one presupposition, namely that the avant-gardes' view of history differed from, or, better, was against, the default notion of history in historicism, and against its perceived art and literary historical extension: Realism. Admittedly, much is to be argued for this. As Hayden White reminds us, around 1900 'the term "history" had come […] to be synonymous with "reality," so much so that the phrase "historical reality" had become a pleonasm'.[14] Nowhere was this assumption as clear as in professional history. Here a variety of at times conflicting views which ranged from hypertrophic positivism to unbridled relativism, and which today we commonly lump together under the label of 'historicism', upheld that all social and cultural phenomena were determined by history, that is, by the context in which they figure. As is well known, this rather general assumption around 1900 was not characteristic of historians alone. It pervaded European culture, which in a panoply of ways prided itself on its advanced understanding and mastery of the past as it supposedly had once existed. This wider cultural interest in the past, as a real thing that had to be cherished and studied, was of course also mirrored in the emanations of Realism in the arts – the realist novel, for instance, perfectly mirrored the cultural significance attributed to the past, as its default tense was the past tense; the novel, and the *Bildungsroman* especially, thus made its readers witness to past events moving towards the future; whence also the success of the historical novel. Because reality was perceived as historical, and all that can be known for certain was the past, so, eventually, the present came to be viewed as the history of tomorrow in an ever-faster-changing world. The future, in turn, as Reinhart Koselleck has shown, came to be looked upon as a *vergange Zukunft*, a former future or future past on the way forward.[15]

To read the avant-gardes as a reaction against this dominant view of history is entirely justified. For, in part following Friedrich Nietzsche's critique of history as it was understood in the nineteenth century, the avant-gardes unmistakably assailed historicism and left the conventions of Realism behind. Yet it is perhaps less justifiable to reduce the avant-gardes' entire understanding of history to a mere after-effect of the historical emanations of Realism in the arts, and historicism in professional history. Indeed, while critics in other cases often compare the avant-gardes to a large variety of other than nineteenth-century European periods and styles, when it comes to 'history', with a few exceptions (such as Walter Benjamin's ruminations on the Baroque), we most often tend to pull the card of nineteenth-century Realism and its historiographical cognates. By so doing, we not only remain caught in a fixed set of presuppositions, if not ourselves entrenched in exclusively contextualizing and historicizing analyses of the avant-gardes. At the risk of stating the obvious, we thereby also operate with a rather narrow understanding of history, reducing it to a single, albeit supposedly 'long', century.

Polytemporality and anachronicity

That avant-garde works frequently move beyond and outside the parameters of nineteenth-century European culture is no secret. Synthetic Cubist collages or *papiers-collés* such as Picasso's visually punning and anti-illusionist *Guitare, partition, verre* (Guitar, Sheet Music, Glass, 1912, Figure 7.1), for instance, leave no doubt about the avant-gardes' departure from nineteenth-century Realist conventions. This still-life can also be read as anti-historicist, in that in defiance of Realist painting it further incorporates a newspaper snippet referencing a historical battle in part to claim a place for the everyday as constitutive of, or at least conterminous to, historicity. The moment or the present, Picasso here suggests, is always more than itself; it has the potentiality of the implex, as Paul Valéry called it in *L'idée fixe* (1932), it can go in various, albeit conditioned directions, and it belongs to all not the few. As such, this same work can also be interpreted as a response to its immediate historical context, that is, a short phase before the First World War, during which the arrival of global war still seemed a possibility, not a necessity. In addition, critics often couple this work to the brief phase in Picasso's oeuvre during the early 1910s in which he

Figure 7.1 Pablo Picasso, *Guitar, Sheet Music, Glass* (1912). Cut-and-pasted wallpaper, newspaper (*Le Journal*, 18 November 1912), sheet music, coloured paper, paper and hand-painted faux bois paper, charcoal and gouache on paperboard, 47.9 × 36.5 cm. McNay Art Museum, San Antonio. Bequest of Marion Koogler McNay © McNay Art Museum/Art Resource, NY/Scala, Florence © 2021 Succession Picasso/SABAM Belgium.

produced a whole series of works portraying stringed instruments,[16] a phase that coincidentally ended with the arrival of the Great War, thereby suggesting that the redemptive song of the guitar collage came to a close when the war began. Picasso, in sum, elevated the sign of the guitar to malleable material, turning it into a site of possibility and openness, to abandon it in the end. Yet, sitting somewhat uneasily with our historicizing and contextualizing gaze, this same sign of course also invites us to consider the enormously rich history of visual art works portraying chordophones, a history whose materiality Picasso pulls on the plank of this work as well. This history is almost boundless and reaches well beyond the Middle Ages; it also comes with a wide variety of views of the relations between past, present and future that differ at times radically from those in the nineteenth century.

The creation of 'shapes of time', as George Kubler called them,[17] the development of temporal cross-referencing complexes we encounter in Picasso's collage, is not typical of the avant-gardes alone, but of all art. Exploiting the potential of *polytemporality*, as Bruno Latour defines it,[18] that is, bringing together material or materialities with different historical origins, is indeed not only characteristic of avant-garde collages, textual experiments, assemblages or performances. Such polytemporality can also be located in, say, the plays of Shakespeare with their well-studied bricolage of building blocks and sources stemming from various periods. We can read any twenty-first-century novel as a polytemporal object – the basic narrative make-up or 'exoskeleton' of the novel[19] after all is a late eighteenth-century generic convention – and even the Realism of a Courbet, whose scandalous *Un Enterrement à Ornans* (1849–50), for instance, derived from its adoption of a genre previously reserved for the depiction of nobility, is polytemporal in this sense. Such diachronic intertextuality, as it is known in literary studies, this ability to reverse even the pro- and retentional consciousness of time, abounds in all art.

As Werner Hofmann, Alexander Nagel and others have argued, this ultimately points to the *anachronic* nature of all art, which as a rule relativizes temporal and historical distance and which follows a temporality of its own, one that can fold, bend, crack, wrinkle, split or loop the linear arrow or arrows of time, the multidimensional strip of time we commonly evoke to conceive of history.[20] This makes clear that art in whatever medium travels through time and history in ways that mostly do not mesh with the dominant view of history in the nineteenth century. Pointing at the anachronic nature of all art is not to deny that concrete art works are at the same time also situated and dated events, however. Historicization or contextualization should therefore not simply be thrown overboard. (Far from it – I will conclude on a contextualizing note myself.) Yet, if we take this anachronic aspect or material-force of art seriously, if we recognize that art is a mode of transmission that continues to produce effects into the future while also altering and changing the past, then we might also want to enquire whether the classic avant-gardes in some way stand out here as an artistic formation.

Indeed, what, if anything, did the avant-gardes make of the anachronic nature of art? And what does 'history' in these avant-gardes look like if we for a brief stint bracket our inclination to look at them as post-Realist or post-historicist, and also drop our habit of historicizing and contextualizing them? How, for instance, is history presented in a text or score such as Kurt Schwitters' *Ursonate* (1922–32)? What perspective on history is yielded by, say, László Moholy-Nagy's *Licht-Raum-Modulator* (1922–1930)? Where is history here? And where is history in Marcel Duchamp's *Le Grand verre* (1915–23)? How do these and all other so-called classic or historical avant-garde works relate or present history?

Metahistory and interchronicity

To answer the above questions, even if it were just partially, it is worth considering the view of history in the avant-gardes from a metahistorical perspective – and the prefix *meta-* is of course key here, in that it implies that we do not anchor the discourses, works and practices of the avant-gardes in any context that surrounded them. Instead, we jump straight away from an initial close reading of a work to a meta-perspective and ask how that work imagines, projects or calibrates the relationships between past, present and future, and how it considers something like a context. As Roland Barthes famously stated in his essay 'Le mythe, aujourd'hui': 'un peu de formalisme éloigne de l'Histoire, mais [...] beaucoup y ramène.'[21] This holds true in our case, too, because an attentive analysis of avant-garde works, discourses and practices does allow for some general conclusions about the nature of 'history' in the classic avant-gardes, for a different *hermeneutics* of history, we will see. In fact, when we approach the archive of works and artefacts the avant-gardes left us today as carriers of 'tertiary memory', as Bernard Stiegler defines it,[22] that is, as temporal objects or prostheses which allow us to experience history and time, it further becomes clear that we may want to revise our common view that the avant-gardes simply favoured the present or the future over the past.

Let us turn to an example: Max Ernst's *Katharina Ondulata* (1920, Figure 7.2). One of Ernst's so-called *Übermalereien* or 'overpaintings', it consists of a piece of paper on which Ernst first printed certain elements and then subsequently painted over. Its structure, in other words, is laminar or layered, and as such it can be read not just as an index, but also as a manifestation of its own construction in

Figure 7.2 Max Ernst, *Katharina Ondulata d.i. frau wirtin a.d. lahn* (1920). Gouache, pencil and ink on printed paper, 31.2 × 27 cm. Inscribed: 'Katharina ondulata d.i. frau wirtin a.d. lahn erscheint als der deutschen engelin u. perlmütter auf korksohlen im tierbild des krebses'. Scottish National Gallery of Modern Art, Edinburgh. Purchased with the support of the Heritage Lottery Fund and the Art Fund 1995. © Scala, Florence © 2021 SABAM Belgium.

time. Evoking a landscape of sorts, its motives are dazzling. Centre right we see a mountain, which is actually named: it is an almost verist drawing of Mount Fuji on the Japanese island of Honsu, the tallest mountain of the country, an iconic piece of *japonisme*, and, notably, a volcano. This motif is further elaborated at the bottom, where we appear to be confronted with a cross-cut of geological or techtonic layers, the top crust of which consists of the volcano. These layers or strata are interesting as one of them contains a signature and a date: 'Max Ernst, 20'. As other layers find themselves on top of this one, it is difficult to resist reading this work as a projection of some future. This is, at some point in the future, how the world will look. An accretion of strata, the landmass at the bottom is anything but uniform. It evokes processes of metallization, crystallization, dissolution and saturation. The blue layers of water, and above all the red dotted section bottom left, further hint at a process of liquefaction that is still evolving. Yet there is little happening, it seems. This work invites us to be patient, and, while being patient, to consider how things came about, how they can be un-happened, scraped off, again and again, layer after layer – as Ernst himself would come to do elsewhere through the technique of *grattage*.

Of course, taking the differently coloured zones at the bottom for geological strata implies that we also undo Euclidean perspective, and simply look at this work as evoking a flat surface foregrounding its own materiality. When, alternatively, we look at this landscape as having depth, then these are not strata, but a river, a lake or even a sea, surrounded by differently coloured patches of land that remove themselves further from us one after the other. In this case, however, we no longer find ourselves in the future, but in the now, the present.

It is at this critical junction or folding of temporalities, at a point upon which the past becomes visible from the future and the present from the past, that at the centre we find two entities, left and right, both of which suggest a sense of dynamism.[23] To the right, on a pedestal, a zigzagging arrow-construction. Just like the faux-bois layer or zone at the bottom, this in part mechanomorphic shape consists of man-made remnants: tubes, wall-papered matter, a set of flags. The figure suggests dynamism in two ways. First, through a process of excretion. Out of the blue tube far right pulverized material is ejected, the dust-like matter landing on Mount Fuji and thus the whole contraption apparently transforming the landscape over time. Second, the faux-bois pedestal finds itself on water; perhaps what we are seeing is not something static, but a figure in the process of moving and floating by. This tension between movement and stasis, time evolving and standing still, is further emphasized by the zigzagging shape of the arrow-like member. If what we are witnessing is a cross-cut of geological strata, however, then all this figure does, it seems, is to displace land (as the picture as a whole seems to be doing as well), while being stuck in the ground.

To the left we find an organic shape or figure, perhaps set in motion by the feathery insect or caterpillar-like creature tied to the blue cog. A *vulva dentata* – if we extend the title's assonance and take the Katharina of this title as a reference to Catherine the Great – or the opposite, an emblem of chastity – when we interpret the same Katharina as a reference to the saintly Catherine of Alexandria – this 'female' figure as well is engaged in an act of excretion. Unlike the 'male' figure on the right, whose labour seems to yield something *informe*, an ash-like un-form, the 'female' figure produces form. For the cinders 'she' produces form a stone or bone-like statue, a work in progress that clearly introduces something new into this landscape and does not just displace it. Whether this new life or entity is rooted in the past, buried under layers of ground, or whether it is completely visible in the now, in its turn excreting a substance that yet again takes on a red un-form, is not to be determined. Yet together these three figures (the 'male' land displacer, the 'female' creator of form and the statue-like 'child' excreting a substance) do suggest a cyclical process. This further upsets any attempt to place or locate this tableau in time.

This work holds much more secrets. Constellations of stars in the sky, for instance, introduce an astrological temporality, a cosmological sense of time, if not an eternity that renders the difference between past, present, future irrelevant. The 'male' shape, with the ladder leading to its top, also intimates the Cross, suggesting we are long past the morning of deposition, perhaps even long past Apocalypse. The mention of waves in the work's title alludes to Greek mythology and to Hercules more specifically. If we take the organic life-form in the 'female' figure to resemble a crab, this figure might actually be a portion of Hercules, as he got pinched in the toe by a crab sent by Hera.[24] It is an estranging state, to say the least, that this late Dada work allows us a glimpse of, and we could easily interpret it in a variety of ways. In fact, the work explicitly invites us to do so. The text at the bottom reads: 'Undulating Katharina, i.e., mistress of the inn on the Lahn appears as guardian angel and mother-of-pearl of the Germans on cork soles in the zodiac sign of cancer.' The expression 'mistress of the inn on the Lahn' is the first line of a popular schoolboy song, which is of a type that can be extended indefinitely with the addition of new verses. As such it is also a reference to the openness of interpretation of this image.

Crucial to observe, however, is that this openness rests on the temporal indeterminacy of the work. Like any piece of art or writing, this is an anachronic work that moves through time freely by the connections and references it makes through art and cultural history. It is also manifestly polytemporal, in that it is clearly a work composed of remnants of human labour: wallpaper, cogs, etc. Yet its most important building block is time, that is, it collates culturally coded objects and themes associated with time in an assemblage or *agencement* that resists decoding and territorialization in a Deleuzian sense. For *Katharina Ondulata* allows us to simultaneously see the past, the present and the future, and forces upon us a hermeneutical point of entry to all three without determining their relations. Thus, it conditions us as interpreters to recalibrate these relations ourselves. It does not, significantly, push us outside of its temporal universe; it cannot in a way, as this is a work made of time. Rather, it places us in-between past, present and future, and as such it is also *interchronic*, making us see a phase of pre- and posthistory at once, a point upon which even the future and the past can be regarded as imbricated, the future taking place before the past. The metahistorical view or conception of history to emerge from *Katharina Ondulata* is thus anything but a stable one, as the interchronic nature of the work demands from us that we contemplate and try to experience a variety of temporalities and forms of historicity at once.

Interchronicity in context

Katharina Ondulata's interchronicity does not stand alone in the archive of the classic avant-gardes. Different yet cognate instances of interchronicity proliferate in the works and practices of these avant-gardes. We encounter such instances in the various points of entry or perspectives analytic Cubist works enforce upon us at the same time, in the space between the three- and four-dimensional worlds evoked by Duchamp's *Grand verre*, in the Metaphysical painting of De Chirico or the massive turn to objects in surrealism, and in the colour theory, in part inspired by Chevreul, of the Simultanéiste Robert Delaunay, with its implied suspension between the states of seeing and non-seeing, as in the act of awakening and opening one's eyes. In fact, all instances we usually describe as emanations of *simultaneity* appear to have been developed to effect interchronicity. When, for example, Tristan Tzara, Marcel Janco and Richard Huelsenbeck devised their so-called simultaneous poem 'L'Amiral cherche une maison à louer' (1916), what was at stake was perhaps not so much the depiction of several things unravelling at the same time. At stake, rather, was the opening of a hermeneutical point of entry in time and history, a moment-in-between

History in the European avant-gardes   153

all of these different temporalities and trajectories that conditions the reader, viewer or listener to experience this simultaneity.

Interchronicity also surfaces in many other practices, protocols and procedures developed by the avant-gardes. The exploration of unmotivated

Figure 7.3 Sophie Täuber & Hans Arp, *Untitled* (Duo-Collage, 1918). Paper, board and silver leaf on board, 82 × 62 cm. © bpk, Nationalgalerie, Staatliche Museen zu Berlin, Jörg P. Anders © 2021 SABAM Belgium.

action and chance operations, for instance, provided avant-gardists themselves with a vantage point from which to experience an aperture in time, a moment that opened, and permitted them to tinker with, what comes before and after, what causes what and what changes what – chance operations after all suspend the present and anticipate a renewed future understanding of the past. Also in the exercise of geometric abstraction by the avant-gardes the interchronic stands out, in that it is most frequently the equality of geometric elements in time that is thematized in such grid-like works. Indeed, however we approach Hans Arp's and Sophie Täuber's duo-collage (Figure 7.3), for instance, it refuses to establish or fix a before, now and after, past, present or future. Its visual rhythm is created, foregrounded even, by glitches and intervals, by the interchangeability of non-identical matter in time. (Paul Klee, in his Bauhaus *Pädagogisches Skizzenbuch* (1925), would bring these insights to full bloom a few years later.)

Manifested by all of these cases – and given world and time many more could be added – is, first of all, that the classic avant-gardes *actively* seized upon the potential of the anachronic nature of art in general to forge or impose a multitude of experiences of time and views of history on an audience. Second, these cases thereby also illustrate that it is perhaps oversimplifying to claim that the avant-gardes adhered to a generic futurism or a shared presentism. Isolating one or several dominant regimes of historicity hides that at bottom the avant-gardes were perhaps indifferent to any hierarchy or stratification among past, present and future. To them, there was no ontological primacy of the present or future over the past. Yet neither was the past to be endowed with authority over today or tomorrow. This indifference might be interpreted as proof of an a- or antihistorical stance after all, but the actual knowledge of history produced by such aesthetic experiments becomes rather clear when we return to the context in which it was produced.

Let us go back to where we began: the avant-gardes' patience in the wake of historicism and Realism. If historicism means that context is key, then not just Leopold von Ranke's work, but also Oswald Spengler's speculative ruminations on the nature of two millennia of civilization were historicist – Spengler just worked with a different ontology of context. So did Giambattista Vico, whose work regained new prominence in the early 1910s, or the Earl of Birkenhead, whose *The World in 2030 A.D.* (1930), illustrated by former Vorticist Edward McKnight Kauffer, simply invented a context for wild conjectures about future global history. While the avant-gardes were developing their interchronic time assemblages, there was, in short, no dearth of philosophical, scientific, historiographical, cosmological and ideological context-models. Laws, rhythms, patterns, they were seen everywhere. Theories and philosophies of history and time of the widest possible variety became weapons also in political debates over the legitimation of power. On its own terms, Carl Einstein observed in his study *Georges Braque* (1934), historicism thus incited a 'vacation from causality'.[25]

Anti-historicism, as David Myers has argued,[26] thereby began a history of its own, not least in the sphere of religion, where the sprawling of contexts was felt to lead to a complete overhaul of eternal truths and values. The avant-gardes, in all of this, were a minor voice. Yet not within the history of the arts. Aware of the fact that reality could only be seen as a context by their contemporaries, and that those defining the right context most convincingly could also lay claim to power, they exploited art's given anachronic nature to the full in time assemblages that derailed the basic presuppositions of contextual logic. For when neither the past nor the present nor the future can be shown to have ontological primacy, if even determining which of these age-old temporal units comes first proves impossible, then little remains of 'context', and a truly different understanding of history takes off. Indeed, avant-gardists of all isms portrayed themselves as the 'primitives' of a new era to come, but this new era was not located in some distant future or in a new social or political context to come. It would begin with history beyond history. Until then patience was key.

Today, in our own, so-called post-avant-garde times, claims abound about the 'historical turn', 'the temporal turn', the fascination, both conceptual and artistic, with 'the contemporary': these are all said to be typical of our current predicament in the arts. Perhaps the classic avant-gardes' patience is soon to be awarded, and a *chronoaesthetics* that further explores their experiments with temporality and historicity across the arts will finally be developed.

Notes

1 Renato Poggioli, *The Theory of the Avant-Garde*, trans. Gerald Fitzgerald (Cambridge, MA: The Belknap Press of the Harvard University Press, 1968), 68–74. Compare Marjorie Perloff's *The Futurist Moment: Avant-Garde, Avant Guerre, and the Language of Rupture* (Chicago, Illinois: University of Chicago Press, 1986).

2 François Hartog, *Régimes d'historicité. Présentisme et expériences du temps* (Paris: Seuil, 2003). Compare, among others, Maria Stavrinaki's study *Dada Presentism. An Essay on Art and History*, trans. Daniela Ginsburg (Stanford, CA: Stanford University Presss, 2016).

3 F. T. Marinetti, 'Fondazione e Manifesto del Futurismo', in *Teoria e invenzione futurista*, ed. Luciano De Maria (Milan: Mondadori, 1968), 13.

4   F. T. Marinetti, 'The Foundation and Manifesto of Futurism', in F.T. Marinetti, *Critical Writings*, ed. Günter Berghaus, trans. Doug Thomson (New York: Farrar, Straus and Giroux, 2006), 16.

5   Kurt Pinthus, 'Rede für die Zukunft', in *Die Erhebung: Jahrbuch für neue Dichtung und Wertung*, ed. Alfred Wolfenstein (Berlin 1919), 1, 411; cited in translation from Stavrinaki, *Dada Presentism*, 8.

6   Wassily Kandinsky, *Concerning the Spiritual in Art*, rev. ed., trans. M. T. H. Sadler (London: Dover, 2012), 19.

7   Kasimir Malevich, 'Suprematism' (1927), in *Modern Artists on Art*, ed. Robert L. Herbert (Englewood Cliffs, NJ: Prentice-Hall, 1964), 94.

8   For a collection of these materials, see Hans-Jürgen Schmitt (ed.), *Die Expressionismusdebatte; Materialen zu einer marxistischen Realismuskonzeption* (Frankfurt: Suhrkamp, 1973). This debate has been revisited time and again, becoming one of the most vexed yet perhaps also most inconclusive international controversies of twentieth-century intellectual life.

9   Krzysztof Ziarek, *The Historicity of Experience: Modernity, the Avant-Garde, and the Event* (Evanston: Northwestern University Press, 2001), 3–21. See also Ziarek's *The Force of Art* (Stanford, CA: Stanford University Press, 2004).

10 Andrew Benjamin, *Art, Mimesis and the Avant-garde: Aspects of a Philosophy of Difference* (London: Routledge, 1991), especially 1–5.

11 See *inter Alia*, David Cunningham, 'Architecture, Utopia and the Futures of the Avant-Garde', *The Journal of Architecture* 6, no. 2 (2001): 169–82; 'A Time for Dissonance and Noise: On Adorno, Music, and the Concept of Modernism', *Angelaki* 8, no. 1 (2003): 61–74; 'The Futures of Surrealism: Hegelianism, Romanticism, and the Avant-Garde', *SubStance* 34, no. 2 (2005): 47–65.

12 Peter Osborne, *The Politics of Time: Modernity and Avant-Garde* (London: Verso, 1995; 2nd ed. 2011), ix–x, 1–5, 13–16, 23.

13 Susan Buck-Morss, 'Revolutionary Time: The Vanguard and the Avant-Garde', in *Benjamin Studien/Studies: Perception and Experience in Modernity*, ed. Helga Geyer-Ryan (Amsterdam: Rodopi, 2002), 209–25; *Dreamworld and Catastrophe: The Passing of Mass Utopia in East and West* (Cambridge, MA: MIT Press, 2000).

14 Hayden White, 'Modernism and the Sense of History', *Journal of Art Historiography* 15 (2016): 1–15.

15 Reinhart Koselleck, *Vergangene Zukunft. Zur Semantik geschichtlicher Zeiten* (Frankfurt a/Main: Suhrkamp, 1979).

16 See, among others, David Cottington's still excellent analysis in 'What the Papers Say: Politics and Ideology in Picasso's Collages of 1912', *Art Journal* 47, no. 4 (1988), 350–9.

17 George Kubler, *The Shape of Time. Remarks on the History of Things* (New Haven: Yale University Press, 1962).

18 Bruno Latour, *Nous n'avons jamais été modernes: Essai d'anthropologie symétrique* (Paris: La Découverte, 1991). Compare also Michel Serres, *Eclaircissements. Cinq entretiens avec Bruno Latour* (Paris: François Bourin, 1992), where Serres launches the term 'polychronicity' to refer to the same phenomenon.
19 I borrow this metaphor from Fredric Jameson, *The Political Unconscious, Narrative as a Socially Symbolical Act* (London: Methuen, 1981).
20 Werner Hofmann, *Die Moderne im Rückblick. Hauptwege der Kunstgeschichte* (München: Beck, 1998); Alexander Nagel, *Medieval Modern: Art Out of Time* (London: Thames and Hudson, 2012).
21 Roland Barthes, *Mythologies* (Paris: Editions du Seuil, 1957), 184.
22 Bernard Stiegler, *Technics and Time, 1: The Fault of Epimetheus*, trans. R. Beardsworth and G. Collins (Stanford: Stanford University Press, 1998).
23 For a reading of this work that also compares it to similar experiments by Francis Picabia and Man Ray, see: Diana Walden, 'Max Ernst', in the Catalogue *Max Ernst. A Retrospective* (New York: The Solomon R. Guggenheim Foundation, 1975), 15–61, especially 25–6.
24 For a more elaborate discussion of this work's astrological references and allusions to Greek mythology, see John J. Hatch, 'Desire, Heavenly Bodies, and a Surrealist's Fascination with the Celestial Theatre', *Culture and Cosmos* 8, nos. 1–2 (2004), 87–106.
25 Carl Einstein, *Werke—Berliner Ausgabe, Band 3: 1929–1940*, ed. Hermann Haarmann et al. (Berlin: Fannei & Walz, 1996), 299, my translation.
26 David N. Myers, *Resisting History. Historicism and Its Discontents in German-Jewish Thought* (New Jersey: Princeton University Press, 2003).

8

Clement Greenberg's modernism: Historicizable or ahistorical?

Rahma Khazam

'We have never been modern,'[1] claimed Bruno Latour, on the grounds that modernity's distinction between nature and culture was never as watertight as it was made out to be. The same may be said, I will argue, about the conventional perception of modernism as ahistorical: like the nature/culture distinction, modernism's claim to ahistoricity was not truly watertight either. If modernism has indeed never been truly or solely timeless or ahistorical, just as we have never been truly modern, then it may be historicized and connected to the broader context of the political, social and scientific developments of its time. In my essay, I will explore this claim in relation to Clement Greenberg's modernism, which can and has been contextualized historically, despite the latter's emphasis on its autonomy and timelessness. I will also consider the historicism/ahistoricity dichotomy in relation to movements or worldviews that preceded or followed Greenberg's modernism. My intention is to show not only that some of these movements have more in common with Greenberg's modernism than it might initially appear, but also that the issue of ahistoricity vs. historicism is a fundamental distinction that crops up in different guises throughout the history of artistic modernism and beyond – leading to inconsistencies and contradictions that question the divisions it implies. First, I highlight its recurrence in Greenberg's modernism, then its re-emergence in analyses of the contemporary, and finally, I show how a similar dichotomy pervaded earlier modern movements. Just as the purifying practice of modernity exists alongside nature/culture hybrids in Latour's scheme, so do Greenbergian modernism's purifying and ahistoricizing practices likewise go hand in hand with its historicization and proximity to certain non-modern approaches to time.

Greenberg's modernism

The issue of timelessness vs. historicity loomed large in Greenberg's modernism, linking up with related binaries such as purity and autonomy vs. context and continuity: indeed, ahistoricity, purity and autonomy all presuppose distance and aloofness with respect to historical and contextual concerns. Yet Greenberg was unable to keep the two sides of these dichotomies apart: he co-opted all these notions into his articles on modernist painting in an ongoing dialectic that was never fully resolved. For example, he argued in favour of the continuity, and therefore historicization, of modernist art in his article 'Modernist Painting' (1960–5): 'Modernism has never meant anything like a break with the past. It may mean a devolution, an unraveling of anterior tradition, but it also means its continuation.'[2] Indeed, Greenberg needed this continuity to legitimate his approach to modernist painting, as he himself admitted, noting that modernist painting would not be worthy of its name if it did not take into account art's past and the standards of quality on which it was based.[3]

Yet at the same time, Greenberg's position was ahistoricist: he argued that each art had to ascertain the effect that was uniquely and durably associated with it through a process of narrowing and reduction.[4] Michael Fried acknowledged this ahistoricity: 'Dispensable conventions were progressively discarded until [...] one arrived at a kind of timeless, irreducible core (in painting, flatness and the delimitation of flatness). The implication of this account was that such a core had been the essence of painting all along, a view that seemed to me ahistorical.'[5] Yet, as James Meyer emphasizes, in 'Art and Objecthood' ([1967] 2003), Fried not only rejected minimalism but also asserted his independence from that ahistoricity:[6] in that essay, Fried wrote that flatness and its delimitation should be regarded not as 'the "irreducible essence of pictorial art" but [...] the *minimal conditions for something's being seen as a painting*; and that the crucial question is not what these minimal and, so to speak, timeless conditions are, but rather what, at a given moment, is capable [...] of succeeding as painting'.[7] As Fried showed, Greenberg's ahistoricism was hard to defend.

A similar dialectic pervaded Greenberg's reflections on the subject of medium-specificity: he ascribed purity and autonomy to modernist painting, while nonetheless allowing it to incorporate historical or methodological references that were foreign to it. For instance, in 'Avant-Garde and Kitsch' (1939), Greenberg foregrounded the need to exclude everything extraneous to painting: 'Picasso, Braque [...] derive their chief inspiration from the medium they work in. The excitement of their art seems to lie [...] in its pure preoccupation with the invention and arrangement of spaces, surfaces, shapes, colors, etc., to the exclusion of whatever is not necessarily implicated in these factors.'[8] In 'Modernist Painting', he likewise emphasized the importance of eliminating any quality that might belong to another art: 'The task of self-criticism became to eliminate from the effects of each art any and every effect that might conceivably be borrowed from or by the medium of any other art. Thereby each art would be rendered "pure", and in its "purity" find the guarantee [...] of its independence.'[9] For Greenberg, it was especially important to eliminate the effects of sculpture, and particularly its three-dimensionality, of which painting needed to be entirely free if it was to ensure its autonomy.[10]

Yet despite his repeated insistence on purity and autonomy, Greenberg nonetheless engaged with historical and methodological references pertaining to other disciplines. In 'Towards a Newer Laocoon' (1940), he recommended borrowing the method of music, insofar as it was an art that could only be conceived in terms of the sense of hearing: 'Only by [...] defining each of the other arts solely in the terms of the sense or faculty which perceived its effect and by excluding [...] whatever is intelligible in the terms of any other sense [...] would the non-musical arts attain the "purity" and self-sufficiency which they desired.'[11] Greenberg claimed to be merely borrowing the method of music rather than its effects, yet even this contravenes his requirement that each art should exclude whatever was intelligible to any other sense.

Another way in which Greenbergian modernism allowed itself to be shaped by external influences – thereby once again contradicting its claims to timelessness – was through its deliberate non-engagement with political events, non-engagement being a political position in itself. Benjamin Buchloh accounts for Greenberg's disidentification with the trauma of the Second World War in the following terms: 'Either you confront that history or you don't. And if you don't, it's easier to claim access to a new identity-formation in relation to American liberal-democratic culture: that lies at the foundation of the new painting in New York as well.'[12] The horror of the Second World War was clearly out of place in the context of the affirmative post-war modernist narrative that Greenberg was putting together – a narrative of renewal that, as Hal Foster suggests, institutions in this period of reconstruction wanted to hear.[13] The potential links between the traumatic history of the Second World War and Greenberg's modernism considerably weaken the latter's claim to ahistoricity.

Above and beyond its connections to politics or music however, it was Greenberg's repeated involvement with science that most undermined his claim to autonomy and ahistoricity. For example, he evoked a parallel between painting and scientific methodology, as he had done with music: 'That visual art should confine itself exclusively to what is given in visual experience [...] is a notion whose only justification lies, notionally, in scientific consistency. Scientific method alone asks that a situation be resolved in exactly the same kind of terms as that in which it is presented.'[14] Yet in the case of science he went a step further, noting that its convergence with art was based on historical and cultural affinities: 'From the point of view of art itself its convergence of spirit with science happens to be a mere accident [...] What their convergence does show, however, is the degree to which Modernist art belongs to the same historical and cultural tendency as modern science.'[15]

There were even closer affinities between Greenberg's modernism and the history and culture of science. In her book *Eyesight Alone* (2005), Caroline A. Jones makes significant connections between Greenberg's theories and the scientific culture that was permeating everyday life in the United States at the time, noting that in Greenberg's writing, abstract art was to occupy spaces already opened up by scientific discourse.[16] The testable, normative criteria he sought to apply to painting were an example of this: 'Was a particular painting its own kind of pictorial "fact," or did it seem to rely on some other art form for its effects? Did it exhibit illusionism (bad) or rigorously exclude it (good)? Was it "illustrative" or self-reflexive? Did it appropriately acknowledge the means of its own production?'[17] Even more telling are the parallels Jones draws between Greenberg's focus on vision and 'opticality', and technological developments such as hi-fi. Hi-fi was one instance of the segmenting of the senses resulting from the processes of rationalization spreading across mid-century United States, and just as hi-fi targeted the ear, so did Greenberg's modernism target the eye. As Jones writes: 'The "culture" being authenticated was pre-eminently the acoustic culture of the "dead" room (and the white cube) [...] Hi-fidelity listeners created their own fiercely separate world, as intensely regulated as Greenberg's optical one, for the purposes of entering a similarly purified and artificial acoustical regime.'[18]

Convergences between modernist painting, technology and science also took place on the level of the works themselves. As Jones observes, scientists were taking human movements apart, using photographic technologies to transform them into measurable fragments, and a number of artists followed these developments.[19] She points in particular to the formal connection, first made by Jeremy Lewison, between the left–right walk of the figure in Thomas Eakins's Marey-inspired photographs of human movement from 1884 and the left–right movement of the figures in Jackson Pollock's *Mural* (1943).[20] For

Jones, Pollock's *Mural* 'fueled Greenberg's desire to ordinate the senses through a programme of rationalized body disciplines that could integrate industrial labour into modernist décor. Cubist geometries and segmented movement were both aspects of the march of industrial progress'.[21] *Mural* thereby testified to the links between Greenberg's modernism and the socio-historical developments of its time.

Greenberg even went so far as to use the term positivism, although he did not appear to have engaged seriously with it.[22] Nineteenth-century positivism as developed by the philosopher Auguste Comte was based on the premise that observation, experiment and the scientific method constituted the means of attaining truth, yet as Jones observes, 'Greenberg's repetitive, vernacular invocation [...] somehow summoned these tenets without concern for their philosophical rigor. Positivism, in this context, is signified by a set of reading protocols in which the "disinterested" objective observer measures sense-data against testable criteria'.[23] Greenberg's use of positivism nonetheless reinforced modernism's links with science.

To the extent that his brand of modernism was positivist, investigative and quasi-scientific, it was also a break with the art of his predecessors. According to Jones, Kandinsky and Rothko emphasized the spiritual dimension of their art, whereas Greenberg did the opposite: 'Nonobjective painting and sculpture, in his writing, became comprehensible – not in terms of "the spirit," that nineteenth-century ideal, but as deeply related to rationalization, efficiency, and the rapidly industrializing public sphere.'[24] In other words, Greenberg replaced the quest for the spiritual by verifiable criteria, jeopardizing art's purity as well as its ahistoricity, by allowing it to reflect the scientific and economic developments of its time.

Greenberg's continual vacillations make the question as to whether modernist painting was truly ahistorical, pure or autonomous hard to answer. It would appear that the new painting was a quest for a timeless purity, for works that obeyed their own laws and logic but nonetheless borrowed from other disciplines or were legitimated by the art of the past, and so not entirely autonomous or ahistorical after all. Indeed, as he himself admitted in his essay 'Detached Observations' (1976): '"Purity" of and in art [...] is an illusory notion, of course. It may be remotely conceivable or imaginable, but it can't be realized [...] All the same, for Western art in its Modernist phase "purity" has been a useful idea and ideal.'[25] Greenberg thus juxtaposed the ahistorical, purity and autonomy with consideration of historical, social or political developments: in other words, modernist painting was both timeless and of its time, and these two characteristics coexisted alongside one another in an undecidable ongoing interplay.

In view of the above, we may conclude that it is impossible to enforce a strict separation between historicization and the ahistorical in modernist art, just as, in Latour's scheme, nature and culture cannot be kept apart. Indeed, for Latour the term 'modern' refers to two different types of practices that need to be considered in isolation from one another if they are to retain their validity: the first operates by means of 'translation', producing nature/culture hybrids that link together such factors as the composition of the atmosphere and scientific strategies, whereas the second operates by purification, distinguishing sharply between human and nonhuman, society and nature.[26] The first is essential to the second, for if there were no hybrids, there would be no need for separation. As Latour notes: 'So long as we consider these two practices of translation and purification separately, we are truly modern [...] As soon as we direct our attention simultaneously to the work of purification and the work of hybridization, we immediately stop being wholly modern, and our future begins to change.'[27]

We might make a similar point about Greenberg's modernism. Greenberg may be said to have been truly modern when he concerned himself with such issues as autonomy and ahistoricization, but as soon as he began to associate the historical and the ahistorical, he ceased to be entirely modern, paving the way for a different future in which these oppositions could disappear. As the next section will show, however, they have not entirely disappeared but continue to exert an impact on critical thinking about art up until today.

Post-Greenberg

Commonly defined as an art of the present,[28] the contemporary is likewise marked by the ahistoricity/historicization dichotomy. Not only do certain theorists of the contemporary shed new light on the distinction, but they also warrant consideration insofar as they refute or support Greenberg's thinking. At one extreme, Lionel Ruffel (2015) eschews modernism's ethos of separation and division, emphasizing that the contemporary exposes the modern for what it is, an ideology premised on sequentiality that views time as a unidirectional linear sequence.[29] Rejecting the assumption that the contemporary is just the newest stage or sequence in this time-line and so merely follows on from the modern, he proposes that the contemporary suspends the notion that time is an arrow: 'It reconnects with what time is: heterogeneous, a mixture, whether on a subjective or a collective level. In this sense the contemporary really is [...] not modern or a-modern [...] It is another mode of being in time, in history, in the world.'[30] For Ruffel, who defines the flow of modern time in terms of a coherent whole, that whole no longer exists, for the non-modern human multitudes have torn it apart.[31]

Ruffel claims that the contemporary includes all other representational systems and is thus transhistorical, proceeding not by sequentiality but by superimposition and thus including the modern within it.[32] The contemporary is thus premised on the layering of highly diverse temporalities and experiences.[33] Referencing Benjamin, Ruffel goes so far as to posit the co-temporality in the present of all historical eras, offering an 'archaeological' approach that allows the remains of the past to be read in the present, while eschewing detachment in favour of an engagement with everyday life.[34]

Whereas Ruffel's definition of the contemporary contradicts Greenberg's position on nearly every count, Giorgio Agamben reinstates disengagement and separation in his essay 'What Is the Contemporary?' [2008]. Agamben writes: 'Those who are truly contemporary, who truly belong to their time, are those who neither perfectly coincide with it nor adjust themselves to its demands [...] But precisely [...] through this disconnection and this anachronism, they are more capable than others of perceiving and grasping their own time.'[35] As Ruffel himself notes, Agamben's formulation of the contemporary is a counter-model to his: premised on distance and disconnection, it eschews direct engagement with daily life, adopting a detachment akin to the modern.[36]

Yet in the final analysis the difference between Ruffel and Agamben may not be as great as Ruffel thinks. Agamben's contemporary constitutes 'an ahistorical concept; not a label of periodization, but an existential marker',[37] and as such, it elicits comparison with Ruffel. For as mentioned earlier, Ruffel's contemporary also rejects a purely historical perspective: it is premised instead on the superimposition or co-temporality of all historical eras, thereby questioning the centrality of sequentiality, chronology and periodization in the writing of history and, as a result, the very possibility of history itself.

Likewise contesting the modern approach, Terry Smith's *The Contemporary Condition: The Contemporary Composition* (2016) contrasts the work of Gertrude Stein with contemporary composition: 'Stein composes by writing a composition about explaining artistic composition that not only articulates a modernist argument about what it is to compose, but which also becomes, in itself, a model of a modernist literary composition.'[38] Contemporary composition, on the other hand, is concerned with place making, world picturing and connectivity, thereby transcending notions of style or ideology.[39] It may be divided into three contemporaneous currents, the remodernist tendency that reverts to modernist, postmodern and late modernist art, a second current based on critical nationalist and identitarian perspectives and a third consisting of small-scale, do-it-yourself initiatives concerned with precarity or futurity.[40] Yet here too, the simultaneity of these currents and the juxtaposition of different temporalities transcends the sequentiality of periodization, chronology and history in general, and may thus be described as ahistorical. In other words, despite the differences between them, the definitions of the contemporary formulated by Ruffel, Smith and Agamben function ahistorically: by avoiding sequentiality or periodization, they attain Greenberg's stated, but unrealized aim.

The post-contemporary, on the other hand, retains a sequential conception of time. Contesting the modernist perception according to which the past, present and future follow on from one another, it proposes that it is the future, and not the past, that shapes the present. The future thus becomes the main principle for structuring time and provides the impetus for the new. Armen Avanessian writes: 'Concrete examples [...] are phenomena that usually start with the prefix "pre," like preemptive strikes, preemptive policing, the preemptive personality [...] What happens in the present is based on a preemption of the future.'[41]

Yet despite the challenges the post-contemporary presents to modernism, there are nonetheless commonalities between them. For a start, the prefix 'post' in post-contemporary recalls the sequentiality of the modern, even though in the post-contemporary it is the future that has priority. In the second place, both the post-contemporary and modernism are future-oriented. The post-contemporary emphasizes the hegemony of the future over the present, thereby invalidating the contemporary, as Avanessian observes: 'The logic of the contemporary with its fixation on the present – [...] this presentism has difficulties or even completely fails in dealing with the logic of being constituted by the future.'[42]

Greenberg's modernism also had to do with the future: insofar it was teleologically determined, it was constituted and pre-defined by the goal of flatness, such that its future could be said to have pre-empted its present as well as its past. The successive generations of modernist painters who tested and experimented with painting's norms[43] may thus be retrospectively regarded as having contributed to its ongoing goal. In his article 'Towards a Newer Laocoon', Greenberg noted the shifts within art history from imitation to abstraction and from tonality to primary colours, shifts that were historically explicable but also goal-oriented, pointing inexorably forward: 'The history of avant-garde painting is that of a progressive surrender to the resistance of its medium [...] The picture plane itself grows shallower and shallower, flattening out and pressing together the fictive planes of depth until they meet as one upon the [...] surface of the canvas.'[44] Somewhat like the post-contemporary, Greenberg's modernism was determined by developments that were yet to come, by a future that was brought to bear on events that had already taken place in the past.

We may conclude from this brief and necessarily incomplete survey of the relation between contemporary and modern that because of its sequentiality, Greenberg's modernism could not be truly ahistorical – and that it has more affinities with the post-contemporary than the contemporary. As such, it is not so much turned towards the present as obsessed with the future. This fixation on progress and developments to come likewise confirms that it was never entirely timeless or ahistorical.

Pre-Greenberg

The ahistorical/historicist dichotomy also plays itself out in the modern movements prior to Greenberg, highlighting the context and background in relation to which the latter's views developed and generating, as in the case of the contemporary, overlaps, contradictions and inconsistencies between the different theorists of the modern. At one extreme, the art historian Catherine Grenier argues in favour of modern art's ahistoricity and autonomy. Pointing out that all modern artists take an interest in the distant or ancient past, she notes that the German expressionists were continually referencing the Middle Ages and children's drawings, while the Russians were fascinated by vernacular styles, and that recalling the origins of art was a trait all these artists shared with other modern art movements from Cobra to abstract expressionism.[45] Indeed, for Grenier, this same openness to the past characterizes the work of artists from Matisse and Duchamp to Picabia and Beckmann, and defines it more satisfactorily than the idea of the rejection of the past, a goal that is all too often attributed to modern art.[46] Her views thus echo those of Greenberg, to the extent that she emphasizes continuity and the past of art.

As much as Greenberg, albeit on different grounds, Grenier defends modern art's lack of political engagement, arguing that art historians have mistakenly linked the desire for political and social change that marked the late nineteenth and early twentieth centuries with the concurrent revolution in art – to the point where it has become just about impossible to extricate art from the humanist project of remedying political inadequacies.⁴⁷ For those who mistakenly link art and politics, the modern revolution was a failure, a historical event like so many others, and in the same way, modern art has become just another style that has had its day. However Grenier herself resists this interpretation, emphasizing that the advent of modern art has to be viewed in isolation from politics and thus as ahistorical.⁴⁸ After all, neither Duchamp nor Apollinaire held progressive political views: they engaged with modern art on an artistic level,⁴⁹ as was also the case of the artists Greenberg championed.

Indeed, for Grenier, modern art is inherently apolitical, for it was not so much a revolution as a kind of revelation. Drawing on the writings of the literary theorist Hans Robert Jauss, she posits that the old and the new are not two different time frames, nor does the old give rise to the new. Instead, the old contains the premise of the new, which itself encompasses the old.⁵⁰ Accordingly, modern artists such as Matisse or Picasso described their experience as a revelation or realization, but not in terms of a political or social upheaval.⁵¹ On this reading, the modern art movements prior to Greenberg, like Greenberg's modernism itself, appear to be disconnected from political and historical time.

Yet Grenier fails to take into account those modern artists who were politically engaged. In this, she resembles Greenberg. At the other extreme from Grenier and Greenberg, Colin Trodd points out: 'It should come as no surprise that Greenberg's model of modernism found no place for Dada, surrealism and constructivism, all of which sought [...] to generate visions of social and cultural emancipation. In all three cases modernism involved disputing and contesting the shape and nature of modern society.'⁵² Dada, surrealism and constructivism did, however, find a place in Peter Bürger's historical avant-garde, which rejected the notion of the autonomy of art in favour of the integration of art and life.

Alexei Penzin likewise rejects the ahistoricism of Greenberg's model in favour of the historicized, politically oriented model of modernism defended by the avant-garde. In 'The Biopolitics of the Soviet Avant-Garde', he highlights the anti-autonomous stance of certain modern art movements, explicitly referencing Peter Bürger's distinction between modernism and the avant-garde – according to which modernism is viewed in the context of the institutionalization of art's autonomy, and the avant-garde as contesting the notion of autonomy.⁵³ As Penzin states, analogous dualisms have been formulated by other thinkers, for example, Benjamin's concept of *Jetztzeit* – a time of revolutionary possibility opposed to the homogeneity of chronological time – or the notion of the two modernities put forward by Antonio Negri and Michael Hardt.[54] As Penzin notes, one of their two modernities has to do with the nation-state and its system of domination and the other with struggle and contestation, thereby substantiating 'the difference between avant-garde and modernism, placing them in the global perspective of two rival modernities'.[55] Even more important for the purposes of the present study, this difference may also be expressed in terms of the ahistorical/historicist dichotomy, such that the first modernity seeks to preserve its autonomy, while the second is more attuned to change and historical reality, as in the case of the avant-garde.

As I argue throughout this essay, an analogous split may be identified in the work of Greenberg himself. In 1939, Greenberg referred to the avant-garde culture he was defending in explicitly historical terms: 'A part of Western bourgeois society has produced something unheard of heretofore: – avant-garde culture. A superior consciousness of history – more precisely, the appearance of a new kind of criticism of society, an historical criticism – made this possible.'[56] Likewise, in 'Towards a Newer Laocoon', he wrote: 'I find that I have offered no other justification for the present superiority of abstract art than its historical justification.'[57] Indeed, for T. J. Clark, both 'Avant-Garde and Kitsch' and 'Towards a Newer Laocoon', those two early essays on art written in 1939 and 1940, respectively, were 'historical explanations of the course of avant-garde art since the mid-nineteenth century. They are seized with the strangeness of the avant-garde moment [...] a peculiar, indeed unique, reaction to a far from unprecedented cultural situation – to put it bluntly, the decadence of a society'.[58] Yet Clark was not convinced by Greenberg's arguments, noting that his account of flatness was not as rich, vivid and meaningful as that espoused by the avant-garde.[59] As it turned out, Greenberg's subsequent writings increasingly addressed formal concerns, to the point where if we were to try to link Greenberg's later modernism to one of the two modernities described by Penzin, we would associate it with the modernity that institutionalizes art's autonomy, and not with the modernity of struggle and contestation associated with the historical avant-garde. Greenberg's modernism thus shifted from political awareness to ahistoricism.

That said, the roots of the dichotomy between historicism and ahistoricism may be traced even further back than the avant-garde – to the eighteenth and nineteenth centuries, according to the philosopher Peter Osborne. Osborne likewise differentiates between Greenberg's modernism and other types of art on the basis of their autonomy or ahistoricity on the one hand, and their capacity for critique, contestation and political engagement on the other. Indeed the first of the two traditions that he proposes designates Kant and Lessing as predecessors of Greenberg – opposing them to the second more recent tradition connecting Dada, Duchamp and the Russian avant-gardes to conceptual art and after.[60] For Osborne, the main tradition today is the second, insofar as the Greenbergian approach of limiting the qualities of medium-specificity and aesthetic judgement to a fixed grouping of historically recognized arts has proved problematic.[61] As Osborne notes: 'While critically dominant in the United States in the decade-and-a-half immediately following the Second World War and currently resurgent in a marginal and modified form, the medium-specific modernism of a plurality of arts is essentially a nineteenth-century tradition.'[62]

Finally, the modernist historicist/ahistoricist dichotomy spills over into broader developments, as Rosalind Krauss stresses in her discussion of the historicist foundations of American critical thought, to which Greenberg, on her reading, subscribed: for Krauss, these foundations were called into question by structuralism, which was later to be itself denounced for its ahistoricism.[63] The shift from autonomy to politicization, from the ahistorical to the historicized and back again, thus recurs over and over again in the modernist period, in a seemingly endless cycle. That – as I have been arguing – this same historicist/ahistoricist duality also traverses the work of Greenberg himself is corroborated by Krauss (1985), when she writes: 'Profoundly historicist, Greenberg's method conceives the field of art as at once timeless and in constant flux [...] Certain things, like art itself [...] are universal, transhistorical forms. But in the same breath it is to assert that the life of these forms is dependent upon constant renewal.'[64]

Such a perspective allows us to conclude that like the nature/culture binary, the notions of ahistoricity and historicism, autonomy and politicization or contextualization, are not so much diametrically opposed as shifting, overlapping in certain respects, and even, on occasion, intertwined – thereby supporting the claim that Greenberg's modernism was never truly or solely ahistorical. As Latour writes: 'If we have never been modern [...] the tortuous relations that we have maintained with the other nature-cultures would also be transformed. Relativism, domination, imperialism, false consciousness, syncretism – all the problems that anthropologists summarize under the loose expression of "Great Divide" – would be explained differently.'[65] In the same way, if modernism has never been completely ahistorical, we would need to provide, as this essay has begun to do, a new and different account of modernist painting and of its relation to the movements that followed and preceded it – that is to say, of the last hundred and fifty odd years of the history of art.

Notes

1. See Bruno Latour, *We Have Never Been Modern* [1991], trans. Catherine Porter (Cambridge: Harvard University Press, 1993).
2. Clement Greenberg, 'Modernist Painting' [1960–65], in *Art in Theory 1900–2000*, ed. Charles Harrison and Paul Wood (Malden/Oxford/Carlton: Blackwell, 2003), 778.
3. Ibid., 779.
4. Ibid., 774.
5. Michael Fried, 'Theories of Art after Minimalism and Pop' (1987), in *Discussions in Contemporary Culture* no. 1, ed. Hal Foster (Seattle: Bay Press, 1987), 56–7.
6. James Meyer, *Minimalism: Art and Polemics in the Sixties* (New Haven: Yale University Press, 2004), 231.
7. Michael Fried, footnote 3, 'Art and Objecthood' [1967], in *Art in Theory 1900–2000*, 845.
8. Clement Greenberg, 'Avant-Garde and Kitsch' [1939], in *Art in Theory 1900–2000*, 541.
9. Greenberg, 'Modernist Painting', 775.
10. Ibid., 776.
11. Greenberg, 'Towards a Newer Laocoon' [1940], in *Art in Theory 1900–2000*, 565.
12. Benjamin H. D. Buchloh, Roundtable 'Art at mid-century', in *Art since 1900*, ed. Hal Foster, Rosalind Krauss, Yve-Alain Bois and Benjamin H. D. Buchloh (London: Thames & Hudson, 2004), 321.
13. Hal Foster, Roundtable 'Art at mid-century', in ibid., 320.
14. Greenberg, 'Modernist Painting', 777.
15. Ibid., 778.
16. Caroline A. Jones, *Eyesight Alone: Clement Greenberg's Modernism and the Bureaucratization of the Senses* (Chicago/London: The University of Chicago Press, 2005), 139.
17. Ibid., 137.
18. Ibid., 409.
19. Ibid., 243.
20. Ibid. See also footnote 88, 475.
21. Ibid., 248.
22. Ibid., 105.
23. Ibid.
24. Ibid., xxi.
25. Clement Greenberg, 'Detached Observations', *Arts Magazine*, (Dec. 1976). Available online: http://www.sharecom.ca/greenberg/detached.html (accessed 18 October 2018).
26. Latour, *We Have Never Been Modern*, 10.

27 Ibid., 11.
28 Geoff Cox and Jacob Lund, *The Contemporary Condition: Introductory Thoughts on Contemporaneity & Contemporary Art* (Berlin: Sternberg Press, 2016), 9.
29 Lionel Ruffel, 'Displaying the Contemporary/the Contemporary On Display', trans. R. MacKenzie, *The Drouth*, Issue no. 52, Summer 2015: 6. Available online: https://issuu.com/drouth/docs/lionel_ruffel_displaying_the_contem (accessed 18 October 2018).
30 Ibid., 7.
31 Ibid.
32 Ibid.
33 Ibid., 15.
34 Lionel Ruffel, *Brouhaha: Worlds of the Contemporary* [2016], trans. R. MacKenzie (Minneapolis: University of Minnesota Press, 2017).
35 Giorgio Agamben [2008], 'What Is the Contemporary?' in *'What Is an Apparatus?' and Other Essays*, trans. David Kishik and Stefan Pedatella (Stanford: Stanford University Press, 2009), 40.
36 See Ruffel, *Brouhaha*.
37 James Riley, 'What Is the Contemporary?', University of Cambridge Contemporary Research Group (15 March 2013). Available online: https://www.english.cam.ac.uk/research/contemporary/?p=257 (accessed 24 August 2020).
38 Terry Smith, *The Contemporary Condition: The Contemporary Composition* (Berlin: Sternberg Press, 2016), 17.
39 Ibid., 21.
40 Ibid., 24–5.
41 Armen Avanessian in Armen Avanessian and Suhail Malik, 'The Speculative Time Complex', in *The Time Complex. Post-Contemporary*, ed. Armen Avanessian and Suhail Malik (Miami: NAME Publications, 2016), 10–11.
42 Ibid., 15.
43 Greenberg, 'Modernist Painting', 776–7.
44 Greenberg, 'Towards a Newer Laocoon', 566.
45 Catherine Grenier, 'Modernité: révolution ou révélation ?', in *La Parenthèse du moderne*, edited by Marianne Alphant, (Paris: Centre Pompidou, 2005), 77.
46 Ibid.
47 Ibid., 71.
48 Ibid., 72.
49 Ibid., 76.
50 Ibid., 72.
51 Ibid., 74.
52 Colin Trodd, 'Postmodernism and Art', in *The Icon Critical Dictionary of Postmodern Thought*, ed. Stuart Sim (Cambridge: Icon Books, 1998), 91.

53 Alexei Penzin, 'The Biopolitics of the Soviet Avant-Garde', in *Pedagogical Poem: The Archive of the Future Museum of History*, ed. Ilya Budraitskis and Arseniy Zhilyaev (Moscow/Venice: V-A-C Foundation/ Marsilio, 2014), 91.
54 Ibid., 92.
55 Ibid.
56 Greenberg, 'Avant-Garde and Kitsch', 540.
57 Greenberg, 'Towards a Newer Laocoon', 567.
58 T.J. Clark, 'Clement Greenberg's Theory of Art', *Critical Inquiry* 9, no. 1 (September 1982): 143.
59 Ibid., 152.
60 Peter Osborne, *Anywhere or Not At All: Philosophy of Contemporary Art* (London/Brooklyn: Verso, 2013), 46.
61 Ibid., 81.
62 Ibid.
63 Rosalind E. Krauss, *The Originality of the Avant-Garde and Other Modernist Myths* (Cambridge: The MIT Press, 1985), 2.
64 Ibid., 1.
65 Latour, *We Have Never Been Modern*, 11–12.

9

Beer in Bohemian Paris: A symbol of the Third Republic

Alexandra Bickley Trott

Symbols of the republic

On 30 June 1878, Claude Monet began a series of paintings of Haussmann's Paris, which on this summer's day was shrouded in hundreds of tricolours, alive in the breeze and flying above the crowds filling the Parisian boulevards (Figure 9.1). Édouard Manet depicts the same day on a street further to the north of the city (Figure 9.2). With the same palette we again see the tricolour and the sandy colour of the street and buildings. But in this harsh realism, the flurry of flags – some tangled in their pole – are hung oblivious to the scene's destitution. The grand buildings of Monet's boulevard are replaced by a mound of rubble, and instead of a bustling crowd we see the back of a single one-legged pensioner, hobbling down the cobbled street. Seen side by side they show differing views of modern Paris. One affirming the official version: the vibrant gathering of people, celebrating a moment of republican liberty. The other highlighting the ruin of Paris: of buildings destroyed, and men crippled by war.

Just a few years earlier, in 1870, France had lost its war against Prussia, and through it the country lost its elected leader, Louis Napoléon, the nephew of the great Napoléon Bonaparte who for many had symbolized stability, and the nationalist spirit of France's re-emerging imperial might. In his place sprung a conservative provisional government led by President Adolphe Thiers, a royalist driven by the right-wing agenda to reinstate the Bourbon Monarchy.[1] A republic only by name, his was a government willing to slaughter thousands of its own people to defend its aims, as evidenced during the annihilation of the Commune when Theirs's army 'gunned down' ordinary men, women and children of Paris.[2]

Figure 9.1 Claude Monet, *Rue Montorgueil*, 1878, oil on canvas, Musée d'Orsay, Paris. Reproduction permission granted by Musée d'Orsay, Paris.

Figure 9.2 Édouard Manet, *Rue Mosnier*, 1878, oil on canvas, J. Paul Getty Museum, Los Angeles. Digital image courtesy of the Getty's Open Content programme.

Following this dark chapter in France's history, the fête of the 30 June 1878 celebrated peace and productivity, and promoted the country's recovery from war. Taking place alongside the *Exposition Universelle*, this was part of the state's wider agenda to project a rejuvenated image of French society: one that was innovative and culturally progressive, which embraced modernity and was not held back by archaic traditions. Yet, this was a country still divided by an intensely partisan political environment. While France remained under conservative leadership, by this time under the presidency of Patrice de MacMahon and his policy of 'Moral Order', the elections sparked by the Crisis of May 1877 had handed a substantial majority to the republicans in the Chamber of Deputies. The left was starting to gather pace.

In the aftermath of the Paris Commune, socialist activity had been curtailed by the loss of left-wing revolutionaries, either through fatalities suffered during the massacre of 1871, or by the subsequent imprisonment and exile of communards. While amnesty was not granted until 1880, socialist and working-class political activism began to re-emerge in France as early as the mid-1870s, and by 1879 (the year the Presidency was won by the republican Jules Grévy) Jules Guesde and Paul Lafargue founded the Parti Ouvrir Français. This was a Marxist political party with a 'radical republican programme' that campaigned to subvert royalist conservativism, and embed republican ideology in the French legislature, and in society more broadly.[3] The tricolour, whose three stripes came to represent the three tenets of the democratic nation – *Liberté, Égalité, Fraternité* – had been a symbol of the republic since the years of the First Revolution. And following the Bourbon Monarchy's reinstatement of the white flag during its brief restoration in 1815, the subsequent re-adoption of the tricolour as the national flag had symbolized republican victory during the July Revolution of 1830. Seen in 1878 in the works of Monet and Manet, the tricolour is once again raised to symbolize growing republican strength, starting to emerge victorious over their royalist adversaries in this long-fought battle for the republic.

In this chapter I turn away from the more prestigious Fine Arts, to instead examine how the bohemian clubs of the time responded to this struggle between republicans and royalists: a battle for the soul of France. This analysis focuses specifically on two associated clubs, the Hydropathes and the Bon Bocks. If republicans promoted their ideology through symbols such as the tricolour, for the bohemian clubs, it was beer that became an unlikely symbol of their beliefs in sovereignty, *laïcité*, and the rights of the common man.

This is an atypical look at Paris's bohemian clubs, and a view at odds with the notion of the forward-thinking, absinthe-drinking, bohemians usually associated with artists of Montmartre around the turn of the century. Seemingly motivated by aesthetic progression and social freedoms, such clubs are more widely understood in sharp contrast to previous generations of communards, anarchists and Realist painters, who confronted fraught socio-political tensions. Indeed, the clubs themselves reinforced the idea that they had no political agenda: at the Hydropathe club all talk of politics was expressly forbidden. I will show how beer was employed as a symbol to promote a more radical opposition to the royalist, catholic factions that still threatened to return the country to a conservative monarchist state, as well as how it became a symbol of sovereignty: a weapon in the battle against the ascendency of foreign authority and culture.

The Hydropathes: a secular Eucharist

Founded in 1878, the Hydropathe club was active at the turning point between conservatism and liberal republicanism in France's early Third Republic. Taking place just before the social liberalization of the 1880s, the club was still subjected to the laws and censorships of MacMahon's Moral Order. Yet, despite the state's suspicion of its people and anxiety of further uprisings, new social liberties were instigated, and the Hydropathe club was one of the first artistic societies to successfully take advantage of the ability to gather in large numbers.[4]

For almost two years the club hosted soirées twice a week for artists, poets, musicians and the youth of the Latin Quarter. In contrast with the radical political action of artists in previous decades, the young men who attended the Hydropathe club were forbidden from discussing politics, and its president Émile Goudeau consistently claimed that they were interested only in matters of the arts: 'The Latin Quarter, numb from inflexible politics, and from religious questions that are of little interest today, wakes to listen to verse and song. It devises its philosophical-poetic works, allowing fantasy to hover with its wings deployed.'[5] Its members produced and performed poetry, music and song, and while artistic talent was appreciated, it was by no means required, and was secondary to the need to participate socially within the club's fraternal spirit. The club was highly successful, attracting a crowd of several hundred young Parisians each week. It was also hugely influential, not least for being the birthplace of the Fumiste movement, a humorous, satirical form of proto-performance art. In 1880 the Fumiste was described to be at odds with the typical man of letters:

> To abandon one's senses and to make him give the quintessence of his imbecility, is characteristic of Fumisme. The spirit of bourgeois culture demands to be

rewarded with cheering and discreet smiles; Fumisme on the other hand carries its own reward within itself: it is art for art's sake. In order to be considered a man of bourgeois spirit it will often suffice to be an ass in a lion's skin; to be a good Fumiste it is often essential to be a lion in the skin of an ass.[6]

At the heart of Fumiste philosophy was a cutting, yet obscure, satire, which sought to subvert the political order through seemingly nonsensical actions and absurdity in daily life. This was a proto-anti-art, and a basis for conceptual art as we would understand it today. After the Hydropathe club, Fumisme was soon developed by the *Arts Incohérents*, the *Chat Noir* (co-founded by Goudeau), and the notorious Alfred Jarry. These in turn inspired the twentieth-century anti-art of Paris Dada, therein sparking an historical lineage that spanned numerous subsequent generations.

At the Hydropathe club, alcohol helped to create a carefree environment of unrestrained artistic creativity; and in a room of several hundred young men, drinking songs helped to both unite and provoke the often boisterous crowd. Despite later claims that the Hydropathes indulged in a vast array of drinks, in the club's earliest months, beer was the only drink that was consumed.[7] As Francisque Sarcey wrote in 1878: 'There, we speak verse, we make music, we sing and we talk. No drink other than beer is permitted.'[8] In the following decades associated bars followed the same trend. In the early twentieth century the Cabaret Zut opened in Montmartre as a homage to the Zutistes – the 1870s collective including Verlaine, Rimbaud and Hydropathe Charles Cros – and likewise prided itself on only selling beer.[9] Furthermore, Aristide Bruant's *Le Mirliton*, which took over the lease of the Chat Noir's original venue on the rue Rochechouart, also only stocked beer.[10]

Given the ubiquity of wine in French society, its economic importance and symbolic value to the nation's cultural identity, it is conspicuous by its absence at these events. Much is known of the 'cultural landscape of viticulture' in French history, and according to statistics gathered in 1899, wine accounted for over 72 per cent of the country's alcohol intake.[11] A further 22 per cent was made up by spirits, and only 5.5 per cent by beer. This is in contrast with Britain, whose tastes are shown to have been almost exactly opposite, with beer accounting for 72 per cent of the total alcohol consumed, and only 2.2 per cent by wine. Given this, the choice made by these clubs to sell only beer is notable.

The widespread contamination of phylloxera (otherwise known as the Great Wine Blight) may have been a potential cause of this phenomenon. From the 1850s through to the mid-1870s, aphids devastated French vines, causing unprecedented damage to the country's wine industry. The quality and availability of wine were both severely affected. Poor-quality synthetic substitutes and expensive foreign imports became a common, though unwelcome sight. As stocks ran dry the prices escalated, and although the worst of the disease was vanquished by 1875, its repercussion on the industry lasted until the end of the century. The Hydropathe club was active as the cost of a bottle of wine was near its peak, and as prices more than doubled its consumption decreased to less than half.[12] Although this might suggest that beer provided a necessary alternative during a difficult time for the French wine industry, for the beer-drinking cultures such as the Hydropathes, the consumption of beer also helped to distance the club from dominant cultural practices in French society, not least dissociating it from symbolic reference to the Eucharist. During the Holy Sacrament of the Catholic church, Christians gather to 'celebrate' the Eucharist, breaking bread, drinking a sip of wine, singing and praying as a mass to reinforce and confirm their collective beliefs. The Hydropathes similarly gathered en masse, drinking and singing together to confirm their belief in a modern, secular way of life. In the years leading up to *laïcité* – the official separation of church and state – this celebration of a secular Eucharist, in which the blood of Christ was replaced with a symbol of the working man – was a loaded political gesture denoting this generation's separation from the liturgical rites of the church, and the 'anti-republican' conservatives who continued to follow it.

Outside of the Hydropathe meetings, particularly after the club's close, many of its leading figures were associated with anticlerical discourse. Such views, for instance, surfaced overtly at Goudeau's Chat Noir, and the increasingly controversial matter of the church's authority was confronted in the first edition of the cabaret's journal: 'It is high time to correct an error which has weighed down on more than sixty entire generations ... The writing which we call holy – I don't really know why – has done nothing more, to put it politely, than make a mockery of the people.'[13] As Julian Brigstocke has argued, in opposition to the Catholic church's tactical construction of the Basilica de Sacré Cœur, such articles attempted to re-imagine Montmartre as a place characterized by 'anti-clericalism and anti-traditionalism'.[14] While anticlerical views are not so vehemently confronted in the Hydropathes' own journal, *l'Hydropathe*, potentially due to persistent surveillance at this earlier moment, such beliefs nonetheless occasionally surfaced. In the final few issues of the journal (by this point publishing under the title *Tout-Paris*), there are a number of advertisements for anticlerical publications. Unlike the advertisements for local bars and bookshops that appear in a designated advertising space on the back page, the promotion of anticlerical literature occurs on the inside cover. They sit alongside the artists' poetry and prose, and the texts are given full endorsement by the Hydropathe club. Publicity for the anticlerical publication, *Le Jésuite Rouge* by Alfred Sirven and Henri Le Verdier appeared in the journal's final issue; and the following promotion of Pompeu Gener's *La Mort et le Diable* was published in four consecutive issues:[15]

> In these times of conflict between the church and the state, between superstition and reason, it is good fortune to find work of a profound analysis of dogmas and religious myths of diverse races and ages, in which the beliefs of theologians are reduced to their meagre value compared to the omnipotent truth of positivist science. It is to this text that we are happy to signal an important work published by Reinwald, with a preface by Littré, and entitled: La Mort et le Diable: Histoire et philosophie de deux négations suprêmes. This study, which exposes all the obstacles that man must overcome to extend civilization on Earth, is due to a young Spaniard, Mr. Pompejo [sic] Gener, member of the Société d'anthropologie de Paris, and correspondent member of the Cercle des Hydropathes.[16]

Gener was a Catalan writer who was influential in late nineteenth-century Spanish modernism, not least for introducing Nietzschean ideas to the country before the appearance of authorized translations of Nietzsche's texts.[17] The journal's declaration of Gener as a 'correspondent member of the *Cercle des Hydropathes*' indicates the club's attempts to link with a wider network of anticlerical European intellectuals.[18] As well as being a proponent of Nietzschean ideals, Gener is closely aligned with Positivist theories. The preface for his text was written by Émile Littré himself, the student of the founder of Positivist thought, Auguste Comte.

As many historians agree, it was from Comtean Positivism that the seed of *laïcité* grew. The term was coined in the early 1870s to define 'the principle of separation of civil society and religious society.'[19] It formulated a scenario by which the state held no power over religion; and in return the church held no influence over politics.[20] In practical terms, within the context of the 1870s, *laïcité* represented the idea of tolerance of religious faiths, but only under the precept that they were practised in the private domain, without interference in the public realm, and renounced all influence upon state institutions:[21]

> Meanwhile, it must ensure that religions remain in the private domain. Private does not mean individual; there is a possibility of private organizations. The public domain, that which the Republic is responsible for, which begins with the school, should be influenced as little as possible by religions.[22]

It was with the introduction of *laïcité* that the republican politician Jules Ferry made his name in the late 1870s.[23] The republicans still held only a minority in the French legislature for most of the decade, yet due to the lack of a formal party system, it was possible for political figures to hold senior positions under a de facto opposition government. Ferry was one such figure, and in February 1875 he was appointed as Minister of Public Instruction and Fine Arts. Ferry understood the importance of culture and education in society, and saw how it could be mobilized to influence public opinion. This is clearly demonstrated by his choice to continue in this role as head of arts and culture after he was elected as prime minister in 1880, and again in 1883. Convention dictated that the head of government take the role of Minister of Foreign Affairs, taking charge of war and defence, and Ferry was the first and only prime minister to do otherwise, giving greater emphasis to the cultural pursuits within the nation. As part of his responsibilities for the country's cultural institutions, Ferry was involved in the official state Salon. Diverging from the standard, mundane speeches made at the awards ceremony, in 1879 Ferry spoke against the Institute for its suppression of modern painters in favour of academic traditions:

> The Institute conceived the plan to force all of French art to submit to its discipline and obey its rules. To this end, the learned society set itself up as the vigilant guardian of the doors of the Salon [...] Contemporary art is at the same time very strong and absolutely individual [...] It would be difficult to find it in any traditional schools or influences like those of years past. We might say that right now individualism overflows its banks.[24]

In essence, Ferry exploited the arts as a weapon in the battle between conservatives and republicans. While conservatives continued their long-established relationship with Academicism, the republicans aligned themselves alongside modernist art practice. Where the Academic traditionalists attempted to impose restrictions on artists, demanding they follow rigid standards of quality and value, the republicans, Ferry claimed, saw that what made their country great was the 'individualism' of its citizens. In making this claim he distanced the debate from partisan political divides. Instead, the argument focused on defending the natural character of *all* French citizens against oppressive state institutions such as the Academy. This oppression, it was proposed, would hold back the nation, and everything that made it great. Republican individualism, on the other hand, would *support* the citizens of France in freedom of thought and expressions of liberty. As Patricia Mainardi has stated, Ferry asserted the republican position in favour of art's liberty, championing the French pursuit of individualism.[25] This accords with Tamar

Garb's claims that although the diversification of style, genre and the place of exhibition was not new to the Third Republic, it expanded within the liberal democratic system, which promoted the free market economy under the republican 'political credo of individualism'.[26] And as Nicholas Green concisely asserts, the 'independence of artists [...] was actively produced by state sponsorship'.[27]

In aligning the republic with the avant-garde, which he deemed representative of the nation's greatness, Ferry poses them as allies against the common enemy: the traditionalist gatekeepers that suppressed the arts with 'rules' and 'discipline'. While at times seeming to be subversive, the Hydropathes were therefore part of a cultural realignment that worked in favour of republican ideology, by providing a space to perform individuality through a novel anti-art aesthetic that rejected conservative judgements of value; and by promoting, within this space, associated beliefs in anticlericalism.[28]

While the consumption of beer may seem innocuous, within this context it was a small gesture that connected the young group of artists to this heated debate. In rejecting the loaded symbol of the Eucharist, the group disconnected itself from conservatism and the Catholic church, and replaced it with a symbol of a rural, working-class ideal, unpretentious and befitting of a culture for a brave new world that was yet to be won.

Although this republican debate stimulated support for 'individuality', it was not intended to reject patriotic sentiment. On the contrary, it was part of an attempt to reinforce French identity in the image of the republican citizen, and partook of Gambetta's controversial declaration that one could not be both catholic *and* a patriot. To support the Catholic church, he claimed, was to support an authority based outside of the nation, and whose allegiance was not to the people of France, but to Catholics worldwide. This, Gambetta asserted with the approval of his republican compatriots, undermined their nation's sovereignty, which must be reclaimed as a matter of priority.[29] Intricate gestures that undermined the traditional cultures and values of the church and autocratic regimes were a crucial way in which this was achieved on the streets.

The Bon Bocks: anti-modern modernists

The implication that beer represented a symbol of French patriotism may well be countered by the drink's simultaneous reference to Britain or Germany, since beer was a prominent element of these national cultures. However, as I shall now argue, for parts of the avant-garde its consumption symbolized artists' rejection of a standardized, stereotypical national identity, and the pursuit to construct a French persona that was not influenced by official doctrine.[30] This can be seen most acutely at the Bon Bock club: a society of artists that met for lively monthly dinners during the early Third Republic. These meetings continued, rather extraordinarily, for over fifty years, with the only recess forced by the First World War.[31] The lunches combined arts and music in an exclusive social space. Among this privileged crowd were figures such as Charles and Antoine Cros, André Gill, Georges Lorin and Coquelin Cadet, who were all central members of the Hydropathe club, and regular contributors at the Chat Noir, therefore closely linking the Bon Bock club with the avant-garde circles of bohemian Paris.

The term 'Le Bon Bock' translates into English as 'The Good Pint', and the club was so-named in honour of Manet's well-known painting of the same title which received critical acclaim at the Salon of 1873 (Figure 9.3).[32] The portrait depicted Émile Bellot, an engraver and future founder of the Bon Bock lunches, who Manet portrayed sat calmly with a pipe and a glass of beer, in a style reminiscent of the Dutch Golden Age. Instead of rejecting such classical cultural connotations, the Bon Bocks embraced them. They drew on these cultural roots at their monthly lunches, as they recited classical music, and poetry – the forms of high culture that might seem at odds with the avant-garde spirit of bohemian Montmartre. Yet they revelled in this kind of high-brow education, and awareness of the country's cultural history that also included the coarse humour, exaggerated characters, and carnivalesque spirit of Rabelais, who Bellot referenced in his *Album du Bon Bock*: 'beloved brothers, I pray our immortal master, Rabelais, to maintain you in good bodily health and joyous frame of mind.'[33] The Bon Bocks were searching for a contemporary French identity, and here they found an affinity with historical cultures that seemed to offer a more genuine Gallic persona than could be found in their own changeable society.[34] This is paralleled in Manet's image of Bellot as a rural champion; the rustic brass table, characteristic agrarian clothing, the pipe and beer, all create a timeless image that rejects the temporality of Parisian urbanism and modernity.

The name 'Bon Bock' also alluded to the cultural heritage of the society's leaders, many of whom were from the region of Alsace. One of the reasons Manet received such acclaim for Bellot's portrait was due to its apparently conservative subject matter and style. This united left- and right-wing press, appearing as respite from the previous controversies of 'Olympia' and 'Le Déjeuner sur l'Herbe'. Yet this view does not account for the painting's political undercurrent, such as those alluded to by Jules Claretie when he asserted that this calm, dignified figure was likely 'a good *Alsatian* philosopher and patriot, quietly enjoying his tobacco and hops'.[35] Alsace had long been the main producer of French beer, and for the Bon Bocks, the pint of beer referenced in its name was a symbolic allusion to the region, which had recently been lost to Germany following the Franco-Prussian War.[36] The Bon Bock meetings had strong links with Alsace, held as they were at the Alsatian restaurant 'Krauteimer' on the rue Rochechouart in Montmartre. Before the war this was a local haunt of artists and actors of German and Alsatian origin.[37] This Alsatian connection was evident from the first Bon Bock meeting, which was co-organized by the Alsatian satirist Eugène Cottin, during which the caricaturist Étienne Carjat 'recited his "Toast to Alsace-Lorraine"', which was said to 'stir the emotions of all those in attendance'.[38] The Bon Bocks' reference to beer, as well as the Hydropathes' consumption of beer at their séances in 1878, was a symbol of solidarity with the Alsatian people, and the communities alienated by political agenda.

Figure 9.3 Édouard Manet, *Le Bon Bock*, 1873, oil on canvas, Philadelphia Museum of Art: The Mr. and Mrs. Carroll S. Tyson, Jr., Collection, 1963, 1963-116-9.

Figure 9.4 Eugène Cottin, 'La Lutte à Entreprendre', *Le Bon Bock*, no. 1, 21 February 1885, p.3. Courtesy of BnF.

Figure 9.5 Eugène Cottin, 'Les Effets de la Bière en Allemagne', *Le Bon Bock*, no. 10, 2 May 1885, p. 1. Courtesy of BnF.

Beer in Bohemian Paris

Figure 9.6 Eugène Cottin, 'Les Effets de la Bière Française', *Le Bon Bock*, no. 11, 9 May 1885, p.1. Courtesy of BnF.

Ten years after the inaugural Bon Bock dinner, this was confirmed in the *Journal du Bon Bock*, which was published weekly by the group's leading members for at least six months.[39] This is no doubt a peculiar magazine to be published by so-called bohemian artists. Beer was its sole subject. It included poetry and cartoons, as typical of artistic magazines of the period. But it also included historical articles on the history of French beer, reported the fluctuating costs of hops and barley in the capital, and published studies by pre-eminent scientists supposedly proving unequivocally that French beer was superior to its foreign rivals. In all it was an odd mix of satirical literary magazine, trade journal and nationalistic propaganda. Throughout this range of articles, it championed the superiority of French beer, in particular above the German counterpart. In the opening article of the first issue Bellot stated explicitly that this was a 'battle – albeit a passive one – against the Germans'.[40] In this same issue the leading caricature expressed that the battle was underway. Here we see a handsome young Frenchman, clean-shaven showing his chiselled jaw, and wearing clothing reminiscent of the sans-culottes – clearly of the peasantry, but nonetheless clean and respectable (Figure 9.4). He is the personification of French beer battling his German counterpart, imagined as a Prussian soldier, somewhat bestial with his thick beard, and despite being armed with a long dagger, unable to fight off the stoic might of the French revolutionary. Such rivalry continues throughout the journal. In issue ten, we see the supposed 'effects of German beer' (Figure 9.5). Once again pictured as soldiers, the Germans are, under the influence of their own country's beer, turning on each other as they brawl in the streets. On the other hand, when shown the 'effects of French beer', we see patrons as civilized clientele, engaged in conversation over a game of cards or billiards (Figure 9.6). In the presence of women (who they are subtly leering over) they represent the kind of macho masculinity that, we can assume, its readers could have identified with.

The Bon Bock caricatures argued against the consumption of German beer not only for the sake of patriotism, but for health reasons too. German beer, they argued, was mass-manufactured. It used scientific brewing methods, and large quantities of the controversial Salicylic Acid as a preservative. This we can see satirized in issue thirteen, where we are shown a crowd of scientists learning German brewing methods in a scientific laboratory (Figure 9.7). If the message here wasn't transparent enough, the text below clears up any misunderstanding: 'the use of salicylic acid prevents beer from spoiling. The beers do not spoil, it is true, but the health of the drinkers is spoiled. Do not drink beers from Germany: they are all salicylic.' The message had already been made a few months earlier in the image entitled 'A Dream', in which Cottin invokes the death of German beer, killed by her own deadly poison (Figure 9.8). As inscribed on the headstone: 'Here lies Lady German Beer of Munich [...] Deceased victim of her own germs. Eternal regrets for all who they poisoned.' And there in the funeral march are the embodied figures of apoplexy and paralysis: the supposed side-effects of this controversial substance. French beer, on the other hand, was supposedly brewed with traditional, rural techniques, and was the healthy choice against the poisonous German alternative. Thus, for the Bon Bocks, the consumption of beer was not about youthful liberation and bohemian ideals. Its message was to oppose scientific methods of modernity, and to instead stimulate support for a rejuvenation of rural values, rallying against the modern urban ways that were influenced by the invasion of foreign (in this case, German) cultures. By expressing this message through the long-established language of visual satire they appear to maintain a voice of the young free-thinkers, mocking the authority of science, and all the while promoting the reinstatement of a more ancient way of life.

The symbolism adopted by the Bon Bocks had been used in recent times, notably by the revolutionary Realist painter, Gustave Courbet, who

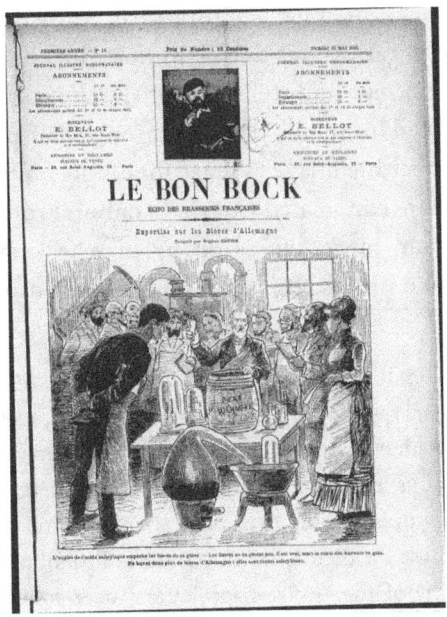

Figure 9.7 Eugène Cottin, 'Expertise sur les Bières d'Allemagne', *Le Bon Bock*, no. 13, 23 May 1885, p.1. Courtesy of BnF.

Figure 9.8 Eugène Cottin, 'Un Rêve', *Le Bon Bock*, no. 5, 28 March 1885, p.3. Courtesy of BnF.

often frequented the Alsatian bar, the Brasserie Andler in Paris, and in the extensive collection of caricatures during his later life, he was rarely pictured without his customary pipe and stein of beer (Figure 9.9). For Courbet, who frequently manipulated his public persona through self-portraiture, the beer stein completed his real-life image of masculine, anti-bourgeois 'naïvety'. Just as much as the substance indicated Courbet's cultural roots, its consumption dictated his behaviour, ideas, the company that he kept and the physical state of the writing he produced often on beer-stained paper, as T. J. Clark describes:

> [Courbet] thrived on [the Brasserie Andler's] mixture of the gross and the intellectual; the others sat and laughed at his hour-long tirades against the Ideal and in favour of Alsatian beer: they laughed but they listened, night after night. Courbet was, in fact as in legend, a naïf, almost an illiterate, with wild spelling and disintegrating syntax spilling over page after page. Yet he was also, in his own cantankerous way, a theorist, a doctrinaire. Proudhon himself groaned under the onslaught of the twelve-page letters, beer-stained and crumpled, which greeted his drafts of *Du principe de l'art*.[41]

Courbet exemplified beer drinking as a rejection of refined culture and etiquette; and offered a glimpse of a world in which intellectualism, vulgarity and naivety were complimentary, rather than conflicting traits. Fearing further imprisonment for his role in the Commune, Courbet was exiled to Switzerland in 1873, the same year Manet's portrait of Bellot was exhibited. And it is perhaps no coincidence that the Bon Bock subject – with his pipe and glass of beer – uses a palette and tone remarkably similar to that of Courbet's own *After Dinner at Ornans* (1848). While the Bon Bock club equally drew on this idealized image of the rural man, it was, however, far from matching Courbet's more radical anarchism. While the journal empathizes with the common Frenchman, and a rural character in particular, by 1885 – at the height of the Tonkin military campaign that sought to establish a French protectorate in Vietnam – this empathy lay specifically with the French infantryman. In two separate issues of 1885, the reader is invited to identify with the French foot soldier fighting for the colonial empire (Figures 9.10 and 9.11). In sharp contrast to the representations of the Prussian military as drunken aggressors, the courageous French soldiers gather to drink beer in the spirit of community. Rather than attempting to subvert the authority of the state, the group encouraged the reader to support the state's military agenda, inviting them to toast to the health of their valiant soldiers with a glass of French beer.

Figure 9.9 Léonce Petit, 'G. Courbet', *Le Hanneton*, 13 June 1867, p.1. Léonce Justin Alexandre Petit (1839–1884), Public domain, via Wikimedia Commons.

Figure 9.10 Eugène Cottin, 'Un Toast à l'armée française au Tonkin, *Le Bon Bock*, no. 7, 11 April 1885, p. 3. Courtesy of BnF.

Figure 9.11 Eugène Cottin, 'Notre Armée dans l'est', *Le Bon Bock*, no. 16, 13 June 1885, p.1. Courtesy of BnF.

Conclusion

National celebrations, such as the fête of 30 June 1878 as depicted by Monet and Manet, were a means by which the emerging liberal Republic entrenched its ideology within French society. They provided a means to collectively engage with common ideals, under the flurry of tricolours that symbolized the victory of the left over the conservative royalists and the Catholic church. The bohemian cultures of the Hydropathes and the Bon Bocks performed an equivalent role on a smaller scale. As we have seen, this was wholeheartedly in support of the republic; but the agency permitted through their own cultural expressions allowed these artists to define what they understood to be the essential characteristics of the new republican citizen. The Bon Bocks championed masculinity, a carnivalesque spirit of Rabelais, the quiet dignity of the rural Frenchman and the regaining of sovereignty from the German invasion (both military and cultural). The Hydropathes were similarly focused on regaining sovereignty, partaking of Ferry's and Gambetta's left-wing agendas that sought to supplant the power of the Catholic church. For both, beer symbolized their defiance and acted as an agent to create and maintain unity in support of their republican cause.

As roots of twentieth-century anti-arts and avant-garde practice, the two clubs under question thus appear to be suitably subversive in respect of their rejection of authority and pursuit of independence. Yet, as I hope to have shown, this nonetheless acted in favour of the emerging liberal republican state, and aided the promotion of its ideology to the Parisian youth. Given the widespread violence against catholic communities, which were expelled from France due to suspicion of the church's authority, and distain for a religious way of life, to understand this to occur within the context and name of liberty, only highlights a certain hypocrisy at the source of avant-garde practice. Similarly, their engagement with a hypermasculine aesthetic, and distrust of the apparent influx of foreign cultural influence, may be less palatable to today's liberal western values. The Bon Bocks, furthermore, did not practice what they preached. Despite what they so doggedly express in their journal, at the Bon Bock lunches they didn't drink beer: in practice, within their exclusive circle they were comfortable with more bourgeois pursuits, toasting their ideas over a glass of fine French wine.

Notes

1. Kevin Passmore, *The Right in France from the Third Republic to Vichy* (Oxford: Oxford University Press, 2013), 18.
2. Monarchists held a majority in the National Assembly with up to 400 seats, compared to 250 republicans, making restoration of the monarchy a distinct possibility. See William Fortescue, *The Third Republic in France 1970–1940: Conflicts and Continuities* (London: Routledge, 2000), 24. John M. Merriman, *Massacre: The Life and Death of the Paris Commune of 1871* (New Haven and London: Yale University Press, 2014), 2.
3. Fortescue, *The Third Republic*, 28.
4. Alan R.H. Baker, *Fraternity among the Peasantry: Sociability and Voluntary Associations in the Loire Valley, 1815–1914* (Cambridge: Cambridge University Press, 1999), 37.
5. Émile Goudeau, *Dix ans de bohème* ([1888]; Paris: Éditions Champs Vallon, 2000), 324.
6. Georges Fragerolle, 'Le Fumisme', *L'Hydropathe* 2, no. 8 (12 May 1880): 2–3. (All translations are my own, unless otherwise stated.)
7. Charles Cros, 'Udadushkhînam – Çruti', *Le Chat Noir*, no. 77 (30 June 1883): 4.
8. Francisque Sarcey, 'Les Hydropathes', *XIX Siècle* (28 November 1878): 1.
9. Dan Franck, *Bohemian Paris: Picasso Modigliani, Matisse, and the Birth of Modern Art*, trans. Cynthia Liebow (New York: Grove Press, 2003).

10 Steven Moore Whiting, *Satie the Bohemian: From Cabaret to Concert Hall* (Oxford: Clarendon Press, 1999), 46.
11 Kolleen M. Guy, 'Wine, Champagne and the Making of French Identity in the Belle Epoque', in *Food, Drink and Identity: Cooking Eating and Drinking in Europe since the Middle Ages*, ed. Peter Scholliers (Oxford: Berg, 2001), 165. David Grigg, 'Convergence in European Diets: The Case of Alcoholic Beverages,' *GeoJournal* 44, no. 1 (January 1998): 11.
12 James Simpson, 'Cooperation and Conflicts: Institutional Innovation in France's Wine Markets, 1870–1911', *The Business History Review* 79, no. 3 (autumn 2005): 534.
13 Jacques Lehardy (Clément Privé), 'Montmartre', *Le Chat Noir*, no. 1 (14 January 1882).
14 Julian Brigstocke, 'Defiant Laughter: Humour and the Aesthetics of Place in Late Nineteenth-Century Montmartre', *Cultural Geographies* 19, no. 2 (2012): 220–1. Construction of the Sacré-Cœur began in Montmartre in 1875.
15 Alfred Sirven and Henri Le Verdier, *Le Jésuite Rouge* (Paris: Dentu, 1879). Pompeu Gener, *La Mort et le Diable: Histoire et Philosophie des deux Négations Suprêmes* (Paris: Reinwald, 1880).
16 *Tout-Paris*, nos. 9–12 (1880): 2.
17 Paul Ilie, 'Nietzsche in Spain: 1890–1910', *PMLA* 79, no. 1 (March 1964): 8. My thanks to Jordi Larios for discussion regarding this obscure figure connected to Catalan Modernisme (not to be confused with Anglo-Saxon Modernism).
18 *Tout-Paris*, nos. 9–12 (1880): 2.
19 Caroline C. Ford, *Divided Houses: Religion and Gender in Modern France* (Ithaca, NY: Cornell University Press, 2005). Guy Bedouelle and Jean-Paul Costa, *Les laïcités à la française* (Paris: Presses universitaires de France, 1998), 11.
20 Ibid.
21 John F. V. Keiger, *Raymond Poincaré* (Cambridge: Cambridge University Press, 1997), 61.
22 Claude Nicolet, *Histoire, Nation, République* (Paris: Odile Jacob, 2000), 248.
23 Pierre Chevallier, *La séparation de l'Eglise et de l'Ecole* (Paris: Fayard, 1981), 228.
24 Jules Ferry speech at the 1879 Salon, reproduced in the 1880 Salon catalogue, v–xiv, cited in Patricia Mainardi, *End of the Salon: Art and the State in the Early Third Republic* (Cambridge: Cambridge University Press, 1993), 61.
25 Mainardi, *End of the Salon*, 61.
26 Tamar Garb, 'Revising the Revisionists: The Formation of the Union des Femmes Peintres et Sculpteurs', *Art Journal* 48, no. 1, 'Nineteenth-Century French Art Institutions' (spring 1989): 64–6.
27 Nicholas Green, '"All the Flowers of the Field": The State, Liberalism and Art in France under the Early Third Republic', *Oxford Art Journal* 10, no. 1, 'Art and the French State' (1987): 71.

28 Charles Rearick, *Pleasures of the Belle Époque: Entertainment and Festivity in Turn of the Century France* (New Haven and London: Yale University Press, 1985).
29 Fortescue, *The Third Republic*, 33.
30 Grigg, 'Convergence in European Diets', 11. According to statistics from Rowntree and Sherwell, in the German Empire, beer made up nearly 50 per cent of all alcohol consumed.
31 Philip Dennis Cate, and Mary Shaw, *The Spirit of Montmartre* (New Brunswick, NJ: Rutgers, 1996), 3.
32 Ibid., 2.
33 Émile Bellot, 'Preface', *Album du Bon Bock* (Paris: Ludovic Baschet, 1878). Translation from Cate and Shaw, *The Spirit of Montmartre*, 4.
34 Romy Golan, *Modernity and Nostalgia: Art and Politics in France between the Wars* (New Haven and London: Yale University Press, 1995). Golan looks in detail at representations of the rural landscape, regional cultures and rustic symbols in art during the modernist period.
35 Jules Claretie, *Le Soir*, cited in Eric Darragon, *Manet* (Paris: Fayard, 1989), 217.
36 Katharina Vajta, 'Linguistic Religious and National Loyalties in Alsace', *International Journal of the Sociology of Language*, no. 220 (March 2013): 110. As is well known, the region changed between French and German rule since the Early Middle Ages, but it had been a region of France since the rule of Louis XVI in 1648.
37 Cate and Shaw, 'Spirit of Montmartre', 3.
38 Ibid. Carjat was a journalist, and co-founded the journal *Le Diogène*. He is perhaps best remembered for having produced a number of well-known photographic portraits, including of Charles Baudelaire and Arthur Rimbaud. Cottin produced illustrations for a number of journals, including front-page designs for *Le Grelot*, *Le Sifflet* and *Le Chat Noir*.
39 It was published for at least six months, between January and June 1885.
40 Émile Bellot, 'Notre Programme,' *Le Bon Bock*, no. 1 (21 February 1885): 1.
41 T. J. Clark, *Image of the People: Gustave Courbet and the 1848 Revolution* (London: Thames & Hudson, 1982), 30.

10

From the marvellous to the managerial: Life at the Surrealist Research Bureau

Rachel Silveri

On Friday, 20 June 1924, the newspaper *Paris-Soir* dutifully reprinted the announcement by André Breton that he had decided to end the publication of his journal *Littérature*. The magazine, it reported, 'has published its last issue, not due to the lack of material resources but for sufficient reasons of existence. The usual collaborators of this journal have the intention of dedicating themselves to Surrealism in poetry and *above all else in life*'.[1] And so it was declared that Surrealism would enter life, indeed that it was already residing within life and required further action, further dedication, further pursuit.

As to what Surrealism in life might look like, by September it was already becoming clearer. Discussions were in the works for a new journal to be called *La Révolution surréaliste*, aimed at liberating 'the unconscious activity of the mind' and 'penetrating the unexplored field of Dreams'.[2] But equally important it was decided that this journal would have a dedicated office, an office, in fact, that was to be open to the public. In a group meeting, the Surrealists decided on the name – the Bureau de recherches surréalistes – and envisioned the types of people they would attract, divided into three categories: first, those who wanted information on Surrealism; second, those who wanted to 'abandon themselves' to dreams and automatic writing; and third, those who wanted to bring new ideas for the movement.[3]

For the office's location, Pierre Naville, a younger addition to the group, offered one of his family's properties, a bi-level apartment at 15 rue de Grenelle, in the seventh arrondissement of Paris. Artworks and posters were brought in to decorate the space; manuscripts and publications were collected to form a library; basic furniture and equipment were procured – a table, chairs and at least one portable typewriter. A large, black cahier was purchased as a logbook.

The Surrealists decided on their hours of operation – Monday through Saturday, from 4:30 pm to 6:30 pm. They ordered official business stamps; they printed various letterheads. They made advertisements and sent announcements to various newspapers to publicize the space. And so on Friday, 10 October 1924, just five days prior to the publication of Breton's first *Manifeste du surréalisme*, the doors of the Surrealist Research Bureau opened to the public.

In the histories of Surrealism, with a few notable exceptions, the Bureau is frequently overlooked.[4] When mentioned, its account is usually in passing or delivered in a somewhat embellished language. Consider Maurice Nadeau's seminal *Histoire du Surréalisme*, in which the Bureau was 'the generator of new energies', a place for 'inventors', 'revolutionaries' and 'dreamers', a site for 'all those who had something to say, to confess, to create'.[5]

In contrast to this type of romanticized description, this essay proposes a study of the concrete power dynamics at place within the Bureau – of what work was accomplished, how such work was distributed and especially how it became supervised. In so doing, I argue for a different type of history for Surrealism, one that foregrounds a different historical context. Scholars of Surrealism have long privileged psychoanalytic theory, as both context and method, in their analyses of this movement.[6] Yet given the aims of *Historical Modernisms* – of rethinking the historicization of early-twentieth-century art afresh and better placing the avant-gardes 'in the historical contexts of their production and reception' – one might argue that the Surrealist workplace warrants a perspective outside the psychoanalytic and instead rooted in the socio-historical.[7] Towards this end, I situate the Bureau in relation to a broader set of historical discourses, including the rationalization of office work, the gendered division of labour and the rise of management practices in interwar France, treating its production as less a product of psychic drives and rather something closer to what T. J. Clark has described as 'a series of actions *in* but also *on* history'.[8]

In 1924, the office was neither a new nor a neutral space: debates about labour and organization were thriving. The fact that the Surrealists chose to create an official, organized and public Bureau at a time when Breton had otherwise called upon its members to '*lâchez tout*', to 'leave everything', merits some explanation.[9] What the Bureau reveals is not only that a handful of writers suddenly became employees of Surrealism, but also that a few members began fashioning themselves as managers, in a manner complicit with contemporary theories of administration. Neither marginal nor insignificant, the Bureau was the ground through which André Breton refined his leadership skills. His abilities to shape and consolidate Surrealism, I contend, rest on this period in which, on the office floor, he worked at governing and managing others.

In the beginning, the Bureau was staffed by ten different Surrealists, each assigned to work on different days. Breton and Louis Aragon worked on Mondays. Paul Éluard and Benjamin Péret staffed the office on Tuesdays. Simone Breton and Jacques-André Boiffard came in on Wednesdays, while Pierre Naville and Francis Gérard handled Thursdays. On Fridays, Max Morise and Roger Vitrac were present at the office. And on Saturdays, Simone and Boiffard assumed an additional shift. From its very inception, the Bureau was thus predicated on an unequal distribution of labour.

Those on duty accomplished specific tasks, at times tedious or mundane. If any visitors came by the office, the members on staff were responsible for them. Despite the Surrealists' initial planning, archival records clearly show that only about four guests per week visited the office, the vast majority of them other Surrealists and writers.[10] When not engaging the public, indeed most of the time, the Bureau's staff had other duties. They signed a daily logbook and recorded their work accomplished, a gesture akin to the attendance sheet and record-keeping notecards described in office literature.[11] They kept inventory and organized the library, documented press clippings, maintained correspondence, coordinated with printers and publishers, mailed pamphlets and other materials. They worked on the production of the journal and managed subscriptions. The day the office opened, Morise and Vitrac sent letters to newspapers and handled the 'Material organization of the Bureau'.[12] The next day, Simone completed an extensive inventory, which was updated a week later by Boiffard.

If one starts to wonder whether the Surrealists were somehow being ironic in all of this mundane office work, consider the nature of some of their correspondence. It was penned on the most banal of stationery – no icons, no graphics, no typographical experimentation. Contrast it with Tristan Tzara's infamous Dada Movement letterhead from 1921 and the differences are clear enough: against the latter's playful, vertiginous alternation of scale in its lettering, a clear mockery of corporate authority, the Surrealist stationery, with its lack of illustrations and bolded serif font, appears sober and serious. They used it to send letters of rectification to the press. For in the fall of 1924, there were a number of other artists, notably Yvan Goll and Paul Dermée, who were attempting to use the label of 'Surrealism'.[13] Whenever those figures received any mention in the press, the Bureau sent a letter to the newspaper, correcting usage of the term.[14] Rather than mocking authority, the Bureau, with its official stationery and stamps, with its public office and monthly journal, wanted to appear legitimate, powerful, the definitive organization of Surrealism.

Beyond the collective commitment to staffing, a few leadership roles within the office were nominally determined. Gérard was declared the general secretary, while Naville and Péret were made the directors of the new journal. Yet the precise roles of such titles were nonetheless kept open and the result was that a few members – mainly Breton and Naville – began vying for power, a struggle that has been left recorded in the office's daily notebook.

Consider one of the earliest entries in the Bureau's Cahier, written on 13 October. Breton declares: 'Put forward these vows: 1. Suppression of all communication for a period of 15 days. 2. Complete suppression of every personal letter that has no experimental interest. 3. Multiplication by every means possible of individual Surrealist initiatives … Communicate to this Bureau the results of such experiences.'[15] Articulated as *vœux*, as vows or wishes, the enumerated statements are blunt, declarative, non-questionable; they are aimed at directing the behaviour of the collective group. Reading the list, Naville decided to endorse the first item, adding, 'I approve' with his initials. As will soon be apparent, this was but one of many such statements. And so already within the first pages of the Bureau's Cahier, it becomes clear that there are certain Surrealists who openly direct the actions of others, certain Surrealists who approve or disapprove such actions, and still others who either silently obey or disobey while they continue their work at the office. It is here, within these distinctions, that we begin to see the Bureau staff mimic contemporary theories of labour management.

Such theories were so widespread at the time that France has been described as living within an 'age of organization'.[16] The writings of Frederick Wilson Taylor advocated the breakdown of labour into highly efficient movements; they were translated as early as 1906 and spread widely – by 1916, readers of the popular *La Nature* (including the Surrealists) could find long profiles written on Taylor within the pages of their journal.[17] While Taylor's work was primarily associated with factory labour, French businessmen found his system of rationalized tasks readily applicable to various industries. Thus as early as 1909, with the founding of *Mon Bureau* by the Ravisse brothers, office trade journals began avidly embracing Taylor's methods and theorizing the multitude of ways in which they could be applied to the white-collar space of the office floor. Throughout the 1910s and 1920s subsequent journals such as *Organisation et outillage du Bureau* and *La Revue du Bureau* made clear that theories of rationalization could be successfully applied to clerical work, office administration and the classification of information. Filing and typing soon became Taylorized activities.[18] Within the layout of the office, desks were to be rearranged so as to provide minimal interruption yet constant supervision. A proper series of movements were established for a broad range of clerical tasks, from opening letters to filing papers, each with their own system of accounting and supervision.

Taylor's system of focusing on the individualized and fragmented motions of workers found its complement in the theories of Henri Fayol, a French engineer, whose writings appeared contemporaneously with that of the American theorist. While Taylor focused on measuring the tasks of labourers, Fayol directed his attention to that of the administration, outlining an entire system of proper management in his widely popular *Administration industrielle et générale* (General and Industrial Administration, 1916). Aimed at outlining the basic functions of executive leadership, Fayol regarded his work as not only applicable to industry but to 'the government of affairs, of every affair, large or small, industrial, commercial, political, religious, or any other'.[19] For Fayol, leadership was part of the 'natural order'; it was applicable to any and every 'human organization' and undertaking.[20] It was a system that ranged from the supervision of one to that of many. His envisioning of administration at once naturalized leadership and deified it.[21]

Fayol identified five elements as central to the activity of management: 'Administration,' he wrote, 'is to plan, organize, command, coordinate, and control.'[22] To plan was to evaluate the business, develop concrete goals and formulate a plan of action to achieve those goals. To organize was to ensure that the business had all it needed to function and implement the plan of action. Command was to maintain and supervise all staff. The goal was to discipline them, sanction them if necessary and 'acquire the optimum return from all employees'.[23] Central to Fayol's administrative system was that command was unified and singular: 'for any action, an employee must receive orders from only one leader.'[24] This leader was to combine both 'personal qualities' (such as 'integrity', 'perseverance' and 'high moral character') and a 'general knowledge of administration', establishing his authority as much by setting a good example as by eliminating unnecessary employees, conducting audits and overviews, and utilizing sanctions.[25] To coordinate was to harmonize all the activities of the business. And finally to control was to ensure that the leader's command was properly respected, to maintain order and rule.

Fayol's tenets on administration spread rapidly. *Administration industrielle et générale* was republished in 1917 and then reprinted in 1918, 1920 and 1925. Beyond his publications, Fayol formed the Centre d'études administratives in

1919, a school that offered management classes, lectures, programming and publishing opportunities. This organization was to merge with the Taylorist Comité Michelin in 1926 to form the Comité national d'organisation française (CNOF). Directed by several of Fayol's students, the CNOF promoted the scientific organization of labour and management alike throughout French industries. Inspired by Fayol's administrative theory, the market was flooded by a variety of texts emphasizing the importance of managerial abilities.[26] In short, during the exact moment when the Surrealists decided to open and operate an office space, the social environment of France was profoundly marked by a series of discourses that at once sought to rationalize such spaces and to stress that above all else such spaces required a clear, commanding and singular leadership. Under this 'age of organization', as the historian Jackie Clarke has described, leadership was a type of 'ethos', a technique of managing people that was to be embodied and exemplified by a certain cast of administrators.[27] And while Fayol's work was widespread, it should also be noted that strong management was not the only option. Against such theories of administration, there existed a variety of individual writers (such as Hyacinthe Dubreuil) and institutions (such as the Confédération générale du travail unitaire) within France that publicly hewed to a tradition of communitarian socialism and called for worker's autonomy and collective effort.[28] This, however, was not the model embraced by the Surrealists.

Consider some further examples in the Cahier. Around 20 October, Breton writes: 'The activity of the office leaves much to be desired and this is due to the seven or eight of us who should not be here. It is absolutely important that the two Surrealists on duty have the ability to work in peace. The others should only stay on the second floor.'[29] Immediately beneath this command, Naville added, 'I approve.' What could have been a collective decision – to separate the bi-level space of the office according to function – was one demanded by Breton and approved by Naville.

When the policy had difficulty taking into effect, Naville proclaimed on 30 October,

> Starting today, it is ESTABLISHED that: a) Only those on duty have the right to be in the principle room on the ground floor. b) The staff on duty must accomplish an effective action during their two-hour shift ... They will record in this cahier, very succinctly and without poetic development, the result of their work. c) Those who are uncooperative will be punished.[30]

Not quite the liberation of dreams, this was Surrealism as a disciplinary endeavour: segregated into an enclosed space, employees were given a precise two-hour frame to be filled with precise duties, 'effective action' and proper notation. Those who refused to follow orders would now be subject to sanctions.

And sanctions were indeed put into effect. On 2 December, Éluard wrote in the Cahier: 'Given what I said earlier about the presence of Vitrac at the Office, the latter being here, I am leaving and from now on will not return to any meeting concerning *la Révolution surréaliste* [sic].'[31] Then it is written, in Éluard's script: 'Naville expels Vitrac.'[32] While the precise reasons are unclear, Vitrac was thus abruptly subject to sanctions.[33] Dismissed from the Bureau, he was not to return. Recall that for Fayol sanctions were key to good command. In order to get that 'optimum return from all employees', one needed to 'eliminate the incompetent', eliminate any employee who had 'become incapable of carrying out his function'.[34] A benefit, Fayol theorized, was that eliminations could create 'unity' throughout the personnel.[35] In expelling Vitrac, Naville at once appeased Éluard, a senior member of the group, increasing his 'optimum return', and bolstered his own authority over the office. Surrealism, in short, was now something that one could be fired from.

While Naville was asserting more and more power over the Bureau's daily existence, Breton was also performing his own type of command and control. Around 20 October, he wrote, 'The press clippings album has not been kept up-to-date. Very annoying.'[36] Rather than updating the album himself, Breton chose to supervise the activity, shaming the staff who should have felt obliged. Then he added another list of directives:

> 1. I ask that this evening we examine *very closely* the texts for the journal that we have gathered. Ensure that the collaboration is not monotonous, I insist on this ...
> 2. A visit to the flea market should be imposed. 3. I ask instantly that each of us contributes ... to the rigorous establishment of the documentary part of Surrealism.[37]

Throughout this passage, Breton uses what Mary Ann Caws has described as a 'style of demand', in which Breton 'calls for our attention, and secures it: "I ask...," "I demand," "I claim."'[38] Deeming this a language of 'noncompromise', Caws describes Breton's voice as 'categorical, stubborn'.[39] While her discussion was in reference to Breton's manifestos, it is clear that it was also the language used at the Bureau. Whenever Breton articulated his views it was done in manner to render discussion obsolete, aimed at disguising what was mere opinion into undisputed rule, aimed at bolstering what Fayol described as a unified and singular command.

In another instance, Breton critiqued the workings of the office, claiming that there was 'too much useless spirit'.[40] 'The scope of Surrealist activity still has yet to be defined. No serious plan of action has been proposed,' he wrote, calling for a programme of action in precisely Fayol's terms.[41] Breton urged members to undertake a 'broader offensive' and he began an active supervision of the staff.[42]

On Friday, 31 October, he visited the Bureau and recorded what he saw: 'It follows from my benevolent inspection today that Morise passed the time typing, and that Vitrac did absolutely nothing (at 5:15pm he declared that there was nothing to do but wait).'[43] While Vitrac immediately denounced such surveillance, no other Surrealist openly protested Breton's decision to act as manager of the office floor, conducting what Fayol would describe as a 'periodic inspection of the organization', a necessary activity of good command.[44]

As Breton adapted his engagement with the Bureau from that of participant to supervisor, he notably abandoned his original duties as a staff member. His extensive critique and so-called 'benevolent inspection' occurred between two Monday shifts in which Breton effectively abandoned his Bureau post. Failing to sign into the logbook on both days, Aragon wrote, 'Breton excuses himself.'[45] Such behaviour continued with the production of *La Révolution surréaliste*. When several staff members travelled to the printer to oversee the publication of the first issue, they were met with what Naville described as '*un travail ingrat*', 'a thankless work', of making mock-ups and proofing pages.[46] 'I was extremely tired,' Naville wrote in a series of letters; 'We worked a day and half at the printer,' while Breton was 'of course at a café'.[47] And when the journal was printed, it was Naville, Boiffard and Morise who attended to the mailing of copies and subscription cards, to their delivery at various bookstores.[48] Breton's avoidance of such work was again in line with Fayol's directives: 'A great leader must always seek to retain for himself the liberty of thought and action necessary for the examination, direction, and control of the main business issues. He must offload on to his subordinates and staff all of the difficult labour which he himself is not strictly bound to carry out.'[49]

Out of all the 'thankless work' present at the Bureau, perhaps the most prominent was that of typing. Consider that when the office received responses to their first questionnaire, 'Is Suicide a Solution?' someone had to type the handwritten answers for publication in the journal. That someone was Simone Breton, who transcribed the texts over two weeks of work, coming into the Bureau on days beyond her assigned shifts, typing up handwritten answers even from other members of the Bureau (such as Aragon) who had access to the office typewriter.[50]

We have, in fact, a photograph of the Surrealists with their writing machine (Figure 10.1). Taken by Man Ray in November 1924 it features nearly a dozen

From the Marvellous to the Managerial 205

Figure 10.1 Man Ray, *Surrealist Group 'Waking dream séance'*, 1924. Photograph of the Bureau de recherches surréalistes (Surrealist Research Bureau) in November 1924. Standing (left to right): Max Morise, Roger Vitrac, Jacques-André Boiffard, André Breton, Paul Éluard, Pierre Naville, Giorgio de Chirico, Philippe Soupault. Seated (left to right): Simone Breton, Robert Desnos, Jacques Baron. © Man Ray 2015 Trust/Artists Rights Society (ARS), NY/ADAGP, Paris [2020], image: Telimage, Paris.

Figure 10.2 Man Ray, *Centrale surréaliste (Surrealist group)*, 1924. Photograph of the Bureau de recherches surréalistes (Surrealist Research Bureau) in November 1924. Standing (left to right): Jacques Baron, Raymond Queneau, André Breton, Jacques-André Boiffard, Giorgio de Chirico, Roger Vitrac, Paul Éluard, Philippe Soupault, Robert Desnos, Louis Aragon. Seated (left to right): Pierre Naville, Simone Breton, Max Morise, Louise (Mick) Soupault. © Man Ray 2015 Trust/Artists Rights Society (ARS), NY/ADAGP, Paris [2020], image: Telimage, Paris.

Surrealists crowded into a corner of the Bureau. Robert Desnos sits above the bottom-right frame; with his left hand, he tilts a box inwards towards the rest of the group, while his right hand is open, gesturing. The gaze of almost every Surrealist is directed towards this space: the emptiness that lies between the palm of Desnos' hand and the container, whose contents, if any, are hidden from the viewer's sight. One after another, Morise and Vitrac, Boiffard, Breton and Naville incline their heads, bend their backs, tilt forward and gaze towards the Surrealist below. In the very centre of this circular grouping sits Simone at a small desk with a small portable typewriter. Like the others, her gaze travels downwards towards Desnos' gesture. Her hands touch the base of the keyboard, though her fingers are no longer extended. The typewriter is set midway through the page and the dark ink of a few words appears across the paper. The transcription has occurred or, perhaps, was still mid-process. The transcriber was Simone. If Desnos was considered the 'prophet' of Surrealism in the words of André Breton, then Simone was its typist.[51]

This group portrait of the Surrealists has been described in the literature as a type of 'waking dream séance', a 'waking dream session'.[52] Yet Desnos' body – his gaze downcast yet pointed, his hands active, articulating – has little resemblance to the passive states that have been recorded in other images depicting his trances (such as the photograph of Desnos that appears in Breton's *Nadja*), where his body was limp, reclining, in a liminal state between awakening and slumber. Other scholars have described this activity as a 'collective automatic writing process'.[53] To be clear, however, the Surrealists who practised automatic writing did so by hand, and never in a group so numerous. Breton's own instructions for automatic writing in his first *Manifeste du surréalisme* state that the goal was to 'write quickly without a preconceived subject', and mentioned nothing of typing.[54]

Indeed this photograph is neither a 'waking dream séance' nor a collective automatic writing session, but rather a publicity image. Note the eyes of Éluard and Giorgio de Chirico, who, rather than gazing downwards towards Desnos, look up and stare directly into Man Ray's camera, revealing that this is less an absorbed activity than a staged spectacle. The Surrealists were on display and they knew it, from Breton's performed concentration with a monocled eye to de Chirico's confrontational mug. The photograph is part of a series of images that Man Ray took to document the Bureau's opening.[55] In another portrait taken on the same day, we glimpse fourteen Surrealists lined up against the Bureau's walls, a table with papers and books in disarray nestled in the foreground (Figure 10.2). That disarray was itself performed, as archival notes indicate that Aragon pressed the Bureau members to 'take care' of the library and to 'not leave the papers on the table in disorder'.[56] As for the artists themselves, the same group that was huddled around Simone reappears here in the exact same dress. In each image, the number of represented Surrealists exceeded those who routinely staffed the office. Viewers could see Desnos, de Chirico, Philippe Soupault and his wife Louise – figures who had very little to do with the running of the Bureau and the journal. But the idea was to have images that could be used to represent and promote the movement, photographs that recorded the Surrealists in action, investigative, serious, a formidable (and numerous) group. Along with a third photograph (now lost), the publicity photographs appeared on the front cover of the first issue of *La Révolution surréaliste*. These were the very first images one encountered from the self-declared revolutionary movement, a variety of artists, dressed in suits, posing in their office space.

Indeed, what the photograph of the Surrealists grouped around Simone ultimately publicizes is the latter's role as a transcriber, as a labourer who copies or reproduces one form of writing (*l'écriture automatique*) into another (document, record, testament). The image shows Simone as the *dactylo-copiste*, the typist-copier, attached to her machine, nearly an extension of it. With her head bowed in dutiful attention, her hands at the base of the typewriter, the transcription underway, she appears as a replica of the various typists seen across contemporaneous office trade journals (Figures 10.3 and 10.4). Such a gendered division of labour, between (feminine) typists and (masculine) administrators, reflects a deep complicity with interwar office culture.

Delegating the tasks of typing to others, abandoning his Bureau post, foregoing the material production of the journal, Breton, simply put, was no longer working. He was supervising. The staff at the Bureau felt the effects of such management. Vitrac was fired. Morise and others became accustomed to having their work monitored and critiqued. Aragon eventually complained that staffing the Bureau was a '*corvée*', a chore.[57] Not work, not duty, but *chore*, what the dictionary tells us is an 'annoying obligation', one 'unavoidable and without interest'.[58] This was what Surrealism 'in life' had become. It was the same word that Simone used when she finally decided to quit the Bureau. Several weeks after the typing frenzy of the suicide questionnaire, on 7 January 1925, Simone wrote and signed in the office notebook: 'I protest the procedures [*les procédés*] used towards certain female staff members [*permanentes*] who have come to take care of certain chores and are treated as *instruments*. I understand that we do not keep them up to date with the detailed functioning of the journal and the Bureau at all.'[59] Note how encompassing Simone's critique is: she protests '*les procédés*',

Figure 10.3 Detail of advertisement for La Machine Comptable Ellis, *Mon Bureau* 164 (October 1927): page 603. Source gallica.bnf.fr/Bibliothèque nationale de France.

Figure 10.4 Advertisement for Société des Machines à Écrire MAP, *Mon Bureau* 139 (September 1925): page 664. Source gallica.bnf.fr/Bibliothèque nationale de France.

'the procedures', of certain staff members (a word that describes methods, a way of doing something, a general attitude). She objects to a specifically gendered condition, writing '*permanentes*', 'staff members', in the feminine plural. She protests being treated like an *instrument*, a tool, an extension of a machine. She disputes the lack of information provided to certain members, and their exclusion from the overall decision-making processes concerning the journal, the office and the movement at large. After realizing that the revolutionary concerns of Surrealism were blinded to her position, that the Bureau itself was founded on an unequal division of labour, Simone left and never returned. Breton made no commentary on her departure. Carrying little for the protest that was occurring within the very walls of 15 rue de Grenelle, he was busy drafting 'The Last Strike', a text in which he called for intellectuals to stop work and show solidarity with 'our friends, the true workers'.[60]

The Bureau ended in April 1925, once Breton had grown tired of his squabbling employees, once he had grown tired of dealing with Naville, claiming outright that he was 'annoyed' by his behaviour.[61] Utilizing the authority he had been refining, Breton moved the journal's headquarters to his own apartment and opened the fourth issue of the magazine with the editorial 'Why I Have Taken Direction of *La Révolution surréaliste*'. When he later learned that Naville was protesting to other members of the group, Breton's choice of words could not have been more revealing: '*Je vais le sacquer à la première occasion*', 'I'm going to fire him at the first opportunity.'[62]

In the literature on Surrealism, Breton's ascent has been described in various terms. He was 'naturally the head', due to his 'charisma', his 'particular magnetism'.[63] Breton was said to have a personality that provoked 'fascination', a 'physical seduction', a 'sphere of attraction'.[64] He was a sorcerer, a 'spiritual compass', the 'arbiter of Surrealism', the 'arbiter of the entire avant-garde'.[65] He was a 'pope', 'priest', 'guru', 'teacher', the recipient of 'a certain form of *faith*'.[66] In the more sobering accounts, he was simply the one 'who had done the most to shape the movement'.[67]

Metaphors abound in these narratives, from electromagnetic fields to magic. The terms I wish to add to this description – planning, organization, command, coordination, control – are not nearly as poetic, yet not nearly as vague. If Breton became the leader of Surrealism, it was not because of charisma or faith, but because he actively espoused management qualities, the very qualities that were being theorized contemporaneously with his movement.

And if Surrealism was to enter life, as it did, it would not just be found in the socializing in cafes, the wanderings through the street, the cinema, the flea market, the arcades. Neither elusive pursuit nor romantic ideal, Surrealism 'in life' was found in the mire of power relationships surrounding Breton. Here, depending on one's place within the group, Surrealism 'in life' became an opportunity for exerting command or it became a type of 'thankless work'. Neither marvellous, nor liberating, nor revolutionary, what the Bureau gives us is an image of artists performing and re-performing the dominant norms that structured the 'age of organization' in France.

The history of Surrealism after the closure of the Bureau is well known. The group that Breton was now strictly administering would become affiliated with the Communist Party. Debates would ensue. Novels would be written. Art would be made. By 1930, Breton made sure to publicly denounce Naville, Vitrac and Gérard along with the others who should be 'abandoned silently to their sad fate': André Masson, Philippe Soupault, Robert Desnos, Antonin Artaud, Jean Carrive, Joseph Delteil.[68] Breton declared that Naville had an 'insatiable thirst for fame'; he was blinded by a 'revolutionary allure'.[69] Vitrac was 'a veritable swine of ideas'.[70] Gérard suffered from 'congenital imbecility'.[71] Such lengthy, acerbic and public denunciations within the *Second Manifeste du surréalisme* were merely sanctions of a different sort. With office or without, Surrealism was now a defined group, a group that one was either permitted to join or was not, an organization commanded and controlled by Breton. Such a view of Breton as manager, as supervisor, as bureaucratic leader is not necessarily to discredit his subsequent political writings, his firm commitment to a pro-Trotskyite, anti-Stalin, anti-Fascist, anti-nationalist politics that he articulated throughout the 1930s. But it is to remind us that Breton rose to that position – spokesperson of Surrealism – through the governance debates that marked the life at the Bureau and the acts of sanctions and firings that ensued.[72]

The Surrealist Research Bureau – its structure, supervision and organization, the thematics of work – would continue to haunt some of its members. Naville, too, joined the Communist Party and became a sociologist of labour, writing over thirty books on the politics of work.[73] Gérard became the secretary of Leon Trotsky.[74] Simone continued her independent spirit and avoided the fate of a typist. And Breton? Well, Breton continued to manage.

Notes

1   'À Tous Échos', *Paris-Soir*, 20 June 1924, 2, original emphasis. Unless otherwise noted, all translations from the French are my own.

2 *La Révolution surréaliste* Bulletin de souscription, reproduced in *Histoire du Surréalisme: Documents surréalistes*, ed. Maurice Nadeau (Paris: Éditions du Seuil, 1948), 16.

3 See '2009. [Artaud, Antonin]. Bureau de Recherches Surréalistes: Manuscrits autographes et textes ronéotypés, réunion du 2 avril 1925,' in *André Breton: 42 rue Fontaine: Tome III: Manuscrits* (Paris: CalmelsCohen, 2003), 94.

4 Notable exceptions include Julia Kelly, 'The Bureau of Surrealist Research', in *Twilight Visions: Surrealism and Paris*, ed. Therese Lichtenstein (Nashville: Frist Center for the Visual Arts, with University of California Press, 2009), 79–101; Sven Spieker, *The Big Archive: Art from Bureaucracy* (Cambridge, MA: MIT Press, 2008), 85–104; and Abigail Susik, *Surrealist Sabotage and the War on Work* (Manchester: Manchester University Press, 2021).

5 Maurice Nadeau, *Histoire du Surréalisme* (first published 1944; Paris: Éditions du Seuil, 1964), 61–2.

6 For an engagement of Surrealism and psychoanalytic theory, see, among others, Hal Foster, *Compulsive Beauty* (Cambridge, MA: MIT Press, 1993); Hal Foster, *Prosthetic Gods* (Cambridge, MA: MIT Press, 2004), 225–54; David Lomas, *The Haunted Self: Surrealism, Psychoanalysis, Subjectivity* (New Haven: Yale University Press, 2000); and Natalya Lusty, *Surrealism, Feminism, Psychoanalysis* (Burlington, VT: Ashgate, 2007).

7 Angeliki Spiropoulou, Proposal for *Historical Modernisms Symposium*, Institute of English Studies, School of Advanced Study, University of London, 12–13 December 2016.

8 See T. J. Clark, *Image of the People: Gustave Courbet and the 1848 Revolution* (Berkeley: University of California Press, 1973), 15, emphasis added.

9 André Breton, 'Lâchez tout', in *Œuvres complètes: Tome I*, ed. Marguerite Bonnet (Paris: Gallimard, 1988), 262–3.

10 See Paule Thévenin, ed., *Bureau de recherches surréalistes: Cahier de la permanence: Octobre 1924—avril 1925* (Paris: Gallimard, 1988).

11 See, for example, Gabriel Chavet, *Ce que doit savoir l'employé de bureau* (Paris: Gauthier-Villars & Cie., 1921), 149.

12 Thévenin, ed., *Bureau de recherches surréalistes*, 17.

13 For a detailed overview of this debate, see Jeremy Stubbs, 'Goll versus Breton: The Battle for Surrealism', in *Yvan Goll—Claire Goll: Texts and Contexts*, ed. Eric Robertson and Robert Vilain (Amsterdam: Rodopi B.V., 1997), 69–82.

14 Thévenin, ed., *Bureau de recherches surréalistes*, 17–19.

15 Ibid., 19–21.

16 Jackie Clarke, *France in the Age of Organization: Factory, Home and Nation from the 1920s to Vichy* (New York: Berghahn Books, 2001), 6–8 and passim.

17 Ibid., 14. See also Anson Rabinbach, *The Human Motor: Energy, Fatigue, and the Origins of Modernity* (Berkeley: University of California Press, 1992), 271–88.

The Surrealists modelled *La Révolution surréaliste* on the design of *La Nature*. For coverage of Taylor in the latter publication, see A. Breton, 'L'Organisation du travail et le système Taylor', *La Nature*, quarante-quatrième année, deuxième semestre, no. 2246 (14 October 1916): 246–51.

18 See Delphine Gardey, 'The Standardization of a Technical Practice: Typing (1883–1930)', *History and Technology* 15, no. 4 (1999): 313–43.
19 Henri Fayol, *Administration industrielle et générale* (Paris: Dunod et Pinat, 1917), 5, original emphasis.
20 Ibid., 26, 33.
21 Clarke, *France in the Age of Organization*, 28–34. See also Marjorie A. Beale, *The Modernist Enterprise: French Elites and the Threat of Modernity, 1900–1940* (Stanford: Stanford University Press, 1999), 97.
22 Fayol, *Administration industrielle et générale*, 11.
23 Ibid., 138.
24 Ibid., 31.
25 Ibid., 138, 103, 29.
26 See, among others, Joseph Carlioz, *Le Gouvernement des entreprises commerciales et industrielles* (Paris: Dunod, 1921); Joseph Wilbois, *Le Chef d'entreprise: sa fonction et sa personne* (Paris: Alcan, 1926); and Jules Billard, *Un essai de doctrine, le fayolisme* (Paris: Jouve, 1924).
27 Clarke, *France in the Age of Organization*, 49.
28 For an overview, see ibid., 51–6.
29 Thévenin, ed., *Bureau de recherches surréalistes*, 26.
30 Ibid., 39.
31 Ibid., 65.
32 Ibid.
33 A series of private letters reveal that Naville and other Surrealists were upset with Vitrac's 'moral attitude' and the fact that he 'made these rather terrible scenes'. Pierre Naville, Letters to Denise Lévy (November 1924), Archives Pierre Naville, CEDIAS Musée social bibliothèque.
34 Fayol, *Administration industrielle et générale*, 138, 140.
35 Ibid., 145.
36 Thévenin, ed., *Bureau de recherches surréalistes*, 26.
37 Ibid., 26.
38 Mary Ann Caws, *André Breton* (New York: Twayne, 1996), 100.
39 Ibid., 25–6.
40 Thévenin, ed., *Bureau de recherches surréalistes*, 36.
41 Ibid.
42 Ibid.
43 Ibid., 40.

44 Fayol, *Administration industrielle et générale*, 138.
45 Thévenin, ed., *Bureau de recherches surréalistes*, 35, 45.
46 Pierre Naville, Letter to Denise Lévy (7 December 1924), Archives Pierre Naville, CEDIAS Musée social bibliothèque.
47 Pierre Naville, Letters to Denise Lévy (6 and 7 December 1924), Archives Pierre Naville, CEDIAS Musée social bibliothèque.
48 Thévenin, ed., *Bureau de recherches surréalistes*, 70–84.
49 Fayol, *Administration industrielle et générale*, 145.
50 See accounts in Thévenin, ed., *Bureau de recherches surréalistes*, 67–9.
51 André Breton, 'Robert Desnos', in *Œuvres complètes: Tome I*, 473.
52 Rosalind E. Krauss and Jane Livingston, eds., *L'Amour fou: Photography and Surrealism* (Washington DC: The Corcoran Gallery of Art, with Abbeville Press, 1985), 12. See also Kelly, 'The Bureau of Surrealist Research', 83; and Rudolf Kuenzli, 'Surrealism and Misogyny', in *Surrealism and Women*, ed. Mary Ann Caws, Rudolf Kuenzli, and Gwen Raaberg (Cambridge, MA: MIT Press, 1991), 18–19. *Waking Dream Séance* is also the official title given by the Man Ray Archives and Estate.
53 Martine Antle, 'Breton, Portrait and Anti-Portrait: From the Figural to the Spectral', in *André Breton Today*, ed. Anna Balakian and Rudolf Kuenzli (New York: Willis Locker & Owens, 1989), 49–50. See also Spieker, *The Big Archive*, 89.
54 André Breton, 'Manifeste du surréalisme', in *Œuvres complètes: Tome I*, 332.
55 Pierre Naville, Letter to Denise Lévy (November 1924), Archives Pierre Naville, CEDIAS Musée social bibliothèque.
56 See reproduction of archival notes by Louis Aragon in Gérard Durozoi, *History of the Surrealist Movement*, trans. Alison Anderson (Chicago: University of Chicago Press, 2002), 64.
57 Ibid.
58 'corvée, n. 3', *Le Grand Robert de la langue française*, version 4.1 (Paris: Dictionnaires Le Robert, November 2017), https://grandrobert.lerobert.com/robert.asp (accessed 12 September 2020).
59 Thévenin, ed., *Bureau de recherches surréalistes*, 75, emphasis added.
60 André Breton, 'La Dernière grève', *La Révolution surréaliste* 2 (15 January 1925): 1–3.
61 Pierre Naville, Letter to Denise Lévy (30 April 1925), in Archives Pierre Naville, CEDIAS Musée social bibliothèque.
62 André Breton, Letter to Simone Kahn (20 September 1925), reprinted in André Breton, *Lettres à Simone*, ed. Jean-Michel Goutier (Paris: Gallimard, 2016), 264.
63 Henri Béhar, *André Breton: Le grand indésirable* (Paris: Calmann-Lévy, 1990), 166–7. Nadeau, *Histoire du Surréalisme*, 55–6.

64 Julien Gracq, *André Breton: Quelques aspects de l'écrivain* (first published 1948, Paris: José Corti, 1977), 56, 52, 54. Sarane Alexandrian, *André Breton par lui-même* (Paris: Éditions du Seuil, 1971), 25.

65 Marguerite Bonnet, 'Avant-propos', in *Les Critiques de notre temps et Breton*, ed. Marguerite Bonnet (Paris: Garnier Frères, 1974), 17. Clifford Browder, *André Breton: Arbiter of Surrealism* (Geneva: Librairie Drosz, 1967). Alexandrian, *André Breton par lui-même*, 27.

66 Mark Polizzotti, *Revolution of the Mind: The Life of André Breton* (Boston: Black Widow Press, 2005), 191–2. Gracq, *André Breton*, 51, original emphasis.

67 Polizzotti, *Revolution of the Mind*, 191.

68 André Breton, 'Second manifeste du surréalisme', in *Œuvres complètes: Tome I*, 786.

69 Ibid., 798–9.

70 Ibid., 789.

71 Ibid., 788–9.

72 I am grateful to Jean-Michel Rabaté for the prompt to think further about Breton's politics in the 1930s.

73 For more on Naville's political life, see Françoise Blum, with Sylvie Le Dantec, eds., *Les vies de Pierre Naville* (Villeneuve-d'Ascq: Presses Universitaires du Septentrion, 2007).

74 See Gérard's account of this in his memoirs, Gérard Rosenthal, *L'Avocat de Trotsky* (Paris: Robert Laffront, 1975).

11

History and active thought: The Belgrade surrealist circle's transforming praxis

Sanja Bahun

Activating thought

'Thought is a product of matter … Yet, thought, albeit consequential to matter, is never a passive product, a mere reflection of matter; rather, it possesses an active role … it is working, operative, capable of transforming the material world, which, in turn, may transform thought itself … and on *ad libitum*.'[1] So begins an ambitious philosophical treatise entitled *Outline for a Phenomenology of the Irrational* (Nacrt za jednu fenomenologiju iracionalnog), written by Koča Popović and Marko Ristić, two key members of the Belgrade Surrealist Circle (and recent philosophy graduates), published by Surrealist Publishing in Belgrade in 1931. A unique text in the history of global surrealisms, *Outline for a Phenomenology of the Irrational* tiptoes the discursive fields of Aristotle, Kant, Hegel, Husserl, Freud and Einstein over more than hundred pages to posit an approach to matter, history and art-making through the category of the irrational. The idea of a perpetually transformative, mutually corrective interaction of thought and matter is key to Popović and Ristić's argumentation in this book. One such interaction dynamizes both thought and the material world from within, Popović and Ristić argue, so that they can only appear to us as one joint dialectical process; in turn, its processual and dynamic nature endows thought-assumed-as-matter with the capacity to be subversive, revolutionary and to transform history. Yet, to release this potential one must challenge another natural propensity of thought, namely, its tendency to reify itself into abstractions, categories like spirit, freedom, history, unconscious – a step which, Ristić and Popović argue, even the likes of Freud and Hegel have failed to take. In order to avoid the petrification of thought into a passive object (an abstraction), then, we should exploit the inherent potential of thought for its own negation and self-critique, resident in the vast repositories of the unconscious. It is in eliciting and activating this negational background of thought and overriding the static positivism of the rational mode of thinking that the crucial achievement of surrealism as an enunciative mode lies. Surrealist dialectic negation, the authors argue, naturally engenders aesthetic modes and strategies of representation that are most suitable for continual rebellion and self-critique: identifying and opposing the dictates of petrified thought in each expressive act, privileging communal and participatory modes of thinking and performing over Western individualism, and using transposition, irony, simulation. The category of the irrational, always in dialectic tension with the rational, stands at the centre of this aesthetic operation in history: it is a hermeneutic and psychological point in which the world of material phenomena and the unconscious coalesce, each serving as an incessant corrective to the other.

Nibbling on the morsels of material history of the locale which engendered and conditioned these thoughts on the irrational, and engaging surrealist activities of different types, this essay zooms in on the Belgrade Surrealist Circle's efforts to dynamize the interaction between historical matter, thought and its representation and to use it for strategic political purposes. Taking as my case study one of the most influential art-practices in the liminal (and, history will prove, transient) zone of Yugoslavia will enable me to pose questions that are more capacious: How does material history turn itself into continuously active forms/represented objects? What implications may the Belgrade surrealists' mandate for active thought have for our understanding of modernism and history? And what mode of interpretation befits this vision of historically-politically engaged art?

Activating history

There have been few better vantage points for appreciating that history is not static than the region of Yugoslavia in the early twentieth century. Politically and cognitively located at the intersection of two demising empires (Austro-Hungarian and Ottoman), and between the demands of an imported notion of nation-state and the indigenous styles of political action, the region was a charged locus of political contests, cultural interpellations and dissenting practices. The legacy of interacting empires and human motions between and against those empires created intense awareness of the region's inter-positionality and the latter shaped the regional conceptualizations of history and the manoeuvres and investments of artists that aspired to convey them. Founded in 1918, Yugoslavia constituted the first union of the South Slavs, peoples living in the territories that gained independence from colonial rule in a series of processes following the mid-nineteenth-century liberation wars. The very foundation of the country was contingent upon a historical incident that in itself came to epitomize global inter-imperial fissures.[2] On 28 June 1914, Gavrilo Princip, an impressionable youth whose farmer-father had participated in the Herzegovina Uprising against the Ottomans in 1875–7 and later supplemented his meagre income by transporting illegal migrants across the border between the Ottoman and the Austro-Hungarian Empires, assassinated the Austro-Hungarian Archduke Franz Ferdinand at Latin Bridge in Sarajevo. The event sparked the First World War, the outcome of which (among many other things) was the political possibility for a sovereign state of the South Slavs. The new state, initially named the Kingdom of Serbs, Croats, and Slovenes, operated as constitutional monarchy from 1918 to 1929, then, renamed the Kingdom of Yugoslavia (the land of South Slavs), as absolute monarchy/dictatorship from 1929 to 1934 (the period of the most intense activity of the Belgrade Surrealist Circle), and as shaky constitutional monarchy, increasingly economically and politically dependent on the Nazi Germany from 1934 to 1945. Caught between the desire for independence and the legacy of imperial claims, and between the modernizing aspirations and an anti-modernizing political set-up, it was a highly repressive state, with a notorious impressment law and swiftly developing penitentiary system for the dissenting. In the cultural sphere, the Turks, French, Germans, Italians and Russians had battled for hegemony in the region for nearly a century; in one significant case of strategic aid, France provided shelter and schooling to more than 3,500 Serbian children in France during the First World War, including almost all future members of the Belgrade Surrealist Circle. These cultural interpellations only intensified as the new, strategically positioned, country came into being, but they were now stratified, their complex operation reflecting global political reconstellations. For one, the Soviet influence, while officially denounced, grew steadily among the members of undercover resistance organizations; and these counted in their ranks many members and associates of the Belgrade Surrealist Circle.

In 1922, the same year when the Kingdom of Serbs, Croats, and Slovenes was officially ratified and internationally recognized at the Conference of Ambassadors in Paris (coincidentally, also known as the year of modernist miracles), young Marko Ristić published his first poetry, started international correspondence, and took up the editorship of *Ways*, a Belgrade-based little magazine dedicated to contemporary literature. Over the course of following year, Ristić transformed the journal into a voice of international proto-surrealism and started conversations and text and gift exchanges with André Breton. In the years to follow, Ristić coordinated Yugoslav surrealists through a period of individual and collective art practices and publications (1922–9) and the operation of the Circle as a self-declared public organization (1929–33), and he served as a coalescing point for surrealist practices after the dissipation/banning of the Circle (post-1934). Hundreds of preserved visual artefacts, more than twenty books of poetry, prose and theory, several manifestoes, fanzines, magazines and bilingual journals, and one group exhibition/conceptual presentation came out of these endeavours. But the Circle's long-term legacy is the unique endurance, even exultation, of modernist art and development of neo-avant-gardes in post–Second World War, socialist Yugoslavia. I have traced this history in more detail elsewhere.[3] Here it is important to highlight only that, while the Belgrade collective invested their energy in recognizable surrealist concerns such as the nature of poetic creation, madness, and the functioning of dreams, they also placed particular emphasis on the issues of artistic and social responsibility and the role of artist in a participation-oriented society. Not only anti-bourgeois and anti-establishment but also actively committed to a proletarian revolution, the Belgrade surrealists understood their artistic enterprise as a subversive act, 'boundless, unselfish, and moral',[4] in the face of which the contemporaneous French surrealist activities – even at their most radical – were somewhat naïve and/or purely rhetorical. The Belgrade surrealists viewed the bourgeois society in monarchical Yugoslavia as incompetent, myopic and repressive in its racing capitalism and displaced nationalism. In turn, the Yugoslav monarchical state authorities perceived the Circle as rather a dangerous political party, at times even a terrorist organization, than an artistic grouping. The group itself dissipated upon the arrest and detention without trial of several key members in December 1932 – an incident reported in an emotionally charged article by René Crevel in *Le surréalisme au service de la révolution* in May 1933; Crevel astutely likens the terror of the Yugoslav pro-fascistic government to the contemporaneous rise of Nazism in Europe.[5]

This history suggests that site-specific convergences between material history and intellectual history and the local meanings that art production acquires in each setting matter greatly when approaching global movements like surrealism. The artwork that the Belgrade Surrealist Circle produced must be understood as 'emplaced' in the historic-political context of a newly independent, oppressive state; inter-imperial position of the region; violent history of colonial rule;

both appropriation and wariness of foreign cultural influence; and cohort-specificities such as their commitment to the surrealist blend of Marxism and psychoanalysis, engagement with revolutionary organizations, multilingualism and higher-level education in disciplines of philosophy and law.[6] It is out of this geo-cognitively hybrid terrain that the Belgrade surrealists' art emerged as a site-specific aesthetic ethnography that insists on an understanding of thought, representation and history itself as dynamic, unfinished and continuously embroiled in dialectical self-critique.

Interactive artwork, interactive history

The members of the Belgrade Surrealist Circle were mostly the merchant class youth, many of them of Jewish or Tsintsar descent, educated in France or Switzerland, and most of them living in the Belgrade neighbourhood of Dorćol and surrounding zones. Spreading around the crossroads of four major trade routes ('dört yol' means 'four roads' or 'crossroads' in Turkish), leading to, respectively, Vienna, Widdin, Istanbul and Dubrovnik, Dorćol fronts the Danube river which was for centuries the border between the Ottoman and Austro-Hungarian empires. Sited on this marker of division, the neighbourhood also positioned itself as defying the border, and, through all the legitimate and illicit commerce of goods and people that took place there, blurring the physical and cultural boundaries between the imperial zones; a hub for the placeless, homeless and transient. By the early twentieth century, the area had become an eclectic architectural composite befitting the fractured histories of peoples inhabiting it – Serbs, Turks, Jews, Armenians, Aromanians, Roma, Greeks, Germans; within a square mile one could find a synagogue, a mosque, an Orthodox Christian and a Catholic church. The early-twentieth-century architectural revamping of this terrain and, in particular, intense building of monuments in service of nation-building and bourgeois civil culture promotion provoked irritation among the Belgrade surrealists. While French surrealists found evocative potential in monuments in Paris, whose scriptural function seems to be to deaden the past and thus, paradoxically, liberate the present, the members of the Belgrade Circle found such potential in dilapidated walls, almost deprived of any outward signs of historical specificity – except that it is precisely their dilapidated, forcefully erased condition that testifies to the workings of history.

One such wall fronts a piece of conceptual engagement art called *Facing a Wall: A Simulation of the Paranoiac Delirium of Interpretation. Survey*, authored/

signed by Belgrade surrealists M(arko) R(istić), V(ane) B(or), Ž(ivanović) N(oe), M(ilan) D(edinac), D(ušan) M(atić) and R(astko) P(etrović). The collective took a frontal-view close-up photo of a dilapidated Dorćol wall and then asked its members to 'simulate delirium' (or simply freely associate) and develop their own artistic responses to the photograph – autobiographical, intertextual, abstract, affective – in the form of six interventions. The interventions were subsequently arranged around the incentive-photo, reproduced on two pages in the third issue of the Belgrade surrealist journal *Nadrealizam danas i ovde* (*Surrealism Today and Here*, 1932), and accompanied by Ristić's article 'Facing a Wall – An Explanation of the Eponymous Illustration Page' ('Pred jednim zidom – objašnjenje istoimene strane ilustracija'). Ristić explains that the four phases/facets of the artwork – photographing of the wall, free-associating on the photograph, materialization of the idea (interventions), and reflection about the work (that is, the article itself) – aim to elicit the traces of the unconscious and to insert and activate these in the public sphere.[7] One may remember here both Salvador Dalí's 1930 essay 'The Stinking Ass' ['L'âne pourri', 1930] and Breton and Paul Éluard's *The Immaculate Conception* [*L'Immaculée conception*, 1930], but the immediate context for this installation is Ristić and Popović's 1931 *Outline for a Phenomenology of the Irrational*. As *Outline* defines it, 'simulation' is a volitional, historically engaged, phenomenological activity which purports to awaken the latent content through an external, conscious impetus like a material phenomenon or an image thereof. Its result is a simulacrum which dynamizes the image/received matter and activates thought. Far from being a product of a solitary simulation of paranoid state, simulation emerges through the collaborative 'paranoiac' activity of the producer of the work of art and its interpreter. Being phenomenological and collaborative, such simulacra are also markedly historical, Ristić and Popović insist: they articulate the dialectical struggle between activated thought/matter and the unthought/not-yet-matter, a struggle that governs and shapes the historical subject-in-becoming.[8]

A good example of such operation in history is Vane Bor's 1935 pair of photographs of a semi-deserted Dorćol underpass, *Milica S. Lazović as a Shadow, or Two Minutes before Crime* (*Milica S. Lazović kao senka ili dva minuta pre zločina*) and *One Minute before Murder* (*Jedan minut pre ubistva*). Capturing the perspective of someone looking down at a female (Figure 11.1) and a female and a male (Figure 11.2) figures in the white roadway below, this series of photographs was probably taken during a random walk but was carefully staged as a pair of film-frames showing a cobble-stone road on one side and the other side of a bridge. The road is demarcated by tall cement walls, creating two

Figure 11.1 Vane Bor (Stevan Živadinović), *Milica S. Lazović as a Shadow, or Two Minutes Before Crime*, 1935, vintage photograph, 90 × 60 mm, Inv. No. M112. Courtesy of the Museum of Contemporary Art, Belgrade.

Figure 11.2 Vane Bor (Stevan Živadinović), *One Minute Before Murder*, 1935, vintage photograph, 87 × 62 mm, Inv. No. M111. Courtesy of the Museum of Contemporary Art, Belgrade.

main compositional lines that converge towards the horizon of each image. The two horizons in Bor's photographs embody the contrasts that characterized 1930s Belgrade: in the Dubrovačka street-facing photograph (*Milica S. Lazović ...*), the horizon is a dense mixture of heterogeneous abodes – ground-level Turkish-style houses, two-floor baroque edifices, and, towards Upper Dorćol, modern buildings, all bearing witness to architectural and historical transformations of the city; in the photograph facing the Danube river-bank (*One Minute before Murder*), the horizon is ominously consumed by the unpopulated river bank and a recently constructed canal that would allow cargo ships to bring coal for the new power plant 'Power and Light' in the Lower Dorćol quay. The titular crime is oddly absent in Bor's photographs, but it looms in the surprising emptiness of urban space and the interplay of geometrical lines and shapes, darkness and light. An in situ Hellenistic necropolis with an architrave 'gate' to Hades, a temple dedicated to Greek goddess Hecate was dug up close to the location in 1935, and Bor must have been aware of this discovery. Furthermore, these photographs remind one of Eugène Atget's snapshots of deserted Parisian streets, which Camille Recht and Walter Benjamin, respectively, linked to the scenes of crime. Unlike Atget's photographs, however, Bor's series foregrounds the human and the (possible) violation of the human, and it is oriented towards interaction. In *Milica S. Lazović ...*, the slanted-vertical occlusion that tantalizingly diminishes the view draws the viewer into an uncomfortable hermeneutic effort: the blurred bordure signals the mythic operation of bridge as passage to death but the uncanny close-up also suggests that the viewer is somehow implicated in this passage. On her way to the river (of death?) in *One Minute before Murder*, then, the girl has suddenly turned back; she looks away with a half-smile, as if interacting with someone under or on the other side of the bridge, while a passer-by is approaching her, hands in his pockets, unnoticed yet. Will someone warn her? And against what? Where is the threat situated, exactly? The careful spatial arrangement of the actants in Bor's artwork positions the viewer as not only a witness of a crime, but also, hypothetically, its perpetrator; or a rescuer.

While mythic in tenor, Bor's series also indexes some events in the region's recent history. In April 1934, less than a year before these photographs were taken, the workers constructing a twin-underpass in the immediate vicinity unearthed the skeletons of the soldiers who had unsuccessfully defended Belgrade against the Central Powers in a decisive First World War battle; on 1 May 1934 Yugoslavia signed a major trade treaty with Nazi Germany, whereupon German Foreign Minister Hermann Göring became a frequent guest in Belgrade;[9] and, on 9 October 1934 King Alexander of Yugoslavia was assassinated, along with the French Foreign Minister, Louis Bartou, in Marseilles, France. Taken at a cusp historical moment, Bor's photographs foreground the claustrophobic enclosure of horizon-paths between two tall, bare walls, and the human's entanglement in crime. There is more than an inkling that we, too, are responsible for this unfolding of history, or, at least, the narrative of Bor's photographs. The cinematicity of the series forces the viewer to become a co-creator of this film, to supplant an edit between the two film-frames, and, importantly, imagine the dénouement of the action. Like installation *Facing a Wall*, then, Bor's photographs rely for their operation on an extraordinarily active relationship between the text, its producer(s) and its recipient(s), and they materialize the interaction between the matter, thought/affect, and articulation that Popović and Ristić keenly examined in *Outline*. This is a lesson for the interpreters of these artworks, then: as much as the exterior impetus does not deprive the artefacts in question of the quality of being a 'representation' of the unconscious flow (and thus also participants in an international surrealist conversation), so the intention to elicit the interior affective content that binds objects and observing subjects does not take away from the artefact the quality of being a representation of a particular physical infrastructure of Belgrade, metonymically linked to the deep and contemporary history of the area.

Dialectic self-critique and unfinalizable work of art

The active relationship between the text, its producer and its recipient, and the idea of a perpetually transformative interaction of thought and matter put forward in *Outline* and articulated in *Facing a Wall* and Bor's photographs had already been conceptualized and specifically linked to the mode of self-critique in an earlier text, Marko Ristić's 1928 novel entitled *Without Measure*. The novel, written from 1926 to 1928 in Paris and Belgrade, is a fragmentary piece of prose that runs like a novel but simultaneously undermines its own generic status. The quasi-autobiographical narrator/detective follows the wanderings of a man named Roman ('roman' means the 'novel' in both Serbo-Croatian and French), strolling in and out of the supposed reality, into a hyper-reality, the collective unconscious, and from history into the mythic supra-history, and back into the current political and cultural debates. The fragmentary storyline follows the negotiation of the protagonist's passage through alternating experiences of fascination, political resentment and radicalization, all punctuated by the oblique references to specific sites in Belgrade, Paris, Vrnjačka banja and several seashore locations. While the narrative tension rises and murders, dream-murders and executions accrue, the entities of the narrator and the protagonist become progressively indistinguishable from each other until they finally transform into a writer penning a polemic response to Ivan Nevistić, a Yugoslav scholar who had previously published a critical article on the Belgrade surrealists.

Insofar as the temporal and spatial coordinates of the protagonist's actions and utterances and his bodily boundaries are blurred, or hard to 'measure', focalization is shifting (or incalculable), and the subject (narrator)-object (protagonist) relation is indeterminate (impossible to measure), Ristić's *Without Measure* might seem comparable to Breton's *Nadja*, written at the same time and during the period of intense interaction between the two writers. Yet, Ristić presents the reader with a markedly different text. He opts for a male protagonist in interaction with an assumedly male narrator, a choice that helps him avoid the objectivization of the female and the narrative distraction of love affair and foreground, instead, the textual line of maladjustment, resentment and social revolt. The narrator-writer, involved in the story yet strategically distanced and psychologically undecided, continuously probes the quality and integrity of their own writing and is more comparable to the later developments of the role in Nouveau Roman (e.g. Alain Robbe-Grillet) than to the emphatically subjective narrator of a surrealist novel. The protagonist operates as, simultaneously, the subject of the work of art, the activity of its production, the artwork itself and its formal, generic and contextual interpretation, and is, in this respect, just like the narrator, rather a metatextual trace than an iconographically embodied being. Meanwhile, the metapoetic and intertextual games proliferate. Genres (a detective chronicle, a Gothic novel, a symbolist play a manifesto, a film script, a fairy tale, a scholarly article), narrative modes, tonalities of address and focalization all constantly shift in the text. To make the matters even more complicated, the novel consists of not only the loose plot outlined above, but also its own paratext and visuals, accrued across the three editions of the text (1928, 1962, 1986): the 1928 acknowledgements, motto and footnotes; the 1962 author's prologue and endnotes; the 1928 kabalistic pictographs and illustration from the first edition of Jules Verne's *Twenty Thousand Leagues Under the Sea* (*Vingt mille lieues sous les mers: Tour du monde sous-marin*, 1870), the 1962 reproduction of Max Ernst's 'Owl (A Bird in a Cage)' (owned by Ristić since 1927), the 1986 reproduction of Giorgio de Chirico's 1914 *Piazza d'Italia* and others. As contextualized by the chatty narrator in one of his copious discursive footnotes, this interaction of textual modes and formats and the exultation of the book's unfinizability is both the condition for rejuvenating the genre of the novel and a performance of a specific historical mandate: the novel should serve as 'a silent witness' to history.[10]

While the surrealist revolt tends to be oriented by a notion of freedom that is overarching but also abstract, the target and historical tenor of Ristić's novel are specific. It was with dismay that, in 1927, Ristić wrote from Paris to his Belgrade friends about the sudden lapse in communication between the two surrealist circles, a lack of understanding in both political and aesthetic matters. Yugoslav surrealist Milan Dedinac wrote back to Ristić: 'I cannot advize you to pass over certain differences ... Our position is immeasurably more absurd and more brutal than theirs in France ... For, just think what freedom means in our country ... and what in theirs (not to mention our impressment law!).'[11] In the novel written in this context, then, the search for unconditional freedom segues seamlessly in a dialectical challenge to the very notion of freedom as enshrined in, and appropriated by the philosophical discourse and moves into the pursuit of a specific freedom (revolution). The last is addressed through the metonymic extension of leitmotifs such as revolver and 'atentat' ('assassination'), wherein the 'atentat' of 'a certain artistic convention' becomes, across three editions, inextricably linked to the past, present and future history of the region and beyond: to the assassination of Franz Ferdinand in 1914; that of five Croatian MPs in the Parliament in 1928; that of King Alexander in 1934; and subsequent history of global political assassinations, especially those related to liberation struggles, for example, that of Patrice Lumumba. This expansion is not accidental. Already in the first edition of the novel Ristić suggests that the South Slavs' yearning for freedom is intensified by another kind of captivity, an incarceration in regional and global imperial inscriptions, which, parenthetically, the French group might have also unwittingly deployed. These are meticulously related in *Without Measure*: 'East, West, Catholicism, Mediterranean Culture, Europe in Danger, Balkan Man, Racial Expression, the Slavic Mission, Reslavicization – what are all those games and toys to me?' queries Ristić's narrator, 'and what is love for homeland, nurturing beauty, belief in good, and other abstractions?'[12] As an impassionate and lengthy footnote to the text at this point further explicates, it is the concept and discourse of 'racial art', whose rise and global spread we can date to 1925–30, that bother Ristić most: he deems it a doubly limited, superficial way to refer to identity through entity, entrapping us, sometimes unawares, in an imperial construction. And 'imperialism itself, including imperialism of the spirit', the footnote-voice argues, is 'the most facile form of dogmatism' (233). In the face of an abstract, or mediated notion of freedom, the narrator of Ristić's text muses, the only 'position which remains fruitful for the spirit', is 'a MORAL and REAL attitude [...]: a working, active rejection of a certain order which has proven itself as dead and artificially maintained', that is, 'a bloody dialectic'. For, 'passive resistance is insufficient' (233–34).

How, in this context, one pursues freedom relevant to one's integrity – one that would be beyond all abstraction and yet 'immanent to ... our existence' – and makes art revolutionary and resistant to the imposition of an identity in the name of (sometimes myopic) idealism, Ristić's narrator ponders.[13] Rejecting imposed measures and demarcations, *Without Measure* itself is the answer to this question. The novel as a whole may be understood as a performative of Hegelian philosophy, compulsively explored by Ristić, a PhD student of Philosophy at Sorbonne, in the period 1922-7.[14] This ambition is synopsized in one strategic peripheral character, who describes his name, Jan, as being derived from 'Ja-Ne', meaning 'I-Not I' in Serbo-Croatian, and his existence as being shaped by dialectical tension. The same kind of dialectic, we infer, determines the very status as an anti-novel: 'it is from the interiority of the book that its very negation erupts', the narrator reiterates (204). In line with this dialectical procedure, the first-person narration also stages a pamphlet against its own writer, framed as 'I against itself' ('This [text] is a pamphlet against myself, perpetuated for years, and in vain', 234) and enacts one of the governing principles of the Belgrade surrealist project: permanent self-critique. And the text rallies 'against the reader', that is, against the passive reader habituated into the 'logical' or 'consequential' progression of narrative and history. It is not only the bourgeois literature of the yesteryear and the obsolete political system that are targeted here. This proclamation should be understood, I suggest, as a challenge to, or a call for, a more active readerly entity, at once a co-creator and an interpreter of the novel, thus an entity which would assist in consistently activating thought. Chapter entitled 'Against the reader' opens with the assertion that the book that we are reading does not end or stop with its last page. The narrator entreats the reader to abandon 'belting' and 'belt measure-taking' (both implied in 'kaišarenje') and to continue reading even after the last word in the novel, to turn back the pages and start from the beginning or to branch out down any side routes that the book suggests (64). The textual monster's existence and shape, indeed its very coming into being, are thus conditional upon our commitment to read against the grain. The two postulates articulated by *Facing a Wall* and Bor's photographs thus shape Ristić's novel, too. The figurative space we traverse embodies the space and time of a specific historical subject-in-becoming, but this embodiment is itself subject to a condition: Roman – the protagonist and the novel itself – is figuratively constituted only through the collaboration of the producer and recipient/interpreter of the work of art.

Unsurprisingly, then, *Without Measure* also renounces its prerogatives as a text: rather, it describes itself as an 'activity', or 'being active' ['aktivitet']' (47), thus a processual entity, a dynamism at the heart of the object. The term 'aktivitet' has limited currency in colloquial Serbo-Croatian; what Ristić doubtlessly has in mind here is the specific way in which the term was used by Hegel in his *Lectures on the History of Philosophy* (Vorlesungen über die Geschichte der Philosophie). Responding to Aristotle's *Nicomachean Ethics*, Hegel describes the circumstances governing the abrogation of passivity in the face of thought's propensity for reification. Because thought reifies its own content as being (a certain subject-matter, an object, *Gegenstand*), Hegel reasons, it must be receptive. Dialectically understood, then, thought-assumed-as-matter must be simultaneously an instance of active thinking, wherein 'the object [subject-matter] reverses into activity' ('der Gegenstand schlägt um in

Aktivität'; 162).¹⁵ In Ristić's reworking of this insight, an endless, committed readerly pursuit would continuously galvanize the inner capacity of thought to dynamize itself into activity and thus, in turn, co-create the activity that is the text; this dialectic activity, Ristić believes, is deeply political. Here the producer and the user of art become one, enjoined in the 'aktivitet' of endlessly co-creating and co-witnessing history, what, in a 1969 interview, Ristić (after Marx) called 'reversing, or transforming praxis' ('umwälzende Praxis'). In 1984, at the end of his life and after two published editions of the novel, Marko Ristić still treated *Without Measure* as a work in progress.

The (political) futures of Surrealism

Ristić's *Without Measure* proposes a bold vision of artwork as reliant on the (hope of) continuous writing-reading-reworking of artwork and history, thence appreciated and cognizable only in the context of an expansive temporality that multilaterally connects the past, the present and the future. While attentive to unequally paces and divergences in international modernisms, our pursuit of a more global, more multi-levelled, and more multi-sectoral account of modernism still lacks flexible temporal thinking, one that would be more profoundly attuned to the diverse handling of time – and thus also modernity – in each locale and under each circumstances. The never-ending nature of creating art and history that Ristić identifies points us in the direction of just such flexible historical thinking. It is with Ristić's mandate to capture the past but also the futurity of modernist artefacts in mind that I sketch here the future of the Belgrade Surrealist Circle's historically charged practices. These 'future perfect' snapshots of the figures and spaces we have engaged so far host further lessons for scholars of global modernisms.

Image 1: In 1937 Koča Popović joined a contingent of Yugoslav volunteers (*brigadistas yugoslavos*) in Spain, fighting besides the Republican Army in the Spanish Civil War until 1939. With the outbreak of the Second World War, he became a leading figure in the partisan movement, and the Commander of the First Proletarian Division of the Yugoslav Partisans. After the war, Popović became the Chief of the General Staff of the Yugoslav People's Army, then the Minister of Foreign Affairs – a position which he held for more than ten years – and then the Vice-President of Yugoslavia. As the Yugoslav Minister of Foreign Affairs (1953–65), Popović was instrumental in establishing the first alliance of a European country with the postcolonial South. Among Popović's diplomatic accomplishments, one can single out the organization of the legendary 1954–5 long boat trip for the Yugoslav president Josip Broz Tito, during which Tito visited one by one newly independent states in Asia and Africa, forging not only political and cultural links but also affective rapports between global communities (Tito, for one, was the first European head of state to visit independent India, and the Yugoslav Declaration was the first to bring the demands of the Algerian National Liberation Front to the United Nations); orchestration of the 1956 meeting of Yugoslav president, Indian Jawaharlal Nehru and Egypt's Gamal Abdel Nasser at the islands of Brijuni (Yugoslavia), widely seen as the inaugural step in the creation of the non-aligned movement; and the organization of the First Summit of Non-aligned Movement itself.

Image 2: In 1938 Marko Ristić published his long surrealist poem 'Turpituda/e: A Paranoiac-Didactic Rhapsody' ('Turpituda: paranojačko-didaktička rapsodija'), together with surrealist-expressionist artwork by Krsto Hegedušić, as an intermedial work entitled *Turpituda/e* [Turpituda]. The poem ends with the image of 'wolves sharpening their teeth' at the prospect of 'a manic fete' where the concrete and iron of financial watchtowers will spin, the earth will slide down a tangent, seas will fume, and lava will pour out of history. This prophetic imagery of war and revolution, and the visual–verbal blend of daydreaming and eroticism, did not please the authorities: the book was identified as incendiary and almost the entirety of the edition of 500 copies was confiscated and destroyed, under the Kingdom of Yugoslavia Law on the Protection of State Public Security and Order. Fewer than ten copies of the original book have survived, including the author's own copy. After the Second World War, Ristić became socialist Yugoslavia's first ambassador to France, then served as the Head of the influential Special Committee for International Cultural Exchange, and the President of the Yugoslav Permanent Delegation to UNESCO since 1952, where he worked enthusiastically on the promotion and implementation of the Universal Declaration of Human Rights. He was a member of SEC (Société Européenne de Culture), a prominent cultural pan-organization set up in response to the partitioning of Europe, whose first East-West Dialogue conference in Venice in 1956 he attended alongside some key figures of mid-century international modernism – philosophers like Marice Merleau-Ponty and Jean-Paul Sartre; writers like Stephen Spender, Giuseppe Ungaretti and Jarosław Iwaszkiewicz; and art historians like Mikhail Alpatov. He wrote inspiring articles in French and Serbo-Croatian on the necessity of cultural exchanges and dignity and service of translator,[16] and was one of the key figures credited for the persistence of modernism in Yugoslav literatures and arts.

Image 3: It was under the same bridge that Vane Bor memorialized in his photographs that a large group of Jews and Roma from Dorćol passed in 1941, on their way to the train station or Banjica concentration camp, herded into their tragic future by German and Belgrade police. One of those few who escaped this fate was a Sephardic Jew named Oskar Davičo, an acclaimed surrealist poet and one of the foremost members of the Belgrade Surrealist Circle. Davičo was arrested in Italian-occupied Split, and then interned in the region of Parma (Italy), wherefrom he escaped just before German occupation in 1943 and joined the partisan movement. In 1945 he was the Yugoslav court reporter at the Nuremberg war crimes trials. A few years later he re-performed some of the key principles of the Belgrade Surrealist Circle in his series of poems/book-length poem *Human's Human* (*Čovekov čovek*, 1953): permanent self-critique (including the critique of ideology for which one oneself has fought), revolutionary humanism and commitment to an unrelenting pursuit of freedom – a freedom whose content always transforms in interaction between thought and matter. 'I believe in the inventiveness of the human,/who can think freedom to death,' he writes in 'Facts', the central poem in the book. Davičo visited African countries one by one as they gained independence in the late 1950s and early 1960s and subsequently published a travelogue entitled *Black on White* (1962), in which he self-consciously rejects the Orientalizing gaze and highlights his own inadequate knowledge, whilst suggesting a transhemispheric solidarity of the formerly 'downtrodden' and a commonality that, he believes, effectively circumvents Western prejudices and racialized inscriptions. With its sustained critique of racism and its poignant reflections on the author's own 'whiteness' which he now wishes to denounce, Davičo's book also targets the tone of cultural superiority that tainted some of the earlier Yugoslav travelogues of the post-war period.[17]

Image 4: The First Summit Conference of Heads of State or Government of Non-Aligned Countries (later known as the Non-aligned Movement [NAM]) was held in Belgrade from 1 to 6 September 1961.[18] As a socialist country which had won independence through a liberation war and, since 1948, had been precariously but inventively navigating the Cold War international relations, Yugoslavia found natural allies in recently independent Asian, African and Central and South American states. Already in *Outline*, Popović and Ristić were arguing for the inevitable demise of Western individualism and the rise of an ethics and aesthetics of participation modelled on 'the communitarian practices of peoples and native communities from the Global South' and building of multilateral and multi-plane bridges between communities that challenge the state-and-border-based thinking about human habitats.[19] Twenty years later, in their positions as the Minister of Foreign Affairs and Head of Foreign Cultural Exchange, respectively, Popović and Ristić were able to put these thoughts in practice. A hidden punctum of modernism and history emerges here: while the non-aligned movement was a result of increasing cooperation and brainstorming of Tito, Nehru, Nasser, Sukarno of Indonesia and Kwame Nkrumah of Ghana, it was philosophically and politically prepared and organized by the once-surrealist Popović and vitally aided by diplomatic and cultural exchange efforts of other members of the Belgrade Surrealist Circle, including Ristić, Davičo, Dedinac and Matić. From the movement's foundational documents onwards, the NAM named and condemned cultural imperialism, critiqued the developmentalist and linear understanding of history, and promoted what Tito called a 'resolute struggle for decolonization in the field of culture'.[20]

The movement sparked vibrant cultural exchanges. According to some records, more than 40,000 students from the non-aligned countries studied in Yugoslavia between 1961 and 1991, often supported by Yugoslav scholarships; cultural councils were established at quick pace; architecture and urban projects exchanges proliferated; non-Western and minor languages were included in Yugoslav higher education curriculum; multilateral literary translations abounded and unique postcolonial museums like the Museum of African Art (Belgrade, 1977) and the Josip Broz Tito Art Gallery of the Non-aligned Countries in Titograd (Titograd, 1981), which acquired art solely through donations and gifts, were established, serving as models of a new type of cross-cultural cooperation and insight.[21] Post-war international surrealist art and literature thrived and developed along South–South axis in these exchanges. Geo-historically located in Europe and involved in surrealism from the very beginning, Yugoslavia was nevertheless devoid of any imperial historical baggage and without statehood precedence. It was an openly anti-colonial cultural space with committed resources for cultural aid and exchange, and with repeatedly professed aspiration to enable rather than occlude the indigenous types and means of expression and local redefinitions of 'West-originating' artistic movements like surrealism. Positioned as such, for global surrealists, Yugoslavia served as a safe conduit, preferred partner, and an exemplary fringe redefiner/displacer of the cultural material from a 'centre'.[22] For Yugoslav artists and writers, encounters with their non-aligned peers were often an opportunity to engage in self-critique and negotiate their own racial positionality as the white or the white subaltern. Scattered across different countries with histories of disruption (Yugoslavia itself being a prime example here), the archival traces of these encounters are unfortunately scant, random, disorganized. We do have testimonies, however, that Aimé Césaire, Leopold Senghor, Agostinho Neto and many other global South writers with surrealist strand in their poetic portfolio spent time in Yugoslavia;[23] that artists, both heirs and developers of indigenous surrealist practices, interacted and even jointly presented at international art biennales like the International Biennale in Alexandria, the São Paulo Biennial, International Graphic Art Biennial in Ljubljana, Triennale India in New Delhi and festivals of culture like those in Kinshasa, Dakar, Algiers and Lagos; and that one 'non-aligned gift', a Yoruba Gelede mask, features prominently in Marko Ristić's 'The Wall of Surrealism' – an installation-wall in his household, methodically assembled from 1930 to 1970, now regarded as the first installation in Yugoslav art, and on permanent display at the Museum of Contemporary Art in Belgrade.

What lessons about historical modernisms does this temporally expanded look at an avant-garde collective provide in closure? One above all: there is no history that is not a human history and thus the ultimate purpose of any creative activity can only be, as Ristić claims, the 'affirmation of the human' (*BM* 20) – that is, a man's or a woman's realization as a human, always on its own (cultural, historical, individual) terms, and others' acknowledgement of this condition. Believing in infinite creative capacities of the thinking human to transform material world, the Belgrade surrealists not only bequeathed to us some inspiring artwork but also effected a change in real history in a long span and across multiple sites – a change whose contours we have only begun to delineate. Inherent to humans as the anchoring points in the ever-lasting, mutually corrective interaction of thought and matter, the potential for transformation will be released whenever a human self-critically battles thought's proclivity to reify itself by engaging in practices of activation, 'aktivitets'. That such practices, as well as our tools to assess them, must remain unfinalizable and subject to permanent self-critique is an insight with which I would like to close this essay.

Notes

ACKNOWLEDGEMENT. The bulk of my discussion in the middle part of this essay appeared, with a different purpose, as an article: Sanja Bahun, 'Gaps, or the Dialectics of Inter-imperial Art: The Case of the Belgrade Surrealist Circle', *MFS Modern Fiction Studies* 64, no. 3 (Fall 2018): 458–87. I am grateful to *Modern Fiction Studies* and the Johns Hopkins University Press for allowing me to reproduce select material from that publication. I would also like to thank the following institutions which made this work possible: Historical Archives of Belgrade; the Archive and Documentation section of the Museum of Contemporary Art, Belgrade; The Legacy of Marko Ristić in the Archive of the Serbian Academy of Sciences and Arts (SASA), Belgrade; the Library Legacy of Marko Ristić in SASA, Belgrade.

1. Koča Popović and Marko Ristić, *Nacrt za jednu fenomenologiju iracionalnog* [Outline for a Phenomenology of the Irrational], ed. Gojko Tešić (Belgrade: Prosveta, 1985 [1931]), 7–8. For a French translation, see *Esquisse d'une phénoménologie de l'irrationnel* (Sesto San Giovanni: Mimesis, 2016).
2. On inter-imperiality and modernism, see Laura Doyle, 'Modernist Studies and Inter-Imperiality in the Longue Durée', in *The Oxford Handbook of Global Modernisms*, ed. Mark Wollaeger (Oxford: Oxford University Press, 2012), 669–96. On inter-imperial contexts of the Belgrade Surrealist Circle's production, see Bahun, 'Gaps.'
3. Sanja Bahun-Radunović, 'The Value of the Oblique (Notes on Relational Funhouses, Historical Occlusions, and Serbian Surrealism),' in *The Avant-garde and the Margin: New Territories of Modernism*, ed. Sanja Bahun-Radunović and Marinos Pourgouris (Newcastle: Cambridge Scholars Publishing, 2006), 26–52.
4. Marko Ristić, *Oko nadrealizma* I [*Around Surrealism*] (Belgrade: Clio, 2003), 166.
5. René Crevel, 'Des surrealists yougoslaves sont au bagne', *Le surréalisme au service de la revolution* 6 (May 1933): 36–9.
6. On 'placedness', see Laura Doyle and Laura Winkiel, 'Introduction', in *Geomodernisms: Race, Modernism, Modernity*, ed. Doyle and Winkiel (Bloomington: Indiana University Press, 2005), 1–4. The level of education and foreign language knowledge was an occasionally uncomfortable point of distinction between the Paris Centrale and the Belgrade Circle. In a 1931 letter to Ristić from Paris, Popović relates how he translated large chunks of Hegel's text from German into French to André Thirion at a meeting on previous day, apparently in an effort to introduce their *Outline* to the French group and solicit their help in publishing their own text in French. Koča Popović, letter of 6 November 1931. The Legacy of Marko Ristić, SANU Archives, Belgrade, unit of archival preservation 14882, box 2.
7. M(arko) R(istić), 'Pred jednim zidom – objasnjenje istoimene strane ilustracija' ('In Front of a Wall – An Explanation of the Eponymous Illustration Page'), *Nadrealizam danas i ovde* 3 (1932): 51.
8. Ristić and Popović, *Outline*, 49–52.
9. The ratification coincided with the establishment of a one-party Austrofascist state in Austria, Hitler's May Day speech at Tempelhof Air Field and the establishment of the notorious People's Court (Volksgerichtshof), empowered to mete out death sentences for high treason in Berlin, Germany.

10　Marko Ristić, *Bez mere* [*Without Measure*] (Belgrade: Nolit, 1986, henceforth *BM*), 91.
11　Milan Dedinac, letter of 15 February 1927, The Legacy of Marko Ristić.
12　*BM*, 232–3.
13　Ibid., 233.
14　Ristić started his PhD study in Philosophy in 1927, but never finished it. The surviving drafts of his doctoral thesis, 'La Métaphysique des faits divers' ('Metaphysics of News'), focus on the flaws of traditional metaphysics, circulation of news and the category of the dialectic moment (Ristić 1985: 243–54).
15　G. W. F. Hegel, 'Metaphysik' ['Metaphysics'], in *Vorlesungen über die Geschichte der Philosophie II* [Lectures on the History of Philosophy II]. Vol. 19, ed. Eva Moldenhauer and Karl Markus Michel (Berlin: Suhrkamp, 1986), 162.
16　Marko Ristić, 'Dignité et Servitude du Traducteur', *Babel* 9, no. 3 (1963): 123–4.
17　Oskar Davičo, *Crno na belo* [*Black on White*] (Belgrade: Prosveta, 1962), 9, 20, et passim.
18　The first Summit was attended by Afghanistan, Algeria, Yemen, Myanmar, Cambodia, Sri Lanka, Congo, Cuba, Cyprus, Egypt, Ethiopia, Ghana, Guinea, India, Indonesia, Iraq, Lebanon, Mali, Morocco, Nepal, Saudi Arabia, Somalia, Sudan, Syria, Tunisia and Yugoslavia. Some historians erroneously suggest the Bandung Asian-African Conference (18–24 April 1955, Bandung, Indonesia) was an antecedent for the establishment of the non-aligned movement, but this is erroneous since nonalignment as a concept and political strategy emerged distinctly only in the period 1956–61 and some key figures in the movement like Tito and Kwame Nkrumah of Ghana were not present at Bandung. For survey, see *The Non Aligned Movement and the Cold War*, ed. Nataša Mišković, Harald Fischer Tine and Nada Boškovska (London: Routledge, 2014).
19　Ristić and Popović, *Outline*, 116–17.
20　Josip Broz Tito, 'Address to the Sixth Conference of Heads of State or Government of Non-aligned Countries', Havana, September 4, 1979 (Red Hill, A.C.T.: Embassy of the Socialist Federal Republic of Yugoslavia, 1979), 24.
21　See Bojana Piškur, 'Yugoslavia: Other Modernities, Other Histories', *Inter-Asia Cultural Studies* 20, no. 1 (2019): 131–9; Ana Sladojević, *Slike o Africi/ Images of Africa*, Non-aligned Modernisms, Vol. 1 (Belgrade: Museum of Contemporary Art, 2015).
22　On such operation, see Homi Bhabha, 'The Third Space', in *Identity, Community, Culture, Difference*, ed., Jonathan Rutherford (London: Lawrence & Wishart 1990), 210.
23　Aimé Césaire first travelled to the Kingdom of Yugoslavia in 1935, when his visit to Martinska island, off the Adriatic coast, prompted him to start writing *Notebook of a Return to the Native Land* (*Cahier d'un retour au pays natal*, 1939).

Bibliography

Adams, Henry. *The Education of Henry Adams: An Autobiography*. Cambridge, MA: The Riverside Press, 1918.

Adorno, Theodor W. *Aesthetic Theory*, edited and translated by Robert Hullot-Kentor. London and New York: Continuum, 2002.

Agamben, Giorgio. *Infancy and History: The Destruction of Experience*, translated by Liz Heron. London and New York: Verso, 1993.

Agamben, Giorgio. *Potentialities: Collected Essays in Philosophy*, edited and translated by Daniel Heller-Roazen. Stanford: Stanford University Press, 1999.

Agamben, Giorgio. *The Time That Remains: A Commentary on the Letter to the Romans*, translated by Patricia Dailey. Stanford: Stanford University Press, 2005.

Agamben, Giorgio. *'What Is an Apparatus?' and Other Essays*, translated by David Kishik and Stefan Pedatella. Redwood City: Stanford University Press, 2009.

Alexandrian, Sarane. *André Breton par lui-même*. Paris: Éditions du Seuil, 1971.

Alt, Suvi. 'Darkness in a Blink of an Eye', *Angelaki* 21, no. 2 (June 2016): 17–31.

Appadurai, Arjun. *Modernity at Large: Cultural Dimensions of Globalization*. Minneapolis, MN: University of Minnesota Press, 1996.

Ardis, Ann and Patrick Collier. Eds. *Transatlantic Print Culture, 1880–1940: Emerging Media, Emerging Modernisms*. Basingstoke: Palgrave Macmillan, 2008.

Arendt, Hannah. *The Jewish Writings*. New York: Schocken, 2007.

Aristotle. *Poetics*. *The Complete Works of Aristotle*; *The Revised Oxford Translation Vol. 2*, edited by Jonathan Barnes, translated by Ingram Baywater. New Jersey: Princeton University Press, 1984.

Aristotle. *Physics, Vol. 1: Books 1–4*, translated by P. H. Wicksteed and F. M. Cornford. Cambridge, MA: Harvard University Press Loeb Classical Library, 1989.

Arvatov, Boris. *Art and Production*, translated by Shushan Avagyan. London: Pluto Press, 2017.

Avanessian, Armen and Suhail Malik. 'The Speculative Time Complex'. In *The Time-Complex. Post-Contemporary*, edited by Armen Avanessian and Suhail Malik, 5–56. Miami: NAME Publications, 2016.

Avanessian, Armen and Suhail Malik. Eds. *The Time-Complex. Post-Contemporary*. Miami: NAME Publications, 2016.

Bachelard, Gaston. *The Poetics of Space*, translated by Maria Jolas. Boston: Beacon Press, 1994.

Badiou, Alain. *Saint Paul: The Foundation of Universalism*, translated by Ray Brassier. Stanford CA: Stanford University Press, 2003.

Badiou, Alain. *Handbook of Inaesthetics*, translated by Alberto Toscano. Stanford: Stanford University Press, 2005.

Badiou, Alain. *The Century*, translated by Alberto Toscano. Cambridge: Polity Press, 2007.

Bahun-Radunović, Sanja. 'The Value of the Oblique (Notes on Relational Funhouses, Historical Occlusions, and Serbian Surrealism)'. In *The Avant-garde and the Margin: New Territories of Modernism*, edited by Sanja Bahun-Radunović and Marinos Pourgouris, 26–52. Newcastle: Cambridge Scholars Publishing, 2006.

Bahun-Radunović, Sanja and Marinos Pourgouris. Eds. *The Avant-garde and the Margin: New Territories of Modernism*. Newcastle: Cambridge Scholars Publishing, 2006.

Bahun, Sanja. 'The Burden of the Past, The Dialectics of the Present: Notes on Virginia Woolf's and Walter Benjamin's Philosophies of History', *Modernist Cultures* 3, no. 2 (2008): 100–15.

Baker, Alan R.H. *Fraternity among the Peasantry: Sociability and Voluntary Associations in the Loire Valley, 1815–1914*. Cambridge: Cambridge University Press, 1999.

Balakian, Anna and Rudolf Kuenzli. *André Breton Today*. New York: Willis Locker & Owens, 1989.

Bart, Pauline B. 'The Myth of Value-Free Psychotherapy'. In *The Sociology of the Future: Theory, Cases, and Annotated Bibliography*, edited by Wendell Bell and James A. Mau, 113–59. New York: Russell Sage Foundation, 1971.

Barthes, Roland. *Mythologies*. Paris: Editions du Seuil, 1957.

Barthes, Roland. *The Rustle of Language*, translated by Richard Howard. New York: Hill & Wang, 1986.

Bazin, Victoria. *Modernism Edited: Marianne Moore and the Dial Magazine*. Edinburgh: Edinburgh University Press, 2019.

Beale, Marjorie A. *The Modernist Enterprise: French Elites and the Threat of Modernity 1900–1940*. Stanford: Stanford University Press, 1999.

Beckett, Samuel. *Letters Vol. II: 1941–1956*. Cambridge: Cambridge University Press, 2012.

Beckett, Samuel. *Letters Vol. IV: 1966–1989*. Cambridge: Cambridge University Press, 2016.

Beckett, Samuel and others. *Our Exagmination Round His Factification for Incamination of Work in Progress*. London: Faber, 1972.

Bedouelle, Guy and Jean-Paul Costa. *Les laïcités à la française*. Paris: Presses universitaires de France, 1998.

Bell, Wendell and James A. Mau. Eds. *The Sociology of the Future: Theory, Cases, and Annotated Bibliography*. New York: Russell Sage Foundation, 1971.

Bellot, Émile. *Album du Bon Bock*. Paris: Ludovic Baschet, 1878.

Benjamin, Andrew. *Art, Mimesis and the Avant-garde: Aspects of a Philosophy of Difference*. London: Routledge, 1991.

Benjamin, Walter. *Städtebilder*: 'Nachwort' von Peter Szondi. Frankfurt: Suhrkamp, 1963.

Benjamin, Walter. *Illuminations*, edited with an Introduction by Hannah Arendt, translated by Harry Zohn. New York: Schocken Books, 1969.

Benjamin, Walter. *Berliner Kindheit um neunzehnhundert*, 'Nachwort' von Theodor W. Adorno. Frankfurt: Suhrkamp, 1987.

Benjamin, Walter. *The Correspondence of Walter Benjamin, 1910–1940*, edited by Gershom Scholem and Theodor Adorno, translated by Manfred Jacobson and Evelyn Jacobson. Chicago: University of Chicago Press, 1994.

Benjamin, Walter. *One-Way Street*, translated by Edmund Jephcott. In *Selected Writings Vol. 1*, edited by Marcus Bullock and Michael W. Jennings, 456–7. Cambridge, MA: The Belknap Press of the Harvard University Press, 1996.

Benjamin, Walter. *Selected Writings Vol. 1: 1913–1926*, edited by Marcus Bullock and Michael W. Jennings. Cambridge, MA: The Belknap Press of the Harvard University Press, 1996.

Benjamin, Walter. *The Arcades Project*, translated by Howard Eiland and Kevin McLaughlin. Cambridge, MA: Harvard University Press, 1999.

Benjamin, Walter. *Gesammelte Briefe Vol. 5*, edited by Christoph Gödde. Frankfurt am Main: Suhrkamp, 1999.

Benjamin, Walter. *Selected Writings Vol. 2: 1927–1934*, edited by Marcus Bullock, Howard Eiland and Garry Smith, translated by Rodney Livingstone and Others. Cambridge, MA: Harvard University Press, 1999.

Benjamin, Walter. *Selected Writings Vol. 3:1935–1938*, edited by Howard Eiland and Michael Jennings, translated by Edmund Jephcott and Others. Cambridge, MA: Harvard University Press, 2002.

Benjamin, Walter. *Selected Writings Vol. 4: 1938–1940*, edited by Howard Eiland and Michael W. Jennings, translated by Edmund Jephcott and Others. Cambridge, MA: Harvard University Press, 2006.

Benson, Peter. *Black Orpheus, Transition, and Modern Cultural Awakening in Africa*. Berkeley, CA: University of California Press, 1986.

Bergson, Henri. *Time and Free Will: An Essay on the Immediate Data of Consciousness*. 1880, translated by F.L. Pogson. London: George Allen & Unwin Ltd, 1910.

Bergson, Henri. *Creative Evolution*. 1907, translated by Arthur Mitchell. New York: Henry Holt and Company, 1911.

Berman, Jessica. *Modernist Commitments: Ethics, Politics, and Transnational Modernism*. New York: Columbia University Press, 2011.

Bernstein, J.M. Ed. *Classic and Romantic German Aesthetics*. Cambridge: Cambridge University Press, 2003.

Bhabha, Homi. 'The Third Space'. In *Identity, Community, Culture, Difference*, edited by Jonathan Rutherford. London: Lawrence & Wishart, 1990.

Billard, Jules. *Un essai de doctrine, le fayolisme*. Paris: Jouve, 1924.

Bishop, Tom. *Le Passeur d'Océan: carnets d'un ami américain*. Paris: Payot, 1989.

Blacker, C. P. *Birth Control and the State*. London: Kegan Paul, 1926.

Blum, Françoise with Sylvie Le Dantec. Eds. *Les vies de Pierre Naville*. Villeneuve-d'Ascq: Presses Universitaires du Septentrion, 2007.

Boer, Roland. 'The Immeasurably Creative Politics of Job: Antonio Negri and the Bible'. *SubStance* 41, no. 3 (2012): 93–108.

Bohrer, Karl Heinz. *Suddenness: On the Moment of Aesthetic Appearance*, translated by Ruth Crowley. New York: Columbia University Press, 1994.

Bonnet, Marguerite. Ed. *Les Critiques de notre temps et Breton*. Paris: Garnier Frères, 1974.

Boulez, Pierre. *Orientations: Collected Writings*, edited by Jean-Jacques Nattiez, translated by Martin Cooper. Cambridge, MA: Harvard University Press, 1986.

Bourdieu, Pierre. *The Rules of Art: Genesis and Structure of the Literary Field*, translated by Susan Emanuel. Stanford: Stanford University Press, 1995.

Brake, Laurel. 'The Case of W. T. Stead'. In *Transatlantic Print Culture, 1880–1940: Emerging Media, Emerging Modernisms*, edited by Ann Ardis and Patrick Collier. Basingstoke: Palgrave Macmillan, 2008.

Bredbeck, Gregory W. 'Missionary Positions: Reading the Bible in E.M. Forster's "The Life to Come"'. In *Reclaiming the Sacred: The Bible in Gay and Lesbian Culture*, edited by Raymond-Jean Frontain, 137–60. New York: Harington Park Press, 2003.

Breton, André. *Œuvres complètes: Tome I*, edited by Marguerite Bonnet. Paris: Gallimard, 1988.

Breton, André. 'L'Organisation du travail et le système Taylor'. *La Nature*, quarante-quatrième année, deuxième semestre, no. 2246 (14 October 1916): 246–51.

Breton, André. 'La Dernière grève'. *La Révolution surréaliste* 2 (15 January 1925): 1–3.

Breton, André. *Nadja*, translated by Richard Howard. New York: Grove Press, 1960.

Breton, André. *What Is Surrealism? Selected Writings*, edited by Franklin Rosemont, translated by Samuel Beckett et al. New York: Pathfinder, 1978.

Breton, André. *42 rue Fontaine: Tome III: Manuscrits*. Paris: Calmels Cohen, 2003.

Breton, André. *Lettres à Simone*, edited by Jean-Michel Goutier. Paris: Gallimard, 2016.

Brigstocke, Julian. 'Defiant Laughter: Humour and the Aesthetics of Place in Late Nineteenth-Century Montmartre'. *Cultural Geographies* 19, no. 2 (2012): 217–35.

Brooker, Peter and Andrew Thacker. Eds. *Geographies of Modernism*. London: Routledge, 2005.

Brooker, Peter and Andrew Thacker. Eds. *The Oxford Critical and Cultural History of Modernist Magazines Vol. I: Britain and Ireland 1880–1955*. Oxford: Oxford University Press, 2009.

Brooker, Peter and Andrew Thacker. Eds. *The Oxford Critical and Cultural History of Modernist Magazines Vol. II: North America, 1894–1960*. Oxford: Oxford University Press, 2012.

Brooker, Peter, Sascha Bru, Andrew Thacker and Christian Weiko. Eds. *The Oxford Critical and Cultural History of Modernist Magazines: Vol. III: Europe 1880–1940*. Oxford: Oxford University Press, 2013.

Browder, Clifford. *André Breton: Arbiter of Surrealism*. Geneva: Librairie Drosz, 1967.

Bryher. 'Paris, 1900', *Life and Letters To-day* 16, no 8 (Summer 1937): 33–42.
Bryher. *The Heart to Artemis: A Writer's Memoir*. London: Collins, 1963.
Buck-Morss, Susan. *Dreamworld and Catastrophe: The Passing of Mass Utopia in East and West*. Cambridge, MA: MIT Press, 2000.
Buck-Morss, Susan. 'Revolutionary Time: The Vanguard and the Avant-Garde'. In *Benjamin Studien/Studies: Perception and Experience in Modernity*, edited by Helga Geyer-Ryan, 209–25. Amsterdam: Rodopi, 2002.
Budraitskis, Ilya and Arseniy Zhilyaev. Eds. *Pedagogical Poem: The Archive of the Future Museum of History*. Moscow/Venice: V-A-C Foundation/Marsilio, 2014.
Bulson, Eric. *Little Magazine, World Form*. New York: Columbia University Press, 2017.
Butler, Christopher. *Early Modernism: Literature, Music and Painting in Europe 1900–1916*. Oxford: Clarendon Press, 1994.
Cage, John. *Silence*. Middletown, Connecticut: Wesleyan University Press, 1961.
Carlioz, Joseph. *Le Gouvernement des entreprises commerciales et industrielles*. Paris: Dunod, 1921.
Carr, Helen. *The Verse Revolutionaries: Ezra Pound, H.D. and the Imagists*. London: Jonathan Cape, 2009.
Carter, E. H. and C. K. Ogden. *General History: In Outline and Story*. London: Thomas Nelson, 1938.
Cate, Philip Dennis and Mary Shaw. *The Spirit of Montmartre*. New Brunswick, NJ: Rutgers, 1996.
Cavell, Stanley. *The World Viewed: Reflections on the Ontology of Film*. Cambridge, MA: Harvard University Press, 1979.
Caws, Mary Ann, Rudolf Kuenzli and Gwen Raaberg. Eds. *Surrealism and Women*. Cambridge, MA: MIT Press, 1991.
Caws, Mary Ann. *André Breton*. New York: Twayne, 1996.
Césaire, Aimé. *Notebook of a Return to the Native Land/Cahier d'un retour au pays natal*. 1939, translated by Mireille Rosello with Annie Pritchard. Newcastle upon Tyne: Bloodaxe, 1995.
Chakrabarty, Dipesh. 'Postcoloniality and the Artifice of History: Who Speaks of Indian Pasts? *Representations*, no. 37 (Winter 1992): 1–26.
Chaney, Lisa. *Coco Chanel: An Intimate Life*. New York: Viking, 2011.
Chavet, Gabriel. *Ce que doit savoir l'employé de bureau*. Paris: Gauthier-Villars & Cie., 1921.
Chevallier, Pierre. *La séparation de l'Eglise et de l'Ecole*. Paris: Fayard, 1981.
Chielens, Edward E. Ed. *American Literary Magazines: The Twentieth Century*. Westport, CN: Greenwood Press, 1992.
Churchill, Suzanne and Adam McKible. 'Little Magazines and Modernism: An Introduction'. *American Periodicals: A Journal of History, Criticism and Bibliography* 15, no. 1 (2005): 1–5.
Clark, Timothy James. 'Clement Greenberg's Theory of Art'. *Critical Inquiry* 9, no. 1 (September 1982): 139–56.

Clark, Timothy James. *Image of the People: Gustave Courbet and the 1848 Revolution*. London: Thames & Hudson, 1982.

Clarke, Jackie. *France in the Age of Organization: Factory, Home and Nation from the 1920s to Vichy*. New York: Berghahn Books, 2001.

Cole, Lori. '*Légitime Défense*: From Communism and Surrealism to Caribbean Self-Definition'. *Journal of Surrealism and the Americas* 4, no. 1 (2010): 15–30.

Collier, Patrick. 'What Is Modern Periodical Studies?' *Journal of Modern Periodical Studies* 6, no. 2 (2015): 92–111.

Cottington, David. 'What the Papers Say: Politics and Ideology in Picasso's Collages of 1912'. *Art Journal* 47, no. 4 (1988): 350–9.

Crevel, René. 'Des surrealists yougoslaves sont au bagne'. *Le surréalisme au service de la revolution* 6 (May 1933): 36–9.

Crow, Thomas. *Modern Art in the Common Culture*. New Haven: Yale University Press, 1998.

Cunningham, David. 'A Time for Dissonance and Noise: On Adorno, Music, and the Concept of Modernism'. *Angelaki* 8, no. 1 (2003): 61–74.

Cunningham, David. 'Architecture, Utopia and the Futures of the Avant-Garde'. *The Journal of Architecture* 6, no. 2 (2001): 169–82.

Cunningham, David. 'The Futures of Surrealism: Hegelianism, Romanticism, and the Avant-Garde'. *SubStance* 34, no. 2 (2005): 47–65.

Darragon, Eric. *Manet*. Paris: Fayard, 1989.

Davičo, Oskar. *Crno na belo* [*Black on White*]. Belgrade: Prosveta, 1962.

de Gourmont, Remy. *Les Petites Revues, essai de bibliographie*. Paris: Librairie du Mercure de France, 1900.

de Man, Paul. *Blindness and Insight: Essays in the Rhetoric of Contemporary Criticism*. London: Routledge, 1989.

de Quincey, Thomas. *Confessions of an English Opium Eater*. Harmondsworth: Penguin, 1986.

Dilthey, Wilhelm. *Selected Writings Vol. 5: Poetry and Experience*, edited by Rudolf Makkreel and Frithjof Rodi, translated by Louis Agosta, Rudolf Makkreel and Michael Neville. Princeton, NJ: Princeton University Press, 1985.

Dobrée, Bonamy. *Timotheus; The Future of the Theatre*. London: Kegan Paul, 1925.

Doyle, Laura. 'Modernist Studies and Inter-Imperiality in the Longue Durée'. In *The Oxford Handbook of Global Modernisms*, edited by Mark Wollaeger, 669–96. Oxford: Oxford University Press, 2012.

Doyle, Laura and Laura Winkiel. Eds. *Geomodernisms: Race, Modernism, Modernity*. Bloomington: Indiana University Press, 2005.

Drouin, Jeff. 'Close and Distant Reading Modernism'. *Journal of Modern Periodical Studies* 5, no. 1 (2014): 115.

Durozoi, Gérard. *History of the Surrealist Movement*, translated by Alison Anderson. Chicago: University of Chicago Press, 2002.

Duthuit, Georges. 'Matisse and Byzantine Space'. *Transition Forty-Nine*, no. 5 (1949): 20–39.

Dworkin, Craig. *No Medium*. Cambridge, MA: The MIT Press, 2013.

Edwards, Brent Hayes. *The Practice of Diaspora: Literature, Translation, and the Rise of Black Internationalism*. Cambridge, MA: Harvard University Press, 2003.

Einstein, Carl. *Werke—Berliner Ausgabe, Band 3: 1929–1940*, edited by Hermann Haarmann et al. Berlin: Fannei & Walz, 1996.

Eisenstein, Sergei. *Film Form: Essays in Film Theory*, edited and translated by Jay Leyda. New York and London: Harcourt Brace Jovanovich, 1949.

Eliot, T. S. *Selected Prose of T. S. Eliot*, edited by Frank Kermode. London: Faber/New York: Farrar, Straus and Giroux, 1975.

Eliot, T. S. *Selected Essays 1917–1932*. London: Faber & Faber, 1980.

Eliot, T. S. *The Poems of T. S. Eliot Vol. 1*, edited by Christopher Ricks and Jim McCue. London: Faber, 2015.

Ellmann, Richard. *James Joyce*. Rev. edn. Oxford: Oxford University Press, 1982.

Emden, Christian J. *Walter Benjamins Archäologie der Moderne: Kulturwissenschaft um 1930*. Munich: Wilhelm Fink Verlag, 2006.

Eric Robertson and Robert Vilain. Eds. *Yvan Goll—Claire Goll: Texts and Contexts*. Amsterdam: Rodopi B.V., 1997.

Eugène Jolas, 'From Jabberwocky to "Lettrism"', *Transition Forty-Eight*, no 1, ed. Georges Duthuit (January 1948): 104–20.

Ezra Pound. *Literary Essays of Ezra Pound*, edited by T.S. Eliot. London: Faber and Faber, 1954.

Faxon, Frederick Winthrop. *Ephemeral Bibelots: A Bibliography of the Modern Chap Books and Their Imitators*. Boston: Boston Book Company, 1903.

Fayol, Henri. *Administration industrielle et générale*. Paris: Dunod et Pinat, 1917.

Fenellosa, Ernest and Ezra Pound. *The Chinese Written Character as a Medium for Poetry: A Critical Edition*, edited by Haun Saussy, Jonathan Stalling and Lucas Klein. New York: Fordham University Press, 2008.

Fijałkowski, Krzysztof and Michael Richardson. Eds. *Refusal of the Shadow: Surrealism and the Caribbean*. London: Verso, 1996.

Ford, Caroline C. *Divided Houses: Religion and Gender in Modern France*. Ithaca, NY: Cornell University Press, 2005.

Ford, Ford Madox. *It Was the Nightingale*. London: Heinemann, 1934.

Ford, Ford Madox. *A History of Our Own Times*, edited by Sondra Stang and Solon Beinfeld. Bloomington: Indiana University Press, 1988.

Ford, Ford Madox. *A Man Could Stand Up*, edited by Sara Haslam. Manchester: Carcanet, 2011.

Ford, Ford Madox and Joseph Conrad. *Romance*. London: Smith, Elder & Co., 1903.

Forster, E. M. *Howards End*. London: Edward Arnold, 1910.

Forster, E. M. *Collected Short Stories*. Harmondsworth: Penguin Books, 1954.

Forster, E. M. *The Life to Come and Other Stories*, edited by Oliver Stallybrass. London: Edward Arnold, 1972.

Forster, E. M. *Two Cheers for Democracy*. London: Edward Arnold, 1972.
Forster, E. M. *A Passage to India*. London: Penguin Classics, 2005.
Forster, E. M. *Maurice*. London: Penguin Classics, 2005.
Fortescue, William. *The Third Republic in France 1970–1940: Conflicts and Continuities*. London: Routledge, 2000.
Foster, Hal. *Compulsive Beauty*. Cambridge, MA: MIT Press, 1993.
Foster, Hal. *Prosthetic Gods*. Cambridge, MA: MIT Press, 2004.
Foster, Hal and Rosalind Krauss, Yve-Alain Bois and Benjamin H.D. Buchloh. *Art Since 1900*. London: Thames & Hudson, 2004.
Franck, Dan. *Bohemian Paris: Picasso Modigliani, Matisse, and the Birth of Modern Art*, translated by Cynthia Liebow. New York: Grove Press, 2003.
Freud, Sigmund, Stefan Zweig. *Correspondance*. Paris: Rivages, 1995.
Fried, Michael. 'Theories of Art after Minimalism and Pop'. In *Discussions in Contemporary Culture 1*, edited by Hal Foster, 55–8. Seattle: Bay Press, 1987.
Fried, Michael. 'Art and Objecthood'. In *Art in Theory 1900–2000*, edited by Charles Harrison and Paul Wood, 835–46. Malden/Oxford/Carlton: Blackwell, 2003.
Friedman, Susan Stanford. *Planetary Modernisms: Provocations on Modernity across Time*. New York: Columbia University Press, 2018.
Frontain, Raymond-Jean. Ed. *Reclaiming the Sacred: The Bible in Gay and Lesbian Culture*. New York: Harington Park Press, 2003.
Fukuyama, Francis. 'The End of History?' *The National Interest*, no. 16 (1989): 3–18.
Gadamer, Hans-Georg. *Truth and Method*. 2nd edn., edited by John Cumming and Garret Barden, translated by W. Glen-Doepel. New York: Crossroad, 1989.
Garb, Tamar. 'Revising the Revisionists: The Formation of the Union des Femmes Peintres et Sculpteurs'. *Art Journal* 48, no. 1 (Spring 1989): 63–70.
Gardey, Delphine. 'The Standardization of a Technical Practice: Typing (1883–1930)'. *History and Technology* 15, no. 4 (1999): 313–43.
Garland, David. 'What Is a "History of the Present"? On Foucault's Genealogies and Their Critical Preconditions'. *Punishment & Society* 16, no. 4 (2014): 365–84. DOI:10.1177/1462474514541711.
Gelber, Mark H. Ed. *Stefan Zweig Reconsidered: New Perspectives on His Literary and Biographical Writings*. Tübingen: Max Niemeyer Verlag, 2007.
Gener, Pompeu. *La Mort et le Diable: Histoire et Philosophie des deux Négations Suprêmes*. Paris: Reinwald, 1880.
Geyer-Ryan, Helga. Ed. *Benjamin Studien/Studies: Perception and Experience in Modernity*. Amsterdam: Rodopi, 2002.
Giddens, Anthony. *Conversations with Anthony Giddens: Making Sense of Modernity*. Stanford, CA: Stanford University Press, 1998.
Gilbert, Sandra M. and Susan Gubar. *No Man's Land: The Place of the Woman Writer in the Twentieth Century*. 3 Vols. New Haven: Yale University Press, 1988.
Gillies, Mary Ann. *Bergson and British Modernism*. Montréal, QC: McGill-Queen's University Press, 1996.

Goethe, Johann Wolfgang von. *Dichtung und Wahrheit. Aus meinem Leben*. Munich: Carl Hanser, 1960.

Golan, Romy. *Modernity and Nostalgia: Art and Politics in France between the Wars*. New Haven and London: Yale University Press, 1995.

Goldman, Jane. *Modernism, 1910–1945 Image to Apocalypse*. Basingstoke: Palgrave Macmillan, 2004.

Goodman, Nelson. *Languages of Art*. Indianapolis: Bobbs-Merrill, 1968.

Goudeau, Émile. *Dix ans de bohème*. 1888. Reprinted with notes and introduction. Paris: Éditions Champs Vallon, 2000.

Gracq, Julien. *André Breton: Quelques aspects de l'écrivain*. Paris: José Corti, 1977.

Green, Nicholas. '"All the Flowers of the Field": The State, Liberalism and Art in France under the Early Third Republic'. *Oxford Art Journal* 10, no. 1 (1987): 71–84.

Greenberg, Clement. 'Detached Observations'. *Arts Magazine* (December 1976). Available online: http://www.sharecom.ca/greenberg/detached.html (accessed 18 October 2018).

Greenberg, Clement. *The Collected Essays and Criticism Vol. 1: 1939–1944*, edited by John O'Brian. Chicago: The University of Chicago Press, 1986.

Greenberg, Clement. *The Collected Essays and Criticism Vol. 4: Modernism with a Vengeance, 1957–1969*. Chicago: Chicago University Press, 1993.

Greenberg, Clement. 'Avant-Garde and Kitsch'. 1939. In *Art in Theory 1900–2000*, edited by Charles Harrison and Paul Wood, 539–49. Malden/Oxford/Carlton: Blackwell, 2003.

Greenberg, Clement. 'Modernist Painting'. 1960–65. In *Art in Theory 1900–2000*, edited by Charles Harrison and Paul Wood, 773–9. Malden/Oxford/Carlton: Blackwell, 2003.

Greenberg, Clement. 'Towards a Newer Laocoon'. 1940. In *Art in Theory 1900–2000*, edited by Charles Harrison and Paul Wood, 562–8. Malden/Oxford/Carlton: Blackwell, 2003.

Greenhalgh, Chris. *Coco Chanel & Igor Stravinsky*. New York: Riverhead books, 2002.

Grenier, Catherine. 'Modernité: révolution ou révélation ?' In *La Parenthèse du moderne*, edited by Marianne Alphant: 71–82. Paris: Centre Pompidou, 2005.

Griffiths, Sian. Ed. *Predictions*. Oxford: Oxford University Press, 1999.

Grigg, David. 'Convergence in European Diets: The Case of Alcoholic Beverages'. *GeoJournal* 44, no. 1 (January 1998): 9–18.

Guy, Kolleen M. 'Wine, Champagne and the Making of French Identity in the Belle Epoque'. In *Food, Drink and Identity: Cooking Eating and Drinking in Europe since the Middle Ages*, edited by Peter Scholliers. Oxford: Berg, 2001.

Hal Foster. Ed. *Discussions in Contemporary Culture*, no. 1. Seattle: Bay Press, 1987.

Haldane, J.B.S. *Daedalus; or, Science and the Future*. London: Kegan Paul, Trench and Trübner, 1923.

Harding, Jason. *The Criterion: Cultural Politics and Periodical Networks in Interwar Britain*. Oxford: Oxford University Press, 2002.

Harpham, Geoffrey Galt. *Language Alone: The Critical Fetish of Modernity*. New York: Routledge, 2002.

Harrison, Charles and Paul Wood. Eds. *Art in Theory 1900–2000*. Malden/Oxford/Carlton: Blackwell, 2003.

Harrison, Thomas. *1910: The Emancipation of Dissonance*. Berkeley: University of California Press, 1996.

Hartog, François. *Régimes d'historicité. Présentisme et expériences du temps*. Paris: Seuil, 2003.

Hatch, John J. 'Desire, Heavenly Bodies, and a Surrealist's Fascination with the Celestial Theatre'. *Culture and Cosmos* 8, nos. 1–2 (2004): 87–106.

Hegel, G. W. F. 'Metaphysik'. *Vorlesungen über die Geschichte der Philosophie II Vol. 19*, edited by Eva Moldenhauer and Karl Markus Michel. Berlin: Suhrkamp, 1986.

Hoffman, Frederick, Charles Allen and Carolyn F. Ulrich. *The Little Magazine: A History and a Bibliography*. Princeton, NJ: Princeton University Press, 1947.

Hofmann, Werner. *Die Moderne im Rückblick. Hauptwege der Kunstgeschichte*. München: Beck, 1998.

Hulme, T. E. *Selected Writings*, edited by Patrick McGuinness. New York: Routledge, 2003.

Huyssens, Andreas. 'Geographies of Modernism in a Globalizing World'. In *Geographies of Modernism*, edited by Peter Brooker and Andrew Thacker, 6–18. London: Routledge, 2005.

Ilie, Paul. 'Nietzsche in Spain: 1890–1910'. *PMLA* 79, no. 1 (March 1964): 8–96.

James, Henry. *Letters of Henry James Vol. 2*, edited by Percy Lubbock. New York: Charles Scriber's Sons, 1920.

Jameson, Fredric. *The Political Unconscious, Narrative as a Socially Symbolical Act*. London: Methuen, 1981.

Jolas, Eugène. *Critical Writings, 1924–1951*, edited and with an introduction by Klaus H. Kiefer and Rainer Rumold. Evanston: Northwestern University Press, 2009.

Jones, Caroline A. *Eyesight Alone: Clement Greenberg's Modernism and the Bureaucratization of the Senses*. Chicago/London: The University of Chicago Press, 2005.

Joyce, James. 'Exiles'. In *Poems and Exiles*, edited with Introduction by J. C. C. Mays. London: Penguin, 1992.

Joyce, Stanislaus. *My Brother's Keeper: James Joyce's Early Years*. Cambridge: Da Capo Press, 2003.

Kahane, Benjamin. 'Queer Modernism'. In *A Handbook of Modernism Studies*, edited by Jean-Michel Rabaté, 347–61. Oxford: Wiley, 2013.

Kandiah, Michael D. 'Contemporary History', https://www.history.ac.uk/makinghistory/resources/articles/contemporary_history.html.

Kandinsky, Wassily. *Concerning the Spiritual in Art*. Rev. edn., translated by M.T.H. Sadler. London: Dover, 2012.

Kaplan, Carola M. and Anne B. Simpson. Eds. *Seeing Double: Revisioning Edwardian and Modern Literature*. London: Macmillan, 1996.

Keiger, John F.V. *Raymond Poincaré*. Cambridge: Cambridge University Press, 1997.

Kelly, Julia. 'The Bureau of Surrealist Research'. In *Twilight Visions: Surrealism and Paris*, edited by Therese Lichtenstein, 79–101. Nashville: Frist Center for the Visual Arts, with University of California Press, 2009.

Kermode, Frank. *The Sense of an Ending: Studies in the Theory of Fiction*. Oxford and New York: Oxford University Press, 2000.

Kern, Stephen. *The Culture of Time and Space, 1880–1918*. Cambridge, MA: Harvard University Press, 1983.

Kim, Sharon. *Literary Epiphany in the Novel, 1850–1950: Constellations of the Soul*. New York: Palgrave Macmillan, 2012.

Kime Scott, Bonnie. Ed. *The Gender of Modernism: A Critical Anthology*. Bloomington: Indiana University Press, 1990.

Knowlson, James. *Damned to Fame: The Life of Samuel Beckett*. London: Bloomsbury, 1997.

Koestler, Arthur. *Arrow in the Blue*. London: Readers Union, William Collins and Hamish Hamilton, 1954.

Koestler, Arthur. *The Invisible Journey. Autobiography 1931–53*. London: Collins with Hamish Hamilton, 1954.

Koselleck, Reinhart. *Vergangene Zukunft. Zur Semantik geschichtlicher Zeiten*. Frankfurt a/Main: Suhrkamp, 1979.

Krauss, Rosalind. *Passages in Modern Sculpture*. Cambridge, MA: The MIT Press, 1981.

Krauss, Rosalind. *The Originality of the Avant-Garde and Other Modernist Myths*. Cambridge: The MIT Press, 1985.

Krauss, Rosalind. *Under Blue Cup*. Cambridge, MA: The MIT Press, 2011.

Krauss, Rosalind E. and Jane Livingston. Eds. *L'Amour fou: Photography and Surrealism*. Washington DC: The Corcoran Gallery of Art, with Abbeville Press, 1985.

Kubler, George. *The Shape of Time. Remarks on the History of Things*. New Haven: Yale University Press, 1962.

Küenzlen, Gottfried. *Der Neue Mensch*. Munich: Wilhelm Fink Verlag, 1994.

Lacoue-Labarthe, Philippe and Jean-Luc Nancy. *The Literary Absolute: The Theory of Literature in German Romanticism*, translated by Philip Barnard and Cheryl Lester. Albany: State University of New York Press, 1988.

Lane, Christopher. *The Ruling Passion: British Colonial Allegory and the Paradox of Homosexual Desire*. Durham, NC: Duke University Press, 1995.

Larcati, Arturo, Klemens Renoldner and Martina Wörgötter. Eds. *Stefan-Zweig-Handbuch*. Berlin: De Gruyter, 2018.

Latour, Bruno. *Nous n'avons jamais été modernes: Essai d'anthropologie symétrique*. Paris: La Découverte, 1991.

Latour, Bruno. *We Have Never Been Modern*, translated by C. Porter. Cambridge, MA: Harvard University Press, 1993.

Leddy, Annette and Donna Conwell. Eds. *Farewell to Surrealism: The Dyn Circle in Mexico*. Los Angeles, CA: Getty Research Institute, 2012.

Lehardy, Jacques (Clément Privé). 'Montmartre'. *Le Chat Noir*, no. 1 (14 January 1882).

Léro, Etienne. 'Civilisation'. *Légitime Défense*, no. 1 (1932): 9.

Lessing, Gotthold Ephraim. *Laocoön: An Essay on the Limits of Painting and Poetry*. 1766. In *Classic and Romantic German Aesthetics*, edited by J. M. Bernstein, 25–129. Cambridge: Cambridge University Press, 2003.

Lewis, Wyndham. *Time and Western Man*, edited by Paul Edwards. Santa Rosa: Black Sparrow Press, 1993.

Lichtenstein, Therese. Ed. *Twilight Visions: Surrealism and Paris*. Nashville: Frist Center for the Visual Arts, with University of California Press, 2009.

Liddle, Dallas. 'Genre: "Distant Reading" and the Goals of Periodicals Research'. *Victorian Periodicals Review* 48, no. 3 (Fall 2015): 383–402.

Lomas, David. *The Haunted Self: Surrealism, Psychoanalysis, Subjectivity*. New Haven: Yale University Press, 2000.

Lukács, Georg. *The Meaning of Contemporary Realism*, translated by John & Necke Mander. London: Merlin Press, 1963.

Lusty, Natalya. *Surrealism, Feminism, Psychoanalysis*. Burlington, VT: Ashgate, 2007.

MacLeod, Kirsten. 'The Fine Art of Cheap Print: Turn of the Century American Little Magazines'. In *Transatlantic Print Culture, 1880–1940: Emerging Media, Emerging Modernisms*, edited by Ann Ardis and Collier Patrick, 182–98. Basingstoke: Palgrave Macmillan, 2008.

MacLeod, Kirsten. *American Magazines of the Fin de Siècle: Art, Protest, and Cultural Transformation*. Toronto: University of Toronto Press, 2018.

Mageean, Michael. '*The Secret Agent*'s (T)extimacies: A Traumatic Reading beyond Rhetoric'. In *Seeing Double: Revisioning Edwardian and Modern Literature*, edited by Carola M. Kaplan and Anne B. Simpson, 235–58. London: Macmillan, 1996.

Mainardi, Patricia. *End of the Salon: Art and the State in the Early Third Republic*. Cambridge: Cambridge University Press, 1993.

Malevich, Kasimir. 'Suprematism'. 1927. In *Modern Artists on Art*, edited by Robert L. Herbert, 92–102. Englewood Cliffs, NJ: Prentice-Hall, 1964.

Mallarmé, Stéphane. *Selected Poetry and Prose*, edited and co-translated by Mary Ann Caws. New York: New Directions, 1982.

Mallarmé, Stéphane. *The Book*, translated by Sylvia Gorelick. Cambridge, MA: Exact Change, 2018.

Mandelstam, Osip. *The Noise of Time and Other Prose Pieces*, translated by Clarence Brown. London: Quartet, 1988.

Mannheim, Karl. *Essays in the Sociology of Knowledge*, edited and translated by Paul Kecskemeti. London: Routledge, 1952.

Mao, Douglas and Rebecca L. Walkowitz. 'The New Modernist Studies'. *PMLA* 123, no. 3 (2008): 737–48.

Marcus, Laura. *Dreams of Modernity: Psychoanalysis, Literature, Cinema*. Cambridge: Cambridge University Press, 2014.

Marcus, Laura. 'Experiments in Form: Modernism and Autobiography in Woolf, Eliot, Mansfield, Lawrence, Joyce, and Richardson'. In *A History of English Autobiography*, edited by Adam Smyth, 298–312. New York: Cambridge University Press, 2016.

Marcus, Laura, Michèle Mendelssohn and Kirsten E. Shepherd-Barr. Eds. *Late Victorian into Modern*. Oxford: Oxford University Press, 2016.

Marinetti, Filippo Tommaso. *Teoria e invenzione futurista*, edited by Luciano de Maria. Milan: Mondadori, 1968.

Marinetti, Filippo Tommaso. *Critical Writings*, edited by Günter Berghaus, translated by Doug Thomson. New York: Farrar, Straus and Giroux, 2006.

Mason, Gregory. 'In Praise of *Kairos* in the Arts: Critical Time, East and West'. In *Rhetoric and Kairos: Essays in History, Theory, and Praxis*, edited by Phillip Sipiora and James S. Bauman, 199–210. New York: State University of New York Press, 2002.

McCole, John. *Walter Benjamin and the Antinomies of Tradition*. Ithaca, NY: Cornell University Press, 1993.

McLuhan, Marshall. *The Interior Landscape: The Literary Criticism of Marshall McLuhan, 1943/1962*, edited by Eugene McNamara. New York: McGraw-Hill, 1969.

McLuhan, Marshall. *Understanding Media: The Extensions of Man*. Cambridge, MA: The MIT Press, 1994.

McLuhan, Marshall. *Counterblast: 1954 Edition*. Berkeley: Ginko Press, 2011.

McLuhan, Marshall and Eric. *Laws of Media: The New Science*. Toronto: University of Toronto Press, 1988.

McNamara, Andrew. *Surpassing Modernity: Ambivalence in Art, Politics and Society*. New York: Bloomsbury, 2019.

McNeill, William. *The Glance of the Eye: Heidegger, Aristotle, and the Ends of Theory*. Albany: State University of New York Press, 1999.

Meisel, Perry. *The Absent Father: Virginia Woolf and Walter Pater*. New Haven, CT: Yale University Press, 1980.

Meisel, Perry. *The Myth of the Modern: A Study in British Literature and Criticism after 1850*. New Haven, CT: Yale University Press, 1989.

Merriman, John M. *Massacre: The Life and Death of the Paris Commune of 1871*. New Haven and London: Yale University Press, 2014.

Meyer, James. *Minimalism: Art and Polemics in the Sixties*. New Haven: Yale University Press, 2004.

Miller, Carolyn R. 'Foreword'. In *Rhetoric and Kairos: Essays in History, Theory, and Praxis*, edited by Philip Sipiora and James S. Baumlin, xi–xiv. Albany: State University of New York Press, 2002.

Miller, Tyrus. *Singular Examples: Artistic Politics and the Neo-Avant-Garde*. Evanston, Illinois: Northwestern University Press, 2009.

Miller, Tyrus. 'Mimesis of the New Man: The 1930s from Ideology to Anthropolitics'. In *Encounters with the 30s*. Madrid: Reina Sofia, Museo Nacional Centro de Arte, 2012.

Mišković, Nataša, Harald Fischer Tine and Nada Boškovska. Eds. *The Non Aligned Movement and the Cold War*. London: Routledge, 2014.

Mitchell, W.J.T. *Picture Theory: Essays on Verbal and Visual Representation*. Chicago: University of Chicago Press, 1994.

Moholy-Nagy, László. *The New Vision and Abstract of an Artist*. New York: Wittenborn, Schultz, 1947.

Monnier, Adrienne. *Les Gazettes d'Monnier 1925–1945*. Paris: René Julliard, 1953.

Moretti, Franco. *Distant Reading*. London: Verso, 2013.

Moser, Thomas C. *The Life in the Fiction of Ford Madox Ford*. Princeton: Princeton University Press, 1980.

Mueller, Dawn M. Ed. *Creating Sustainable Community: The Proceedings of the ACRL 2015 Conference*. Chicago: Association of College and Research Libraries, 2015.

Mussell, James. 'Repetition: Or, 'In Our Last''. *Victorian Periodicals Review* 48, no. 3 (Fall 2015): 343–58.

Myers, David N. *Resisting History. Historicism and Its Discontents in German-Jewish Thought*. Princeton, NJ: Princeton University Press, 2003.

Nadeau, Maurice. Ed. *Histoire du Surréalisme: Documents surréalistes*. Paris: Éditions du Seuil, 1964.

Nagel, Alexander. *Medieval Modern. Art Out of Time*. London: Thames and Hudson, 2012.

Nancy, Jean-Luc. *The Muses*, translated by Peggy Kamuf. Stanford: Stanford University Press, 1994.

Naville, Pierre. *Archives*. CEDIAS Musée social bibliothèque, 1924–1989.

Negri, Antonio. *Time for Revolution*, translated by Matteo Mandarini. London: Continuum, 2003.

Nichols, Ashton. 'Browning's Modernism: The Infinite Moment as Epiphany'. *Browning Institute Studies* 11 (1983): 81–99.

Nicolet, Claude. *Histoire, Nation, République*. Paris: Odile Jacob, 2000.

Nicolson, Harold. *The Development of English Biography*. London: The Hogarth Press, 1927.

Nietzsche, Friedrich. 'The Birth of Tragedy Out of the Spirit of Music'. In *The Birth of Tragedy and Other Writings*, edited by Raymond Geuss and Ronald Spiers, translated by Ronald Spiers. Cambridge: Cambridge University Press, 1999.

North, Michael. 'The Making of "Make It New"'. *Guernica* (15 August, 2013): https://www.guernicamag.com/the-making-of-making-it-new/, accessed 24 July 2019.

O'Malley, Seamus. *Making History New: Modernism and Historical Narrative*. New York: Oxford University Press, 2014.

Ogden, C.K. *ABC of Psychology*. London: Kegan Paul, 1929.

Osborne, Peter. *The Politics of Time: Modernity and Avant-Garde*. London: Verso, 2011.

Osborne, Peter. *Anywhere or Not at All: Philosophy of Contemporary Art*. London/Brooklyn: Verso, 2013.

Parker, Richard. 'Walter Pater – Imagism – Objectivist Verse'. *Victorian Network* 3, no. 1 (Special Bulletin 2011): 22–40.

Parkes, Adam. *A Sense of Shock: The Impact of Impressionism on Modern British and Irish Writing*. New York: Oxford University Press, 2011.

Passmore, Kevin. *The Right in France from the Third Republic to Vichy*. Oxford: Oxford University Press, 2013.

Pater, Walter. *Studies in the History of the Renaissance*, edited by Matthew Beaumont. Oxford: Oxford University Press, 2010.

Paz, Octavio. *Children of the Mire: Modern Poetry from Romanticism to the Avant-Garde*. Cambridge, MA: Harvard University Press, 1991.

Penzin, Alexei. 'The Biopolitics of the Soviet Avant-Garde'. In *Pedagogical Poem: The Archive of the Future Museum of History*, edited by Ilya Budraitskis and Arseniy Zhilyaev, 76–94. Moscow/Venice: V-A-C Foundation/Marsilio, 2014.

Perloff, Marjorie. *The Futurist Moment. Avant-Garde, Avant Guerre, and the Language of Rupture*. Chicago, IL: University of Chicago Press, 1986.

Philpotts, Matthew. 'The Role of the Periodical Editor'. *Modern Language Review* 107, no. 1 (January 2012): 39–64.

Philpotts, Matthew. 'Defining the Thick Journal: Periodical Codes and Common Habitus', 2013. http://blogs.tandf.co.uk/jvc/files/2012/12/mla2013_philpotts.pdf.

Pinthus, Kurt. 'Rede für die Zukunft'. In *Die Erhebung: Jahrbuch für neue Dichtung und Wertung*, edited by Alfred Wolfenstein. Berlin: S. Fischer, 1919.

Pinthus, Kurt. *Menschheitsdämmerung: Ein Document des Expressionismus*. Hamburg: Rowohlt, 1955.

Piškur, Bojana. 'Yugoslavia: Other Modernities, Other Histories'. *Inter-Asia Cultural Studies* 20, no. 1 (2019): 131–9.

Pittard, Eugène. *Race and History*. London: Kegan Paul, Trench and Trübner, 1926.

Poggioli, Renato. *The Theory of the Avant-Garde*, translated by Gerald Fitzgerald. Cambridge, MA: The Belknap Press of the Harvard University Press, 1968.

Polizzotti, Mark. *Revolution of the Mind: The Life of André Breton*. Boston: Black Widow Press, 2005.

Popper, Karl. *The Poverty of Historicism*. London: Routledge, 2002.

Pound, Ezra. 'A Few Don'ts by an Imagiste'. *Poetry* 1, no. 6 (March 1913): 200–6.

Pound, Ezra. 'Epstein, Belgion and Meaning'. *The Criterion* 9, no. 36 (April 1930): 470–5.

Pound, Ezra. *Literary Essays of Ezra Pound*, edited with Introduction by T.S. Eliot. London: Faber and Faber, 1954.

Pound, Ezra. *The ABC of Reading*. London: Faber, 1951.

Pound, Ezra. *Guide to Kulchur*. New York: New Directions, 1970.

Prater, D. A. *European of Yesterday. A Biography of Stefan Zweig*. Oxford: Clarendon Press, 1972.

Prochnik, George. *The Impossible Exile: Stefan Zweig at the End of the World*. London: Granta, 2014.

Rabaté, Jean-Michel. *1913: The Cradle of Modernism*. Malden, MA: Blackwell, 2007.

Rabaté, Jean-Michel. Ed. *A Handbook of Modernism Studies*. Oxford: Wiley, 2013.

Rabinbach, Anson. *The Human Motor: Energy, Fatigue, and the Origins of Modernity*. Berkeley: University of California Press, 1992.

Rancière, Jacques. *The Names of History: On the Poetics of Knowledge*, translated by Hassan Melehy. Minneapolis: University of Minnesota Press, 1994.

Rancière, Jacques. *Mute Speech: Literature, Critical Theory, and Politics*, translated by James Swenson. New York: Columbia University Press, 2011.

Rearick, Charles. *Pleasures of the Belle Époque: Entertainment and Festivity in Turn of the Century France*. New Haven and London: Yale University Press, 1985.

Richter, Gerhard. *Walter Benjamin and the Corpus of Autobiography*. Detroit: Wayne State University Press, 2000.

Ricoeur, Paul. *Time and Narrative Vol. 1*, translated by Kathleen Mclaughlin and David Pellauer. Chicago: University of Chicago Press, 1984.

Ricoeur, Paul. *Time and Narrative Vol. 3*, translated by Kathleen Blamey and David Pellauer. Chicago: Chicago University Press, 1990.

Rieger, Stefan. *Die Individualität der Medien: Eine Geschichte der Wissenschaften vom Menschen*. Frankfurt a/M: Suhrkamp Verlag, 2000.

Riley, James. 'What Is the Contemporary?' University of Cambridge Contemporary Research Group (15 March 2013). Available online: https://www.english.cam.ac.uk/research/contemporary/?p=257 (accessed 24 August 2020).

Ristić, Marko. 'Dignité et Servitude du Traducteur'. *Babel* 9, no. 3 (1963): 123–4.

Ristić, Marko. *Bez mere*. Belgrade: Nolit, 1986.

Ristić, Marko. *Oko nadrealizma I*. Belgrade: Clio, 2003.

Rivers, W. H. R. *Social Organization*, edited by W. J. Perry. London: Kegan Paul, Trench and Trübner, 1924.

Roberts, John. *Philosophizing the Everyday: Revolutionary Praxis and the Fate of Cultural Theory*. London and Ann Arbor: Pluto Press, 2006.

Rosenthal, Gérard. *L'Avocat de Trotsky*. Paris: Robert Laffront, 1975.

Rowse, A. L. *On History: A Study of Present Tendencies*. London: Kegan Paul, Trench, Trübner & Co., 1927.

Ruffel, Lionel. 'Displaying the Contemporary/the Contemporary On Display', translated by R. MacKenzie. *The Drouth*, no. 52 (Summer 2015): 5–12. Available online: https://issuu.com/drouth/docs/lionel_ruffel_displaying_the_contem (accessed 18 October 2018).

Ruffel, Lionel. *Brouhaha: Worlds of the Contemporary*. Translated by R. MacKenzie. Minneapolis: University of Minnesota Press, 2017.

Rutherford, Jonathan. Ed. *Identity, Community, Culture, Difference*. London: Lawrence & Wishart, 1990.

San Juan Jr., E. 'Aimé Césaire's Insurrectionary Poetics'. In *Surrealism, Politics and Culture*, edited by Raymond Siteri and Donald LaCoss, 226–45. Aldershot: Ashgate, 2003.

Sarcey, Francisque. 'Les Hydropathes'. *XIX Siècle* (28 November 1878).

Saunders, Max. *Ford Madox Ford: A Dual Life Vol. 1*. Oxford: Oxford University Press, 1996.

Saunders, Max. *Imagined Futures, Writing, Science, and Modernity in the To-Day and To-Morrow Book Series, 1923–31*. Oxford: Oxford University Press, 2019.

Saunders, Max. *Self Impression: Life-Writing, Autobiografiction, and the Forms of Modern Literature*. Oxford: Oxford University Press, 2010.

Saussy, Haun. *Great Walls of Discourse and Other Adventures in Cultural China*. Cambridge, MA: Harvard University Press, 2001.

Sayeau, Michael. *Against the Event. The Everyday and the Evolution of Modernist Narrative*. Oxford: OUP, 2013.

Schmitt, Hans-Jürgen. Ed. *Die Expressionismusdebatte; Materialen zu einer marxistischen Realismuskonzeption*. Frankfurt: Suhrkamp, 1973.

Scholes, Robert and Clifford Wulfman. *Modernism in the Magazines: An Introduction.* New Haven: Yale University Press, 2010.

Scholliers, Peter. Ed. *Food, Drink and Identity: Cooking Eating and Drinking in Europe since the Middle Ages.* Oxford: Berg, 2001.

Serres, Michel. *Eclaircissements. Cinq entretiens avec Bruno Latour.* Paris: François Bourin, 1992.

Shew, Melissa. 'The *Kairos* of Philosophy'. *Journal of Speculative Philosophy* 27, no. 1 (2013): 47–66.

Shirazi, Roxanne. 'A Digital Wasteland: Modernist Periodical Studies, Digital Remediation, and Copyright'. In *Creating Sustainable Community: The Proceedings of the ACRL 2015 Conference*, edited by Dawn M. Mueller, 192–9. Chicago: Association of College and Research Libraries, 2015. http://www.ala.org/acrl/sites/ala.org.acrl/files/content/conferences/confsandpreconfs/2015/ACRL2015_A.pdf.

Sim, Stuart. Ed. *The Icon Critical Dictionary of Postmodern Thought.* Cambridge: Icon Books, 1998.

Simpson, James. 'Cooperation and Conflicts: Institutional Innovation in France's Wine Markets, 1870–1911'. *The Business History Review* 79, no. 3 (Autumn 2005): 527–58.

Sipiora, Phillip and James S. Bauman. Eds. *Rhetoric and Kairos: Essays in History, Theory, and Praxis.* New York: State University of New York Press, 2002.

Sirven, Alfred and Henri Le Verdier. *Le Jésuite Rouge.* Paris: Dentu, 1879.

Siteri, Raymond and Donald LaCoss. Eds. *Surrealism, Politics and Culture.* Aldershot: Ashgate, 2003.

Sladojević, Ana. *Slike o Africi/Images of Africa, Non-aligned Modernisms Vol. 1.* Belgrade: Museum of Contemporary Art, 2015.

Smith, John E. 'Time and Qualitative Time'. In *Rhetoric and Kairos: Essays in History, Theory, and Praxis*, edited by Phillip Sipiora and James S. Bauman, 46–57. New York: State University of New York Press, 2002.

Smith, Terry. *The Contemporary Condition: The Contemporary Composition.* Berlin: Sternberg Press, 2016.

Smyth, Adam. *A History of English Autobiography.* New York: Cambridge University Press, 2016.

Spieker, Sven. *The Big Archive: Art from Bureaucracy.* Cambridge, MA: MIT Press, 2008.

Spinney, Laura. *Pale Rider: The Spanish Flu of 1918 and How It Changed the World.* New York: Public Affairs, 2017.

Spiropoulou, Angeliki. *Virginia Woolf, Modernity and History. Constellations with Walter Benjamin.* London and New York: Palgrave Macmillan, 2010.

Spiteri, Raymond. 'Surrealism and the Political Physiognomy of the Marvellous'. In *Surrealism, Politics and Culture*, edited by Raymond Spiteri and Donald LaCoss, 52–72. Aldershot: Ashgate, 2003.

Spiteri, Raymond and Donald LaCoss. Eds. *Surrealism, Politics and Culture.* Aldershot: Ashgate, 2003.

Stallman, R. W. 'Time and *The Secret Agent*'. *Texas Studies in Literature and Language* 1, no. 1 (Spring 1959): 101–22.

Stanford Friedman, Susan. *Planetary Modernisms: Provocations on Modernity across Time*. New York: Columbia University Press, 2015.

Stavrinaki, Maria. *Dada Presentism. An Essay on Art and History*, translated by Daniela Ginsburg. Stanford, CA: Stanford University Press, 2016.

Steele, Valerie. *Paris Fashion: A Cultural History*. Rev. edn. New York: Bloomsbury, 2017.

Steinberg, Leo. *Other Criteria: Confrontations With Twentieth-Century Art*. Oxford: Oxford University Press, 1972.

Steinberg, Michael. 'Hannah Arendt and the Cultural Style of the German Jews'. *Social Research* 74, no. 3 (Fall 2007): 879–902.

Stevenson, Randall. *Reading the Times: Temporality and History in Twentieth-Century Fiction*. Edinburgh: Edinburgh University Press, 2018.

Stiegler, Bernard. *Technics and Time, 1: The Fault of Epimetheus*, translated by R. Beardsworth and G. Collins. Stanford, CA: Stanford University Press, 1998.

Subrahmanyam, Sanjay. 'On World Historians in the Sixteenth Century'. *Representations*, 91, no. 1 (Summer 2005): 26–8.

Susik, Abigail. *Surrealist Sabotage and the War on Work*. Manchester: Manchester University Press, 2021.

Szondi, Peter. 'Nachwort'. In Walter Benjamin, *Städtebilder*. Frankfurt: Suhrkamp, 1963.

Thévenin, Paule. Ed. *Bureau de recherches surréalistes: Cahier de la permanence: Octobre 1924—avril 1925*. Paris: Gallimard, 1988.

Tito, Josip Broz. 'Address to the Sixth Conference of Heads of State or Government of Non-aligned Countries'. Havana, 4 September 1979, Red Hill, A.C.T.: Embassy of the Socialist Federal Republic of Yugoslavia, 1979.

Trodd, Colin. 'Postmodernism and Art'. In *The Icon Critical Dictionary of Postmodern Thought*, edited by Stuart Sim, 89–100. Cambridge: Icon Books, 1998.

Turner, David. 'History as Popular Story: On the Rhetoric of Stefan Zweig's "Sternstunden der Menschheit"'. *The Modern Language Review* 84, no. 2 (April 1989): 393–405.

Unger, Nikolaus. 'Remembering Identity in *Die Welt von Gestern*: Stefan Zweig, Austrian German Identity Construction and the First World War'. *Focus on German Studies* 12 (2005): 95–116.

Vajta, Katharina. 'Linguistic Religious and National Loyalties in Alsace'. *International Journal of the Sociology of Language*, no. 220 (March 2013): 109–25.

Valéry, Paul. *The Art of Poetry*, translated by Denise Folliot. Princeton: Princeton University Press, 1958.

Waldman, Diane. *Max Ernst: A Retrospective*. New York: The Solomon R. Guggenheim Foundation, 1975.

Weigel, Sigrid. *Body- and Image-Space. Re-reading Walter Benjamin*. London: Routledge, 1996.

Wells, H. G. *The Discovery of the Future*. London: T. Fisher Unwin, 1902.
White, Hayden. *Metahistory: The Historical Imagination in Nineteenth-Century Europe*. Baltimore: Johns Hopkins University Press, 1973.
White, Hayden. *Tropics of Discourse: Essays in Cultural Criticism*. Baltimore: Johns Hopkins University Press, 1978.
White, Hayden. *Figural Realism: Studies in the Mimesis Effect*. Baltimore: Johns Hopkins University Press, 1999.
White, Hayden. 'The Historical Event'. *Differences: A Journal of Feminist Cultural Studies* 19, no. 2 (2008): 9–34.
White, Hayden. 'Modernism and the Sense of History'. *Journal of Art Historiography* 15 (2016): 1–15.
Whiting, Steven Moore. *Satie the Bohemian: From Cabaret to Concert Hall*. Oxford: Clarendon Press, 1999.
Wilbois, Joseph. *Le Chef d'entreprise: sa fonction et sa personne*. Paris: Alcan, 1926.
Wilde, Alan. 'Modernism and the Aesthetics of Crisis'. *Contemporary Literature* 20, no. 1 (Winter 1979): 13–50.
Wilder, Gary. *The French Imperial Nation-State: Negritude and Colonial Humanism between the Two World Wars*. Chicago: Chicago University Press, 2005.
Williams, Raymond. *Marxism and Literature*. Oxford: Oxford University Press, 1977.
Willmott, Glenn. *McLuhan, or Modernism in Reverse*. Toronto: University of Toronto Press, 1996.
Wistrich, Robert S. 'Stefan Zweig and the "World of Yesterday"'. In *Stefan Zweig Reconsidered. New Perspectives on His Literary and Biographical Writings*, edited by Mark H. Gelber. 59–77. Tübingen: Max Niemeyer Verlag, 2007.
Wolfe, Tom. *The Electric Kool-Aid Acid Test*. London: Black Swan, 1989.
Wolfenstein, Alfred. *Die Erhebung: Jahrbuch für neue Dichtung und Wertung*. Berlin: S. Fischer, 1919.
Wollaeger, Mark and Matt Eatough. Eds. *The Oxford Handbook of Global Modernism*. Oxford: Oxford University Press, 2012.
Woolf, Virginia. *The Essays of Virginia Woolf Vol. 4*, edited by Andrew McNeille. London: The Hogarth Press, 1984.
Woolf, Virginia. *The Death of the Moth, and Other Essays*. London: The Hogarth Press, 1942.
Woolf, Virginia. *Moments of Being*, edited by Jeanne Schulkind. London: Pimlico, 2002.
Woolf, Virginia. *The Essays of Virginia Woolf Vol. 5*, edited by Stuart N. Clarke. London: Hogarth Press, 2009.
Ziarek, Krzysztof. *The Historicity of Experience: Modernity, the Avant-Garde, and the Event*. Evanston: Northwestern University Press, 2001.
Ziarek, Krzysztof. *The Force of Art*. Stanford, CA: Stanford University Press, 2004.
Zweig, Stefan. *The World of Yesterday*. London: Cassell, 1987.
Zweig, Stefan. 'Die Geschichte als Dichterin'. Reed Library – Stefan Zweig Collection, SZ-AP2/W-H234.1. In stefanzweig.digital, edited by Literaturarchiv Salzburg. Last Update 17.12.2019, URL: stefanzweig.digital/o:szd.werke#SZDMSK.211.

Index

Absolute, the xxiii, 11
Academicism 182
Aching, Gerard 70n. 28
Adams, Henry 40–1, 51n. 44
Adorno, T. W. 14, 45, 52n. 70, 53n. 89, 79, 81, 87n. 35
aesthetics xix, 14, 15, 18, 121–4, 129, 229
   chronoaesthetics 155 (*see also* temporality)
Agamben, Giorgio 77, 84, 165–6
ahistoricism/ahistoricity/ahistorization 13, 20, 112, 159–70
Allen, Charles 70n.23
alphabetic script 123
anachronism/anachronicity 7, 23, 25, 145–8, 151, 154–5, 165
Angelus Novus 16 *See also* Klee, Paul
   Angel of History 84, 95, 137n. 27 (*see also* Benjamin, Walter)
Annales School, the 1, 21
anti-art 179, 183, 193
anti-Historicism 155
apolitical 39, 168 *See also* ahistoricism
Apollinaire, Guillaume 1, 127, 130, 132, 168
Appadurai, Arjun 62, 71n. 39
Arab Spring 1
Aragon, Louis xi 199, 204–6, 207, 213n. 56
Ardis, Ann 69n.17
Arendt, Hannah 51n. 33
Aristotle 16, 18, 77–8, 87n. 27, 215, 226
Arp, Hans x, 153–4
Art Nouveau 42, 44
Artaud, Antonin 12, 210
Arts and Crafts 59
Arts Incohérents 179
Arvatov, Boris 136n. 14
assemblage 23, 25, 132–3, 141, 147, 152–5
Atget, Eugène 222
automatism 127–8
   automatic writing (*see* Surrealism)

autonomy 13, 15, 24, 159–61, 163–4, 167–70
Avanessian, Armen 166
avant-garde xxii, xv, 8, 10, 12, 17, 20–1, 23, 25–6, 56–7, 61, 63, 67, 119, 126–7, 132, 137n. 23, 137, 138n. 36, 141–5, 147–8, 152–5, 160–1, 166, 168–70, 183, 184, 193, 198, 209, 218, 231 *See also* Bohemian Clubs; the New York Poets; *Noucentrisme*
Black Mountain Poets 60
Constructivism 141, 168
Cobra 138n. 36, 167
Cubism 10, 13–14, 141, 168, 170, 179, 199
Dada/Dadaism xix, xxiii, 6, 10, 14, 61, 131, 141, 151
Expressionism 141, 143
   Abstract Expressionism 13, 167
Futurism xxiv, 25, 40, 66, 141–3, 154
Imagism 73
Passéisme 40
Simultaneisme 152
Suprematism 143
Surrealism 6, 10, 13, 26, 63, 115, 138n. 36, 141, 152, 168, 197–210, 215–32
   automatic writing (*l'écriture automatique*) 197, 206, 207
   Belgrade Surrealist Circle, the 26, 215–19, 227, 229–30, 131
   Bureau de recherches surréaliste (Surrealist Research Bureau) 197–207
   Manifeste du surréalisme 198, 206, 210 (*see also* Manifesto)
   La Révolution surréaliste (*see* Periodicals)
Vorticism 67
avant-gardism 22
   neo-avant-garde 127, 137n. 22, 138n. 36, 218

Bachelard, Gaston 47
  The Poetics of Space 47
Badiou, Alain 23, 66, 75, 81
Bahun, Sanja 26, 49n. 2
Baker, Alan R. H. 193n. 4
Barthes, Roland 19, 114, 148
Baudelaire, Charles 5, 16, 21, 44, 195n. 38
Bauhaus 67, 154
Bazin, Victoria 70n. 22
Beats, the 60
Beckett, Samuel 3, 4, 11, 14, 79, 82
Bedouelle, Guy 194n. 19
Belgrade Surrealist Circle, the *See* Avant-garde: Surrealism
Belloc, Hilaire 95
Bellot, Émile 184, 187, 190
Benjamin, Andrew 144
Benjamin, Walter xxiii, xxvi, 1, 14–17, 25, 33–4, 39, 40–8, 77, 84, 96, 112, 117, 128, 130–1, 137n. 27, 143, 145, 165, 168, 222
  The Arcades Project 44, 45
  A Berlin Chronicle 45–7
  'Berlin Childhood Around 1900' 44
  'On the Concept of History' xxvi, 34
  'On the Image of Proust' 52n.72
  'Literary History and the Study of Literature' 25
  One-Way Street 138n. 35
  'The Storyteller' 39
  'The Work of Art in the Age of Mechanical Reproducibility', 44
Benson, C. A. 95
Benson, Peter 72n. 55
Bergson, Henri xxiv, 23
  durée réelle 23, 30n. 52
  élan vital 23
    Creative Evolution 30n. 52
    Time and Free Will: An Essay on the Immediate Data of Consciousness 30n. 52
Berman, Jessica 71n. 34
Bernal, J. D. 95, 97
  The World, the Flesh and the Devil 97
Berr, Henri
  L'Evolution de l'Humanité 103–4
Bickley Trott, Alexandra 25
Bildungsroman 22, 33, 144 *See also* Künstlerroman
biography 34, 49–50n. 9, 93, 100–2, 108n. 30

autobiography 21, 22, 33–5, 37–40, 45, 49, 93
Bishop, Tom 9
Blake, William 25
Blue Mountain Project 56
Bochner, Jay 57
Boer War, the 41, 115
Bohemian Clubs/Bohemianism 25, 175, 177, 184, 187–8, 192 *See also* Avant-garde
  Bon Bock, les 25, 183–92
  Fumisme 178–9
  Hydropathes, les 25, 177–81, 183–4, 185, 192
  Zutistes, les 179
Boiffard, Jacques-André 199, 204, 205, 206
Bor, Vane (Stevan Živadinović) 220, 221–2, 223, 226, 229
Boulez, Pierre 132, 138n. 39
Bourbon Monarchy 175, 177, 198
Bourdieu, Pierre 14, 69n. 7
Brake, Laurel 57
Braudel, Fernand 1
Breton, André 9–10, 13, 14, 63, 75, 127, 197–210, 218, 220, 223
Breton, Simone (née Simone Kahn, also Simone Collinet) 199, 204–10
Brexit 3
Brigstocke, Julian 180
Brittain, Vera 95, 98
  Halcyon 108n. 19
Brooker, Peter 68 n5
Brooks, Cleanth 56
Bru, Sacha 25, 68 n5
Bryher (Annie Winifred Ellerman) 33, 40–7
  Heart to Artemis 40, 43
  'Paris, 1900' 41, 43
Buck-Morss, Susan 144
Bulson, Eric 61, 67
Bureau de recherches surréaliste (Surrealist Research Bureau) *See* Avant-garde: Surrealism
Bürger, Peter 168
Byzantine (art) 9, 12

Cadet, Coquelin 184
Cage, John 121, 132
Camus, Albert 2
Capitalism 18, 115, 116, 218
Carjat, Étienne 185, 195n. 38

Carnivalesque 184, 192
Carrive, Jean 210
Carter, E. H. 105
  General History: in Outline and Story
    105 (*see also* Ogden, C. K.)
Castoriadis, Cornelius 113
Cate, Philip Dennis 195n. 31
Catholicism 12, 225
Cavell, Stanley 127–8
Césaire, Aimé 62, 231, 233n. 23
Chakrabarty, Dipesh 27n. 15
Chanel, Coco (Gabrielle Bonheur) 6–8
Chaney, Lisa 8
Chesterton, G. K. 95, 101
Chevallier, Pierre 194n. 23
Chronoaesthetics *See* aesthetics;
  temporality
Churchill, Suzanne 70n. 23
Claretie, Jules 184
Clark, Timothy James 190, 198, 202
Classics, the 5
Claudel, Camille 3
Cole, Lori 63
Collier, Patrick 58, 69n. 16
colonial xxiii, 62, 63, 66, 67, 83, 84, 116, 190, 217, 218
  anti-colonial 62, 63
  post-colonial xx, 62, 67, 227, 230
colonialism xix, 9
Communism 63, 210
  The Communist Manifesto 22 (*see also* manifesto)
Comte, Auguste 163, 181
Conrad, Joseph 20, 33, 94, 95
  Nostromo 23
  Romance 94 (*see also* Ford, Ford Madox)
  Secret Agent, The 94
Constructivism *See* Avant-garde
Contemporary, the xxi, xxiv, 13, 15, 92, 95, 99, 105, 125, 114–15, 128, 155, 159, 164–7, 182
Conwell, Donna 71n. 37
Cosmopolitanism 9, 10
Cottin, Eugène 185–7, 188–92
Courbet, Gustave 147, 188–91
Covid-19 2
crisis 13, 22, 23, 73–6, 80, 124–5, 129
Cros, Antoine 184

Cros, Charles 179
Crow, Thomas 5
Cubism *See* Avant-garde

Dada *See* Avant-garde
Dante, Alighieri xxvi, 91
Danto, Arthur 116
Davičo, Oskar 229
de Chirico, Giorgio 152, 205–6, 207, 224
de Gourmont, Remy 59
de MacMahon, Patrice 177
de Man, Paul 26
de Nerval, Gérard 5
De Quincey, Thomas 34, 93
  Confessions of an English Opium-Eater 34, 93
Delaunay, Robert 152
Deleuze, Gilles 152, 143
DeLillo, Don 113, 114
  Underworld 113, 114
Delteil, Joseph 10, 210
Dermée, Paul 199
Derrida, Jacques xxii, 143
Desnos, Robert 205, 206–7, 209
dialectical image xxiii, 16, 17 *See also* Angel of History
Didi-Huberman, Georges 144
digital humanities 58, 69n. 7; 21
Dilthey, Wilhelm 20
Drouin, Jeff 69 n.16
Duchamp, Marcel 14, 116, 127, 148, 152, 167, 170
Durée 76 *See also Annales*; Braudel, Fernard
  Longue durée 1, 4
Duthuit, Georges 8, 12

Eagleton, Terry 22
Eatough, Matt 71n. 34
Edwards, Brent Hayes 66, 71n. 41, 42
Einstein, Albert xxiii, 215
Einstein, Carl 155
Eliot, George
  Middlemarch 20
Eliot, Thomas Stearns xix, xxii, 4, 5, 10, 11, 23, 55, 58, 60, 73, 76, 78, 91–4, 95, 101, 124–5, 129, 138n. 36 *See also* mythical method, the
  Four Quartets 25

'Tradition and the Individual Talent' 124–5
The Waste Land 58, 73, 91, 94
Ellmann, Richard 27n. 5
Éluard, Paul 203, 205
Emden, Christian J. 34
Emery, Mary Lou 71n. 44
Emplotment 111 *See also* White, Hayden
Epiphany 74, 76 *See also* Kairos, Illumination, moment, the
Ernst, Max 149–50, 224
Exposition Universelle See World Exhibition
Expressionism *See* Avant-garde

Faxon, F. W. 59
Fayol, Henri 201–4
Fenellosa, Ernest 122, 123
 Chinese Written Character as a Medium for Poetry 122 (*see also* Pound, Ezra)
Ferry, Jules 182–3, 192
fin-de-siècle 25, 59 *See also* avant-garde; Bohemian clubs
Ford, Ford Madox 33, 59, 92, 94–5, 97, 100
 A History of Our Own Times 92
 Parade's End 100
 Romance 94 (*see also* Conrad, Joseph)
Forster, E. M. 79–85
 'The Life to Come' 80–4
 Maurice 80, 83
Fortuny, Mario 7, 8
Foster, Hal 144, 161
Foucault, Michel 143
Fragerolle, George ₁93n. 6
Frankfurt School, the 143
Freud, Sigmund xxii, 1, 6, 10, 22, 36–7, 46, 47, 215
Fried, Michael 121, 160
Friedman, Susan Stanford 4
Fumisme See Bohemian clubs
Futurism *See* Avant-garde

Galsworthy, John 4
Garb, Tamar 183
Gehry, Frank 116
Gener, Pompeu 181
Giddens, Anthony 96
Golan, Romy 195n. 34
Goll, Claire and Ivan 10, 133, 199

Goudeau, Émile 178, 179
grand narrative xix, 20, 116, 117 *See also* Lyotard, Jean-François
Great Exposition, the *See* World Exhibition
Great War, the *See* World War I
Green, Nicholas 183
Greenberg, Clement 13–14, 24, 121, 159–70
Greenhalgh, Chris 7–8
Grenier, Catherine 167–8
Guesde, Jules 177

H.D. (Hilda Doolittle) 94
Haldane, J. B. S. 95, 97–9, 101
 Daedalus; or, Science and the Future 97–8
Haraway, Donna 117
Hardt, Michael 167
Harrison, Thomas 40
Hartog, François 25, 141
Hauptmann, Gerhart 5
Haussmann, Georges-Eugène 175
Hegedušić, Krsto 228
Hegel, Georg Wilhelm Friedrich xxi, 141, 215, 225–6
Heidegger, Martin 9, 11, 78
Herodotus 18, 113
historical materialism 103
historical sense, the 23 *See* T.S. Eliot
historicism 17, 18, 25, 41, 84, 112, 143–5, 154, 155, 159, 169, 170
historicity 20, 21, 23–4, 25, 48, 129, 141, 143, 145, 152, 160
historiography xxvi, 18, 19–21, 24, 33, 49, 59, 99, 100, 102, 111–17
history
 art history 25, 166
 contemporary history 91–2, 99, 106, 106n. 3, 112, 223
 'future history' 97
 literary history xx, 25, 56–7, 59, 135
 material history 216
 novelesque history 114
 postmodern history
 queer history 116
 universal history 18, 22, 99, 117
 world history 92, 105
  history of civilization 103, 105–6
  (*see also* Ogden, C. K.)
historiography xxvi, 18, 19–21, 24, 26, 33, 49, 49n. 2, 59, 99–100, 102, 111–17

big-data 116
deep historiography 116
eco-historiography 116
Hitler, Adolf 37, 232n. 9
Hofmann, Werner 147
Hoffman, Frederick 61
Huelsenbeck, Richard 152
Hughes, Langston 67
Hugo, Victor 5
humanism 117, 129
Huxley, Aldous 98, 101
　Brave New World 98
Huyssen, Andreas 62, 66, 144
Hydropathes, les See Bohemian clubs

Ibsen, Henrik xxii, xxv, 2, 4
　The Enemy of the People 2
ideogram 122, 123, 127, 130
illumination 46 See also *Kairos*, moment, the
interchronicity 25, 148, 152–3 See also temporality; polytemporality
irrational, the 26, 215–16 See also Surrealism

Janco, Marcel 152
Jarry, Alfred 3, 4, 179
Jolas, Eugène 8–12, 59, 67 See also Periodicals: *transition*
Jones, Caroline A. 162–3
Joyce, James xix, xxvi, 2–4, 6, 9, 10, 12, 67, 74, 91, 92, 94, 95, 101
　A Brilliant Career 2–3
　A Portrait of the Artist as a Young Man 3
　Exile 2–4
　Ulysses xix, 2, 3, 4, 6, 9, 10, 91, 94
Jünger, Ernst 9

Kairos See also Moment, the 23, 73, 76–82
Kandinsky, Wassily 127, 142, 163
Kant, Immanuel 13, 113, 122, 141, 170, 215
Kermode, Frank 79–80
Kern, Stephen 30n. 51
Khazam, Rahma 13
Khlebnikov, Velimir 127, 143
Klee, Paul See also *Angelus Novus* 16, 127, 154
Koestler, Arthur 37, 38–9

Kolocotroni, Vassiliki 23
Koselleck, Reinhart 145
Kouen, Jan 6
Krauss, Rosalind 121, 123, 128, 170
Kreymborg, Alfred 57
Kruchenykh, Aleksei 127, 143
Kubler, George 147
Künstlerroman 22, 33 See also *Bilgunsroman*

labour 124, 134, 152, 163, 198–204, 207, 209–10
Lacan, Jacques 113
Laclau, Ernesto 113
Lacoue-Labarthe, Philippe 11
Lafargue, Paul 177
Laïcité 177, 180–2
Larkin, Philip xxvi
Latour, Bruno 25, 143, 147, 159, 164, 170
Le Verdier, Henri 181
Leddy, Annette 71n. 37
Lehardy, Jacques (Clément Privé) 180
Léro, Etienne 63, 67
Lessing, Gotthold Ephraim 121–4
　Laocoön: An Essay on the Limits of Painting and Poetry 121–2
Lewis, Wyndham 64, 66, 101, 121, 127, 138n. 36
　Time and Western Man 121
Liddle, Dallas 57
little magazines See periodicals
Littré, Émile 181
Longue durée See also the *Annales* School 1, 4
Lorin, Georges 184
Lukács, Georg 17–8, 124
Lyotard, Jean-François 20, 116, 117, 143

MacLeod, Kirsten 59, 70n. 25
McKay, Claude 63, 67
McKnight Kauffer, Edward 154
McNamara, Andrew 15–6
Maeterlinck, Maurice 3
Mainardi, Patricia 182
Malevitch, Kazimir 3
Mallarmé, Stéphane 40, 128–32
　Le Livre 129
Mandelstam, Osip 39
Manet, Édouard 175, 176–7, 184–5, 190, 192

Manifesto xxiii, 10, 63, 66, 67, 103, 127, 135, 142, 203, 218, 224, 230 *See also* avant-garde, Bohemian clubs)
Mann, Thomas xxiv
Mannheim, Karl 34
Mao, Douglas 55
Marcus, Laura 22, 62
Marinetti, Filippo Tommaso 127, 142 *See also* Futurism
Márkus, György 15
Marsden, Dora 9
Marx, Karl xix, xx, 63, 102, 103, 114, 116, 227
Marxism xx, xxiv, 12, 17, 63, 66, 75, 96, 97, 102, 103, 124, 177, 219, 227
Masson, André 12, 13, 210
Matisse, Henri 12, 167, 168
Matyushin, Mikhail 143
Maurois, André 99
 The Next Chapter: The War against the Moon 99
medium 122–35
memory 34, 36, 39, 41, 45–7, 123, 148 *See also* temporality; time
Ménil, René 63
metahistory 111, 148 *See also* history; Hayden White
metamedia 132 *See also* medium
Meyer, James 160
Miller, Tyrus 23, 141
mimesis 18, 48
Mitchell, W. T. J. 121–2, 128, 144
modernisme 60
modernismo 60
Modernist Journals Project (MJP) 55, 64
Modernist Magazines Project 8, 56, 61
modernist painting 13, 121, 160–1, 162–3, 170
modernist studies 25, 55–6, 61
 new modernist studies 55
modernity xix, xxi, xxv, xxvi, 2, 4–5, 7, 9, 15, 16, 21, 23, 26, 34, 42, 44, 60, 96, 98, 114–15, 125, 131, 159, 169, 177, 184, 188, 227
 'Colonial Modernity' 42, 63, 67, 71n. 44 (*see also* colonial)
Moholy-Nagy, László 121, 127, 148
moment, the 25, 46, 73, 75, 80, 82, 84 *See also* Epiphany, *Kairos,* illumination

Monet, Claude 175–6, 177, 192
Monnerot, Jule-Marcel 63
Monnier, Adrienne 43, 44
Monoskop 56
Moore, Marianne 59
Moretti, Franco 57
Morise, Max 199, 204–7
Morrison, Toni
 Beloved 114, 177
Mussell, James 57–8
'mythical method', the 92, 94–5 *See also* Eliot, T. S.

Nadeau, Maurice 12, 198
Nagel, Alexander 147
Nancy, Jean-Luc 11, 85
Napoléon, Bonaparte 115, 175
Napoléon, Louis 175
narrative *See* grand narrative
 anti-narrative 112
naturalism 5, 17
Naville, Pierre 197, 199, 200, 202–6, 209, 210
Nazism 218
Negri, Antonio 78, 85
negritude 62
Neogy, Rajat 67
new, the xxi, 14–17, 91, 100, 106n. 1, 115, 128, 130, 137n. 27, 143, 166, 168 *See also* tradition
 new man, the (*Der Neue Mensch*) 137n. 23
 new painting 161, 163
new criticism 55, 60
New York Poets, the 60 *See also* Avant-garde
Nicolson, Harold 102
Nietzsche, Friedrich xix, xx, 12, 33, 83, 116, 145, 181
nominalism 127, 132
Non-aligned Movement (NAM) 228–30, 233n.18
Noucentrisme 60 *See also* avant-garde
novelty *See* new, the
Nouveau Roman, the 224
Now-time (*Jetztzeit*) 34, 77 *See also* time

O'Malley, Seamus 34
Objet-trouvé 116 *See also* the readymade
Ogden, C. K. 95, 98, 99, 101, 103, 105

General History: in Outline and Story 105 (*see also* E. H. Carter)
Osborne, Peter 144, 169–70

Panofsky, Erwin 23, 76
Paris Commune, the 115, 177
Penzin, Alexei 168–9
Péret, Benjamin 199–200
periodicals ('little magazines') 8–9, 21, 58, 56, 59–68, 132
   291 61
   391 61
   Angry Penguins 61
   Australian New Writing 61
   Blast 57
   The Blind Man 61
   Broom 61
   Cabaret Voltaire 61, 132
   The Century Guild Hobby Horse 59
   Close-Up 61, 62, 220
   Commerce 10
   The Criterion 58, 59, 130
   Dada 61
   Der Dada 61
   The Dia 58, 59
   Dyn 62
   The Egoist 9
   The Fly Leaf 59
   The Freak 59
   The Germ 59
   The Ghorki 59
   Jacket 60
   The Kenyon Review 60
   La Plume 59
   La Révolution surréaliste (*see also* Surrealism)
   La Revue Blanche 59
   The Lark 59
   Le Chat Noir 59, 195n. 38
   Le Diogène 195n. 38
   L'Etudiant Noir 62
   Le Scapin 59
   Légitime Défense 62–4, 65–7
   London Mercury 58
   Les Petites Revues 59
   The Little Review 10, 58, 69n. 20
   m58 60
   Mavo 67
   New York Dada 61
   New Yorker 58

   Nouvelle Revue Française 10
   Origin 60
   Others 57, 60
   The Owl 57
   Revue du monde noir 62–3
   Shearsman 60
   The Smart Set 58
   Transition 8, 10–12, 59, 67
   transatlantic review 59
   Tropiques 62
   Voorslag 61
   The Yellow Book 59
   Yugen 60
periodization 8, 56, 59, 60, 165–6 *See also* time; history
Picabia, Francis 61, 67
Picasso, Pablo 132, 145–7, 168
Pilotin, Michel 63
Pinter, Harold 3
Pinthus, Kurt 132–5, 142, 160
   Menschheitsdämmerung 132, 133, 135
Pirandello, Luigi 4
Plato 82–3
   Phaedrus 82, 83
Poggioli, Renato 25, 141
Poiret, Paul 7–8
polychronicity 157n. 18 *See also* Serres, Michel; temporality
polytemporality *See also* Latour, Bruno; temporality
Popović, Koča 215, 220, 222, 227, 229, 230
positivism 144, 163, 181, 216
post-contemporary, the 166–7
post-medium condition 128 *See also* Krauss, Rosalind
post-colonial *See* colonial
postmodernism xx, xxiv, xxvii, 115–16
potentiality 25, 76–81, 145
Pound, Ezra 4–5, 10–11, 16, 55, 60, 73, 78, 91, 94, 95, 122–3, 125–6, 127, 129, 130, 131, 132
Praxis 26, 75, 78–9
   transforming, or reversing (*umwälzende Praxis*) 227
Pre-Raphaelites 59
Presentism 16, 23, 25, 34, 141, 154, 166
Prochnik, George 39
Productivism 136n. 14
progress xix, xx, xxiv–xxvi, 3, 14, 16–17, 20, 22, 34, 41, 79, 84, 95, 116, 151, 163, 167, 178

Proust, Marce, xxiv, 45–6, 48, 92
  À la recherche du temps perdu xxiii
Psyche Miniatures 101 *See also* Ogden, C.K.
Purnell, Ida 62

Quitman, Maurice-Sabas 63

Rabaté, Jean-Michel 51n. 40, 214n. 72
Rabelais, François 184, 192
Rancière, Jacques 20, 24, 117, 144
Ranke, Leopold von 18, 102, 154
Raphael (Raffaello Sanzio da Urbino) 21
Ray, Man (Emmanuel Radnitzky) 127, 204–6
readymade, the 57, 116, 127 *See also* Objet-trouvé
Realism xx, xxv, xxvii, 5, 19, 22, 99, 141, 143–5, 147, 154, 175
Recht, Camille 222
Réjane, Gabrielle 7
Renaissance, the 101, 116, 121
Richardson, Dorothy 40
Ricoeur, Paul 18, 19
Rimbaud, Arthur xxii, 179
Ristić, Marko 215, 217, 218–31
Romanticism 8, 10–11, 14
Rorty, Richard 115
Rosenberg, Harold 121, 128
Rosenthal, Gérard (Francis Gérard) 210
Roth, Phillip
  American Pastoral 114
Rowse, A. L. 101–3, 105
  On History: A Study of Present Tendencies 101–3
Ruffel, Lionel 164–6

Sarcey, Francisque 179
Saunders, Max 24, 25
Scholes, Robert 55
Schwitters, Kurt 127, 148
Senghor, Leopold 62, 231
sequentiality 13, 164–7
Serres, Michel 143
Shakespeare, William 2, 43, 147
Silveri, Rachel 26
Simulacrum 220
simultaneity 34, 133, 152
Sirven, Alfred 181
Smith, Terry 165, 166

Soupault, Louise 205, 207
Soupault, Philippe 205, 207, 210
Soyinka, Wole 67
Spanish flu 1
Spengler, Oswald 19, 154
  The Decline of the West 117
Spiropoulou, Angeliki 29n.49, 49n. 2, 114, 211
Steele, Valerie 6
Steinberg, Leo 121
Sternstunden 34
Stevenson, Randall 29n. 34
Stiegler, Bernard 148
Stieglitz, Alfred 61
Strachey, Lytton 49n.9 100, 101
  Eminent Victorians 100
Stravinsky, Igor 6–8, 14
subaltern 63, 116, 230
Suprematism *See* avant-garde
Surrealism *See* avant-garde
Szondi, Peter 46

Täuber, Sophie x, 153–4
Taylor, Frederick Wilson 200–2
technology 11, 16, 60, 114, 116, 131, 162, 227
temporality xxi, xxiii, xxiv, xxvi, 16, 21, 23, 78–80, 84, 92, 142–3, 151, 155, 165, 184
  polytemporality 25, 147, 152 (*see also* interchronicity; Latour, Bruno)
Thacker, Andrew 8, 68n. 5
Thayer, Scofield 59
theatricality 121
Thésée, Auguste 63
Thiers, Adolphe 175
Third Republic, the 178, 183, 184
time *See also* chronoaesthetics; temporality
  clock time xxiii, 23, 28n. 34
  cyclical time xxv–xxvi, 22
  linear time xxiii, xxv, 3, 16, 22, 23, 33, 46, 147, 164, 230
To-Day and To-Morrow 24, 95–8, 101, 103
  See also Ogden, C.K.
tradition xix, xx, xxii, 5, 22–4, 62, 91, 95, 124–32, 160, 170, 182–3 *See also* Eliot, T.S.; new, the
transnationalism 61

trauma 6, 76, 94, 100, 114, 115, 161
Trotsky, Leon 74, 75, 103, 210
typography 66, 130, 132
Tzara, Tristan 10, 14, 61, 152, 199

Valery Larbaud 10
Valéry, Paul 129, 145
Verlaine, Paul 179
Verticalism/ Vertigralism 10
Vico, Giambattista 154
Victorian age, the 36, 66, 74, 100
    Victorian periodicals 56–7
Vionnet, Madeleine 7
Vitrac, Roger 199, 203–7, 210
Vorticism *See* avant-garde

Walkowitz, Rebbeca 55
Watson, J. B. 101
Watson, James Sibley 59
Weiko, Christian 68n 5
Wells, H. G. 91, 97, 99, 106
    Outline of History 106
West, Geoffrey 70n. 27
West, Rebecca 33
Wharton, Edith 4
White, Hayden 9, 19, 111–17, 144
Whiting, Steven Moore 194n. 10
Wilder, Gary 72n. 45
Williams, Raymond 123, 124
Wittgenstein, Ludwig 25

Wollaeger, Mark 71n. 34
Woolf, Leonard 36, 101
Woolf, Virginia 6, 21, 22, 24, 33–6, 40, 48,
    74, 76, 79, 100, 102, 114
    Between the Acts 114
    'De Quincey's Autobiography' 34–5
    Jacob's Room 6
    To the Lighthouse 79
    Mrs Dalloway 76
    'The New Biography' 100
    Orlando 79, 100
    'Poetry, Fiction and the Future' 21
    'A Sketch of the Past' 36, 74
    Three Guineas 36
World Exhibition (also *Exposition
    Universelle*; the Great Exposition)
    41–4, 63, 177
World War I (also The Great War) 6, 7, 34,
    61, 222
World War II 161, 170
Wulfman, Clifford 55

Yeats, W. Butler xxvi, 3, 4, 38, 76,
    78, 94
Yoyotte, Pierre 63

Zola, Émile 5
Zutistes *See* Bohemian Clubs
Zweig, Stefan 33, 34–9
    The World of Yesterday 34–9

www.ingramcontent.com/pod-product-compliance
Lightning Source LLC
Chambersburg PA
CBHW052216300426
44115CB00011B/1707